THE MATTER OF DIFFERENCE

Materialist Feminist Criticism of Shakespeare

Edited by

Valerie Wayne

HARVESTER
WHEATSHEAF

New York   London   Toronto   Sydney   Tokyo   Singapore

First published 1991 by
Harvester Wheatsheaf
66 Wood Lane End, Hemel Hempstead
Hertfordshire HP2 4RG
A division of
Simon & Schuster International Group

Typeset in 10/12pt Garamond
by Inforum Typesetting, Portsmouth

Printed and bound in Great Britain by
BPCC Wheatons Ltd, Exeter

British Library Cataloguing in Publication Data

The matter of difference: materialist feminist
criticism of Shakespeare.
I. Wayne, Valerie
822.30082

ISBN 0-7450-0777-5
ISBN 0-7450-0827-5 (pbk)

1 2 3 4 5   95 94 93 92 91

Contents

Acknowledgements   vii
Notes on Contributors   viii

Introduction
Valerie Wayne   1

Part I   *Shakespearean Comedy*   27

1. 'What You Will': Social Mobility and Gender in *Twelfth Night*
   Cristina Malcolmson   29

2. Patrimony and Patriarchy in *The Merchant of Venice*
   Carol Leventen   59

3. Desire and the Differences it Makes
   Valerie Traub   81

Part II   *Shakespearean Tragedy*   115

4. Are There Any Women in *King Lear*?
   Ann Thompson   117

5. 'The Swallowing Womb': Consumed and Consuming
   Women in *Titus Andronicus*
   Marion Wynne–Davies   129

6. Historical Differences: Misogyny and *Othello*
   Valerie Wayne   153

7. Defacing the Feminine in Renaissance Tragedy
   Sara Eaton   181

CONTENTS

Part III   English Renaissance Culture   199

8. The World Turned Upside Down: Inversion, Gender and
    the State
    Peter Stallybrass   201

9. Scripts and/versus Playhouses: Ideological Production and
    the Renaissance Public Stage
    Jean E. Howard   221

10. Nostalgia and the 'Rise of English': Rhetorical Questions
    Stephen Foley   237

Afterword: A Future for Materialist Feminist Criticism?
Catherine Belsey   257

Index   271

Acknowledgements

Materialist feminism makes us aware of how institutional structures affect our own lives, and the effects of the Shakespeare Association of America on the life of this book have been salutory, even formative. My gratitude is not only to the association for arranging the seminar in which contributors to this volume participated, but in maintaining certain policies that resist elitism in the seminar membership and in being generally receptive to new issues that produce intellectual and political debate.

A much less institutionalised gathering that I have the pleasure to thank is the Feminist Theory Group which, since 1986, has met in the inelegance of the Political Science mail room at the University of Hawaii at Manoa. The good humour, political commitment and intelligence of its members have taught me much over the years, in part because they are not especially interested in Renaissance literature.

Renaissance Drama has given permission to reprint Jean E. Howard's essay from volume 20 (1989). My thanks also go to Sarah Callies, Joseph Chadwick, Sara Collins, Carolyn DiPalma, Miriam Fuchs, Mark Heberle, Alan MacGregor, Jared Nakatsu, Nera Nakayama, Gloria Olehoivy, Richard Tillotson, Rieko Thomas, Clifford Young, and Deborah Weiner for their assistance with particular essays; to Cristina Bacchilega and Craig Howes for their help in numerous ways as friends and colleagues; to Ann Thompson for the suggestion that initiated the volume; to Katharine Eisaman Maus for proposing its organisation, and to Jackie Jones at Harvester Wheatsheaf for her consistent attention through its completion. Three persons worked as consultants at various stages of the book's development: I am very grateful to Margaret W. Ferguson, Lisa Jardine and Kathleen McLuskie for the energy and extensive knowledge with which they offered their comments on the essays. Margaret Ferguson was especially generous of her time in responding to revisions of the essays and to the introduction. The book is very much a product of these persons, those who are thanked in the notes and the contributors: all have made telling differences in its matter.

Notes on Contributors

CATHERINE BELSEY chairs the Centre for Critical and Cultural Theory at the University of Wales College of Cardiff. She is author of *Critical Practice* (Methuen, 1980), *The Subject of Tragedy: Identity and Difference in Renaissance Drama* (Methuen, 1985) and *John Milton: Language, Gender, Power* (Blackwell, 1988). She is also co-editor with Jane Moore of *The Feminist Reader: Essays in Gender and the Politics of Literary Criticism* (Macmillan, 1989).

SARA EATON is an Assistant Professor of English at North Central College in Naperville, Illinois. She has published essays on the Renaissance in *Theatre Journal* (reprinted in *Staging the Renaissance: Studies in Elizabethan and Jacobean Drama*, eds. David Scott Kastan and Peter Stallybrass, forthcoming from Routledge in 1991), in *The Iowa State Journal of Research* and in Carole Levin and Jeanie Watson's collection, *Ambiguous Realities: Women in the Middle Ages and Renaissance* (Wayne State University Press, 1987).

STEPHEN FOLEY is an Associate Professor of English at Brown University in Providence, Rhode Island. He is co-editor with Clarence Miller of the *Answer to the Poisoned Book* in the Yale edition of the *Complete Works of Thomas More* (1985), co-author with Joseph Gordon of *Conventions and Choices: A Brief Guide to Style and Usage* (D.C. Heath, 1986) and author of *Sir Thomas Wyatt* in the Twayne English Author Series (1990).

JEAN E. HOWARD is Professor of English at Columbia University, author of *Shakespeare's Art of Orchestration: Stage Technique and Audience Response* (University of Illinois Press, 1984) and co-editor with Marion F. O'Connor of *Shakespeare Reproduced: The Text in History and Ideology* (Methuen, 1987). She is completing a book called *Discourses of the Theater: The Stage and Social Struggle in Early Modern England*, forthcoming from Routledge, of which the present essay is a part.

CAROL LEVENTEN has published articles on Marlowe and Anne Sexton, including 'Marlowe's mixed messages: a model for Shakespeare' in *Medieval and Renaissance Drama in England*, vol. III. Formerly an Assistant Professor of English at Adrian College in Michigan, she decided, as a result of what she learned in the course of writing the essay published here, to let criticism influence life by resigning her teaching position in order to devote more time to managing investments.

CRISTINA MALCOLMSON is currently a Lecturer at Yale University where she teaches courses on Renaissance literature and culture. Her published articles include ' "As tame as the ladies"; politics and gender in *The Changeling*', *English Literary Renaissance* (spring, 1990) and 'George Herbert's *Country Parson* and the character of social identity', *Studies in Philology* (winter, 1988). She is editing the forthcoming *Longman Critical Reader: Renaissance Poetry* and completing a book entitled *George Herbert: Religious Identity and Social Change*.

PETER STALLYBRASS is Professor of English and Chair of the Cultural Studies Committee at the University of Pennsylvania. With Allon White he co-wrote *The Politics and Poetics of Transgression* (Methuen, 1986). His collection of essays, *Staging the Renaissance: Studies in Elizabethan and Jacobean Drama*, which he has co-edited with David Kastan, will be published by Routledge in 1991, and his new book, *Embodied Politics: Enclosure and Transgression in Early Modern England*, will be forthcoming from Routledge in 1992.

ANN THOMPSON is a Senior Lecturer in English at the University of Liverpool. Her publications include *Shakespeare's Chaucer* (Liverpool University Press/Barnes and Noble, 1978); an edition of *The Taming of the Shrew* (Cambridge University Press, 1984); *Shakespeare, Meaning and Metaphor* with joint author John O. Thompson (Harvester Wheatsheaf/ University of Iowa Press, 1987); *'King Lear': The Critics' Debate* (Macmillan/Humanities Press International, 1988); and *Teaching Women: Feminism and English Studies* with joint editor Helen Wilcox (Manchester University Press/St Martin's Press, 1989).

VALERIE TRAUB is an Assistant Professor of Renaissance drama and gender studies at Vanderbilt University. Her publications include 'Prince Hal's Falstaff: positioning psychoanalysis and the female reproductive body', *Shakespeare Quarterly* (winter, 1989) and 'Jewels, statues, and corpses: containment of female erotic power in Shakespeare's plays', *Shakespeare Studies*, 20 (1988). Her book, *Desire & Anxiety: Circulations of Sexuality in Shakespearean Drama*, is forthcoming from Routledge.

VALERIE WAYNE is an Associate Professor of English at the University of Hawaii at Manoa. She has published essays in *Shakespeare Studies*, **17** (1985), in Margaret Hannay's collection, *Silent But For The Word* (Kent State University Press, 1985), and in *Ambiguous Realities: Women in the Middle Ages and Renaissance*, eds. Carole Levin and Jeanie Watson (Wayne State University Press, 1987). Her critical edition of Edmund Tilney's *'The Flower of Friendshippe': A Renaissance Dialogue Contesting Marriage*, is forthcoming from Cornell University Press.

MARION WYNNE-DAVIES was the William Noble Fellow at the University of Liverpool and now teaches in the English department at the University of Lancaster. She has edited *The Bloomsbury Guide to English Literature* (1989) and *Chaucer's Wife of Bath's and Clerk's Tales* (1991) for the Methuen English Text Series. She has also written articles for *The Yeats Annual, English Romances* (Irish University Presses, 1988) and *Gloriana's Face* (Harvester Wheatsheaf, forthcoming).

Introduction

Valerie Wayne

I

Producing history is not an apolitical activity. Rather, everything that we are affects the histories that we construct – our gender, our race and class, the historical moments in which we have been and are situated, the geographical locations and political climates we speak from, the erotic reactions we recognise or repress. These factors and many more have implications for the ways we reproduce the past in the present. The title of this book asserts that 'difference', an abstraction used to denote women's marginality, our marked space apart from the (male) generic and universal, is worthy of being made by historians and literary critics into 'matter' in several senses: as a subject with importance, as a textual presence and as a reading practice. The histories that we make here therefore become a means of renewing our commitments to a feminist politics as distinct from a feminist pluralism. As contributors to this book, we acknowledge the ideological and material implications of our work by actively assuming positions of difference, from which we speak and write. We do not claim that our work applies unilaterally to all humankind because the diversity among us produces differing investments, perspectives and positions for readers and writers alike: hence our title disclaims the universality associated with formalist discourse. Nor do we assume that feminism can conflate all of the differences among women, for if, as Teresa de Lauretis has observed, 'feminism exists despite those differences', she also acknowledges that 'as we are just now beginning to realize, it cannot continue to exist without them.'[1] So we speak from the differences among and within women and from a further recognition of the importance of racial, economic, social and erotic categories to assert the value of individually and collectively situated knowledges.[2]

Many earlier versions of history, literature and myth have obscured women from active or positive roles in shaping the past. From the end of the twelfth century, for instance, the 'Matters' of Britain, France and Rome were terms used to refer to the primary subjects of medieval

1

romance and legend. The 'Matter of Britain' centred upon the mythic life of Arthur and romances associated with the knights of the Round Table; the 'Matter of France' presented the historical Charlemagne as defender and leader of the Christian world, while his nephew, Roland, became the hero of Italian Renaissance epics; the 'Matter of Rome' began with the literary story of Oedipus, took up legends about Alexander the Great, and ended with the Battle of the Seven against Thebes.[3] These 'Matters' were ways in which medieval writers constructed their own past and present by asserting its Trojan origin and relation to the Roman Empire; they were part of the 'history' that Renaissance writers inherited. Versions of history such as these make certain kinds of persons and events matter. They ignore as immaterial, or demonise as alien, other persons, places, occurrences. By contrast we here assert difference, offered as an alternative to those other histories, as mattering because events associated with women and otherwise oppressed persons also deserve to be realised as textual and social practices.

All of the essays in this collection were prepared by members of a seminar on Materialist Feminist Criticism of Shakespeare that met at the Shakespeare Association of America conference in Austin, Texas in April 1989.[4] The seminar continued the debate between feminists, new historicists and cultural materialists that had had its most identifiable beginnings three years earlier at the World Congress of the International Shakespeare Association in West Berlin. After that 1986 conference, the politics of the new historicism were discussed at conference sessions and in published essays by Marguerite Waller, Peter Erickson, Lynda Boose, Walter Cohen, Don Wayne, Carol Thomas Neely, Carolyn Porter and others.[5] By 1988 the very localised dispute among Renaissance critics had so heightened the differences between feminists and new historicists that the violence of a binary opposition was asserting itself through the discourse, offspring of the cultural and linguistic opposition between women and men. It seemed a moment to focus instead on alternative differences within and outside of those groups, to invoke politics for collaborative, not only divisive, purposes. The seminar that I led therefore offered participants an opportunity to write about Shakespeare from perspectives that were more politically explicit than the new historicism, and its materialist feminist approach assumed some compatibility, rather than a complete opposition, between the projects of feminists and other leftist political criticisms.

The occasion for these essays was therefore a dispute among Renaissance critics and particularly critics of Shakespeare. Yet it was developments in feminist theory over the past two decades that enabled the topic of the seminar and the alternative direction for inquiry charted by it. In many ways the most influential text identifying the contemporary critical approach available to us was Judith Newton and Deborah Rosenfelt's collection, *Feminist Criticism and Social Change: Sex, class and race in literature and culture*. The introduction to this book theorises materialist feminist criticism in very helpful ways, as will appear from its citation in a number of the essays that follow in the present book. Newton and Rosenfelt describe the 'double work shift' of this criticism as including

> work on the power relations implied by gender and simultaneously on those implied by class, race and sexual identification; an analysis of literature and an analysis of history and society; an analysis of the circumstances of cultural production and an analysis of the complexities with which at a given moment in history they are inscribed in the text.[6]

While stressing the importance of ideology and language in textual construction, the editors also emphasise the capacity of essays in that collection 'to embrace contradiction. They interpret history not as an assortment of facts in a linear arrangement, not as a static tale of the unrelieved oppression of women or of their unalleviated triumphs, but as a process of transformation' (p. xxiii). And the editors conclude that a criticism

> combining feminist, socialist and anti-racist perspectives, is likely to assume that women are not universally the same . . . ; that social change cannot be conceived of in terms only of women who are white and privileged; that integration into existing social structures is not likely to liberate even white middle-class women; and that unequal relations of power in general must be reconstructed, not only for women but for all the oppressed. (p. xxvii)

As they bring together a group of essays that considers the theory and application of this criticism as explored by many of its most informed and adept practitioners, Newton and Rosenfelt also enable the application of materialist feminism to a wide range of literary texts and historical periods.

The greatest advantage of their book may be that it opens out its critical method to include a range of critical practices and approaches, since 'the boundaries between materialist-feminist criticism and other feminist criticisms are fluid' (p. xviii). Newton and Rosenfelt remark that the term 'materialist-feminist' is more inclusive than 'socialist-feminist' and 'that materialist analysis appears, however unevenly, in the work of many feminist critics who do not consider themselves socialists (especially in the United States where Marxism and socialism are so marginalized and negatively viewed by the culture as a whole)' (p. xviii). This present volume includes a variety of practices associated with materialist feminism deployed upon texts from the same historical period, so that readers may have some sense of the diversity and the continuing concerns of the approach, while most of the contributors also work at a metacritical level to theorise their own practice. Catherine Belsey's 'Afterword' provides an account of what materialist feminist criticism might be and become. In this introduction, I offer some historical notes about where, beyond Newton and Rosenfelt, it has come from.

The purpose of this book is therefore to explore the possibilities for materialist feminism's engagement with history and literature as they were produced at some specific moments during the Renaissance and have been subsequently reproduced. Taken together, I hope the essays will convey the complexity and plenitude of that engagement, rather than the rote exercise of some critical dogma on a particular set of texts. As contributors, we seek ways of relating the material conditions of life in the past, which we see as configured by gender as well as by race, class and erotic practice, to literary texts, critical texts and our own lives in the present. This project is collective and is directed towards social change, but the academic situation of its pursuit and the intellectual independence of its participants also resist any systematised approach to its practice. Differences exist among materialist feminists as they do among women and men in general, and there is much reason to delight in that diversity.

II

While the critical practices applied in this book reflect some collaboration between feminists, new historicists and cultural materialists, they also convey a critique of new historicism for its apolitical or recuperative effects and of feminism for its tendencies to idealise or essentialise women. Some resistance among feminist critics of the Renaissance to new historicism comes, I think, from an awareness of a disparity between the professional rewards given to participants in those two discourses. This disparity prompts one to ask whether our profession, and particularly our specialisation, may have more to gain from the consumption of new historicist discourses than from feminist ones. After a period of stagnation and critical confusion in Renaissance studies, some of the highly visible practitioners of new historicism have achieved an elite position that their own resistance to political theorising may make them more ready to accept. While feminism has also made important advances as a methodology for work in the Renaissance and some of its practitioners have been rewarded for their work, the reaction from the profession appears to differ in degree as well as in kind. The effect of feminism's popularity appears to me more often than not to work against elitism, against a kind of exclusivity, that may be as much a function of the gendered character of those two approaches as of their individual proponents. Forces within the academy contribute far more readily to the establishment of a male elite than a female one. Although feminism has functioned during some periods in history as an elitist movement in support of absolute monarchy,[7] its efforts today are more broadly democratic in character, and many feminists in Renaissance studies actively resist tendencies towards exclusivity: we are not such individualists as to mind having more signers to a letter in *PMLA* than any other in its history.[8] New historicism's preoccupation with the elite in Renaissance texts only exacerbates this problem. Since many new historicists argue that subversion is often contained or deradicalised or appropriated in service of the dominant forces in a society, one wonders how political protest can ever become a means of positive social change in the past or the present.

While feminism is a political movement that advocates social change and affirms its possibilities in analysis and interpretation, some recent defences of feminism in relation to new historicism have called for a return to the methods of *The Woman's Part*[9] and a feminist criticism that is predominantly Freudian. Although I applaud the success of those earlier efforts, critical theory and psychoanalytic theory are now at a different point in their development, and to call for an extension of those earlier approaches is to ignore the productive complexity of this particular moment. Some practices of new historicism and cultural materialism may instead become means of producing a more historically grounded feminism, and feminist criticism of the Renaissance can, I think, benefit from interaction with those knowledges. Much more can be written and said about the relation between Shakespeare's texts and Renaissance discourses on marriage, medicine and theology, for example. Our students are full of questions about the material conditions of life in the Renaissance that our research has yet to answer. Nor have feminists in this field carried out the project of resisting the canon as fully as we might, so that we read Shakespeare's texts alongside other Renaissance drama and the non-canonical literature of the period, some of which was written by women. New historicists have generally been much better at relating canonical to non-canonical texts than feminists have, although Catherine Belsey, Lisa Jardine, Kathleen McLuskie, Mary Beth Rose and Linda Woodbridge have written fine books that show how pertinent those lesser-known works can be.[10]

More fundamentally, feminist critics of the Renaissance have only begun to consider the female subject as 'en-gendered across multiple representations of class, race, language, and social relations',[11] to quote de Lauretis once more. These concerns intersect significantly with the projects of socialist feminists who first theorised the relation between feminism and marxism, especially in their dual attention to the importance of sex and class. Although there were many socialist feminists actively considering these issues before the 1970s, it was the second wave of feminism in this century that led to a theoretical articulation of that relation in such books as Kuhn and Wolpe's *Feminism and Materialism*, Christine Delphy's *Close to Home: A Materialist Analysis of Women's Oppression* and Michèle Barrett's *Women's Oppression Today*. Kuhn and Wolpe begin with the definition of historical materialism as it appears in Engels' preface to the first edition of *The Origin of the Family, Private Property and the State*:

> According to the materialist conception, the determining factor in history is, in the final instance, the production and reproduction of immediate life. This, again, is of a two-fold character: on the one side, the production of the means of existence, of food, clothing and shelter and the tools necessary for that production; on the other side, the production of human beings themselves, the propagation of the species.[12]

While they use this definition to affirm a connection to classical marxist thought, they also articulate their belief that marxists have given inadequate attention to the reproduction and support of biological life and the 'invisible' labour that women perform, which includes food preparation, home maintenance and caring for persons of all ages. Women's work in these areas is usually not compensated or considered in relation to the means of production.

> It is clear . . . that much marxist analysis, in subsuming women to the general categories of that problematic – class relations, labour process, the state, and so on, fails to confront the specificity of women's oppression. There is often an automatic assumption that there is no need to do so.[13]

Given this failure and the insufficient development of marxist feminist theoretical work, Kuhn and Wolpe pursue a materialist feminism that particularly addresses the sexual division of labour, in the hope that their work will transform marxism and contribute to a marxist feminism. Their use of the word 'materialist' therefore signals a focus larger than traditional marxism, while they sustain and extend its critique of history and literature.

Christine Delphy stretched this critique even further by objecting to a pervasive confusion between 'the principles of materialism and the analysis which Marx made of the capitalist mode of production': she did not want materialism to become so fully associated with a critique of capitalism that it was irrelevant for analysing other forms of oppression that Marx also recognised. Since she posited materialism as 'the only theory of history for which oppression is the fundamental reality, the point of departure', Delphy advocated extending a materialist analysis *to* women, for 'it is the absence of women from history, from the representation of history, which has . . . led to the dominance of idealist views of entire sectors of experience.'[14] She proposed patriarchy rather than capitalism as the origin of women's oppression and analysed the relations of production configured by it. Her approach therefore appropriated materialist analysis to the situation of women on the grounds that marxist praxis had unnecessarily limited its own application. Rosalind Coward's *Patriarchal Precedents* adds to this analysis a critique of the concept of patriarchy as it functioned in nineteenth-century ethnography and became an important source for Engels' work on the family.[15]

Michèle Barrett's approach in *Women's Oppression Today: Problems in Marxist Feminist Analysis* does not ask that we replace a marxist analysis of capitalism with a feminist analysis of patriarchy as Delphy did, because for her patriarchy is still a subordinate concept, to be retained only 'in contexts where male domination is expressed through the power of the father over women and over younger men'. Barrett instead sees women's oppression as 'entrenched in the structure of capitalism' and concludes her analysis by claiming that 'the struggle for women's liberation and the struggle for socialism cannot wholly be disengaged.'[16] So while she offers a more extensive analysis of the difficulty of relating marxism to feminism than the authors of the previous books, she still advocates an active engagement with marxism. Kuhn, Wolpe and Delphy, on the other hand, prefer to extend the marxist problematic to women. While these theorists therefore take up different positions in what has been called the 'dual-systems debate', they all exhibit a concern for specifically economic forms of women's oppression. Socialist feminists also invoke differing relations to marxism through the use of the word 'materialism', which can convey both a connection with and a development away from the practices of historical materialism as set forth by Marx and Engels. A similar ambiguity occurs in current applications of the word in critical discourse: it does not fully specify the character of one's association with marxism. That slippage is a further source of diversity among essays in this volume.

The extensive activity associated with these issues in the late 1970s and early 1980s was also accompanied by a change within marxism as a result of the influence of Althusser. Asserting 'the relative autonomy of the superstructure and the reciprocal action of the superstructure on the base', Althusser offered a heightened attention to ideology that simultaneously affirmed its material existence. Since ideologies are present in the activities of a person acting in accordance with what he or she believes, he argued that 'the existence of the ideas of his belief is material in that his ideas are his material actions inserted into material practices governed by material rituals which are themselves defined by the material ideological apparatus from which derive the ideas of that subject.' This passage provides 'four inscriptions of the adjective "material" ' applying in turn to actions, practices, rituals and the ideological state apparatus.

While Althusser does not theorise those states further, his uses of the word clearly extend it beyond a concern with false consciousness or the economic in ways consistent with other aspects of his theory. He remarks in the course of discussing the material existence of ideology that 'at the risk of being taken for a Neo-Aristotelian . . . , I shall say that "matter is discussed in many senses", or rather that it exists in different modalities, all rooted in the last instance in "physical" matter.'[17] Hence he helped effect a diffusion in meanings of the word 'material', ranging from matter or physical substance as realised in physical actions (from which the words 'materialist' and 'materialism' originally derived)[18] to state apparatuses such as education which function at an ideological level. The word 'matter' in the title of this book puns on these multiple meanings and also invokes the association between female nature and the 'lower' realm of matter that appears in Renaissance discourses.[19] While materialist feminism is not simply criticism about the physical matter associated with women's bodies, for instance, it can apply to our bodies as sites for the inscriptions of ideology and power, since we cannot 'know' them in any unmediated form and they, as we, are products of the cultural meanings ascribed to them. Althusser's theory enables critical connections between the various meanings of the word and impedes any simple opposition between mind or consciousness and body.

Michèle Barrett pointed out in 1980 that these two recent events in marxist thought, 'the feminist challenge to Marxism and the critique of economism in Marxism[,] have not merely "coincided" historically.' Rather, 'the rejection of economism has led to a radical re-prioritising of ideology, in which the question of gender division can apparently be situated. Hence it has become possible, within a new form of Marxism, to accommodate the oppression of women as a relatively autonomous element of the social formation.'[20] Yet that change does not mean that we address ourselves only to ideological manifestations of political and economic structures. During the 1980s, the accommodation projected by Barrett did not take place to the degree that some hoped it would, and the forms of feminism that developed apart from the marxist problematic received far more attention than materialist feminism, especially among literary critics. In America it was psychoanalytic feminism associated with Freud that had the largest audience, especially in Shakespeare studies. In France it was psychoanalytic feminism more directly indebted to Lacan. While British feminists continued to offer compelling analyses from a materialist perspective, their work was marginalised even by a critic as important as Toril Moi, despite her claim to have written *Sexual/ Textual Politics* from a materialist feminist position.

In 'Feminism, postmodernism, and style', Moi explains that a materialist feminist approach 'structures my critique of *both* camps' of French and Anglo-American feminism, and asserts that she is contributing 'to the outstanding work of such feminists as Juliet Mitchell, Jacqueline Rose, Rosalind Coward, Kate Belsey, Cora Kaplan, Terry Lovell, and Michèle Barrett.'[21] Yet the absence of any extended treatment of materialist feminism in Moi's survey of feminist criticism, which appeared in 1985, the general preoccupation elsewhere with American and French feminism as compared to British feminism, the relative lack of support for socialist or marxist work in America, and the absence of a well-known history of materialist feminist criticism in the States until Newton and Rosenfelt's introduction in 1985, meant that the capabilities and resources of this approach were less available to American critics than they deserved to be. During the second half of the 1980s, however, critics of Renaissance literature began to address issues on a British–American axis when they considered the similarities and differences between cultural materialism and new historicism. It was this development, combined with the critique of both approaches initiated by American feminists – who found themselves repeating many of the objections that socialist feminists had made to marxist marginalisations of 'women's issues' – which made it more possible to consider a materialist feminist alliance along that British–American axis, and to produce this book.

Critics who want to maintain a connection between feminism and marxism have objected that the practice of materialist feminist criticism is now becoming too diffuse and eclectic. In reviewing *Feminist Criticism and Social Change*, Lillian Robinson remarked that that collection 'is only intermittently Marxist' and offers 'a "marxism" divorced from Marx'.[22] More recently, Rosemary Hennessy and Rajeswari Mohan contend that practitioners of the method have paid insufficient attention to the range of oppressions they claim to address through it. While theorists like Kuhn and Wolpe had advocated a materialist approach primarily to extend historical issues to women's concerns, eleven years later Hennessy and Mohan criticise that extension for privileging gender, ideology and the west, with the result that the project

> has lost its radical edge . . . Materialist feminist and/or socialist feminist interventions into literary studies . . . have involved the recuperation of the most radical features of their critiques by maintaining a privileged status for gender, by failing to extend the materialist understanding of history beyond attention to ideological practice and western culture, and by extending the inclusiveness of 'materialism' so broadly that its radical intervention is diffused into an acceptable eclecticism.

These charges characterise as problems the very strategies that some earlier feminists proposed as solutions to a feminist reinterpretation of marxism, but they do so on the grounds that the expansion of multinational capitalism has caused 'patriarchal and capitalist relations [to] become even more securely imbricated' in the last decade, and that the critical privileging of gender has resulted in an inattention to problems of 'new imperialism, white supremacy, homophobia, and class exploitation'. Hennessy and Mohan therefore call for a 'global reading strategy' that 'attends to the interconnection between various modalities of oppression and exploitation at any one instance of the social while situating that instance in the global deployment of capitalist power relations'.[23]

Although these objections are less relevant to those areas such as the Renaissance where materialist feminist methods have yet to be deployed to any considerable degree, they do offer a warning that, in being practised more widely and in claiming to address the multiple concerns of race, class, gender and erotic practice, materialist feminism may promote as theory an approach that it does not adequately sustain in individual or collective analyses. The circulation of the approach to a larger number of critics may nevertheless be viewed as a positive development at a time when so many are applauding the virtues of a 'free' market for east and west alike, without acknowledging how economic forces oppress some while they liberate others. Walter Cohen's remark in *Shakespeare Reproduced*, which was published in 1987, notes an earlier phase of this change:

> at the very time that Marxism has gone into profound crisis in the Latin countries of Western Europe and apparently lost some of its freshness in the Federal Republic of Germany, it has come into its own, as an intellectual though not as a political paradigm, in the English-speaking world, where its previous influence was far less noteworthy.[24]

The disjunction that this remark describes is even more extreme as I write in 1990, and it raises the question of the relation between intellectual and political paradigms, or between intellectual theory and historical studies, that Hennessy and Mohan also consider. 'The separation of the way of knowing from the object of knowledge is itself ideologically produced and serves to re-secure an idealist understanding of theory as metadiscourse and an empiricist notion of history as data.'[25] Those who practise radical political criticisms are not consistent about the degree to which using a materialist understanding of history implies support for marxist economic and political forms of organisation; yet I think most contributors to this volume do acknowledge the importance of materialist feminism as a much-needed critique of the capitalist and patriarchal structures that are being extended and consolidated in the west and the rest of the world. The diffusion of marxism *into* materialism is in this respect very much a contemporary development, one that may appear even more urgent as structural alternatives to capitalism diminish and the pervasive commodification of women promotes various appropriations of our sexuality and labour as 'natural'. While traditional marxists may lament such a diffusion, others may see it as an important means for applying an historical and cultural critique beyond the designs originally envisioned by Marx.

As literary critics we are still discovering how to relate political commitments to critical practices or how our ways of knowing do change the object of knowledge, and that discovery may well be delayed in those areas of study where the historical past has so often been constructed on conservative and apparently apolitical assumptions. The essays which follow in this collection are not immune from the problems discussed by Hennessy and Mohan, for we have yet to determine the political effects of integrating a variety of concerns in criticism of the Renaissance. Valerie Traub's essay in this volume is especially instructive in showing us how we can and must address issues of erotic practice more responsibly. Her observations provide a crucial critique of former practice and an alternative for future work. My own disappointment is that, as a group, we have been unable to address questions of race to any adequate degree in this book, and we are not exonerated in this deficiency by the most visible complexion of European Renaissance society. Rather, it is its very whiteness that we need to learn to see, as well as the ethnic and racial variety present within it. If feminists and postmodernists have taught us that what is absent from our perspective is precisely what our analyses must consider, then this collection asserts by its own omission the importance of addressing more fully the issue of race in Renaissance literature. At the Shakespeare conference that followed the one in which these essays were produced, Margo Hendricks argued for the significance of race in several forums where the issue was ignored or considered irrelevant. Reminding us that race is a concern that we need to consider may enable more extensive work to be done in the field.

The application of materialist feminism to studies of Shakespeare and Renaissance literature at this time also offers a potentially radical alternative to the depoliticising tendencies of some new historicist practice and to the idealised or essentialised effects of some feminist criticism. If, as Hennessy and Mohan claim, the approach has become less radical over time, in this field of study it serves a political function as an intervention in the dispute among new historicists, cultural materialists and feminists, by offering an alternative built from an alliance between the most radical elements of those approaches. Our work is specifically occasioned by feminist objections to new historicism for failings in its own political critique, especially but not only in relation to women. While these disputes can far too easily collapse into a contest over who is and is not politically correct, the present collection does not dwell on problems in the practice of others. Instead, the critics in this volume explore what

11

materialist feminism can offer as an alternative way of reinscribing the Renaissance. Our focus is not exclusively on gender or on the ideological. It is on money and women's work, rape in English law and drama, prosecutions for sexual crimes and slander, on the circulation of homoerotic desire, the disarticulation between oppressions of class and gender, changes brought about by the material conventions of theatre attendance, and rhetorical practices in this profession. While we have not addressed all of the pressing problems raised by materialist feminism, our critical practice does work in concert with many goals of cultural materialism and new historicism to continue the revision of a very elite and entrenched area of literary study, which has too long been recuperated to serve conservative political causes.

<h1 style="text-align:center">III</h1>

This collection begins with essays that focus on individual texts, to show the efficacy of approaching Shakespeare's plays from a materialist feminist perspective. Then it addresses more general issues in interpreting English Renaissance culture. Yet any simplistic division between theory and practice or text and context that might be inferred from this ordering is undermined by the metacritical and theoretical issues raised by essays in the two earlier sections and the specific interpretations offered by those in section three. Nor are the divisions of 'Shakespearean Comedy' and 'Shakespearean Tragedy' used to imply that literary forms have primacy over other concerns addressed by the contributors. On the contrary, these groupings call into question earlier, more formalist accounts of the comedies as providing a haven of possibilities for women, and the tragedies as summarily confining, condemning and killing them. A dual attention in the essays to the concerns of gender and class, desire and work, love and money, literary and extra-literary texts disrupts the assumptions that comedy and tragedy are separate, self-enclosed worlds with nothing in common, that texts can be isolated from the cultures that produced them, or that responsible interpretations can proceed without an awareness of their critical assumptions.

The opening essay illustrates the importance of sustaining a dual perspective in approaching the plays by arguing that *Twelfth Night* 'transfers anxieties about fluid social relations onto gender relations, and solves the problem through its idea of marriage.' Cristina Malcolmson claims in ' "What You Will" ' that this comedy links Malvolio's ill will with his ambition and Puritanism, since 'his sense of being virtuous is actually a desire for supremacy': he wants to climb the social ladder in order to impose his will upon others. Viola's name, in contrast, is a feminine and more positive form of Malvolio's, 'one whose will has become, let us say, musical, and capable of harmonising society rather than disrupting it.' Hence Viola's loving and erotic desire mediates the issue of social mobility in the play, since her devotion to Orsino rebukes Malvolio's self-interested desire for Olivia. Malcolmson situates her discussion with reference to marriage tracts that convey a fear of female independence and advise men to maintain their wives' self-sacrificing love in order to ensure the survival of the union. Those texts emphasised the importance of personal choice or consent and social equality among the marital partners, but the concepts were qualified by a consistent concern for status and authority: 'both consent and equality fade quickly away before the customary necessities of male authority and female submission.' She also considers connections between the play and Nashe's 'Pierce Pennilesse', Marston's *What You Will* and Jonson's *Cynthia's Revels*, suggesting that Malvolio may be Shakespeare's indirect critique of Jonson's view of self-love as a separatist version of merit, self-indulgent and socially divisive. The contrast between Viola and Malvolio in the play illustrates how fully 'sexual-familial structures are linked . . . to socioeconomic structures', as Joan Kelly suggested when she discussed the doubled vision of feminist theory. Maintaining a concern for both issues and arguing that those associated with one set of structures are displaced onto the other, Malcolmson shows how, in the world of this play, one's social estate becomes 'a matter of desire or will rather than birth or title', and how social relations are sustained by an inferior like Viola (or Shakespeare) 'who elects to preserve the social harmony rather than "put down" her masters'.

A related concern with choice and the familial, social and economic structures that circumscribe or enable it appears in Carol Leventen's essay, 'Patrimony and Patriarchy in *The Merchant of Venice*'. Leventen's approach is to make the silences of the text speak by pursuing some options that the play occludes. Concerning Portia's apparent abdication of her estate to Bassanio, for example, she asks:

> is she renouncing power or indicating subtly that she retains it? . . . [W]hen she learns of Antonio's plight and offers to pay his debt twenty times over, she doesn't say, despite her 'everything I have is yours' avowal, 'hey, lighten up; just write a cheque; it's a joint account now'; she says, in effect, '*I* will write that cheque.'

Leventen's argument is that by focusing primarily upon men and money in the play, critics have overlooked its contrasting assessments of Portia and Jessica and the implications of that contrast for its construction of gender. She compares inheritance laws in England and Venice in order to historicise the play's women in relation to money, and observes that

Portia is rewarded for her dutiful behaviour while Jessica is blamed. '*Of course* the play rewards [Portia's] obedience and forbearance; *of course* Bassanio *does* choose wisely and well: daddy does know best, and Portia has proved herself to be daddy's girl, after all.' The alternative of what would happen if Portia defied the terms of her father's will is not even raised in this play, as it is for Hermia and Isabella. Leventen concludes that *The Merchant of Venice* offers the fundamentally conservative lesson to its audience that submissive daughters will fare better than those who rebel, thereby reinforcing anxieties about the relation between women, money and power.

Valerie Traub initiates her discussion of 'Desire and the Differences it Makes' in the spirit of metacommentary that other essays engage in by quoting Marguerite Waller, Jean Howard and Lisa Jardine, in order to observe a pervasive confusion and conflation, even among some of the best critics of Renaissance literature, between gender and sexuality. 'Gender and sexuality pose as synonymous in our critical discourse in a way that not only despecifies our analyses but denies and delegitimates erotic difference.' She traces this problem to the Lacanian construct of desire that collapses both categories within the supposedly larger matrix of subjectivity, and notes also that Freud, despite his theoretical moves to the contrary, used a concept of homoeroticism based on a gender model of 'masculine' activity and 'feminine' passivity. 'Whenever critics use "desire" to refer simultaneously to gender and eroticism, we implicitly reassert this dualistic, patriarchal, normalising history inherent in "desire's" formulation.' Traub then explores the presence of homoerotic desire in early modern Britain, preferring a vocabulary that uses 'heterosexuality' to refer to the location of identity through sexuality in socially ascribed subject-positions, and 'homoeroticism' to refer to 'a position taken in *relation* to desire – a position, however, that was neither socially mandated nor capable of conferring identity or role.'

When she considers *As You Like It* in relation to the theory she has presented, Traub refuses to fix erotic identity but watches the circulation of homoerotic desire. She first observes the interactions between Phebe and Rosalind/Ganymede, where Phebe's desire for the 'feminine' in Rosalind/Ganymede is met by her/his desire to be the 'masculine' object of Phebe's desire. Orlando's willingness to court the young shepherd further requires that he suspend notions of fixed identities, so that 'as the distance between Rosalind and Ganymede collapses, distinctions between homosexual and heterosexual collapse as well.' Traub's argument is not that any character in the play 'is' 'a' 'homosexual', but that 'at various moments in the play, these characters temporarily inhabit a homoerotic position of desire.' So in general the play resists the binary logic so pervasive in discussions and organisations of desire. Traub closes with

14

some methodological observations implied by her approach: that eroticism is a cultural practice which critics should come to recognise and distinguish, and that problems posed by erotic desire require feminist analysis from a historical materialist approach and from a psychoanalytic perspective, which nonetheless depends upon the continuing deconstruction of psychoanalysts' will to mastery. This essay reorients our approach to eroticism in the early modern period. It also extends a materialist feminism in three directions: to the erotic body as a material site for inscriptions of ideology and power, to the material ways in which our erotic choices position us as agents, and to subjective, psychic experience as having an important role to play in this project.

These concerns are as important for the tragedies as they are for the comedies, yet accounts of Shakespeare's plays often obscure issues of sex, gender, eroticism or their material effects in his tragic texts. The last three essays in the section on tragedy consider inscriptions of the female body, and that section begins by exploring a related issue: how women have been erased in critical interpretations of the plays. By asking if there are any women in *King Lear* and whether they can be restored to the text, Ann Thompson takes up one of the primary objections that feminists have made to the work of cultural materialists and new historicists. She characterises such an erasure as substantively different from the class-conscious readings of earlier critics such as Rosalie Colie, Paul Delaney or Alessandro Serpieri, who focused on male power relationships. Instead, a critic like Leonard Tennenhouse has produced a reading that for her 'strenuously *works at* the exclusion of women' by arguing that the play is about kinship and kingship rather than power and gender. Yet the alternative is not simply to restore women to the text, for Thompson does not give full assent either to the practice of feminist 'over-reading' advocated by Carol Thomas Neely, or to Coppélia Kahn's 'under-reading' through unearthing the maternal subtext of the play. Rejecting the dichotomy set up by the poles of this dispute, which associates the personal level of the play with women and the political level with men, she proposes readings that are simultaneously attentive to gender and to materialist concerns: as examples she cites the work of Peter Erickson and Kate McLuskie.

Marion Wynne-Davies locates her essay on *Titus Andronicus* in legislation about rape. In the Middle Ages, rape was often used as a means of gaining possession of a woman's lands and property, particularly since the offender went unpunished if he married the woman he had raped. An act passed under Henry VII around 1487 removed matrimonial protection for the rapist, and another law formulated under Elizabeth I in 1597 made the crime against the woman's person more significant than the claims against her property. Wynne-Davies emphasises the importance of rape in Shakespeare's play: the compositional dates of *Titus* and *The Rape of*

Lucrece are close, Lavinia is raped by Demetrius and Chiron, the bodies of Martius and Quintus are left to die in a pit or 'swallowing womb', and women's wombs, more generally, are viewed as repositories of familial descent and political stability. The proprietorial assurance with which Titus gives both Lavinia and Tamora away in marriage reflects his approach to women as property without any independent subjectivity, an assumption that was reinforced in the legislation before 1597. Yet Titus's own solution to the problem of the state is that its rule be determined by the laws of primogeniture, and that alternative fails utterly. For Wynne-Davies, the dramatic fulcrum of the play is the scene where Lavinia takes a staff in her mouth and writes the names of her violators in the sand. Having been treated as an object of consumption by Titus and Tamora's two sons, Lavinia then consumes the masculine signifier in order to expose the fact of her rape and its perpetrators. Rather than conveying a simple message of liberated female language, however, her action shows at what price Elizabethan society came to acknowledge women as individual subjects whose bodily integrity had been violated.

This essay admits a complex and even contradictory assertion on the part of Shakespeare's tragic women. My own essay on *Othello* argues for a critical distinction between the misogyny voiced in Shakespeare's plays and the ideological positions affirmed by them. Building on Carolyn Porter's critique of new historicists for framing the discursive field so narrowly that it does not account for alternative ideologies existing at any one time, I argue that *Othello* articulates three different ideologies of women and marriage that were identifiable through the Renaissance debate about women: the residual ideology of misogyny and the dispraise of women, the dominant ideology that advocated marriage and praised women, and the emergent ideology that emphasised the likeness between the sexes, especially in relation to desire. The first two of these positions appear in Act II, scene i, in Iago's repartee with Desdemona. The scene is important as a means of gendering the crimes that are committed in the play, because in it Desdemona characterises Iago's misogyny as slander. Hence the play offers a connection between verbal slander, which was an actionable offence during the Renaissance under some circumstances, and the physical violence against one woman that Othello later enacts against Desdemona. Cutting the scene, ignoring it, or condemning it as critics have done effaces the concerns of gender that the play, as written, raises. When Iago's residual discourse displaces Othello's endorsement for the dominant ideology of marriage, Othello comes to act like a conventional medieval misogynist: once the woman's text that marks Desdemona as maritally chaste has been displaced, he writes 'whore' upon his wife's body. And when a critic like Stephen Greenblatt blames Desdemona for her erotic submission by conflating Catholic and Protestant positions on the place of desire in marriage, he inadvertently colludes with Iago's slander in his assessment of her. Recognising some forms of misogynist discourse as residual in the Renaissance and examining the range of ideologies occurring within a given text may help prevent similar actions on the part of contemporary critics.

The erotic body as a site for the inscriptions of ideology and power is also a concern of Sara Eaton's essay, 'Defacing the Feminine in Renaissance Tragedy'. Beginning with a discussion of the critical gaze as a patriarchal one that assumes the spectator is universal and male, she uses feminist film theory to shown an alignment between the situation of the spectator of film or drama as a privileged, invisible guest and the situation of critics empowered to project their own desires onto accounts of gender relations in plays. The problem for critics of Renaissance drama is that some plays present scenes of suffering that appear to call for our engagement in the spectator sport of re-fetishising representations of women as 'truthful' cultural expressions. Eaton's examples here include Anne Frankford in *A Woman Killed with Kindness*, Desdemona in *Othello*, Hermione in *The Winter's Tale*, the Lady in *The Second Maiden's Tragedy*, Tamyra in *Bussy D'Ambois* and Lavinia in *Titus Andronicus*: all of these plays present 'an idealised, cold, chaste, often dead, female body [which] is placed in juxtaposition to that same body's fleshy failures, whether or not the inhabitant is sexually guilty.' If the transformation of these heroines imitates the re-fetishising that the (male) spectator enacts, then Eaton wants to know 'what, or whose, social construct is being duplicated?' Her answer to this question compares the mutilations of dramatic and political images observed by literary critics like Tennenhouse, Goldberg and Bergeron with accounts by social historians of an increasing privatisation of the process of punishing women for sexual crimes. Since the operations of power become most effective when they are invisible and are internalised by women as moral codes, the scenes of sexualised suffering in Renaissance drama enact this desire for cold, chaste perfection in women at the expense of mutilating women's living bodies and giving the spectator as audience or critic what he wants in order to sustain patriarchal order.

While all of these essays on Shakespeare's plays affirm some relation between the operations of power and the constructions of gender, in 'The World Turned Upside Down: Inversion, Gender and the State', Peter Stallybrass asserts that 'there is no *intrinsic* connection between inversions of class, inversions of gender and inversions of ethnic hierarchies. Politics is precisely the work of *making* such connections, not the reflection of a social order that is already known.' This argument has important implications for the 'double work shift' of materialist feminism because it resists assumptions of 'unity' or an easy alliance between oppressed groups, or the requirement that one struggle be subsumed under another, in favour of a localised analysis of political languages that can help us understand how 'our own alliances fail, are reformed, continue.' Stallybrass takes up a variety of visual and verbal texts to explore these issues. He begins with a sixteenth-century Dutch woodcut that represents inversions of status, of gender, of age and of human and animal, observing that while the images can only be understood within a system of analogy, the figuration of that analogy within different images of the woodcut is not transparent or consistent. He goes on to argue against subversion *and* containment models of inversion, because 'they both tend to take the language of inversion as a given rather than as a problematic construction.' As further instances of local variations among texts, he ranges from accounts of the founding of Rome to representations of the French revolution, pausing to consider Samuel Butler's *Hudibras*, Marvell's 'The Last Instructions to a Painter', a portrait of Elizabeth I in Foxe's *Actes and Monumentes* and the plays *Sir Thomas More* and *Locrine*. Stallybrass concludes by reviewing three 'dominant "waves" ' which have interpreted inversion: Max Gluckman's notion that it served as a safety-valve in order to re-establish the norm, Bakhtin's contrasting argument in *Rabelais and His World* that it celebrated the destruction of norms and regulations, and a third wave that saw subversion as constituting power at the very moment of its negation. Against this third view he proposes Gramsci's model of social practices, 'a model in which conflict and contestation are endemic features, and "social control" is understood as a local manoeuvre rather than posited as an all-embracing explanation'. If such an approach acknowledges its own failure to articulate a relation between different forms of inversion, it also exposes the political labour through which categories of class and gender are formed, articulated and – in this essay – analysed.

Jean Howard's contribution to this collection in 'Scripts and/versus Playhouses: Ideological Production and the Renaissance Public Stage', asks us to consider the ideological consequences of the theatre not only in terms of theatrical scripts and representations, but in relation to the material practices and conventions associated with the stage and theatre attendance. As her title suggests, she even raises the possibility that these different practices may not reinforce one another but may, at least potentially, be in conflict or interpellate subjects in contradictory ways. Her work therefore involves a different conception of the historical from most essays in this collection. Howard begins with a portion of a 1574 Act of the Common Council that sharply differentiates the dangers of public playing from performances in private houses, so that the material practices associated with the former are seen as altering social relations apart from the fictions that were enacted on stage. She then considers one aspect of this difference, that members of the audience in public theatres were ordered by their ability or willingness to pay rather than by rank. 'Money thus stratified the audience in ways at least potentially at odds with older modes of stratification.' Taking up Gosson's counsel in *The Schoole of Abuse* against women attending the theatre because of the threat it posed to their reputations, she interprets him as suggesting that 'the female playgoer is symbolically whored by the gaze of many men, each woman a potential Cressida in the camp of the Greeks'. Yet another implication of Gosson's warnings is that 'in the theatre women were licensed to look – and in a larger sense to judge what they saw and to exercise autonomy – in ways that problematised women's status as object within patriarchy'. Howard then turns to Thomas Heywood's play, *The Wise Woman of Hogsdon*, to speculate on the gap between its ideological implications and the ideological consequences of playgoing. While the play's fiction 'walks a fine line between returning women to their "proper places" and validating them as desiring, active subjects', the dramatisation of this play for a female playgoer within the commercial, public theatre might have realised Gosson's fear that in such a location, the proper, middle-class woman could be more fully transformed into the transgressive, desiring subject who also triumphs in Heywood's text.

In 'Nostalgia and the "Rise of English": Rhetorical Questions', Stephen Foley takes up still another important site where meanings are constructed and contested for materialist feminist critics: the profession of English. He addresses the issue by considering the first professor of English literature at Oxford, Sir Walter Raleigh, who assumed his post in the nineteenth century. Foley's account is partially anecdotal, but he also criticises Terence Hawkes's use of an anecdote which provides the latter's essay with its title, ' "Swisser Swatter" ', on the grounds that Hawkes's rhetoric reproduces the patriarchal order that he critiques. As an alternative to joking about the undoing of a woman's language while she is being undone, or characterising Raleigh's version of Shakespeare as a ' "Phallus of the Golden Age" ', Foley offers Virginia Woolf's version of the professor. Woolf's Raleigh not only represents the dangers of nostalgia and imperialism, but of macho-professional rhetoric, self-promotion, and martial pride as evinced in his jingoistic support for World War I. In contemplating Raleigh, Woolf is led to envisage ' "an era of pure, self-assertive virility, such as the letters of professors (take Sir Walter Raleigh's letters, for instance) seem to forebode, and the rulers of Italy have already brought into being" '. The connection here between rhetoric and politics is blatant. As preferable alternatives to this instance of the academic professional, Foley offers us the figures of F.J. Furnivall, Joseph Wright, E.K. Chambers and Caroline Spurgeon, whose styles differed markedly from Raleigh's. The essay concludes with an anecdote from

Virginia Woolf – a parody of Walter Pater's anecdote about Sir Walter Raleigh – that acknowledges the threat women and their writing encounter in academic communities.

In the 'Afterword' to this volume, Catherine Belsey looks forward to consider the direction and development of materialist feminism. Beginning with the repudiation of idealism identified by Newton and Rosenfelt as characteristic of the approach, she notes materialist feminism's concern with the social and the economic, but adds that the recognition of culture as a material practice since Althusser has meant that 'from now on the categories of "experience" and "meaning" and "mode of address" would be understood to be within the range of concerns of a materialist analysis.' While 'culture exists, in a word, as meanings', the oppressive meanings that women experience through rape, violence, regimes of beauty, marital obligations, domestic labour and childbirth often come into conflict with other meanings such as the rights of individuals to life, liberty and happiness. 'Feminism is born of the anger which is a consequence of those contradictions lived materially as women's experience.' Fiction is a crucial site of cultural meanings, so literary criticism has an important function in feminist analysis and cultural history. Belsey gives as an example the way in which *Macbeth* constructs 'man': 'the definitions and redefinitions lay claim to include nearly all human-kindness in their scope, so that only a tiny, domestic corner is left for the proper, admissible, socially acceptable meanings of woman.' Since feminist criticism is a cultural phenomenon in our present, and since our present has been described as postmodern, Belsey then considers the relation between feminism and postmodernism. For her, unlike Alice Jardine and others,[26] the two are not incompatible because postmodernism undermines rationalist and empiricist modes of knowing and dethrones masculinity. The alliance between the two instead differentiates materialist feminism from other feminisms, which recount a single history of women's oppression under patriarchy or are wholly woman-centred. Materialist feminism instead acknowledges the historicity of culture. Belsey argues that feminism is a politics whose 'modes of resistance are as protean as the patriarchal practices it contests'; its postmodern location enables plurality and opposes the notion of an essence to which feminists must commit themselves. 'Materialist feminist history is supple, subtle and complex: it has no place for a unitary and univocal metanarrative.'

Belsey takes up three further concerns in her essay: the issue of style or how feminists should write, the self-conscious character of materialist feminism as a political intervention, and the dangers of reification that such a category promotes. While she welcomes this approach for its theoretical specificity and political alignment, she also registers a fear that the label will 'obscure the need to re-examine and reconstruct our political commitments'. Hence she reminds us of our freedom to discard the category when it is no longer useful. The diversity of essays in this collection offers support for the heterogeneity that Belsey describes as appropriate to materialist feminism, and their specific historical location in a contemporary critical debate makes them as temporal as the former moments they engage with. While I cannot speak for all of the contributors, as its editor I hope that this gathering of essays resists characterisations of materialist feminism as a unitary project. The matter here is difference, not a single new critical approach. What these essays offer instead are alternative ways of engaging with literature and history through an association between feminism and materialism. This account of their projects perhaps conveys something of their complexity and diversity as they developed within and beyond the seminar in 1989.

IV

On my return home from the Shakespeare meetings in Texas, I settled into a seat on the airplane and noticed that the one next to me was vacant. The thought of being able to stretch out for that long trip back to Hawaii was a pleasant one. But just before the plane took off, someone bustled in and took it. I looked up from my book, a collection of essays called *Teaching Women* edited by friends from Liverpool, and decided in summary fashion that this man was not an especially interesting travelling companion for the flight. While my book looked promising, this fellow had a toughness about him, even a physical stiffness, that I associated with military men. Later I learned that he was an army officer on his way to the Pacific island of Kwajalein to work on an installation for SDI or Star Wars, the defence programme that the Reagan administration refused to give up on.

Yet I was curious about the plastic bag that my companion had hooked over the latch on the seat in front of him. Before long he reached into it and pulled out a large ball of thick thread, which he tucked into the corner of the arm rest that we shared. Then he brought out a crochet needle, drew out some thread, and began to crochet a flower. His work with the needle was relaxed and proficient: he was experienced at this. When the flower was finished, he reached back into the bag and pulled out a large piece of crocheted work, to which he added his most recent flower. No longer even pretending to be uninterested, I remarked on the flower and asked if the larger piece were a table cloth. 'Yep', he replied. 'I made the table, and I thought I'd make the cloth.' Since he enjoyed working with his hands but found himself travelling often for the army, he had taken up crocheting as a means of keeping busy and productive during plane

21

flights. As I considered his quiet disruption of gendered stereotypes of behaviour, I was reminded of Renaissance women, who were advised to engage in needlework and spinning at home in order to ensure their own dutiful preoccupation and to prevent their walking abroad and conversing with strange men.

Placed in the situation of anonymous intimacy that such flights induce, we talked long enough to discover a few mutual concerns and some unsurprising differences. Then he took up his crocheting and I tuned into the movie, which was the Sherlock Holmes spoof, *Without a Clue*. Although I'd seen it before, I wanted to watch it again for signs of the displacement and mystification of women that Kate Belsey has observed in the Sherlock Holmes stories.[27] I wasn't disappointed during the opening scene in the Royal Gallery, where an arrow was diverted by a falling suit of armour, so that instead of hitting Holmes, it flew into the chest of a female dummy. Other scenes also played with displacement, and the movie was looking good from this perspective; but its soundtrack was so bad that the passengers were told we would instead be shown the film planned for the trip back from Hawaii, called *My Stepmother Is an Alien*.

While they were switching tapes, I explained to the army officer why I had enjoyed the opening of *Without a Clue* and that I thought the next film might be fun to consider in light of Madelon Sprengnether's remarks at the conference on the psychoanalytic representation of women as aliens. He replied, 'If you'll give me a feminist interpretation of *Stepmother*, I'll go buy a headset.' We laughed together at the alien woman sent to earth in a seductive red dress, who does not belong at a party because the aliens' idea of appropriate attire is constructed from our planet's media and art, rather than from any direct experience. Yet the seductress is so seduced by all the sensual joys of earthly life, especially food and sex, that she eventually pleads with a hovering trinity of alien patriarchs (who look very familiar) to prevent the destruction of the planet. When her request is granted she remains here in exchange for an earthling bachelor who goes off with the aliens, but her discovery of sensuality and her preservation of the earth occur at the price of her domestication to monogamy and to white, bourgeois society. In the last frame, we see her using what extraordinary powers she has left to help her new teenage daughter achieve some amazing feats at basketball.

Although an earlier feminist concern with the representation of women in strong roles might lead some to applaud this film, which is ludicrously conscious of its manipulation of gender, a materialist feminist approach helps one see at what cost the alien is domesticated, how her power is recuperated to the dominant ideology configuring woman as capitalist consumer and object of exchange among men, and how her newfound sensual pleasures are safely contained within the patriarchal family. It is not surprising that the army officer and I saw this film differently. But as we talked about it, my own notions of military rigidity were undergoing some change as well as his concepts of feminism. I don't propose that an openness to feminist criticism by one member of the military will resolve the problems of Star Wars or world wars. Rather, the heroine in *Stepmother* and my companion on the flight had something in common, because in trying to prevent the earth's annihilation, both were coopted to their societies' values and structures. The heroine in the movie eventually lost her power to save the planet by becoming one of us, and SDI may not be able to save it either, however earnestly my companion hoped it would. Nor do I offer materialist feminism as a full solution to global conflict or an escape from values or structures, as if either alternative were possible. But perhaps some forms of human communication that unsettle the resistance we have to those we call alien are a better means of actualising equity and world peace than the domestication in *Stepmother*, the defence materiel of SDI, or a critical approach like new historicism that sometimes 're-others those voices which were and are marginalized and disempowered by dominant discourses'.[28] What I like about materialist feminism is that it helps us understand how all persons, in ways that we are asked to attend to for their differences as well as their similarities, are constrained by ideologies and social practices.

So if materialist feminism is committed to any project, it is to a relational one – not exclusively woman to woman, or woman to man, or feminism to marxism, for none of these categories constitutes a coherent, extant unity – but a project of intellectual and political dialogue, of contest and cooperation. It asserts value in our continuing to talk to each other across oceans and hemispheres, from continent to continent, continent to island and back, race to race, and gender to gender. While it still claims that the personal is political, it assumes an approach that is simultaneously local and global, for if the challenges that women face are often most compelling at the most intimate levels of experience, the sources of those constraints can be seen in diverse configurations across time and place and are puzzlingly transmuted through differences of race, class and erotic practice. The problems of women in Europe and America are not the same as those of women in India or China, and if the work of Alice Jardine and Toril Moi has helped us cross one ocean, the texts of Gayatri Chakravorty Spivak and Maxine Hong Kingston speak to the importance of crossing another one. Perhaps we repeat the trilogy of race, class and gender with such insistence because the relation between those categories is not a stable one, since each of the determinants acts on others and is affected by still other variants. Our repetition tries to maintain some grounding or focus in a fluid and mobile field, but an alternative approach is to acknowledge the instability and multiplicity of historical subjects and to resist, insofar as that is possible, the critical impulse to freeze them into aesthetic archetypes by our analysis; or, as Gayle Omvedt puts it, to refuse the analytical impulse to reify 'one historically specific social phenomenon . . . into a supra-historical principle'.[29] Materialist feminists observe the politics of movement, of interrelation, without claiming to achieve stability or universality. The contributors to this book work from the present as well as the past, across the expansive fragility of oceans, to create a criticism affirming that difference matters: that it makes meaning, has a material existence and is a construct still in the process of becoming.

NOTES

My thanks to Kathy E. Ferguson, Margaret W. Ferguson, Jean Howard, Cristina Malcolmson, Kathleen McLuskie, Lillian Robinson and Deborah Weiner for their careful and constructive comments on this introduction. They made it better.

1. Teresa de Lauretis, 'Feminist studies/critical studies: issues, terms, and contexts', in de Lauretis, ed., *Feminist Studies/Critical Studies* (Bloomington: Indiana University Press, 1986), p. 14. See also de Lauretis' later essay, 'Eccentric subjects: feminist theory and historical consciousness', *Feminist Studies*, **16** (1990), pp. 115–50.
2. See Donna Haraway, 'Situated knowledges: the science question in feminism and the privilege of partial perspective', *Feminist Studies*, **14** (1988), pp. 575–99, for a discussion of the advantages of embodied knowledges and historical contingency in relation to feminism.
3. My account of these matters derives from Helaine Newstead's entry in Joseph R. Strayer, ed., *Dictionary of the Middle Ages*, vol. 8 (New York: Charles Scribner's Sons, 1987), pp. 223–7.
4. Those participating in the seminar when it met in Texas were: Catherine Belsey, Barbara Bono, Doug Bruster, Sara Eaton, Stephen Foley, Hugh Grady, Jean E. Howard, Carol Leventen, Cristina Malcolmson, Leah Marcus, Catherine Milsum, Gail Kern Paster, Peter Stallybrass, Mihoko Suzuki, Ann Thompson, Valerie Traub and Marion Wynne-Davies.
5. Marguerite Waller, 'Academic Tootsie: the denial of difference and the difference it makes', *Diacritics*, **17** (1987), pp. 2–20; Peter Erickson, 'Rewriting the Renaissance, rewriting ourselves', *Shakespeare Quarterly*, **38** (1987), pp. 327–37; Lynda E. Boose, 'The family in Shakespeare studies; or – studies in the family of Shakespeareans; or – the politics of politics', *Renaissance Quarterly*, **40** (1987), pp. 707–61; Walter Cohen, 'Political Criticism of Shakespeare', in Jean E. Howard and Marion F. O'Connor, eds., *Shakespeare Reproduced: The text in history and ideology* (New York and London: Methuen, 1987), pp. 18–46; Don E. Wayne, 'Power, politics, and the Shakespearean text: recent criticism in England and the United States', also in Howard and O'Connor, pp. 47–67; Carol Thomas Neely, 'Constructing the subject: feminist practice and new Renaissance discourses', *English Literary Renaissance*, **18** (1988), pp. 5–18; Carolyn Porter, 'Are we being historical yet', *South Atlantic Quarterly*, **87** (1988), pp. 743–87, and her further discussion in 'History and literature: "after the new historicism" ', *New Literary History*, **21** (1990), pp. 253–81. See also

the essays in H. Aram Vesser, ed., *The New Historicism* (New York and London: Routledge, 1989); Heather Dubrow and Richard Strier, eds., *The Historical Renaissance: New Essays on Tudor and Stuart Literature and Culture* (Chicago and London: University of Chicago Press, 1988) and Jonathan Dollimore's 'Shakespeare Cultural Materialism, Feminism and Marxist Humanism', *New Literary History*, 21: 3 (1990), pp. 471–93.

6. Judith Newton and Deborah Rosenfelt, 'Introduction: toward a materialist-feminist criticism', in Newton and Rosenfelt, eds., *Feminist Criticism and Social Change* (New York and London: Methuen, 1985), p. xix. Subsequent references to this essay will appear parenthetically.

7. See Catherine Gallagher, 'Embracing the absolute: the politics of the female subject in seventeenth-century England', *Genders*, 1 (1988), pp. 24–39.

8. I am referring to the 24 signatures on a letter to the editors of *PMLA*, 104 (1989), pp. 76–8, written in response to Richard Levin's objections to feminist interpretations of Shakespeare.

9. The full title is *The Woman's Part: Feminist criticism of Shakespeare*, Carolyn Ruth Swift Lenz, Gayle Greene and Carol Thomas Neely, eds. (Urbana: University of Illinois Press, 1980).

10. Catherine Belsey, *The Subject of Tragedy: Identity and difference in Renaissance drama* (London and New York: Methuen, 1985); Lisa Jardine, *Still Harping on Daughters: Women and drama in the age of Shakespeare*, 2nd edn (Hemel Hempstead: Harvester Wheatsheaf, 1989; New York: Columbia University Press, 1989); Kathleen McLuskie, *Renaissance Dramatists* (Hemel Hempstead: Harvester Wheatsheaf, 1989; Atlantic Highlands, N.J.: Humanities Press International, 1989); Mary Beth Rose, *The Expense of Spirit: Love and sexuality in English Renaissance drama* (Ithaca, N.Y.: Cornell University Press, 1988); and Linda Woodbridge, *Women and the English Renaissance: Literature and the Nature of Womankind, 1540–1620* (Urbana: University of Illinois Press, 1984).

11. de Lauretis, 'Feminist studies/critical studies', p. 14.

12. Friedrich Engels, *The Origin of the Family, Private Property and the State* (1884; Middlesex, England: Penguin, 1985), pp. 35–6. The passage is quoted in Annette Kuhn and AnnMarie Wolpe, eds., *Feminism and Materialism: Women and modes of production* (London, Henley and Boston: Routledge & Kegan Paul, 1978), p. 7. See Gail Omvedt, ' "Patriarchy": the analysis of women's oppression', *The Insurgent Sociologist*, 13 (1986), p. 33, for a discussion of Engels' 'crucial contribution', which was 'to bequeath to the working class movement the idea that women were not *naturally* the "second sex" '. Omvedt also notes the discussion of reproduction in relation to historical materialism that appears in Marx and Engels' *The German Ideology*.

13. Kuhn and Wolpe, p. 8. For related critiques of marxism by socialist feminists, see Shulamith Firestone, *The Dialectic of Sex* (New York: Bantam Books, 1970) and Zillah Eisenstein, *Capitalist Patriarchy and the Case for Socialist Feminism* (New York: Monthly Review Press, 1979).

14. Diana Leonard, ed. and trans., *Close to Home: A Materialist Analysis of Women's Oppression* (Amherst: University of Massachusetts Press, 1984), pp. 158, 159, 215–16. The article from which these first two quotations appear, which was a response to reviews of Delphy's work by Michèle Barrett and Mary McIntosh, was first published in *Feminist Review*, 4 (1980). In *Close to Home*, Delphy includes sections of her article that describe what the concerns of feminist criticism should be and 'the various ways in which Barrett and

McIntosh fundamentally misconceive marxism' (Chapter nine, 'A materialist feminism *is* possible', p. 154).

15. Rosalind Coward, *Patriarchal Precedents: Sexuality and Social Relations* (London: Routledge & Kegan Paul, 1983).

16. Michèle Barrett, *Women's Oppression Today: Problems in Marxist feminist analyses* (London: Verso, 1980), pp. 250, 258. For a position related to Barrett's, see also Heidi Hartmann, 'The unhappy marriage of Marxism and feminism: towards a more progressive union', in Lydia Sargent, ed., *Women and Revolution* (Boston: South End Press, 1981), pp. 1–41.

17. Louis Althusser, 'Ideology and ideological state apparatuses (notes towards an investigation)', in Althusser, *Lenin and Philosophy and Other Essays* (New York: Monthly Review Press, 1971), pp. 136, 169, 166.

18. See Raymond Williams, *Keywords: A vocabulary of culture and society*, rev. edn (New York and Oxford: Oxford University Press, 1983), pp. 197–201.

19. See Margaret W. Ferguson, '*Hamlet*: letters and spirits', in Patricia Parker and Geoffrey Hartman, eds., *Shakespeare and the Question of Theory* (New York and London: Methuen), p. 295 and p. 307, n. 10.

20. Barrett, *Women's Oppression Today*, pp. 30–1.

21. Toril Moi, 'Feminism, postmodernism, and style: recent feminist criticism in the United States', *Cultural Critique*, 9 (1988), pp. 3 and 19. For a fuller treatment of British feminism, see Janet Todd's *Feminist Literary History* (New York and London: Routledge, 1988), pp. 86–99. Todd makes the observation that

> women are . . . entering history just as the distinction between the historical account and the happening or the something out there is most unstable, when it is becoming clear that that happening has no natural configuration, no necessary articulation at all. These developments certainly allow women into the construction of history - they may in fact be connected with their arrival just as the destabilizing of the Renaissance or of modernism may be associated with women's appearance, as Jardine and Gilbert and Gubar have speculated – but they may also allow another kind of marginalization through the idea of the deconstruction of *all* history before a 'women's history' has been described. (p. 96)

22. Lillian Robinson, 'The text in the world', *The Women's Review of Books*, 3 (1986), p. 11. I am grateful to Lillian Robinson for a copy of this review.

23. Rosemary Hennessy and Rajeswari Mohan, 'The construction of woman in three popular texts of empire: towards a critique of materialist feminism', *Textual Practice*, 3 (1989), pp. 324–5, 323, 325.

24. Cohen, 'Political Criticism of Shakespeare', p. 21.

25. Hennessy and Mohan, 'The construction of woman', p. 325.

26. For critiques of postmodernism and its relation to feminism, see also Jennifer Wicke, 'Postmodernism: the perfume of information', *The Yale Journal of Criticism*, 1 (1988), pp. 145–60, and Sabina Lovibond, 'Feminism and postmodernism', *New Left Review*, 178 (1989), pp. 5–28.

27. Catherine Belsey, *Critical Practice* (London and New York: Methuen, 1980), pp. 109–17.

28. Porter, 'Are we being historical yet?', p. 781.

29. Omvedt, 'Patriarchy', p. 47.

PART ONE

Shakespearean Comedy

'What You Will':
Social Mobility and Gender in
Twelfth Night

Cristina Malcolmson

When Sebastian enters the last scene of *Twelfth Night* and begins to untangle the various intricacies of the plot, Duke Orsino describes his vision of Sebastian and Viola together in these words:

> One face, one voice, one habit, and two persons –
> A natural perspective that is and is not.

Orsino refers to a set of Renaissance artifacts, including complicated mirrors, which highlighted the effect of perspective on human vision. With some of these 'perspectives', a confusion of images would resolve themselves into clarity if viewed from one indirect position. In others, like Holbein's famous painting of 'The Ambassadors', two images could only be seen clearly from two entirely different points of view. Orsino's reference to a 'natural perspective that is and is not' implies not only that he thinks nature has produced before him what is usually the work of art by bringing two mirroring figures on the stage at once; he also suggests that one of these figures, Viola or Sebastian, is a confusion to the eye, and if one took the proper point of view, the confusion would be cleared. But the play reveals that things are more complicated than he would like: there is no view from which Viola will blend into Sebastian; the play proves that Orsino must learn to accept the confusion or the deeper clarity of two, equally viable, points of view.[1]

Orsino's reference to the 'perspective' reproduces the problem of gender in the play (are women and men twins in their mental and emotional abilities? do they have fundamentally different perspectives?). But it also evokes the play's twin issue: the relationship between gender and status. The play in fact treats these issues as reflections of each other: Viola's relationship to Orsino includes both that of woman to man and that of servant to master. More complexly, Viola's relationship to Orsino mirrors Malvolio's relationship to Olivia: both servants want to marry their masters; both men in these pairs are self-obsessed; both women seem far more intelligent than their male counterparts. Shakespeare considers the compatibility of servants and masters as he considers the comparability of men and women. When Orsino recognises the 'impropriety' of Viola's service to him, he puts it in terms of gender and status:

> So much against the mettle of your sex,
> So far beneath your soft and tender breeding. (V, i, 322–3)

The artful rather than natural perspective of the play moves us to compare men and women, servants and masters, gender and status, and to ask if one can ever get all these issues clearly into view, while respecting their differences and understanding their connections.

The questions evoked by Orsino's reference to the 'perspective' are remarkably similar to those posed by the historian Joan Kelly in her article on gender and class, called 'The doubled vision of feminist theory'. Kelly urges feminist historians to recognise that a *'woman's place is not a separate sphere or domain of existence but a position within social existence generally.'* She claims that feminists can see 'the relations of the sexes as formed by both socio-economic and sexual-familial structures *in their systematic connectedness'.* She posits a critical method which would acknowledge the differences of feminism and Marxism, and yet recognise that the issues of gender and class can only be clearly understood in their relation to each other: 'From this perspective, our personal, social and historical experience is seen to be shaped by *the simultaneous operation* of relations of work and sex; relations that are systematically bound to each other – and always have been so bound.'[2]

Twelfth Night was written during a period before a woman's place was imagined as a separate sphere, since, for the Renaissance, a woman was considered to be analogous to other social inferiors in a hierarchical society. The Anglican homily on obedience substantiates its political claims through a mirroring set of obligations: 'some are in high degree, some in low, some Kings and Princes, some inferiors and subjects, Priests and laymen, Maisters and servauntes, Fathers and children, Husbands and Wives.' English society linked gender and status in its own, Renaissance version of Kelly's 'systematic connectedness'. The homily on marriage teaches wives to 'cease from commanding, and performe subjection' by using the same set of analogies: 'For when we ourselves doe teach our children to obey us as their parents, or when we reforme our servants, and tell them that they should obey their masters . . . If they should tell us againe our dueties, we should not thinke it well done.'[3] The homilies testify to the flexibility of this system of correspondences, since women

30

can be included as parents when it serves the purpose (in the homily on marriage) but excluded when it does not: the homily on obedience prefers 'Fathers and children'. Shakespeare, and other authors, constructed literary representations of these mirroring social estates sometimes to reinforce the ideology preached in the homilies, sometimes to challenge it, but primarily by evoking and manipulating what amounted to a cultural language of the analogies of subordination.

Kelly's article suggests that we need to include a historical perspective of both gender and class in our analysis of literature. My thesis is a development of hers: we can understand how gender operates in Renaissance literature only if we consider its relationship to status or class, and only through focused historical research about socio-economic structures, as Kelly puts it, as well as sexual-familial structures. We have to uncover, first, how representations of gender and status in a particular work operate within the Renaissance language of interconnection, and, second, how these representations express or elide actual conditions. Materialist feminists and, actually, all literary historicists have to create a 'perspective' of their own, in which gender and status, literature and history can be perceived in a modern account of their 'systematic connectedness'.[4]

Twelfth Night dramatises the issue of social mobility through women who, though servants, are as capable as their male masters, and who rise out of their role as servants to become their master's mistresses. Our problem is to tease out the ideological significance inherent in the play's version of the cultural mirroring process, a version which links women and aspiring servants, marriage and social mobility. *Twelfth Night* considers advancement in terms of a marriage market which in the play is much more open to personal choice and status exogamy than it is in traditional society, and which also firmly closes down at particular moments. In the play, both men and women improve their lot through this open market, but the play explicitly compares the success of its women to the failure of particular men, who are excluded from the gifts of fortune for reasons which are culturally significant. Not only are female triumphs compared to male inadequacies; the proper attitude towards marriage becomes the mirroring reflection of the proper attitude towards social advancement.[5] The play therefore transfers anxieties about fluid social relations onto gender relations, and solves the problem through its ideal of marriage. I will argue that the play dramatises the superiority of women to men in order to call into question the rigid structures of the traditional order, and, in the process, to validate certain forms of social mobility. Nevertheless, such questioning is contained through the play's model of marriage, which requires a 'loving' commitment to others. The ideology of the play resides in its formulation of love, which includes

31

both dominant, traditional notions of interdependence, and newly emerging attitudes towards individual choice and personal desire, or, as the play puts it, 'will'.[6]

As all critics of the play have noticed, desire or 'what you will' is the motivating force in the play, but this will or appetite is often hungry not only for music, drink or love, but for an improved social position. Maria's forged letter of love from Olivia to Malvolio, which promises him that 'thou art made, if thou desir'st to be so', is a jesting version of the projects of the other characters (II, v, 150–1). Sir Toby Belch seeks to better Sir Andrew Aguecheek's estate and his own by marrying Sir Andrew to his niece, Olivia. After Olivia marries Sebastian, and meets the unknowing Cesario in Act V, Olivia says:

> Fear not, Cesario; take thy fortunes up,
> Be that thou know'st thou art, and then thou art
> As great as that thou fearest. (V, i, 147–9)

Olivia points out the social distinction between Cesario and Duke Orsino, but exhorts the servant to embrace his new position as her husband, an estate which makes him as 'great' as his master. Marriage may be the goal of desire in the play, but these marriages can also elevate one of the partners to a higher social estate. Love and desire participate in the process of social mobility made most visible in Cesario's association with the Duke. Valentine says, 'If the Duke continue these favours towards you, Cesario, you are like to be much advanced' (I, iv, 1–2). Orsino says:

> Prosper well in this,
> And thou shalt live as freely as thy lord
> To call his fortunes thine. (I, iv, 38–40)

Viola herself has explicitly chosen her place in the play: 'I'll serve this Duke' (I, ii, 55); her marriage to him at the end of the play turns Cesario's advancement into a love-match.

The notion that one's social estate could be subject to one's will or a matter of desire underlies the play's simultaneous consideration of the relation of man to woman, and of master to servant. When Viola woos Olivia for Orsino, but wins her heart for herself, the wonder of it lies not only in that a woman has been mistaken for a man, but that a woman has been mistaken for a gentleman. When alone, Olivia repeats to herself her questioning of Cesario, and reveals her attraction to what she takes to be his 'gentility':

> 'What is your parentage?'
> 'Above my fortunes, yet my state is well.
> I am a gentleman.' I'll be sworn thou art.
> Thy tongue, thy face, thy limbs, actions, and spirit

Do give you fivefold blazon. Not so fast; soft, soft,
Unless the master were the man. How now?
Even so quickly may one catch the plague?
Methinks I feel this youth's perfections
With an invisible and subtle stealth
To creep in at mine eyes. (I, v, 287–96)

Olivia feels the inappropriateness of falling in love with a servant, but we see that she has in fact fallen for a cleverly created illusion, Viola's capable representation of the attributes of an upper-class young man, with his tongue, face, limbs, actions and spirit. As Sir Andrew puts it, 'That youth's a rare courtier' (III, i, 88). The argument of some critics that Viola's nobility shines through her disguise must be qualified by the emphasis that the play puts on manipulating illusions and fashioning appearances.[7] Viola's success at this task is measured by Sir Andrew Aguecheek's failure; he is both male and knight, but his inadequate wit and verbal awkwardness ensure that he will be 'put down' by both Maria and Sir Toby (I, iii, 79).

In the play, a gentleman is 'made' and made loveable not by his title or blood, but by his (or her) will. Olivia makes it quite clear that she cannot love Duke Orsino simply for his aristocratic blood, though he is 'noble' and of 'great estate', 'a gracious person' both 'in dimension and the shape of nature' (I, v, 255–60). Cesario instead wins Olivia's heart when he plays the wilful lover:

Viola	If I did love you in my master's flame,
	With such a suff'ring, such a deadly life,
	In your denial I would find no sense;
	I would not understand it.
Olivia	Why, what would you?
Viola	Make me a willow cabin at your gate
	And call upon my soul within the house;
	Write loyal cantons of contemned love
	And sing them loud even in the dead of night;
	Hallo your name to the reverberate hills
	And make the babbling gossip of the air
	Cry out 'Olivia!' O, you should not rest
	Between the elements of air and earth
	But you should pity me.
Olivia	You might do much. What is your parentage? (I, v, 262–75)

Viola's reference to and demonstration of her verbal talents reveal that a gentleman's 'tongue' and 'spirit' are the result of intelligence and will, rather than gender or the 'great estate' that supports Orsino. Olivia in fact only becomes interested in Cesario's parentage after she is impressed with his linguistic potency. Viola is as able as the clown, whom she commends for the skills that she, he and a successful courtier share:

He must observe their mood on whom he jests,
The quality of persons and the time. (III, i, 63–4)

A good wit can turn a sentence inside out, like a 'chev'ril glove' (III, i, 12); he can turn a woman into a man or a servant into a master. Viola and Maria are twinned in the play because, whereas Viola can produce the appearance of a man, Maria can produce the appearance of her mistress, not only through the similarity of their handwriting, but through the use of language that convinces Malvolio that this is indeed 'my Lady's hand' (II, v, 84). The skilful intelligence of Viola and Maria wins for them marriages which improve their social estate: clearly for Maria, whose role as a gentlewoman-in-waiting places her beneath Sir Toby, kinsman to Olivia; and mostly likely for Viola, whose father's noble position is never precisely identified, and is probably beneath the rank of Duke Orsino.[8] When Sir Toby marries Maria in recompense for her 'device', the play represents through the advancement of a woman by marriage what was occurring for ambitious men in society: verbal agility could turn a servant into a master, make a gentleman into a peer or send a commoner into the ranks of the upper classes.

Commentators on the social order speak frequently and heatedly during this period about a fluidity in the status structure which they take to be common knowledge and objective fact. William Harrison claims that merchants 'often change estate with gentlemen, as gentlemen do with them, by a mutual conversion of the one into the other'. According to Harrison, many obtain gentility through attending the Inns of Court or the University, gaining the money and leisure to 'bear the port, charge, and countenance of a gentleman', and purchasing a coat of arms from the heralds; by this process, they, 'being made so good cheap, bee called master . . . and reputed for a gentleman ever after'. Thomas Smith agrees with Harrison on this point, comments that the prince can 'make' gentlemen, esquires or peers, and, in a section entitled 'Whether the maner of England in making gentlemen so easily is to be allowed', decides that such changes of status are good for the realm, especially for the treasury. He also considers quite sympathetically the yeomen who 'doe come to such wealth, that they are able and daily doe buy the landes of unthriftie gentlemen'. By sending their sons to school and freeing them from manual labour, yeomen 'doe make their saide sonnes by these meanes gentlemen'. Thomas Wilson concurs that gentlemen have been 'overreched' by yeomen, and adds that city lawyers are in pursuit of a country seat: 'they undoe the country people and buy up all the lands that are to be sold.' Smith is less sympathetic to the phenomenon, as are a multitude of preachers and satirists. However, even a churchman like Robert Sanderson, middle-of-the-road Anglican minister, could in 1621 announce that such fluidity was not only the status quo, but to be preferred to a closed system of rank. In a sermon on vocation, Sanderson urges idle 'gallants' to find their own work:

> observe by what steps your worthy Progenitors raised their houses to the height of *Gentry*, or *Nobility*. Scarce shall you find a man of them, that gave an accession, or brought any noted Eminency to his house; but either serving in the *Camp*, or sweating at the *Bar*, or waiting at the *Court*, or adventuring on the *Seas*, or trucking in his *Shop*, or some other way industriously bestirring himself in some settled Calling and Course of Life.

Only by equal labours can these young heirs merit 'those Ensigns of *Honor* and *Gentry* which [their ancestors] by industry atchieved.'[9]

Modern historians who study social mobility agree in general with these views, but argue that the movement actually taking place was far less extensive than these comments imply. In his original account of the situation, Lawrence Stone represented the social mobility of the period as 'a seismic upheaval of unprecedented magnitude', and his figures suggest as much: between 1500 and 1700, the number of the upper classes trebled during a time when the population doubled; the number of peers rose from 60 to 160, of knights from 500 to 1,400, and of armigerous gentry from 'perhaps 5,000 to 15,000'.[10] In his later work, Stone severely restricts his earlier assessment by claiming that newcomers were largely younger sons of the gentry, who, through the professions or trade, re-established their gentility. Nevertheless, he does admit to 'the influx of mercantile wealth into land in the late sixteenth and early seventeenth century'.[11] Keith Wrightson states that 'social mobility was a constant phenomenon in English society', since gentility was based on 'the acquisition and retention of landed wealth' rather than birth. He also claims that the later sixteenth and seventeenth centuries 'produced a quickened pace of upward and downward social mobility'. He cites a study of Lancashire where 278 families lost their place among the gentry between 1600 and 1642, and 210 families (and perhaps 79 more) moved up into it. The rising families were in part those of wealthy townsmen, which Wrightson argues were largely younger sons of the gentry; nevertheless, by far the majority of newcomers were prosperous yeomen.[12] Although Stone had originally defined marriage as 'the easiest road to riches', Wrightson concludes, as does Stone elsewhere, that very few marriages took place across status lines. There were, however, some connections made between those in positions close to each other in rank or wealth: the peerage intermarried with the upper gentry, rich merchants and lawyers; the gentry with mercantile or yeoman families.[13] Both of these historians agree that there was significant movement between ranks; they also believe that contemporary accounts of its range and frequency were exaggerated.

In *Twelfth Night*, Shakespeare creates a unique version of the age's commentary about social mobility, since the play represents as primarily a female achievement the advancement noted by his contemporaries. One would like to classify this as pure myth; on the other hand, there is very little historical evidence about the social mobility of women. According to David Cressy:

> widows and women who were heads of households were the only women assumed to have any independence, but the polity was normally assumed to exclude women of all sorts . . . While a wife in England was accorded the rank or status of her man, she was, nonetheless '*de jure* but the best of servants'.[14]

The analogies of English social theory were quite inaccurate in their identification of wives with male children or male servants, since women were prohibited from most avenues for advancement. There is evidence that some daughters of rich merchants married into the gentry or peerage, but most marriages occurred within particular status groups.[15] It is clear that studies of social mobility are severely lacking in evidence on women; more work needs to be done to investigate whether or not women improved their position through marriage or through trade. We can assume, however, that the play's representation of the mobility of its society through women is historically inaccurate, and curiously and significantly skewed in a way unlike the exaggerations of commentators.

Twelfth Night sets free a fluidity between the roles of man and woman, and master and servant in the case of Viola and Maria, but limits it severely and abruptly in the case of Malvolio. In *A Marxist Study of Shakespeare's Comedies*, Elliot Krieger argues that Malvolio's aspirations are ridiculed and exorcised by the play not in order to preserve the true 'liberty' of saturnalia, but 'to allow the aristocracy to achieve social consolidation.' He claims that whereas identity is generally mutable in the play, Malvolio's attempt to cross the line between servant and master is condemned as transgressive. Whereas Viola's enactment of gentility is rendered legitimate by our discovery at the end of the play of her 'noble' blood, Malvolio's inferior status ensures that his ambition will be viewed as presumption.[16]

Krieger is quite right to point out that the play balances the freedom of Viola's fluid identity against the strictures on Malvolio, and that such strictures finally reinforce class prejudice. But in this play such prejudice is more complex than Krieger suggests. The play includes a tentative but radical disruption of conventional categories of identity which is checked but not erased by its ending, and checked in a complicated way. Reducing Viola's astute role-playing to an expression of her nobility ignores the part she plays in this limited but tangible disruption as well as in its containment. Viola's performance as a courtier wins her prestige and potential financial rewards from Orsino and a proposal of marriage from Olivia; her noble breeding may make such success more likely, but her female gender makes it remarkable. Viola is never simply a noble person masquerading as a gentle person without wealth; her rendition of masculine gentility subtly suggests that all social roles can be impersonated. The play treats Viola very differently from Perdita in *Winter's Tale*, since *Twelfth Night* emphasises Viola's performative talent rather than her 'authentic' nobility. We may be convinced in Viola's first scene that she is no commoner: she speaks to the Captain and his sailors with authority, they defer to her, she pays them 'bounteously' (I, ii, 52). Yet the scene raises questions about whether Orsino's 'name' accurately represents his 'nature', or whether the Captain's 'outward character', either as behaviour or title, is related to his 'mind' (25, 50–1). These questions prepare us for Viola's experiments with appearance, partially because she has to negotiate in a world where titles may not be trustworthy, and partially because she herself will manipulate the relationship between seeming and being. The scene does not explicitly define Viola's status as either noble or gentle; rather, her rank is veiled from us just as Viola veils it from the people she will meet. Such masking has a purpose: we, and the characters, will know her through her role-playing and her 'intent':

> O that I served that lady,
> And might not be delivered to the world,
> Till I had made mine own occasion mellow,
> What my estate is . . .
> Conceal me what I am, and be my aid
> For such disguise as haply shall become
> The form of my intent. (41–4, 53–5)

In these passages, to will or choose her way allows Viola to disrupt conventional definitions of identity: 'my estate', 'what I am.' Not to be 'delivered to the world' is to withhold the details of one's family origins, gender and present situation until one can give birth to oneself at the most propitious moment. Such a self-protective delay replaces birth and status with a flexible identity, since not only can outer appearance be subject to one's will, but this will can also be influenced by the practice of acting: Viola's disguise 'haply shall become / The form of my intent.' The word 'form' reproduces the riddles about inner and outer identity that pervade the scene, and the word 'become' increases the dilemma: will the disguise 'become' or be used as the outward form of her inward intent? Will the 'matter' of her external costume represent decorously the inner structuring 'form' or principle of her willed purpose? Will this disguise itself become or begin to dictate her desires? To what extent do clothes make the man? Not only is rank replaced by intent in Viola's plot, but also the focus of the scene on a correspondence between outer and inner quality is complicated by the suggestion that external forms can determine internal states. When her estate is 'delivered' to us in the last act, it is only after we have seen to what an extent her skilful use of disguise becomes her.

Malvolio also does not fit within Krieger's rigid schema. The play manipulates Malvolio's status titles for dramatic purposes: when Malvolio is to appear presumptuous in his disciplining of Sir Toby, Toby cries, 'Art thou more than a steward?' (II, iii, 113). When we are to recoil and laugh at Malvolio's desire to wed Olivia, his analogy tricks us into overestimating the lowliness of his rank: 'There is example for't. The Lady of the Strachy married the yeoman of the wardrobe' (II, v, 39–40). We find out only in the late prison scene, when our sympathy is needed, that Malvolio is in fact not a commoner but a gentleman (IV, ii, 85; see also V, i, 277, 280). He is therefore not disenfranchised in any technical sense; he has already crossed over the most significant boundary line in the society, and is already a legitimate member of the ruling classes. It is true that a marriage between Malvolio and the Countess Olivia would be viewed as unconventional – it would be analogous to the marriage between the Duchess of Malfi and her steward Antonio.[17] But Malvolio's dream of marrying Olivia is in principle no more socially disruptive than Olivia's dream of marrying what she takes to be the gentleman Cesario. Shakespeare seems less intent on stigmatising characters for behaviour outside their rank than on emphasising status differences at particular moments for particular purposes. The play veils and manipulates the rank of Malvolio and Viola in order to encourage the audience to compare their relative success at winning their desired marriages. When their status is identified, it seems unlikely that the ideological point would be that women of undefined noble blood can marry dukes, whereas gentlemen cannot marry countesses. We must search more deeply for Malvolio's offending characteristic.

The play presents the problem most forcefully in two conjoining scenes: Act II, scene iv, in which the Duke and Cesario debate whether or not a woman's love is equal to a man's, and scene v, in which Malvolio imagines himself to be equal to Olivia and superior to Sir Toby through the marriage that would make him 'Count Malvolio'. It is here that the play's interest in twin characters and twin issues becomes most complex: Cesario is like Malvolio because both are servants who wish to marry their masters; Viola is like Maria because both use language and counterfeited appearances to manage their chosen male subjects; Malvolio is like Orsino because both are self-absorbed men for whom mastery consists in the exercise of power and the exclusion of any consideration of the perspectives of others. The play calls attention to its twin issues by repeating lines: when the Duke asks Cesario what sort of woman he has fallen in love with, Cesario replies, 'Of your complexion' (II, iv, 26). When Malvolio imagines Olivia's love for him, he remembers Olivia's previous remark that, should she love, 'it should be one of my complexion' (II, v, 23–4). The play invites us to consider love from two angles: Viola's self-abnegating, amorous desire and Malvolio's self-deluded dream of power. It also encourages us to consider Orsino's inadequate sense of women in terms of Malvolio's more explicitly identified 'self-love'. It is in the simultaneous exploration of the worthiness of women and the inadequacy of Malvolio that we find the play's ideological bias: the desire of an inferior to be matched with a superior is acceptable as long as it is motivated by love; to the extent that desire is self-interested, it is foolish and dangerous. In the world of the play, Malvolio represents ill will or bad will (*mal*: evil; *voglio*: I will or desire). He pursues his ends for the wrong reasons rather than the right. Viola's name, on the other hand, suggests a female, positive version of Malvolio, one whose will has become, let us say, musical, and capable of harmonising society rather than disrupting it. In this play, desire replaces reverence as the basis of the bond that links master and servant, man and woman; we could say that loving and erotic desire mediates the issue of social mobility in the play, since loving desire acknowledges choice and human will, but it also ensures devotion or a commitment to others. In *Twelfth Night*, ambition is acceptable, as long as it is the ambition to love. Our question is, why is such devoted desire identified with a woman rather than a man? What does such an identification make possible for the play and what does it obscure?

In *Twelfth Night*, the current and popular controversy over women mediates the dilemmas about social mobility. This allows the play to question quite fully the traditional ideology that those who rule are mentally or morally superior to those who are ruled, but it holds such questioning in check through an ideal of marriage and a model of marital contract which guards against the dangers of personal independence. The romantic love in the play acknowledges the power of desire, but ensures that such desire will flow into the channels of traditional, socially instituted bonds.

Act II, scene iv, allows Viola to confront the Duke with the value and power of female intelligence, but such intelligence is only discussed in terms of a woman's capacity to love.[18] The erotic power of this scene consists not only in the Duke's ignorance that his man-to-man talk with Cesario about love finally allows Viola to express what she feels, but also in the fact that the scene stages between two potential lovers the debate about women which usually took place within the confines of contemporary treatises. Shakespeare stages the debate with a bias: Viola's concealed identity and love for Orsino ensure our sympathy for her point of view.

The Duke claims that women cannot love as deeply as he does, but the scene suggests that his love for Olivia is superficial, inconstant and finally repressive, since he seems unwilling to imagine or believe that a woman could initiate a love of her own. The Duke's 'self-love' has already been revealed in the first scene of the play, when he proclaims that, after Olivia's grief over her brother dies out, the Duke himself will take his place as the new male sovereign, the 'one self king' reigning in Olivia's affections (I, i, 40). In their conversation in Act II, scene iv, Viola reminds the Duke that he may not be so successful, and offers him the possibility of seeing things from a woman's point of view:

> Viola   Say that some Lady, as perhaps there is,
> Hath for your love as great a pang of heart
> As you have for Olivia. You cannot love her.
> You tell her so. Must she not then be answered?
> Duke   There is no woman's sides
> Can bide the beating of so strong a passion
> As love doth give my heart; no woman's heart
> So big to hold so much; they lack retention. (II, iv, 89–96)

The Duke refuses to imagine that a woman could initiate desire as he does, and so he loses the point of the scene communicated to us: a woman, Viola, loves as deeply as a man, and recognises that she cannot control her beloved's point of view.

The debate about love in this scene is a submerged exploration of the extent to which Renaissance masculinity depends on denying women a will of their own, and the independent perspective that goes with it. Viola deflates this masculine conceit by her words and her presence:

> Duke   Make no compare
> Between that love a woman can bear me
> And that I owe Olivia.
> Viola   Ay, but I know –
> Duke   What dost thou know?
> Viola   Too well what love women to men may owe.
> In faith, they are as true of heart as we. (101–6)

When Viola interrupts the Duke's masculine and mastering order, 'Make no compare', she asserts that her knowledge and experience constitute an identity comparable to his own: 'Ay, but I know.' But what she knows is her erotic attachment to the Duke, 'what love women to men may owe', an attachment that ensures her willing participation in a marital system which fears more deeply the unattached woman than the brilliant wife. Viola's debate with the Duke exposes as masculine tyranny his desire to be Olivia's 'one self king', but protects him and the audience against the play's deeper fear of female independence, expressed in the Duke's reference to the story of Diana and Actaeon:

O, when mine eyes did see Olivia first,
Methought she purged the air of pestilence,
That instant was I turned into a hart,
And my desires, like fell and cruel hounds,
E'er since pursue me. (I, i, 20–4)

The Duke speaks in the fanciful language of a poetic love, but his words reveal that he already fears rejection, since Olivia, like Diana, might refuse to be married; such a fear must be repressed because it would result in the dismemberment of a sense of masculinity which depends on female subservience. Again, the play questions Orsino's association of masculinity and power, but provides a new protection against the dangers of Diana: women will marry because they want to. When Sir Toby praises Maria for her victory over Malvolio, he calls her 'Penthesilea', the Amazon warrior with whom Achilles fell in love just before he killed her. These dangerous extremes of female independence and masculine tyranny are modified by Toby's affirmation that Maria is 'one that adores me' (II, iii, 176–9).

Viola's response to Orsino in their debate about love is similar to that of Jane Anger in the treatise 'Her Protection for Women' (1589), which answers a lost pamphlet by 'the surfeiting lover'. These two treatises took part in a series of exchanges which fuelled the controversy about women during the period.[19] Like Viola, 'Her Protection for Women' declares that women should be recognised for their 'trueness of love' (p. 181), but the difference between the treatise and the play is registered in the difference between the name Jane Anger and that of Viola. Like Viola, Anger counters male views of female love, but less as a preface to marriage than as a reproof of men, uttered, as she says, in a 'choleric vein' (p. 173). Answering an opponent whose treatise seems to have renounced love and women as well, Anger uses the author's term for himself as 'surfeiting' to consider the destructive effects on women of defining male desire as an appetite. Orsino proclaims his inability to 'suffer surfeit' in his appetite for love, since he 'is all as hungry as the sea / and can digest as much' (II, iv, 100–1), but Anger points out the problem with the metaphor: men 'become ravenous hawks, who do not only seize upon us, but devour us' (p. 178). Her treatise clarifies the contradictory nature of Orsino's love, which he describes as both 'so strong a passion' that 'no woman's heart' is 'so big to hold so much', and as 'more longing, wavering, sooner lost and worn, / Than women's are' (II, iv, 94–6, 33–4). His desire for Olivia is described as infinite, like the sea, but he uses words which suggest that marriage itself would be no solution:

41

> Nought enters there,
> Of what validity and pitch so ever,
> But falls into abatement and low price
> Even in a minute. (I, i, 11–14)

The Duke's description of desire implies that whether the lover surfeits or never surfeits, the fate of his wife will be the same:

> For women are as roses, whose fair flow'r,
> Being once displayed, doth fall that very hour.

Viola's reply is full of pathos:

> And so they are; alas, that they are so;
> To die, even when they to perfection grow. (II, v, 38–42)

Such a reply is quite different from Jane Anger's comment on the subject:

> men's eyes are so curious, as be not all women equal with Venus for beauty, they cannot abide the sight of them; their stomachs so queasy, as do they taste but twice of one dish they straight surfeit, and needs must a new diet be provided for them. (p. 178)

Viola's careful and caring instruction of the Duke as well as our sympathy for her concealed love prepare us for the harmony of their betrothal in the last scene of the play, but keep us from considering what their marriage will finally be like.

Jane Anger's treatise is unusual in its lack of interest in the subject of matrimony, since most pamphlet-writers defending women during this period praised them most highly for their capacity to be able companions to men. Nicholas Breton in 'The Praise of Vertuous Ladies' (1597) claims that a man should see a great part of a woman in himself, since Eve was made out of Adam, and this proves that a woman is 'no other substance but another himself'. For every excellent man, there is an excellent woman, who is 'everie waies his match'. The treatise soon turns to the match it most prizes, that of marriage, but here the equality of women stressed by the treatise becomes a threat. The best companion to a wise man is a witty woman, but 'it is wisdom for a man to take heed that a woman be not wiser than himself.' Finally, the treatise states with a jesting tone, but a serious purpose that the only worthy 'wit' of a maid is to choose a husband well; of a married woman, to love none other; and of a widow, to provide for her children. This treatise suggests that the faculties which made women 'everie waies' a man's 'match' could only usefully be exercised within the institution of marriage, and that even in marriage these capacities had to be restrained.[20]

A woman's love was essential to a successful marriage, according to the manuals of the period, which prized marriage as a form of companionship rather than simply as a necessity for lawful procreation. For William Perkins, the creation of Eve proved that a woman should not rule her husband, since she did not come out of his head, nor be his slave, since she did not come out of his feet, but, since she came out of his side, 'man should take her as his mate.'[21] But the equality that this notion of companionship seems to promise is quickly qualified by the manuals, and the love of a wife for her husband begins to appear as another form of masculine control. Edmund Tilney's *Flower of Friendshippe* (1568) states:

> equalitie is principally to be considered in thys matrimoniall amitie, as well of yeares, as of the gifts of nature, and fortune. For equalnesse herein, maketh friendliness . . . In this long and troublesome journey of matrimonie, the wise man maye not be contented onely with his spouses virginitie, but by little and little must gently procure that he maye also steale away her private will, and appetite, so that of two bodies there may be made one onely hart, which she will soone doe, if love raigne in her, and without this agreeable concord matrimonie hath but small pleasure . . . or none at all, and the man, that is not lyked, and loved of his mate, holdeth his lyfe in continuall perill, his goodes in great jeopardie, his good name in suspect, and his whole house in perdition.

John Dod and Richard Cleaver in *The Godly Form of a Household* (1598) use almost the same words as Tilney, but their sense of the relationship between love and possession has increased: 'The husband ought not to bee satisfied that, he hath robd his wife of her virginitie, but in that he hath possession and use of her will.' Dod and Cleaver recognise the tension between the requirements that men rule and that women love: 'For although the husband shall have power to his wife, to feare and obey him, yet he shall never have strength to force her to love him.'[22]

The marriage manuals emphasise the importance of personal choice and consent by the marriage partners, and such choice includes women as well as men, but the equality of choice does not extend much farther than the original decision. The literature on marriage during this period as well as current historical studies suggest that individual desire did influence marriage negotiations much more than we previously believed: Keith Wrightson has shown that Lawrence Stone overemphasised the capacity of aristocratic parents to determine marriages for their children, and ignored the extent to which lower-class marriages were initiated by the partners. Marriage manuals consistently acknowledge the fact of individual choice in their very structure, at the same time that they insist on parental approval. These manuals include chapters on consent and on the contractual nature of marriage, in order to stress the extent to which the marriage must be a matter of free will. It may finally be the case that marriage manuals were written for the children of the gentry or the 'middling sort' rather than for the aristocracy, whose marriages were more consistently determined by issues of status and wealth rather than personal choice. It is clear that they were written more often for men than for women. The voluntary nature of the marriage vow, in which the promise 'must not come from the lippes alone, but from the wel-liking and consent of the heart', nevertheless preceded a relationship in which a woman's love had to be matched by submission and obedience to her husband's will. Many marriage manuals suggest, in fact, that the only real choice appropriate for a woman after marriage was to choose to love her husband. In Tilney's *The Flower of Friendshippe*, which celebrates 'perfite love' that 'knitteth loving heartes, in an insoluable knot of amitie', the female speaker, Lady Julia, urges women to apply themselves to their duty, not only to revere their husbands, but to love them:

> The first thing, therefore, which the married woman must labour to intende, the first thing which she must with all her force, applie her whole minde unto, and the first thing which she must hartily put in execution, is to lyke, and love well. For reason doth bind us to love them, with whom we must eate, and drinke.[23]

The fear of unloving wives in the marriage manuals is like the fear of female independence in *Twelfth Night*: in both cases, women refuse to authorise as mutually beneficial and as benevolent the form of social control inherent in the Renaissance institution of marriage. But this fear of the independent woman in *Twelfth Night* and the celebration of a romantic love that impels one to choose to be dependent on another mediates and controls the play's twin issue: the danger of self-interested rather than devoted servants. The play and its various literary and social sources testify to a society searching to articulate a new social bond between 'master' and 'servant', one which would acknowledge choice and ensure a new kind of 'dependability', based on contract rather than feudal obligation.[24]

In Act II, scene v, which directly follows the debate about love between Orsino and Viola, Malvolio imagines his new estate as 'Count Malvolio', and the play reveals that such self-interest has always motivated his government within the house. It is clear that Malvolio does not pursue Olivia with the poetic abandon of the other lovers in the play; he sees her as his ticket to a higher social position. His desire for Olivia as well as his ethical severity is a mask for a will-to-power:

Fabian	O, peace! Now he's deeply in. Look how imagination blows him.
Malvolio	Having been three months married to her, sitting in my state –
Toby	O for a stone bow, to hit him in the eye!

Malvolio	Calling my officers about me, in my branched velvet gown; having come from a day-bed, where I have left Olivia sleeping – . . . And then to have the humour of state; and after a demure travel of regard, telling them I know my place, as I would they should do theirs, to ask for my kinsman Toby – . . . Saying, 'Cousin Toby, my fortunes having cast me on your niece, give me this prerogative of speech.'
Toby	What, what?
Malvolio	'You must amend your drunkenness'. (II, v, 40–71)

Malvolio's fantasy reveals that his disciplinary zeal is impelled by a desire to dominate, unlike Viola's gracious deference. His imagined reproof, 'You must amend your drunkeness', is, like his branched velvet gown and his imperious looks, only another means by which he demonstrates his new position of power within the household. Malvolio's imagined reproof of Sir Toby is to be compared to the kindly correction of Orsino by Viola: their motives, according to the play, establish their difference. Malvolio's crime is not that he, as a gentleman, wants to marry a countess, or even that a steward wants to marry his mistress; it is that he will use his new position to disrupt traditional customs and rituals, and that such use of his 'prerogative' will be motivated by an ambition to establish his superiority and to impose his will on others. His sense of being virtuous is actually a desire for supremacy; for this reason, there will be no more cakes and ale, as Toby puts it (II, iii, 116–17). We find during the play that Malvolio has brought Fabian 'out o' favour with my lady' Olivia for bearbaiting, and put Viola's benevolent captain into jail for some unidentified crime (II, v, 6–7; V, i, 275–6). Although Maria calls Malvolio only 'a kind of Puritan', Malvolio's fantasy of power constitutes the play's critique of London disciplinarians, those Puritan aldermen who were perhaps gentlemen but had originally been merchants, who condemned holiday revelry, bearbaiting and the theatre: such a concern for civil rule, according to the play, masks a self-interested desire to govern, an unwillingness to accept traditional social bonds, and a willingness to disrupt rather than harmonise the social order. London Puritans and Malvolio are like the 'politicians' and 'Brownists' that Sir Andrew fears (III, ii, 30–1): each is a type of 'separatist', one who does not respect the bonds that tie the community together, bonds which may be flexible and fluid, but which must continue to hold if society is to survive.

In 'Pierce Pennilesse: His Supplication to the Divell' (1592), Thomas Nash, Gent., attacks those newly rich men who have no respect for the 'noble' virtue of liberality, which he feels is the main source of income for struggling writers. The contempt for tradition on the part of these 'new men' is the result of a frenetic upward movement of tradesmen and lawyers, who dress 'as brave as any . . . Nobleman'. He makes it clear that he does not oppose social mobility *per se*, but only that worthy men are left impoverished, whereas the undeserving obtain higher estates through 'delicious gold' or are unjustly promoted like 'some such obscure upstart gallants, as without desert or service are raised from the plough, to be checkmate with Princes'. Indeed, such social advancement would be appropriate if granted to writers whose talents make them superior to their patrons: 'This is the lamentable condition of our Times, that men of Arte must seeke almes of Cormorants, and those that deserve best, be kept under by Dunces.' Like *Twelfth Night*, Nash questions the traditional notion that social superiors are necessarily better than those they govern, but he also attacks merchants and tradesmen who have no respect for the traditional nobility and no respect for the theatre. 'Pierce' claims that the ethical severity of those citizens who condemn playgoing only masks a desire to usurp the place of the traditional nobility:

> I will defend [the theatre] against any Collier or clubfooted Usurer of them all, there is no immortalitie, can be given a man on earth like unto Playes. What talke I to them of immortalitie, that are the only underminers of Honour, and doe envie any man that is not sprung up by base Brokerie like themselves. They care not if all the ancient houses were rooted out, so that like the Burgomasters of the Low-Countries they might share the government amongst them as States, and be quarter-maisters of our Monarchie . . . [They respect] neither the right of Fame that is due to true Nobilitie deceased, nor what hopes of eternitie are to be proposed to adventurous mindes, to encourage them forward, but only their execrable luker, and filthie unquenchable avarice.

Social advancement is appropriate for 'adventurous mindes' and 'men of Arte', but not for those who seek to mount upward for the wrong reasons: a hunger for money and power over others. Such as these not only have no respect for the ancient houses of nobility, they want to cast society into a different form, so that, like the 'Burgomasters of the Low-Countries', they will be 'quarter-maisters of our Monarchie'. According to the treatise, this disruption of the social order is caused by the devil himself, '*Nicalao Malevolo* . . . the great mister maister of hell'.[25]

In 'Pierce Pennilesse', Nash reacts against Puritan attacks on the theatres and against the influence of the London city government on the Privy Council. *Twelfth Night* (1602) was produced only a few years after the office of the Master of the Revels had affirmed its capacity to license theatrical companies and restrict the days of their performances, as well as the bearbaiting that occurred nearby. Such courtly and civic control over theatrical revelry mirrored the repression of holiday pastimes in the countryside in places like Shakespeare's Stratford. Local Puritan elites were prohibiting many village festivities, including the church ales, in the name of a more thorough 'civil rule' (II, iii, 122).[26]

Nash's pamphlet illuminates one of the most important contexts for *Twelfth Night*: urban satire, including the Harvey–Nash quarrel, in which 'Pierce Pennilesse' figures, but also including the war of the theatres, occurring during this period and referring at times to this play. *What You Will* is one of John Marston's volleys in the war, and its connections to *Twelfth Night, or What You Will* clarify that, for these playwrights, the intersection between disguise and the problem of fluid social relations is commonplace. In a society where status categories are flexible, apparel becomes a 'god', and opinion, or 'what you will', according to Marston, determines all social value, including personal rank and identity. One of the central characters in Marston's play, Albano, is a merchant who for a time loses his wife, his property and his name because people assume that he is dead and the living person standing before them is an imposter. Whether *What You Will* appeared before or after *Twelfth Night*, the attributes they share suggest that *Twelfth Night* was not only about revelry or carnival, but about the difficulties of estimating the value of individuals when the externals of identity, including rank and gender, are so easily imitated. It is therefore relevant that Shakespeare's play and probably Marston's were put on before an Inns of Court audience, incipient lawyers, well versed in urban satire and preparing for the successes and dangers of social advancement in the city. 'What you will' for Marston refers to opinion, and for Shakespeare to desire, but both playwrights testify to a world in which individually initiated attitudes and acts have replaced a shared consensus about appropriate behaviour and the rules for evaluating it. Both plays fear such a world, in which every man and woman can be a phoenix; *Twelfth Night* offers us women and servants who exchange their independence for a willing desire for another and so preserve 'all relation'.[27]

Malvolio may be a kind of Puritan, but he is also the conventional butt of urban satire, the social climber who becomes obsessed with the externals of rank, 'the habit of some sir of note' (III, iv, 77–8), without a sense of 'true' worth and its significance for the community. Viola's decision to trust the Captain at the beginning of the play takes on new importance in this context, because she, like all members of society, must learn to accept and analyse a difference between external appearance and internal value:

> There is a fair behaviour in thee, captain,
> And though that nature with a beauteous wall
> Doth oft close in pollution, yet of thee
> I will believe thou hast a mind that suits
> With this thy fair and outward character. (I, i, 47–51)

Viola's trust in the Captain is a matter of judgement and of will, an opinion not a fact. The problems of disguise in *Twelfth Night* take the play into the world of Ben Jonson's exploration of character and the ambiguous relationship in his plays between inner worth and social rank.

For Jonson, the nobility are to be revered, but only if they

> Study the native frame of a true heart,
> An inward comeliness of bountie, knowledge,
> And spirit that may conforme them actually
> To *God's* high figures.[28]

In *Cynthia's Revels, Or the Fountayne of self-love* (1600), the Jonsonian surrogate Crites unmasks the narcissism that motivates decadent aristocrats as well as ambitious courtiers; the play uses terms that look forward to Shakespeare's presentation of the Duke and Malvolio. But unlike Shakespeare, Jonson proceeds to define a positive version of self-love, which transforms narcissism into an honourable method of establishing publicly one's inner value: 'allowable Self-love' quickens 'minds in the pursuit of honour', and impels individuals to reach a social position which will justly match 'that true measure of one's self' (V, vii, 26–35). In the play, Cynthia the Queen singles out for promotion her playwright Crites, whom she describes as one 'whom learning, virtue, and our favour last / Exempteth from the gloomy multitude' (V, viii, 32–3).

In *Twelfth Night*, Shakespeare pokes fun at a notion of 'allowable self-love' which results in the preferment of its author. He associates such self-love with the colour yellow theatrically attributed to it in *Cynthia's Revels*, and with an overly pretentious, censorious steward, who is convinced that his lady will thrust greatness upon him.[29] Malvolio's 'self-love' satirises Jonson's version of individual value not only as self-indulgent but as socially divisive, because it privileges censuring the faults of others and praising the self over the more difficult task of preserving the harmony of social relations. *Twelfth Night* suggests that Jonson's version of merit is just as 'separatist' as the Puritans he derides in his comedies. The 'railing' that Viola's social music tames is not only that of the Puritans but that of the satirists.

Shakespeare is as interested as Jonson in the relationship between the 'name' and 'nature' of nobility, but he explores the issue through 'Viola' rather than 'Crites'. The name of the Duke, Orsino (or 'the little bear'), indicates that the Duke as well as Malvolio is the subject of the play's bearbaiting. Marston's Duke in *What You Will* is blatantly frivolous and sensual; audiences must have understood that Orsino's attitude towards love and women was not presented uncritically by *Twelfth Night*. But such criticism never becomes biting satire in Shakespeare's play: 'there is no railing in a known discreet man, though he do nothing but reprove' (I, v, 95–6).[30]

In *Twelfth Night*, Shakespeare celebrates the social arts, very like his own, which can turn a servant into a master, a glove-maker's son into a gentleman, a woman into a man, a man into a woman. Nevertheless, he reproves those who would use this social fluidity for their own benefit or as an opportunity to reorder the traditional structure according to new ethical and political principles. Such ethical and political blueprints, he suggests, are simply fantasies of power, which exchange the community good for private profit.

The play links the issues of gender and status in order to make marriage, with its inclusion of desire and its commitment to permanence, the model of all social bonds. The Priest's description of Olivia's marriage betrothal to Sebastian represents the play's dream of a perpetual community, in which each member willingly takes his or her place:

> A contract of eternal bond of love
> Confirmed by mutual joinder of your hands,
> Attested by the holy close of lips,
> Strengthened by interchangment of your rings. (V, i, 156–9)

It is not a coincidence that in the last act, as the cases of mistaken identity mount up, willing service is coordinated with the contract of marriage, and the dangers of infidelity to such a contract are considered: Olivia's sense of her husband Cesario's betrayal is followed by Antonio's sense of his master Sebastian's betrayal, and then by Orsino's sense of his servant Cesario's betrayal. Antonio, of course, is the model for the new servant imagined by the play, since his service is based on desire rather than duty or reverence:

> I could not stay behind you. My desire
> (More sharp than filed steel) did spur me forth;
> . . . My willing love . . . Set forth in your pursuit. (III, iii, 4–5, 11–13)[31]

The marriage bonds that certify the socially acceptable 'willing love' of man and woman are forged by the 'true' priest in the play, who is opposed dramatically to the 'false' priest–fool, Sir Topas, who baits Malvolio. This carnivalesque figure reproaches others in society who have 'dissembled in such a gown' (IV, ii, 5–6), but also members of the aristocracy, who, like Chaucer's Sir Thopas, provide only an empty image of aristocratic superiority. Such an image becomes ridiculous when engendered by a non-aristocratic author–fool, like the narrator of the *Canterbury Tales*, who cannot get a tale of nobility quite right, but also when manipulated by a Sir Toby, whose name is so close to the Sir Topas he concocts that he becomes implicated in his own critique. Such satirists as Sir Toby miss the point when they bait Malvolio: blood is not the issue, but rather some mysterious quality of inner nobility which Sir Toby himself does not possess.

Viola's 'courtesy' is evidence not only of this inner nobility, but of her willingness to use her performative talent for unselfish purposes, to spin out the modes of social behaviour that can preserve the ties that bind. Orsino and Olivia think nostalgically about 'the old age' or the 'merry world' before true love and loyal servants were replaced by 'these most brisk and giddy-paced times' (II, iv, 6, 48; II, i, 100–1). *Twelfth Night* is plagued by a fear that when the witty whirl that is its surface and its plot shuts down, no trustworthy social order will remain: 'with hey, ho, the wind and the rain' (V, i, 391ff).

Perhaps this is one reason why the play so relentlessly excludes the figure of the merchant, although in the sources, the father of Viola and Sebastian is almost always a merchant, and frequently the father of Olivia is so as well.[32] In Marston's play, Albano the merchant most forcefully represents the fragility of an identity based on fortune or chance, since he has achieved his status in the community through the power of wealth rather than the tradition of family lineage. In *Twelfth Night*, a play that is filled with imagery of the sea, merchants are never mentioned, although the play does refer to a new map of the world which includes the West Indies, and which is used to describe the lines on Malvolio's smiling face as he pursues his hopes with Olivia (III, ii, 76–8). The play evokes the sense of treasure that can be obtained from the sea, as well as the riches that can satisfy a desire which is as infinite as the sea. But the treasure from the ocean in this play is Viola and Sebastian; like aspirations for social ascent, commercial interests are turned into romantic appetites.

The play cannot afford the figure of the merchant because such a social role does not fit clearly enough into the traditional hierarchical order of servant and master. The relations of the commercial classes to the classes above them could not easily be described in terms of feudal norms – they are not mentioned in the homily on obedience – since they were constituted more by monetary exchange than by the traditional ideals of reverence and duty. Shakespeare has to consider Malvolio as 'a kind of Puritan'; a real Calvinist merchant would upset the delicate balance of a play which explores the issue of social mobility through the lens of willing servants rather than successful entrepreneurs.[33]

The play solves the problem of self-interested desire through Viola's harmonious social bonding, and so projects anxieties about status relations onto gender relations. The play's fear of independent women is implicated in its fear of independent servants, since Viola's dependence is constituted in opposition to Malvolio's self-interest. Therefore sexual-familial structures are linked rather explicitly to socio-economic structures, as Kelly puts it, in such a way as to suggest that Viola's attitude to her labour as a servant to the Duke is praiseworthy because it partakes of her attitude towards her beloved, Orsino. As such, loving male–female relations mediate master–servant relations: both partners may be quite equal in intelligence and moral capacity, or indeed the subordinate may be superior to his or her master; nevertheless, an appreciative love should tie both together. Such a formula redefines traditional hierarchical bonds as more flexible in themselves, but also turns anything but the most loving commitment to one's superiors into 'self-love'.

The play's superimposition of labour relations onto marital relations results in a model of 'willing service' formed in the image of the 'mutual consent' required in the marriage contract. The history of the various kinds of contract during this period demonstrates that Shakespeare's model of contract is a selective one, since such an agreement could act as either a conservative or a disruptive force. At the time that the play was produced, changes in the law were eroding traditional restraints on business contracts, and strengthening the individual's control over these transactions. Such agreements required voluntary and mutual consent at the cost of feudal models of obligation, since deference to status was replaced with an interest in the market and personal profit. But such 'freedom' was not extended to labouring individuals, whose tendency to move throughout the country in pursuit of work had resulted in the passing of the Statute of Artificers (1563), which prohibited the sudden termination of contracts between employer and employed, and made illegal a horizontal mobility of workers responsive to new commercial developments. Through its labour-contract clauses, the Statute sought to place labourers under the firm control of a 'master', and often within the structure of the employer's family and paternal authority. *Twelfth Night* also mediates between a status and a market society through marriage and the family: it dramatises voluntary consent and 'free' will as mitigating the rigidity of the master–servant relationship, but also as preserving this traditional bond at a time when market forces were wearing away its feudal foundations. Shakespeare may have taken his cue from the marriage manuals of the period, which employ the language of contractual 'freedom', but nevertheless hedge it about with a concern for status and authority: 'consent' includes parental agreement and 'equality' requires likeness in rank; both consent and equality fade quickly away before the customary necessities of male authority and female submission. Like the manuals and marital law during this period, Shakespeare attempts to negotiate between individual interests and those of traditional society. He follows Perkins by making marriage the model for 'the commonwealth'.[34]

Twelfth Night imagines a world in which one's social estate is a matter of desire or will rather than birth or title. Such desire is innocent and successful to the extent that it moves one to be bound unselfishly to another. Shakespeare divides and conquers in his play not only by praising Viola and condemning Malvolio, but also by obscuring what Viola and Malvolio share in the play's various literary and social sources: a connection with a commercial class whose access to money has the power to upset the traditional link between high birth, wealth and status. The ideal that is set before women, servants and merchants in the play is that of loving and willing service, a Viola who chooses her man, but who also chooses to correct gently rather than dethrone the tyrant who will rule over her in the future. We might imagine a play about Mal-Viola (or Jane Anger), who does not wish the Duke well and says so, and whose female desire cannot so easily be presented as 'good will'. Just as Jonson in *Cynthia's Revels* presents himself in Crites, Shakespeare in *Twelfth Night* presents himself in Viola, that figure so well versed in the 'arts' of social behaviour, far more intelligent than her superiors, who elects to preserve the social harmony rather than 'put down' her masters.

NOTES

1. I am grateful for the comments and suggestions made by the participants of the seminar 'Materialist feminist criticism of Shakespeare' held at the 1989 meeting of the Shakespeare Association of America. I would particularly like to thank Catherine Belsey, Barbara Bono, Mihoko Suzuki, Valerie Wayne and Marion Wynne-Davies. 'Perspectives' are discussed in Jurgis Baltrusaitis, *Anamorphic Act*, trans. W.L. Strachan (New York: Harry N. Abrams, 1977), pp. 11–18, 91–114. Orsino's comment on the perspective appears in *Twelfth Night*, V, i, 215–16 in *The Complete Signet Classic Shakespeare*, ed. Sylvan Barnet (New York: Harcourt Brace Jovanich, 1972). Subsequent citations will refer to this edition and appear in the text of the essay.
2. Joan Kelly, 'The doubled vision of feminist theory', in Judith L. Newton, Mary P. Ryan and Judith R. Walkowitz, eds., *Sex and Class in Women's History* (London: Routledge and Kegan Paul, 1983), pp. 264, 265, 266. The emphasis is Kelly's own.
3. 'An exhortation concerning good order, and obedience to rulers and magistrates,' and 'An homilie of the state of matrimonie', in *Certaine Sermons or Homilies appointed by the Queenes Majestie, to be declared and read by all Parsons, Vicars, and Curates . . .* (London, 1595), I3 and Gg7.
4. Of course, several Renaissance critics have already discussed quite successfully the relationship of gender and status in Renaissance drama. Frank Whigham's 'Sexual and social mobility in *The Duchess of Malfi*' (*PMLA*, 100 [1985], pp. 167–86) is the best of this sort, and I am indebted to his discussion of social mobility. Nevertheless, in his essay, the gender issues tend to collapse into the status issues: 'the duchess's enterprise is not primarily private and romantic: it is, rather, a socially adaptive action that extends to the zone of gender conflict a maneuver actively in play in the arena of class conflict' (p. 171). Whigham's quotation from Kenneth Burke on *Venus and Adonis* at the beginning of the essay clarifies this: 'The real subject is not primarily sexual lewdness at all, but "social lewdness" mythically expressed in sexual terms.' If feminist writers in

the 1970s ignored problems of class (Paula Berggren, 'The woman's part: female sexuality as power in Shakespeare's plays', and Clara Claiborne Park, 'As we like it: how a girl can be smart and still popular', both in Carolyn Lenz, Gayle Greene and Carol Neely, eds., *The Woman's Part: Feminist criticism of Shakespeare* [Urbana: University of Illinois Press, 1980], pp. 17–34, 100–16), then new historicists and cultural materialists in the 1980s often reduced gender concerns into a symbolic means of articulating what is 'the real subject': status, or issues of power in general. See Leonard Tennenhouse, *Power on Display: The politics of Shakespeare's genres* (New York and London: Methuen, 1986) for a fascinating discussion of 'Staging carnival', which attends to the role of women and Queen Elizabeth in the process of inheritance, but which finally defines the comedies and Petrarchan literature as 'presenting us with a political crisis which must be understood and resolved in sexual terms' (p. 19). This is the problem, I think, with focusing exclusively on Queen Elizabeth in discussing these issues: the sexual-familial questions can too easily disappear before the political or socio-economic concerns. Jean Howard avoids this difficulty in 'Crossdressing, the theatre, and gender struggle in early modern England', (*SQ*, **39** [1988], pp. 418–40), in which she discusses the 'various manifestations of crossdressing' as 'an interlocking grid through which we can read aspects of class and gender struggle in the period', and the particularity with which she does so is enlightening and refreshing. She interprets *Twelfth Night* quite differently from the way I do, however, because she sees Viola's crossdressing as 'in no way adopted to protest gender inequities' (p. 431).

5. In an essay in this collection, 'The world turned upside down: inversion, gender and the state', Peter Stallybrass argues that 'there is no *intrinsic* connection between inversions of class [and] gender . . . Politics is precisely the work of *making* such connections.' I argue in this essay that *Twelfth Night* performs such work by coordinating the interests of women and servants, and by making female 'good will' the model for socially ambitious men.

6. It is not a coincidence that the centrality of 'will' to the play reproduces the role of 'will' in the sonnets, in which Shakespeare represents his own peculiar linking of love and the potential rewards of patronage. For a largely psychoanalytic account of will in the sonnets, see Joel Fineman, *Shakespeare's Perjured Eye* (Berkeley: University of California Press, 1988). My analysis of traditional and emergent attitudes in the play is indebted to Raymond Williams' discussion of his terms 'dominant', 'emergent' and 'residual' in *Problems in Materialism and Culture* (London: Verso, 1980), pp. 31–49, and in *Marxism and Literature* (Oxford: Oxford University Press, 1977), pp. 121–8.

7. I disagree with those critics who diagnose and/or dismiss Viola's successes in this play as the result of her noble rank (Tennenhouse, *Power on Display*, p. 66; Elliot Krieger, *A Marxist Study of Shakespeare's Comedies* [London: Macmillan Press, 1979], pp. 105–30).

8. As with several other characters, the play confuses us about the status of Maria: she is represented by Sir Toby as 'my niece's chambermaid' (I, iii, 50), but is identified by Olivia as 'my gentlewoman' (I, v, 162). But the play continually groups her with the 'lighter people', as Malvolio puts it (V, i, 341). In her forged letter to Malvolio, Maria herself delineates the line she will eventually cross: 'Be opposite with a kinsman, surly with servants' (II, v, 149–50).

9. William Harrison, 'A description of England' (1577), in F.J. Furnivall, ed., *Elizabethan England* (London: Walter Scott, 1902), pp. 7, 9; Thomas Smith,

De Republica Anglorum (London, 1583), pp. 27–30; Thomas Wilson, *The State of England Anno-dom. 1600*, ed. F.J. Fisher (London: Camden Miscellany xvi, 3rd series lii, 1936), pp. 25, 38; Robert Sanderson, 'Ad populum; the fourth sermon . . . London, Nov. 4, 1621' in *XXXXVI Sermons* (London, 1986), p. 212.

10. Lawrence Stone, 'Social mobility in England, 1500–1700', *Past and Present*, 33 (1966), pp. 16, 23–24; see also David Cressy, 'Describing the social order of Elizabethan and Stuart England,' *Literature and History*, 3 (1976), pp. 29–44.
11. Lawrence Stone, *An Open Elite? England 1540–1880* (Oxford: Clarendon Press, 1984), pp. 399–400; 405–6.
12. Keith Wrightson, *English Society 1580–1680* (London: Hutchinson, 1982), pp. 26–30, 140.
13. Stone, 'Social mobility', p. 38; Wrightson, p. 86, cites Vivien Brodsky Elliott, 'Mobility and marriage in pre-industrial England' (unpubl. Ph.D. thesis, University of Cambridge, 1978), pt. 1, ch. 4; pt. 3, ch. 3. See also Elliott, 'Single women in the London marriage market: age, status, mobility, 1598–1619', in R.B. Outhwaite, ed., *Marriage and Society: Studies in the social history of marriage* (London: Europa Publications, 1981), pp. 81–100; and Stone, *The Family, Sex and Marriage in England, 1500–1800* (London: Weidenfeld and Nicolson, 1977), pp. 60–1, 491.
14. Cressy, 'Describing the social order', pp. 34–5.
15. Stone, 'Social mobility', p. 38; Lawrence Manley, *London in the Age of Shakespeare: An anthology* (London: Croom Helm, 1986), pp. 77–8.
16. Krieger, *A Marxist Study*, pp. 100–1, and throughout.
17. See Whigham, 'Sexual and social mobility in *The Duchess of Malfi*'.
18. See Catherine Belsey's illuminating and convincing reading of this scene in 'Disrupting sexual difference: meaning and gender in the comedies', in John Drakakis, ed., *Alternative Shakespeares* (London: Methuen, 1985), pp. 166–90. Belsey argues that Viola-as-Cesario calls 'into question that set of relations between terms which proposes as inevitable an antithesis between masculine and feminine, men and women' (p. 167). I am arguing that the difference between the categories of servant and master are also questioned by the play, and that Viola's success and 'good will' in disrupting these differences in scene iv are compared to Malvolio's failure in scene v. Viola's noble rank, like her role as a wife, is affirmed at the end of the play, and, as Belsey says, closes off 'the glimpsed transgression . . . But the plays are more than their endings' (pp. 187–8).
19. The full title of Anger's treatise is 'Jane Anger her Protection for Women. To defend them against the Scandalous Reportes of a late Surfeiting Lover, and all other like Venerians that complaine so to bee overcloyed with womens kindness' (London: Richard Jones, 1589). See the abridged text in Katherine Henderson and Barbara McManus, eds., *Half Humankind: Contexts and texts of the controversy about women in England, 1540–1640* (Urbana and Chicago: University of Illinois Press, 1985). Page numbers from this edition will appear in the text of the essay. For commentary on the controversy about women and lists of texts, see Henderson and McManus, *Half Humankind*; Edmund Tilney, *'The Flower of Friendshippe:' A Renaissance Dialogue Contesting Marriage*, ed., Valerie Wayne, forthcoming from Cornell University Press; Linda Woodhouse, *Women and the English Renaissance: Literature and the nature of womankind, 1540–1620* (Urbana: University of Chicago Press, 1984), pp. 139–51; and Louis B. Wright, *Middle-Class Culture in Elizabethan England* (Chapel Hill: University of North Carolina Press, 1935), pp. 481–

502. For a discussion of the intersection of the controversy and later drama, see Sandra Clark, 'Hic Mulier, Haec Vir and the controversy over masculine women', *Studies in Philology*, **82** (1985), pp. 157–83; and Mary Beth Rose, 'Women in men's clothing: apparel and social stability in *The Roaring Girl*', *English Literary Renaissance*, **14** (1984), pp. 139–51.

20. Nicholas Breton, 'The Praise of Vertuous Ladies' in *The Wil of Wit, Wits Will, or Wils Wit, chuse you whether. Containing five discourses.* (London: Thomas Creede, 1597), pp. 65, 69, 67, 70–1.

21. William Perkins, *Christian Oeconomy*, trans. T. Pickering (London: E. Weaver, 1609), p. 125. The first occurrence of this representation of companionship is found in Bullinger, *Christen State of Matrimony* (1541), sig. A4v.

22. Tilney, 'A Brief and Pleasant Discourse of Duties in Marriage, called the Flower of Friendshippe' (London: Henrie Denham, 1568), B2, B6. John Dod and Richard Cleaver include passages from 'The Flower' in *A Godly Form of Householde Government* (London: Thomas Creede, 1598), pp. 167, 165.

23. For discussions on individual choice in marriage, see Stone, *The Family, Sex and Marriage in England, 1500–1800*, pp. 85–93, 117, 178–95, 270–95; Wrightson, *English Society 1580–1680*, pp. 70–88; Susan Dwyer Amussen, *An Ordered Society: Gender and Class in Early Modern England* (Oxford: Basil Blackwell, 1988), pp. 70–6, 105–8; and William and Malleville Haller, 'The Puritan art of love', *Huntington Library Quarterly*, **5** (1941–2), pp. 254–6, 265. Cleaver insists on the 'consent of the heart' (p. 115) and includes discussions on choice, consent, and contract (pp. 96–129). Perkins includes chapters entitled 'Of the Contract', 'Of the choice of persons fit for marriage' and 'Of consent in the Contract' (pp. 18, 23, 68). See Tilney, D4, for Lady Julia's advice on the choice of husbands and the practicality of love after the marriage has occurred.

24. Howard discusses the emerging idea of contractual relations in 'Crossdressing', p. 428. Don Wayne applies it to Jonson's *Bartholomew Fair* in 'Drama and Society in the Age of Jonson: an alternative view', *Renaissance Drama*, **N.S. 13** (1982), pp. 103–29. See Gordon Schochet, *Patriarchalism in Political Thought: The authoritarian family and political speculation and attitudes* (Oxford: Basil Blackwell, 1975) for a consideration of the idea of contract in political relations, although not in socio-economic relations.

25. Thomas Nash, 'Pierce Penilesse: His Supplication to the Divell' (London, 1592), A2, C4, F3.

26. E.K. Chambers, *The Elizabethan Stage*, 4 vols. (Oxford: Clarendon Press, 1923), vol. I, pp. 298–302; vol. II, pp. 355–6, 471; David Underdown, *Revel, Riot and Rebellion: Popular politics and culture in England, 1603–1660* (Oxford: Oxford University Press, 1987), pp. 56–7.

27. For the Nash–Harvey exchange, see Donald McGinn, *Thomas Nashe* (Boston: Twayne Publishers, 1981), pp. 104–51; for the war of the theatres, see Roscoe Small, *The Stage Quarrel between Ben Jonson and the So-Called Poetasters* (Breslau: M. & H. Marcus, 1899), pp. 101–14; and R.W. Ingram, *John Marston* (Boston: Twayne Publishers, 1978), pp. 43–54. For the exploration of the fluidity of social relations in the drama of the period, see Jean-Christophe Agnew, *Worlds Apart: The market and the theatre in Anglo-American thought, 1550–1750* (Cambridge: Cambridge University Press, 1986), especially pp. 57–148; L.C. Knights, *Drama and Society in the Age of Jonson* (London: Chatto and Windus, 1937); Manley, *London in the Age of Shakespeare*, pp. 75–81, 285–90; and Wayne, '*Drama and Society in the Age of*

Jonson: an alternative view'. The date usually attributed to Marston's *What You Will* is 1601, one year before *Twelfth Night*, but this is just conjecture, as Philip Finkelpearl points out in *John Marston of the Middle Temple* (Cambridge, Mass.: Harvard University Press, 1969), pp. 162–3. Donne speaks of the disruption of traditional social bonds in 'An Anatomy of the World: The First Anniversary'.

28. *Cynthia's Revels, Or the Fountayne of self-love* in *Ben Jonson*, eds. C.H. Herford and Percy Simpson, 11 vols. (Oxford: Clarendon Press, 1932), vol. 4, pp. 1–183, V, iv, 643–6. On Jonson's analysis of what constitutes 'nobility,' see Don Wayne, *Penshurst: The semiotics of place and the poetics of history* (Madison: The University of Wisconsin Press, 1984), pp. 129–73.

29. I am not the first to entertain the notion that Malvolio may represent Jonson; John Hollander considers the possibility for reasons quite different from my own in his insightful and informative essay, '*Twelfth Night* and the morality of indulgence', *The Sewanee Review*, 68 (1959), pp. 220–38. Hollander dismisses the possibility, but reminds us that Marston's *What You Will* 'devotes much effort to lampooning Jonson' (p. 238). See V, vii, 26–35 in *Cynthia's Revels* for the yellow colour of 'allowable self-love', which later turns up as Malvolio's stockings.

30. As Hollander points out, the Duke's name and nature are affirmed as equally 'noble' (I, ii, 25), but the name 'Orsino' suggests quite another character. Jean Howard offers a different interpretation of Shakespeare's treatment of Orsino in her article 'Crossdressing' (p. 432).

31. Antonio is also the character left without a clear social position at the end of the play, since Sebastian never explicitly claims him as his man, nor frees him from Orsino's indictment. The play's tentative sympathy for this homoerotic relationship cannot save it from an exclusion from the community produced at the end of the play and most literally from the social legitimacy of marital bonds. Like that of the other characters, the 'desire' of Antonio for Sebastian begins by flowing into the traditional bonds of master and servant; therefore accounts of its homoeroticism have to be historicised. Nevertheless, Antonio is left at the end of the play a 'masterless' man.

32. Emanuel Forde, *The Famous History of Parismus* (1578); *The Novels of Matteo Bandello*, trans. John Payne, 4 vols. (London: Villon Society, 1890), vol. 4, pp. 121–61 (part II, no. 28); *Gl'Ingannati* (1537), ed. and abridged T.L. Peacock (London: Chapman and Hall, 1862). See also the useful Morton Luce, ed., *Rich's 'Apolonius and Silla', An Original of Shakespeare's Twelfth Night* (New York: Duffield and Co., 1912), which discusses all the sources.

33. Manley, *London in the Age of Shakespeare*, pp. 75–81; Ruth Mohl, *The Three Estates in Medieval and Renaissance Literature* (New York: F. Ungar, 1962).

34. On changes in contract law, see David Little, *Religion, Order and Law* (New York: Harper & Row, 1969) pp. 204–5. On the Statute of Artificers and its relation to market influences, see F.J. Fisher, 'Commercial trends and policy in the sixteenth century', *Economic History Review*, 10 (1940), pp. 110–13; and Bernard Supple, *Commercial Crisis and Change in England, 1600–1642* (Cambridge: Cambridge University Press, 1959), p. 251. Martin Ingram comments on the implicit use of the family as a 'little commonwealth' in the Statute in *Church Courts, Sex and Marriage in England, 1570–1640* (Cambridge: Cambridge University Press, 1987), p. 126. Ingram also describes the mediation between individual and family interests in the courts (pp. 200–5). Consent was nothing new to the marriage contract; there were in fact some efforts made during this period to increase family control over individual

decisions; see Ingram, pp. 135–6. On the contrast between a status and a market society, see C.B. Macpherson, *The Political Theory of Possessive Individualism, Hobbes to Locke* (London: Oxford University Press, 1962), pp. 46–70. Perkins described marriage as a 'seminary to church and commonwealth' in *Christian Oeconomy*, chapter 6. Also interesting on this subject is David Zaret, *The Heavenly Contract: Ideology and organization in prerevolutionary Puritanism* (Chicago: University of Chicago, 1985), who comments that 'by modifying Calvinism with ideas about a heavenly contract, Puritan clerics provided greater scope for individual initiative in religion, but they channeled this initiative in ways that maintained their authority' (p. 129).

—2—

Patrimony and Patriarchy in
The Merchant of Venice

Carol Leventen

A work is tied to ideology not so much by what it says as by what it does
not say. It is in the significant *silences* of a text, in its gaps and absences, that
the presence of ideology can be most positively felt. It is these silences
which the critic must make speak.

Terry Eagleton[1]

Narrowly defined, my subject is the relationship between women and
money in *The Merchant of Venice* and the ways in which the play both
problematises and mystifies that relationship. Portia is wealthy – 'richly
left' – and ostensibly answerable to no one but herself, yet she either
cannot or does not conceive of herself as autonomous, self-determining or
able to use her patrimony to free herself from patriarchal control – even
though she defines and experiences that control, manifested in the 'lottery' established by her dead father, as arbitrary and oppressive, and even
though access to far less material wealth is understood by the male characters (especially but not only Bassanio) to confer the possibility of autonomy and freedom. The play, I argue, tends to endorse and reward
Portia's behaviour as that of a dutiful daughter at the same time that it
tends to judge the behaviour of Jessica, who defies paternal authority and
appropriates her father's wealth, as that of an unruly daughter. In both
cases, the play responds to and participates in contemporary anxieties
about women, money and power. Moreover, *Merchant* deflects attention
from materiality and historicity in its construction of gender, presenting
patriarchal authority ahistorically, as a 'given'. Speaking more broadly,
then, I am concerned with the relationship between patrimony and
patriarchy, and with ways in which the play's mimetic strategies serve to
encode patriarchal values.

Even a casual look at *Merchant* criticism indicates the extent to which
we seem to agree – as we agree on virtually nothing else about this play –
that it is steeped in commerce and finance; that it casts personal relationships in economic terms, conflating love and money; and that it is more

explicitly grounded in economic issues than any other work in the canon ('The chink of coins pervades this play as it does no other', A.D. Nuttall says).[2] Numerous aspects of the play's treatment of economic issues have been thoroughly subjected to critical scrutiny and historical analysis. Shylock's occupation has generated detailed studies of changes in con- temporary lending practices and debates about 'proper' rates of interest that accompanied the shift to a mercantile economy. Antonio's financial predicament has been contextualised in terms of the risk-taking inherent in the early days of venture capitalism. And as for Bassanio and the young Venetians, Lars Engle has observed that the use of marriage and credit markets by young aristocrats in crisis 'may be more topical than we have yet discovered. The play's Venetian setting and numerous fantastic elements do not prevent it from fitting Elizabethan patterns of aristocratic indebtedness and cash-raising through marriage.'[3] Several recent studies have emphasised ideological implications of the play's economics. Engle, who sees *Merchant* as 'a meditation on marriage and credit in an emerging modern economy', shows how the play 'offer[s] reassurance [to the landed aristocrats] that inherited blessings will be preserved.'[4] Walter Cohen, focusing on the 'ideology of form', believes that the play attempts to achieve ideological mystification, and reads *Merchant* as a 'procapital- ist' enactment of 'interclass harmony between aristocratic landed wealth and mercantile capital', with the former retaining the upper hand: 'English history evokes fears of capitalism, and Italian history allays those fears.'[5] Thomas Moisan, concerned like Cohen with the text's ideological function, though not working within the same explicitly materialist framework, seeks to identify 'ways in which the play participates in and interrogates the economic mythologies of its time'.[6] He suggests that *Merchant* 'seems to inscribe and affirm an ideological calculus that fused the interests of the state and the assertions of a providentialist Chris- tianity with the prerogatives of an increasingly capitalist marketplace', but cautions that the play may be invoking 'the ideologically sanctioned mythologies of the time only to question and subvert them'.[7]

From this brief overview, one might conclude that we are talking about a text in which all of the players in the game of money and power are men. Where are the women in these interpretations? This is not the Henriad, in which women are virtually displaced, 'out of the beltway': we are dealing with a play whose heroine, not irrelevantly, possesses the fortune on which much of the plot turns, and is the sole representative of the landed aristocracy whose values and privileges the play may be inscribing. Moreover, both heroine and foil are assessed in terms of gender-appropriate attitudes towards the material. How can we ignore Portia and Jessica if we really are to understand, to borrow Moisan's formulation, 'ways in which the play participates in and interrogates the economic mythologies of its time'? We surely cannot beg the question today by saying that Portia is simply a foil to the materialistic Venetians, an embodiment of the 'timeless' – hence uninterrogated and un-historicised – values of Belmont. Studies that focus on men and money ignore the play's assessment of Portia's 'correct' attitude to her wealth (which she uses in deference to her dead father's wishes) and Jessica's 'incorrect' extravagance (which constitutes a repudiation of her living father). As a result, one potentially fruitful way of learning more about the play's construction of gender and about what I believe is, on bal-ance, its inscription of a benevolent 'daddy knows best' patriarchy – interrogating the very different but reciprocally resonant behaviour and circumstances of Portia and Jessica – has been overlooked.

Paradoxically, it is our efforts to historicise the Shylock/pound of flesh plot that account for our conception of *Merchant* as a 'problem play' despite our recognition that such endeavours may be anachronis-tic, informed since the eighteenth century by critical sensitivity to anti-semitism and, more recently, by a post-Holocaust sensibility. As Harold Bloom says in response to J. Middleton Murry's insistence that *The Merchant of Venice* is a 'fairy story' rather than a problem play, 'For us . . . it had better be a problem play and not a fairy story.'[8] In writing about Shylock, we remain aware that our response to and un-derstanding of the complexities of his words and actions is not, and cannot be, Shakespeare's. Nevertheless, we have not attempted to con-textualise the Portia/three caskets fable despite the fact that such an endeavour is not compromised at the outset by anachronism, despite the fact that we have the means to partially reconstruct at least some sixteenth-century concerns about the economic status and impact of women that inform it, and despite the fact that such concerns were perceived as prob-lematical by the Elizabethans. What do we know about late sixteenth-century inheritance practices and ownership or control of property by women, for example, that can help us to identify those moments in which the play seems to interrogate Renaissance attitudes about the relationship between gender and control of the means of production, and those in which it seems to mystify that relationship? How might a contemporary audience have responded to Jessica's 'getting and spending'? To what extent is Por-tia's conception of her own relation to the economic order a stereotypically 'feminine' one? For all our historicising of Shylock, Antonio and Bassanio, we have barely begun to historicise the play's women in these terms, possi-bly because of subtly inscribed textual and cultural cues. If the play itself relegates women to the economic periphery, has the critical establishment also been ready to take that marginalisation at face value? To what extent has *Merchant* criticism tacitly assented to the ideological assumptions in-scribed in the text?[9]

Very simply, I would propose inverting Cohen's syntax: in this play it may well be Venetian history that evokes fears about women with money, and English history that allays those fears. In creating Portia – a daughter, an heiress who is suddenly in control of a lot of land and money and thereby constitutes a challenge to the social order in general and to fathers in particular – Shakespeare evokes cultural anxieties that are both intensified by Portia's formidable intelligence and spirit and neutralised by her deference to and internalisation of patriarchal norms and values. But he also creates a second character, Jessica, who functions as the properly socialised Portia's virtual opposite where issues of money and self-determination intersect. Where Portia gives, Jessica takes; where Portia accepts constraints, Jessica rebels; but in the end, where Jessica wins the battle, Portia wins the war. What is at stake is the extent to which women's control of the means of production, whether as wives or daughters, can be tolerated or accommodated, and the social controls by which it can be contained.

As Margaret Ferguson observes, 'it is still too early for a definitive answer to Joan Kelly-Gadol's famous question, "Did women have a Renaissance?" '[10] Whereas Kelly-Gadol believes that Renaissance women's participation in the economic system tended to contract as a consequence of the shift from a feudal economy to capitalism, other studies indicate that it may actually have expanded – at least for women of certain classes in certain locations.[11] As Judith C. Brown points out, Kelly-Gadol's conclusion that 'There was no Renaissance for women, at least not in the Renaissance' is based heavily on an examination of literary texts rather than on an exploration of 'inheritance laws or the laws regarding the management of property'.[12] An examination of those laws, however, suggests that conditions determining the economic options of privileged women were much more propitious in Venice than in Renaissance England. The effect on privileged English women of an emergent capitalism's concentration of the means of production in the hands of men seems to have been exacerbated by an entrenched tradition that women could neither hold nor dispose of property in their own right. The doctrine that a wife's property belonged wholly to her husband was so well established in English common law, in fact, that Henry Tudor sought passage of a statute to correct one of its abuses: the 1487 act, 'agaynst taking awaye of Women', made it a felony to abduct and then marry an heiress against her will in order to gain control of her assets[13] – a reform that sought to correct a secondary problem but did not challenge the underlying assumption, which in effect it implicitly legitimated. In fact, according to Sheila Ryan Johansson, travellers' reports suggest that Renaissance women in England, who seemed to have ' "the most spirited and independent temperaments and the most freedom from their husbands' supervision" . . . actually had "less protection from economic exploitation" ' than their sisters on the continent.[14]

At the same time, however, other forces combined to put pressure on the established socio-economic system. Paradoxically, tactical changes in English entail and inheritance practices led to an inadvertent increase in the number of female heirs in the second half of the sixteenth and the early seventeenth centuries, Lisa Jardine has found: in order to prevent land passing out of a family's control, successful efforts were made to convert *tail male*, which restricted succession to men, to *tail general*, which permitted families to retain control when no male heirs were available by transmitting estates to women.[15] It is ironic, Jardine writes, that

> the prominent position occupied by female heirs . . . is in striking contrast to the ideology of modesty and dutiful submission. . . . It was certainly not in the minds of lawyers and landowners preoccupied with patrilinear succession that their women might be involved as other than a means to a patriarchal end.[16]

'Where women receive land, the basic means of production, either as a dowry or as part of their inheritance . . . the social implications are greater [than when men inherit] because its ownership is drastically reorganised at every generation', the historian Jack Goody says: 'Land changes hands between the sexes at every marriage or death, and large quantities of land may come under the direct control of women.'[17] Deaths, of course, cannot be arranged, but marriages can, and it is not surprising, then, that an increasing number of female heirs resulted in an increased effort to contain the potential economic impact of daughters who inherit by controlling their marriages. As Lawrence Stone observes, 'the key to the system of controlled marriage was the exchange of property.'[18] A father's virtually absolute authority over his family, which seems to have reached its height in the late sixteenth century, enabled him to protect his family's assets by ensuring their orderly transfer to the succeeding generation, as Stone points out: 'Fathers in their wills were prone to make their bequests conditional upon strict obedience, the 2nd Earl of Southampton ordering both portion and maintenance to be cut off entirely if his daughter disobeyed the executors.'[19]

Nevertheless, it does appear that some deeply entrenched beliefs and practices that limited women's participation in the economic system were contested on the popular level if not in the courts.[20] According to Linda Woodbridge:

> After approving from the pulpit of the 'law of Nations' which denied a married woman the right to own any property, even her own clothing, the Rev. William Gouge was astonished at the public outcry against his views. In his published marriage sermons, *Of Domesticall Duties*, he reminisced, 'I

remember that when these Domesticall Duties were first uttered out of the pulpit, much exception was taken against the application of a wives subiection to the restraining of her from disposing the common goods of the family without, or against her husband's consent.'[21]

Less dramatically, also, a father's ability to dispose of a daughter in a marriage that best served the economic interest of his family was mitigated, to some extent, by the gradual acceptance of a daughter's right of refusal and accompanied by an elaborate system of safeguards that obligated her husband-to-be to provide guarantees of her future financial security.[22]

The situation in Venice, however, seems to have been significantly different. The evidence is incomplete, but it does suggest that privileged Venetian women attained and exercised far more financial independence and influence than was possible for women of similar status in England: possessing money and land independent of marriage settlements, Venetian women invested in business ventures, disposed of property as they saw fit and left it to whom they chose, thereby constituting, even within the limitations imposed by a patriarchal and patrilinear society, a force to be reckoned with. And their rights to do so were explicitly protected by the legal system. 'Given the patriarchal cast of Venetian law and custom one might expect men to enjoy unrestrained dominion over their wives. But the reality was quite different', Stanley Chojnacki argues in a fascinating and carefully researched article, 'Patrician women in early Renaissance Venice'.[23]

The evidence indicates that 'Venetian law went to great lengths to guarantee women's dowry rights, and for that matter their property rights in general. . . . In Venice there were no restrictions on a married woman's use of property that she owned outright', Chojnacki says.[24] 'She could enter into any transaction that she pleased with it, the statutes asserted, "even without her husband's consent." '[25] These rights, moreover, were not just an 'empty formality', but were upheld in practice.[26] In other words, whether a Venetian woman acquired property (for example, by inheritance) and subsequently married or whether she acquired property during the marriage, that property did not come under her husband's control, either in theory or in practice – a far cry from the theory and the practice in England that precipitated both Henry VII's statutory reform and the popular outburst against Gouge, and a far cry from a socioeconomic system bent on patrolling 'the traffic in women': in effect, it short-circuited, *de jure* and *de facto*, the 'commodification of women'.[27] This would not be true, of course, if Venetian women did not actually *acquire* property independently of dowry arrangements. Just as important, therefore, is Chojnacki's demonstration that they did indeed do so.[28] Equally interesting is the fact that they received inheritances not only from their fathers or other male relatives, but also – because previous generations possessed the same prerogatives – directly from their mothers and other female relatives, and in turn frequently willed their own assets to married daughters or sisters.[29] 'It comes as no surprise that women showed an even stronger disposition [than men] to make bequests to their married female kin', Chojnacki concludes,[30] but it is tempting indeed to imagine the surprise (horror? glee? grounds for rebellion?) that the economic rights of Venetian women might have elicited among the Elizabethans!

Finally, all of this seems to have affected the self-concept of women and the attitudes of men toward them. Chojnacki's analysis of women's testamentary bequests and business activities (which included, among other investments, 'putting money into state-run galley voyages to distant ports of call') leads him to infer that 'women had a clear sense of their legal prerogatives and their economic significance.'[31] Male attitudes too were affected by 'the psychological leverage that [Venetian women] came to exercise over their male kinsmen', and may even have been conciliatory, especially since 'women were now able to attach persuasive conditions to their bequests', just as men had done:[32]

> Now women could use the same kind of pressure, but for purposes of their own which seem more behavioral than lineage-centered. . . . This economic leverage that women were now able to exercise in the area of men's behavior is a large matter, with all sorts of cultural implications; and it would repay further study. But in the present context we can at least make the general observation that Venetian men had reason to stay on the good side of their kinswomen, and this gave women a powerful means of influencing male activity.[33]

It is not difficult to understand the destabilising effects of developments that implicitly challenged English women's status – as object, gift, commodity, property – in a social system that had a vested interest in preserving the status quo and defending itself against disruptive change. Nor is it difficult to imagine why Shakespeare might well have been interested in dramatising divergent responses to these pressures and possibilities in such a way as to accommodate, and possibly provoke, similarly divergent audience responses.

My understanding of *Merchant*, still undergoing redefinition, has been altered by the process of framing these issues. Of course, it remains coloured by my own biases and limitations: I invariably seem to hear the play's dissonances more clearly than the harmonies audible to some; I am not a social historian. What I have to say is certainly not aimed at resolving any of the play's incoherences and contradictions; instead – and in part, I suspect, because I try to deal with what the play omits, glosses over or simply posits – my discussion is aimed at raising new questions rather than answering old ones. Nor do I integrate with the play as a whole what emerges here, which admittedly focuses on only part of the action. My present purpose, then, is less to offer a 'new reading' than to articulate some of the issues and possible responses, however tentative and in need of refinement, that a materialist feminist analysis can yield.

Most studies of Portia's relation to patriarchal structures quite naturally focus either on the trial scene, where she disguises herself to enter a male world and triumphs over her adversaries, or on the ring episode, where she squares off with Bassanio to ensure that his primary loyalty will henceforth be to her, not to Antonio, and breaks the stranglehold of the male–male bond to solidify her power base in the marriage.[34] The sheer theatricality of these encounters, as well as the dramatic tension of her behaviour in Act III, scene ii, when Bassanio chooses the correct casket, makes it easy to overlook her earlier appearances. This is regrettable, I think, because it is in her early scenes, where she defines herself as a daughter, that Portia's responses to overt and covert patriarchal power are equally interesting. Moreover, the nature of Shakespeare's departures from both of his major sources (*Il Pecorone*, *The Jew of Malta*) signals his preoccupation with father–daughter relationships in this play: he invents that relationship in Portia's case and rewords it in Jessica's as he dramatises contemporary attitudes about the relationship of women to the economic base.[35]

Consider Act I, scene ii. Taken at face value, its 134 lines perform an expository function: introducing Portia and Nerissa, they also summarise the provisions of the will, outline the rules of the lottery, reveal Portia's opinion of the 'parcel of wooers' assembled at Belmont and – paralleling Bassanio's comments about Portia near the end of Act I, scene v – establish Portia's attraction to Bassanio. An earlier phase of feminist criticism of Shakespeare, looking more closely at this scene, emphasised mutuality and female bonding as well as the differences between the 'alternative world' created by these two rather isolated women and the comparatively exploitative, mercenary male world of Venice.[36] This critical approach, helpful as it has been in its delineation of affective elements, is not without its dangers. Theoretically, as Judith Newton and Deborah Rosenfelt argue, a polarised criticism in which 'female myths' are granted equal or greater power than material conditions and which 'posits women's nurturing and relational qualities as in themselves a counter to male domination' is not only ahistorical in its valorisation of women and denigration of men; in its idealism, they say, it actually tends to 'replicate the habits of thought we intended to change.'[37]

On a practical level – and especially if one shares Newton's and Rosenfelt's working assumption that mental oppression is rooted in material conditions[38] – it is easy to see what the affective or relational approach obscures: that Portia perceives herself as oppressed, and that she exhibits all the symptoms of a classic case of false consciousness in the way she problematises her situation; that Nerissa, far from being a supportive confidante, does not empathise with and actually trivialises Portia's complaint; and that Shakespeare does not really interrogate her 'cover story'.[39]

In her first appearance, Portia is presented as conflicted – depressed, we might say, because she is oppressed – and she experiences her conflict as internal rather than external. Initially, she voices her discomfort in abstractions – 'if to do were as easy as to know what were good to do' and 'it is a good divine that follows his own instructions' (I, ii, 12–13, 14–15)[40] – never questioning the 'good' itself but blaming herself, in effect, as if to say 'I'd like to do good . . . I ought to want to do good . . . I'm not "good" enough because I don't want what Daddy wanted for me', before even articulating the cause of her misery: 'so is the will of a living daughter curb'd by the will of a dead father' (I, ii, 24–5). She confronts two mutually exclusive alternatives: 'I will do anything, Nerissa, ere I will be married to a spunge' and 'I will die as chaste as Diana, unless I be obtain'd by the manner of my father's will' (I, ii, 98–9, 106–8). A psychological reading would doubtless proceed to interpret her ensuing sniping comments about the deficits of the waiting suitors as due to her reluctance or her inability to confront squarely the implications of such unpromising alternatives, and to attribute her opening reference to herself in the diminutive ('my little body' as opposed to this 'great world')[41] to a sense of oppression, of incapacity in the face of such weighty obstacles, and thus to focus on the displacement that can accompany denial. To be sure, the text invites such a reading: it's okay to be depressed, even to manipulate, as long as one doesn't challenge openly; it's okay to express contempt to others, as long as one doesn't express direct anger at the law of the fathers. Later, when she tells Bassanio

> I could teach you
> How to choose right, but then I am forsworn
> . . . You'll make me wish a sin,
> That I had been forsworn, (III, ii, 10–14)

she has thoroughly internalised her father's values: the way she perceives herself is determined by her father's will, and she cannot think well of herself if she considers acting in opposition to him; but where such action was first described in terms of disobedience, possible defiance is now invested with the importance of a 'sin'. Viewing his system for marrying her off as arbitrary, she never voices anger at the parent who subjected her to a game of chance and 'scanted' her, but is reduced to sniping and (in my opinion) subtly stacking the deck (with just enough ambiguity to suggest, perhaps, that her tilt at subversion is harmless and irrelevant). *Of course* the play rewards her obedience and forbearance; *of course* Bassanio *does* choose wisely and well: daddy does know best, and Portia has proved herself to be daddy's girl, after all. The lottery's outcome suggests that Portia has worried unnecessarily, and that she might have had more confidence, not less, in the 'wisdom' of her father, who never would have put his 'little' girl in a really untenable position.

The bottom line, though, is that Portia is a rich and potentially powerful woman. Her circumstances are analogous to those of Olivia who, as Jean Howard observes, is 'a woman of property without any discernable male relatives to control her or her fortune.'[42] As long as she primarily conceives of herself as a daughter, however, Portia never experiences herself as powerful, never owns her power, never seriously questions the necessity of submitting to her father's dictates. But the very fact that Portia's dialogue with Nerissa takes place at all, and the way she problematises her dilemma, establishes that her compliance is a matter of choice; otherwise, that discussion would be redundant. If she has power in the first half of the play, it is the power to obey, to choose to 'do good'; to act otherwise is to do the opposite of 'good'.

Consider the possibility that the character Portia inhabits a theatrical here-and-now, that the will and the three caskets are not just part of the land of make-believe but speak, however indirectly, to contemporary concerns – even though the play's mixed modes tend to discourage such an approach. In contrast to the play's representation of the mercantile world of Venice, its treatment of Belmont is both anachronistic and ahistorical. On the one hand, Portia's secure possession of inherited (landed?) wealth seems a backward glance at a socio-economic system threatened by inflationary pressures and the 'crisis of the aristocracy' (much as the action in Venice anachronistically evokes a long-gone interest-free economic system). On the other hand, in a play that both posits and questions oppositions between Belmont and Venice, Shakespeare endows the former with a source of wealth and a system of patriarchal privilege that belong as much to the nebulous world of fairy tale and 'old tale' as do the legends of the three caskets and the pound of flesh, asking us to accept them as simply given, a matter of dramatic prerogative.[43] Diverting us from the materiality of Portia's circumstances makes it easier to present additional features as givens – for instance, obscuring the difference between her father's 'will' as a binding document and as volition, and hence equating Belmont's disposition of inherited wealth with Belmont's confidence in the appropriateness (the wisdom, in Nerissa's view) of paternalistic control – a world in which dutiful daughters obey their fathers' 'will' without question, no matter how uncomfortable the process or result – without interrogating the equation.

Accordingly, patriarchal power is deftly, unobtrusively posited as existing independent of time and place, independent of history, ideal – a male fantasy of a social contract/gender system compared to which the 'fallen', historicised world of Venice seems a falling-away.

To ask 'what if . . . ?' might at first seem to distort the play's mimetic strategies, but taking seriously the discrepancy between the play's silence on the materiality of Belmont and its insistence on the materiality of Venice, and recalling that Portia's initial conversation with Nerissa is grounded in the assumption that she does have a choice, however difficult, invite us to confront some of the play's 'significant silences' and 'make [them] speak', in Eagleton's words. Considered in their historical context, as a contemporary audience might have understood them, some of Portia's comments to Nerissa suggest that the action in Belmont is more topical than its 'old tale' qualities would indicate. Most obviously, perhaps, in a period of social change in England, not stasis, the increased power of a father to determine whom his daughter would marry was accompanied – 'balanced' is too strong a word – in the second half of the sixteenth century by what Stone terms a 'significant advance': the emergence of a daughter's countervailing right of refusal.[44] Portia laments that she has no such option when she says 'I may neither choose . . . nor refuse. . . . Is it not hard, Nerissa, that I cannot choose one, nor refuse none?' (I, ii, 23–6). Those members of a contemporary audience threatened by the implication of such a change might well have found her lack of veto power reassuring, a reminder of 'the good old days'; wives and daughters in the audience, however, might well have responded differently, reminding themselves of the difference between previous constraint and emerging option. Although the play alludes to the contemporary transition only in passing, its presence suggests that Belmont's 'will', whatever its function as a theatrical device, did not occupy an historical vacuum but may have encoded an important cultural change. Nor does the play mention the standard provisions for the jointure that a husband or his family had to provide,[45] let alone the likelihood of Bassanio's providing anything resembling an appropriate one: as patriarchal prerogatives are protected, patriarchal responsibilities are ignored.

Even more important, I think, is the way the play treats the larger issue of sanctions imposed upon disobedient daughters. In one sense, Shakespeare problematises this issue in a very subtle way; in another sense, he mystifies it. Although we are told precisely what will happen to her suitors if they fail to choose the proper casket (they are to be confined to a celibate life), we do not know what would happen to Portia were she simply to take matters into her own hands and decide not to abide by her father's system, because the question is never asked – very much in contrast to what Shakespeare takes pains to spell out for us of the coercive pressures applied to heroines like Hermia and Isabella, for example. At no time does Portia allude even indirectly to such plausible consequences: at no time does she say, in effect, 'If I defy my father and refuse to go along with his game, I'll lose my inheritance, but maybe being penniless is preferable to being a pawn' (which would be analogous to Hermia's fight/flight response).

She does not need to, because Shakespeare is not dramatising resistance; instead, he is dramatising the transformation of external sanctions into more subtle, and possibly more forceful, modes of social control. Whereas Hermia problematises defiance in terms of evading the sanctions that appear likely to be imposed, Portia problematises defiance as something that is *wrong*, 'a sin' (III, ii, 13), something that she might 'go to hell' for (III, ii, 21). In short, the will of one father has become the law of the fathers. What originated historically as the vested interest of the head of a family in ensuring the preservation of its economic base no longer has any driving force in the will or the play: what was once functional in terms of political economy has become redundant; submission, once a means to an end (controlling the means of production), has become an end in itself.

Quite literally, Portia makes a virtue out of what once was perceived as necessity. In Freudian terms, Portia's words to Nerissa in I, ii, and to Bassanio in III, ii, demonstrate the power of the superego: the internalisation of cultural imperatives. Guilt is so internalised that one can never 'get away with it' because one punishes one's self; the sanctions are no longer 'out there'. In sociological terms, the manifest function has been overshadowed and replaced by the latent function, and Portia's words dramatise the power of ideology. In new historicist terms, Portia herself contains her own potentially subversive tendencies at this point in the play.

From another perspective, however, the same ideological power that is treated with such sophistication is also externalised, refracted, displaced, and thoroughly mystified. First, by making it antecedent to the action, paternal authority acquires a power beyond the grave, so to speak, and the daughter's potential disobedience is fraught with amorphous and undefinable negative consequences. This seems to me to be much more conservative, much more accepting of patriarchal hegemony than, say, *A Midsummer Night's Dream*, the comedy preceding *Merchant*, in which Shakespeare interrogates the father–daughter conflict directly. In her struggle with Egeus, Hermia contests with a living opponent whose limitations are discernible, not with a shadowy internalised image, and although Egeus appeals to and wins the backing of the coercive power of the state, the play clearly suggests the limitations of the state's representative, Theseus, as well.

Second, the father's authority over his daughter is projected onto the suitors, none of whom challenges the conditions imposed upon *them* – a lifetime of celibacy. In fact, both Morocco and Arragon explicitly accept this provision (II, i, 38–43; II, ix, 12–13), and their acceptance further confirms the potency of a shadowy, posthumous patriarchy. Readers and audience members are unlikely to question these conditions either (as the play's critical history suggests), precisely *because* of the fact that they occur in a fable whose mode lures us into suspending disbelief and accepting the possibility that the will could have such impact. Accordingly, the fairy-tale mode inscribes and serves the interests of a patriarchy threatened by forces of change, and simultaneously makes it difficult for the harbingers of change to protest effectively.

Third, it is important to remember that there are *two* equally implausible fairy tales in the play. *The Merchant of Venice* says nothing about how the sanctions imposed upon unsuccessful suitors are to be enforced, even though the coercive power of the pound-of-flesh fable is indeed interrogated and found not to hold up in the light of day.[46] Ironically, it is interrogated by none other than Portia herself. Thus, the victim of one 'old tale' is the demystifier of the other.

Interestingly, once the lottery is concluded and the weight of paternal authority is lifted, Portia's self-concept seems temporarily to undergo a change. Her description of herself as an 'unlesson'd girl, unschool'd, unpractic'd' (III, ii, 159) has often been cited as an example of stereotypically 'feminine' dissembling, but I am not so sure: it is possible that she really does view herself – that is, what she ought to be – in terms of diffidence and deference, which certainly is congruent with the gendered subjectivity of her opening remarks. For a moment, she redefines herself as

> the lord
> Of this fair mansion, master of my servants,
> Queen o'er myself', (III, ii, 167–9)

announcing a sea-change into something rich and powerful and, to the Elizabethans, controversial as well as strange indeed: a woman who wields a lot of clout, economic and otherwise, and knows it. (When talking about property and staff, she employs masculine nouns – 'lord' and 'master' – but when talking about personal autonomy or self-command, she shifts to a feminine descriptor of greater rank: 'Queen'.) But Portia claims such authority and autonomy only to give them away to Bassanio, immediately neutralising cultural fears about the double spectre of a woman asserting control of property and of herself.

Or does she? Is she renouncing power or indicating subtly that she retains it? A few minutes later, when she learns of Antonio's plight and offers to pay his debt twenty times over, she doesn't say, despite her 'everything I have is yours' avowal, 'hey, lighten up; just write a cheque; it's a joint account now'; she says, in effect, '*I* will write that cheque.' Is she speaking as an English woman who graciously acknowledges the imminent transfer of her property to Bassanio? (If so, she is going through the motions, because the issue is moot.) Or are her words equally compatible with the prerogatives of her sisters in Venice? (If so, the money is hers to bestow.) Regardless, she is willing to do for Bassanio and his friend what she has been unwilling to do for herself: dependent upon a man, her father, for money, she seems ready to use it only to alleviate the unhappiness of other men, not her own unhappiness.

The play does not directly confront the fears and expectations raised by Portia's ambiguous status, but comments on them indirectly through Jessica, who functions almost as a split-off side of Portia in her readiness to do what to Portia is unthinkable. Shakespeare's characterisation of Jessica is tricky to sort out because issues of gender and ethnicity converge and are differentially assessed: at times the play seems to expose her as a disobedient, rebellious daughter; at other times, her unruliness seems neutralised, in context, by her willingness to be absorbed into a homogeneous Christian society. In one sense she fulfills a Christian fantasy as the potentially redeemable daughter of an infidel: a daughter who is not to blame for deficiencies attributable to an unfortunate heritage, who seems willing to be instructed by a Lorenzo, and who can be assimilated to a Christian patriarchy to which she may henceforth be expected to defer with gratitude for its benevolence. Add to this the play's multivalence towards Jessica's father, and the critic encounters a quicksand of shifting sympathies and potentially conflicting ideological patterns.

In another sense, however, Portia embodies a patriarchal fantasy of an ideally compliant daughter to which Jessica is contrasted as every father's nightmare. The contrasts are obvious: she helps herself to Shylock's wealth as if she were entitled (which she is not), as if it were her legitimate patrimony (which it is not); she flees Venice to escape her father's control; she marries a man of whom he cannot but categorically disapprove ('Would any of the stock of Barrabas / Had been her husband rather than a Christian' [IV, i, 296–7]). In short, as a foil to Portia she repudiates in every possible way the social norms and ideological imperatives that invest a father with authority. Unlike Portia, who only fleetingly permits herself to acknowledge her dilemma and never to think it through – and unlike the clown whose own dilemma, whether to 'Bouge' or 'Bouge not', prompts an outrageously comic soliloquy that parodies Faustus's psychomachia[47] – the unperturbed Jessica does not hesitate for a moment.

The analogues between the two young women seem anything but accidental. We know that Shakespeare departs from his source, *Il Pecorone*, in making his 'Lady of Belmont' a daughter, so we can reasonably infer that it is the attitude of daughters toward fathers and their wealth that interests him here. In creating Jessica, his divergence from *The Jew of Malta* is similarly pertinent in calling attention to the daughter–father/ submission–control configuration: Barrabas's daughter Abigail – compliant, helpful, loyal, even sympathetic to her father's plight (up to the point at which she discovers that he is responsible for her lover's death) – is as unlike Jessica as Jessica is unlike Portia.

It is tempting to imagine the response of women in a contemporary audience to Jessica's actions in contrast to Portia's.[48] The same kind of women who would vehemently object to Gouge's sermons would very likely be impatient with Portia's compliance, but might well respond enthusiastically to the straightforward, no-nonsense-about-doing-what's-expected way that Jessica takes matters into her own hands: she takes Shylock's money *in order* to marry Lorenzo; she marries whom she chooses *because* she has the means to flout her father's 'will', and she gets away with it. Because the play remains silent on the possible consequences of any hypothetical defiance by Portia, it creates a theatrical space for this kind of response. A spectator who chafes at the constraints imposed upon Portia, let alone those she imposes on herself, can participate vicariously in Jessica's defiance. But to the extent that the play affords a theatrical space for female subversive activity, it also contains that subversion.

To put it as simply as possible, what Jessica does serves to confirm male fears about what will happen when women obtain control of money and, in consequence, the means of controlling their own lives. Jessica's decision to seize the means of fleeing from Shylock's house is treated ambivalently: no benevolent patriarch, Shylock in his early scenes is much closer to the blocking agent of new comedy whose efforts to control his daughter must be squelched, and at that point in the play it is easy to imagine an audience cheering her on. Moreover, in a play that presents Shylock's frugality so negatively, its opposite, prodigality, can't be all that bad.[49] But what Jessica proceeds to do with Shylock's money, once she gets it, is unequivocally portrayed as frivolous, grossly self-indulgent, mindless, irresponsible. She doesn't just take the money and run; she doesn't just run off with a gentile; she embarks, at least by Tubal's report, on a spending spree in which she confirms and fuels every negative stereotype about women and money ('give her an inch and she'll . . .'). She reaches her nadir when she (reputedly) sells Shylock's ring.

Whatever our conception of Shylock, whatever our understanding of Shakespeare's conception of Shylock, and whatever our view of an historical criticism that moots the question of anti-semitism as anachronistic, I do not think that it is possible to mediate our response to

Shylock's distress over the ring by invoking anachronism. Our sympathy for him is probably never less conditional than when he says, 'I would not have given it for a wilderness of monkeys' (III, i, 122–3). Insofar as Jessica acts to free herself from confinement and constraint, the play makes limited allowances for her; insofar as she defers uncritically to Lorenzo's 'little learning', it glances wryly at her; but insofar as she trades her father's gift from Leah (her mother, presumably) for a monkey, it recoils from her. Unlike Bassanio, whose spendthrift behaviour is glossed over, accepted in a 'boys will be boys' spirit, Jessica's is emphasised: self-serving, extravagant young women are far more threatening than self-serving, extravagant young men. And if such women presume to claim financial independence, they do so at their fathers' expense, figuratively as well as literally. Through Jessica, Shakespeare simultaneously speaks to women's insistence on their right to own and control property – and themselves, and men's fears of what will happen when that right is won.

Jean Howard raises the possibility that 'in the theatre women were licensed to look – and in a larger sense to judge what they saw and to exercise autonomy – in ways that problematised women's status as object within patriarchy.'[50] There are moments when Jessica provokes such a contestatory response, but I think they are outweighed by the moments when she serves as a cautionary example. The play leaves open the question of her status in a world where Portia reigns, and leaves open the possibility that Jessica may find herself more object than subject, more tolerated at the periphery than welcomed at its centre. As she and Lorenzo approach Belmont, Gratiano announces the arrival of 'Lorenzo and his infidel' (III, ii, 218), but no one speaks to her or responds directly to her when she speaks briefly; and in contrast to her loquaciousness when with the clown, she is silent (or silenced?) throughout the re-mainder of the play except when she is alone on stage with Launcelot Gobbo or Lorenzo.[51]

Any alteration in Portia's subjectivity in the trial and ring scenes is beyond my present scope, since it derives from her assumption of male disguise and exercise of heretofore concealed analytical and argumenta-tive powers rather than from any increase in her readiness to claim her patrimony. It is true that she is anything but conventionally 'feminine' as Balthazar and Balthazar-unmasked; where she was depressed and silenced, diffident and often indirect, she now seems to exult in her own cleverness and efficacy. I do not mean to discount the extent and import-ance of her very real victory,[52] but I do think it is fair to conclude by asking whether the play permits her to come into her own because of, not in spite of, her earlier acceptance of the limits imposed upon dutiful daughters. Where Portia says, 'I should', Bassanio says, 'I want' – and both are rewarded for what is presented as gender-appropriate behaviour.

Far from repenting his youthful profligacy and indebtedness, Bassanio displays confidence – as Portia did not – in defining his own course. Moreover, Antonio has no more qualms about backing Bassanio than Bassanio has in asking him to do so; he never puts off his client with a 'patron knows best' response, while the play's much more circumspect heroine is deemed, for all practical purposes, insufficiently capable of choosing for herself and in need of strong paternal control to protect her from erring. The play seems to me to offer yet one more 'warning for fair women': where Portia was initially 'scanted', and where Jessica endowed herself, so to speak, they have virtually changed places by the end of Act V, where Portia is unequivocally empowered and Jessica equivocally circumscribed. Ironically, *Merchant* instructs its audience that daughters who submit, who know their place, will ultimately fare better than daughters who rebel.

NOTES

1. Terry Eagleton, *Marxism and Literary Criticism* (London: Methuen, 1976), pp. 34–5. Eagleton is summarising Macherey here.
2. A.D. Nuttall, '*The Merchant of Venice*', in *A New Mimesis: Shakespeare and the representation of reality* (1983), reprinted in Harold Bloom, ed., *William Shakespeare: Comedies and romances* (New York: Chelsea House, 1986), p. 280.
3. Lars Engle, ' "Thrift is blessing": exchange and explanation in *The Merchant of Venice*', *Shakespeare Quarterly*, **37** (1986), pp. 20–1.
4. Engle, 'Thrift is blessing', pp. 21, 37. Engle argues that 'financial transactions in the play reward a more detailed analysis than they have to my knowledge received' (p. 21), but approaches the subject differently to the way I do. He makes a similar point about Portia's 'punning on the emotional and legal senses of "will" ' (p. 20).
5. Walter Cohen, '*The Merchant of Venice* and the possibilities of historical criticism', *ELH*, **49** (1982), pp. 765, 768, 772.
6. Thomas Moisan, ' "Which is the merchant here? and which the Jew?": subversion and recuperation in *The Merchant of Venice*', in Jean E. Howard and Marion F. O'Connor, eds., *Shakespeare Reproduced: The text in history and ideology* (New York and London: Methuen, 1987), p. 190.
7. Moisan, ' "Which is the merchant here?" ' pp. 188, 189.
8. Bloom, *William Shakespeare*, 'Introduction', p. 5.
9. To what extent, in other words, are late twentieth-century attitudes about women and money informed by similar ideological assumptions? I do not in any way mean to equate late sixteenth- and twentieth-century attitudes, of course. Two inquiries, however, shed light on the persistence of men's anxieties about economically powerful women as well as on women's frequent reluctance to address fully the implications of economic empowerment; see Phyllis Chesler and Emily Jane Goodman, *Women, Money and Power* (New York: William Morrow, 1976), and Annette Lieberman and Vicki Lindner, *Unbalanced Accounts: Why women are still afraid of money* (New York:

Atlantic Monthly Press, 1987). Exploring the 'psychoeconomic condition of women' (p. 11), Chesler and Goodman observe that 'The psychosexual aspects of money, wealth, investment are vastly different for each sex' (p. 52). According to Lieberman and Lindner, 'Whereas men see money as a reflection of their desires for power and control, women . . . project their traditional identities onto money, and at the same time, *see in money what men have taught them to see*' (p. xix; my emphasis). That those lessons include denial – a pretence that money simply does not exist, an implication that it is not 'nice' to pay attention to it (or much 'nicer' to be able to ignore it) – can be seen today, for example, in the practice at certain restaurants of handing menus devoid of prices to female patrons 'escorted' by men! As both books point out, little has been written on this topic. To the extent that Chesler/Goodman and Lieberman/Lindner are correct – that women in patriarchal societies have been taught to be 'squeamish' about money – it is not really surprising that criticism has been silent on this issue.

10. 'Introduction' in Margaret W. Ferguson, Maureen Quilligan and Nancy J. Vickers, eds., *Rewriting the Renaissance: The discourses of sexual difference in early modern Europe* (Chicago and London: University of Chicago Press, 1986), pp. xxx–xxxi. See Joan Kelly-Gadol, 'Did women have a Renaissance?', in Renate Bridenthal and Claudia Koonz, eds., *Becoming Visible: Women in European History* (Boston: Houghton Mifflin, 1977), p. 139; see also pp. 139–40, 145, 148–52.

11. The question of Renaissance women's participation in economic life is an extremely complex one, and generalisations are dangerous; recent work by social historians demonstrates the extent to which conditions varied not only from country to country but sometimes from city to city, as well as by class, status and occupation. See, for example, Judith C. Brown, 'A woman's place was in the home: women's work in Renaissance Tuscany', in Ferguson, Quilligan and Vickers, *Rewriting the Renaissance*, pp. 206–24. 'To the extent that increased employment opportunities contributed to greater financial independence, women undoubtedly gained a small measure of economic power', Brown concludes: 'If we limit our assessment, then, to this one area of economic life, without implying that it covers all facets of women's economic experience or even all classes of women, then we can argue that in Florence, and perhaps in other cities as well, there was in the Renaissance, a renaissance for women' (p. 224). In 'Women in the crafts in sixteenth-century Lyon' (*Feminist Studies*, 8 [1982], pp. 47–80), Natalie Zemon Davis argues that 'women's work had . . . an important and complex role to play in the economy of the sixteenth-century French city' (p. 48): examining the opportunities and constraints experienced by 'mere wage earners' and 'independent women artisans', for example, she finds that the latter 'elicited respect and even apprehension and could sometimes defend openly their economic turf' (p. 62). However, Davis also finds evidence of 'efforts to limit female autonomy in the crafts' (p. 70) as well as efforts to restrict women's control of property and freedom to enter into contracts (p. 68). (See also Davis' 'City women and religious change', in her *Society and Culture in Early Modern France: Eight Essays* (Stanford: Stanford University Press, 1975), pp. 65–95.) Merry E. Wiesner's 'Women's defense of their public role' (in Mary Beth Rose, ed., *Women in the Middle Ages and the Renaissance: Literary and historical perspectives* [Syracuse: Syracuse University Press, 1986], pp. 1–27) examines women's perceptions of 'the shrinking of opportunities in a variety of areas' (p. 1), including financial transactions, but also finds evidence that certain limitations sanctioned by law were often circumvented in practice (p. 4); see also

her 'Spinsters and seamstresses: women in cloth and clothing production', in Ferguson, Quilligan and Vickers, *Rewriting the Renaissance*, pp. 191–205. My own discussion is confined to what we know of inheritance patterns and property rights of upper-class women in Renaissance England and Venice.

12. Brown, 'A woman's place', pp. 206–7.
13. E.W. Ives, ' "Agaynst taking awaye of Women": the inception and operation of the Abduction Act of 1487', in E.W. Ives, R.J. Knecht and J.J. Scarisbrick, eds., *Wealth and Power in Tudor England* (London: Athlone Press, 1978), pp. 21–44.
14. Sheila Ryan Johansson, ' "Herstory" as history: a new field or another fad?', in Berenice A. Carroll, ed., *Liberating Women's History: Theoretical and critical essays* (Urbana: University of Illinois, 1976), quoted in Gayle Greene and Coppélia Kahn, 'Feminist scholarship and the social construction of women', in Greene and Kahn, eds., *Making A Difference: Feminist literary criticism* (London and New York: Methuen, 1985), p. 18.
15. Lisa Jardine, *Still Harping on Daughters: Women and drama in the age of Shakespeare* (Hemel Hempstead: Harvester Wheatsheaf, 1983), p. 85. See especially Chapter 3, ' "I am Duchess of Malfi still": wealth, inheritance and the spectre of strong women' (pp. 68–102). Jardine's citations of significant works by social historians are particularly helpful.
16. *ibid.*, p. 87.
17. Jack Goody, 'Inheritance, property and women: some comparative considerations', in Jack Goody, Joan Thisk and E.P. Thompson, eds., *Family and Inheritance: Rural Society in Western Europe, 1200–1800* (Cambridge: Cambridge University Press, 1976), p. 10.
18. Lawrence Stone, *The Family, Sex and Marriage in England, 1500–1800*, abridged edn. (New York: Harper Colophon, 1979), p. 134.
19. Lawrence Stone, *The Crisis of the Aristocracy, 1558–1641* (Oxford: Clarendon Press, 1965), p. 595.
20. Linda Woodbridge, *Women and the English Renaissance: Literature and the nature of womankind, 1540–1620* (Urbana and Chicago: University of Illinois Press, 1984), p. 133.
21. *ibid.*, pp. 129–30.
22. Stone, *Crisis*, pp. 596, 649–50, 635–45.
23. Stanley Chojnacki, 'Patrician women in early Renaissance Venice', *Studies in the Renaissance*, **XXI** (1974), pp. 176–203, 188.
24. *ibid.*, pp. 192, 189.
25. *ibid.*, p. 189.
26. *ibid.*, p. 190.
27. See Gayle Rubin, 'The traffic in women: notes on the "political economy" of sex', in Rayna Reiter, ed., *Toward an Anthropology of Women* (New York: Monthly Review Press, 1975), and Karen Newman, 'Portia's ring: unruly women and structures of exchange in *The Merchant of Venice*', *Shakespeare Quarterly*, **38** (1987), pp. 19–33.
28. Chojnacki, 'Patrician women', p. 190.
29. *ibid.*, p. 190; see also pp. 196–7.
30. *ibid.*, p. 190.
31. *ibid.*, pp. 198, 197.
32. *ibid.*, p. 199.
33. *ibid.*, pp. 199–200. Moreover, he demonstrates that women tended to favour their birth families in their wills where men tended to favour their marital families.
34. See Newman; Jean Howard, 'Crossdressing, the theatre, and gender struggle in early modern England', *Shakespeare Quarterly*, **39** (1988), pp. 418–40; and

Keith Geary, 'The nature of Portia's victory: turning to men in *The Merchant of Venice*', *Shakespeare Survey*, **37** (1984), pp. 55–68.

35. See Geoffrey Bullough, *Narrative and Dramatic Sources of Shakespeare*, 8 vols. (London and New York: Routledge & Kegan Paul/Columbia University Press, 1961), vol. I, pp. 445–515. In Ser Giovanni's *Il Pecorone* (trans., pp. 463–76) the original Lady of Belmont was a rich and powerful widow, very much in control not just of the ring trick but also of the initial ritual by which her would-be suitors were tested.

36. See Carole McKewin's perceptive – despite what are now apparent as its theoretical limitations – 'Counsels of gall and grace: intimate conversations between women in Shakespeare's plays', in Carolyn Lenz, Gayle Greene and Carol Thomas Neely, eds., *The Woman's Part: Feminist Criticism of Shakespeare* (Urbana: University of Illinois Press, 1980), pp. 117–32. McKewin's emphasis on 'the counter-universe of women' leads her to say that Nerissa, although 'the voice of the status quo' (p. 121), 'also offers a more effective comfort to Portia in the invitation to express her feelings' about the assorted suitors and Bassanio (p. 122).

37. Judith Newton and Deborah Rosenfelt, 'Introduction: toward a materialist-feminist criticism', in Newton and Rosenfelt, eds., *Feminist Criticism and Social Change* (New York: Methuen, 1985), p. xvii.

38. Newton and Rosenfelt, 'Introduction', p. xvi.

39. Again, if we view her from a materialist perspective, Portia's 'cover story' seems a paradigmatic example of Eagleton's definition of false consciousness: 'making sense of [one's] experience in a way that prohibits a true understanding of [one's] society, ways that are consequently false' (p. 17).

40. G. Blakemore Evans, ed., *The Riverside Shakespeare* (Boston: Houghton Mifflin, 1974). All references are to this edition.

41. McKewin also points this out ('Counsels of gall', p. 121).

42. Citing Stephen Greenblatt (*Shakespearean Negotiations* (Berkeley: University of California Press, 1988), p. 69), Howard argues (in 'Crossdressing') that Olivia is 'the real threat to the hierarchical gender system' in *Twelfth Night*, 'Viola being but an *apparent* threat. . . . [Olivia] is punished, comically but unmistakably, by being made to fall in love with the crossdressed Viola. The good woman, Viola, thus becomes the vehicle for humiliating the unruly woman in the eyes of the audience, much as Titania is humiliated in *A Midsummer Night's Dream* by her union with an ass' (p. 432).

43. As Cohen notes, 'There is no source of Portia's apparently endless wealth' (*'The Merchant of Venice* and the possibilities of historical criticism', p. 777). Ralph Berry makes an interesting point: 'What can wealth buy? First of all, silence about its origins. . . . before Portia's wealth, the play draws back. She inherits it, that is all. . . . This silence makes its own point, contributing to Belmont's image of great wealth as being, not becoming' (*Shakespeare and Social Class* (Atlantic Highlands, N.J.: Humanities Press International, 1988), pp. 47–8).

44. 'Conditions varied from family to family according to the temperament of the father, and daughters continued to be under heavy parental pressure for several centuries, but on the whole contemporary comment suggests that this significant advance in the history of the emancipation of women took place between 1560 and 1640' (Stone, *Crisis*, p. 597).

45. 'In return for these straightforward payments [the bride's dowry, or portion], the father of the groom had to undertake a far wider set of obligations' (Stone, *Crisis*, p. 633). To obtain a jointure commensurate with the portion to be

settled on a daughter meant, for all practical purposes, that children tended to be married off within their own class; such marriage arrangements, then, had the effect of promoting social-class stability.

46. Even though the pound-of-flesh plot is invested with elements of implausibility that have led critics like Murry to dismiss attempts to historicise its problematical features, Shylock's *desire* for revenge is psychologically and socially plausible, leading critics like Bloom to insist on 'tak[ing] it seriously' (n. 8, above). My point is simply that the three caskets plot, equally implausible from one perspective, is equally plausible from another.

47. The clown, rehearsing the pros and cons of leaving Shylock to seek employment with Bassanio (who 'gives rare new liveries'), recycles Portia's internalised struggle as well as Jessica's flight when he weighs the competing claims of his conscience and the 'fiend' (II, ii, 109). In his case, like Jessica's but unlike Portia's, the 'fiend' carries the day: ' "Conscience", say I, "you counsel well." "Fiend", say I, "you counsel well" . . . and in my conscience, my conscience is but a kind of hard conscience. . . . The fiend gives the more friendly counsel' (II, ii, 21–31). When the time comes to act on his decision, however, deference to rank seems to leave him virtually tongue-tied, dependent upon his father to speak for him, and three times he calls upon Old Gobbo to do so.

48. I am grateful to Leah Marcus for raising this issue in response to an earlier version of this essay, prepared for the seminar on materialist feminist criticism at the 1989 meeting of the Shakespeare Association of America.

49. As Moisan observes in reference to Bassanio, 'That Shylock should find prodigality contemptible obviously gives prodigality something to commend it' (' "Which is the merchant here?" ', p. 198).

50. In 'Scripts and/versus playhouses: ideological production and the Renaissance public stage,' p. 225 in this volume.

51. 'One has to look twice at the passage . . . to realize that [Portia's] "fare you well, Jessica" (3.4.44) is a dismissal of Jessica, not a personal leave-taking', Berry says (p. 48); 'Jessica will be treated with the icy courtesy due to Lorenzo's wife' (p. 49). Berry focuses on the play's treatment of 'class in its relation to money' (p. 43).

52. Recent work indicates ways in which our assessment of the implications of Portia's achievement is linked to our understanding of gender construction in *Merchant* and therefore to our view of the play as contestatory or conciliatory. Newman, arguing that 'Portia evokes the ideal of a proper Renaissance lady and then transgresses it; she becomes an unruly woman' (p. 29), believes that the play 'interrogates the Elizabethan sex/gender system and resists "the traffic in women" ' (p. 31). Howard is more guarded: even though Portia is less 'stereotypically feminine' than Rosalind or Viola, she uses her disguise and manipulation of Bassanio in the ring trick to '[make] her place in a patriarchy more bearable . . . [i]n a play that insists upon the patriarchal authority of fathers to dispose of daughters and that of husbands to govern wives' ('Crossdressing', p. 433). Lynda Boose, acknowledging that Portia succeeds in 'appropriat[ing] every male–male bond in the play', nevertheless maintains, 'I have always suspected that Portia was sitting in the wings listening to Kate's advice. . . . Gone is Kate's openly confrontational challenge to the male system of female suppression; in its place are the covertly manipulative subversions of passive aggression' ('The comic contract and Portia's golden ring', *Shakespeare Studies*, 20 (1988), p. 247).

Desire and the Differences
it Makes

Valerie Traub

I

Shakespeare studies is currently characterised by an intense self-consciousness, a hyper-awareness, of its modes of inquiry and analysis. In a critical moment fractured and energised by the possibility not only of revisioning and reinstituting the literary canon, but of questioning the very notion of canonicity, 'Shakespeare' is being refigured to reflect contemporary political concerns. As metacommentary succeeds commentary it is therefore increasingly imperative for critics not only to situate their own activity, but to reflect on the perhaps unforeseeable implications of their critical positions. In this spirit of metacommentary, I begin by way of Marguerite Waller's deconstruction of the gendered slippages of Stephen Greenblatt's interpretation in *Renaissance Self-Fashioning* of Sir Thomas Wyatt's sonnet, 'Whoso list to hunt':

> Coinciding with the essentializing rhetoric of the passage, there seems to be an assumption that the owner of this absolutist twentieth-century perspective is both male and heterosexual. The pronoun 'he', referring to the male reader implied by Wyatt's poem, is unselfconsciously elided with a 'we', referring to Greenblatt and his readers, who are decidedly, not generically human, but stereotypically male. 'The poet twice addresses the reader as a potential hunter – "Whoso list to hunt, Who list her hunt" – both inviting and dissuading *him*, making *him*, reenact the poet's own drama of involvement and disillusionment. *We* share the passage from fascination to bitterness. . . .' In other words, Greenblatt's text not only exploits the Wyatt poem to enhance its own authority, but, in the bargain, obliterates the position of the female (or nonheterosexual male) reader. The two gestures, in fact, go together. The liberal guilt which Greenblatt so graciously wishes to share with his reader ('*we* are forced to take responsibility as translators in our own right') does not undo the act of usurpation and colonization being perpetrated either on Wyatt's text or on the reader who does not identify with the thrills and disillusionments of the male traffic in women. On the contrary, the expression of guilt is one more indication that the

critic wants his own position to be regarded as 'natural', as politically and epistemologically beyond question. (One feels guilty about that which one assumes one knows and controls.) To put the case conversely, Greenblatt's own rhetoric of critical mastery effectively delegitimates both the past in relation to the present and the female in relation to the male.[1]

I quote Waller at this length because my own subject is also the denial of difference – but not gender difference. Rather, my topic is the erasure of erotic difference – the difference in/of sexuality which since the late nineteenth century has been coded as 'homosexual' – which Waller's passage, dedicated to the exposure of Greenblatt's elisions, paradoxically enacts. Indeed, her passage both includes and then elides erotic difference in precisely the way Greenblatt progresses from reference to 'we our-selves' to 'the reader' to 'potential hunter' to 'him'. As Waller de-constructs Greenblatt's rhetoric, her passage moves from a criticism of his assumption of universal maleness and heterosexuality (line 3), to a subor-dination through parentheses of the '(nonheterosexual male) reader' in relation to the 'female' reader (line 12), to an erasure of that non-heterosexual male reader completely in the summation of 'the female in relation to the male' (final line).

What is it that allows (requires?) the elision of erotic difference at the same time one reasserts gender difference? Let us look at another passage, this time by Jean Howard, who is discussing Olivia in *Twelfth Night*:

> At the beginning of the play she has decided to do without the world of men, and especially to do without Orsino. These are classic marks of un-ruliness. And in this play she is punished, comically but unmistakably, by being made to fall in love with the cross-dressed Viola. The good woman, Viola, thus becomes the vehicle for humiliating the unruly woman in the eyes of the audience, much as Titania is humiliated in *A Midsummer Night's Dream* by her union with an ass.[2]

The syntactical parallelism of the final sentence sets up a semantic equa-tion of two humiliations: for Olivia to fall in love with the cross-dressed Viola is equal to Titania falling in love with an ass. But *are* they equal humiliations within their respective plays? Howard contends that same-sex love between women becomes the marker of the unnatural in *Twelfth Night*, as the play displaces the anti-theatricalists' concern with the poten-tial of male sodomy (occasioned by the boy actors' female costuming) onto women. Her concern is to show how the 'unruly woman' becomes an object of comedy. However, Howard's own admission that Olivia is punished 'comically but unmistakably' begs the question of the subject of this humour. To whom is same-sex love between women funny? Though Howard sees the comic objectification of women's same-sex love as un-fortunate, she assumes (without contextualising this assumption, in an essay replete with historical reference) that love between women was readily available as source of both humour and humiliation for members of Shakespeare's audience.

To pose the question of the historical meaning of homoerotic desire and its erasure in our critical process is not to devalue the work of Howard and Waller, which has been remarkably enabling to feminist criticism of Shakespeare and the early modern period. In fact, I choose as examples the work of such prominent critics to demonstrate that even in the most sophisticated feminist analyses, homoeroticism is the subject of peculiar rhetorical slippages; such slippages, I believe, indicate un-theorised assumptions circulating throughout our critical discourse.

Take, for instance, the work of Lisa Jardine, which, in a radical analysis of cross-dressing, highlights the homoerotic exchanges entailed by the phenomenon of the boy actor. In *Still Harping on Daughters: Women and Drama in the Age of Shakespeare*, she argues that the erotic double entendres of the cross-dresser were culturally accessible to early modern audiences, inviting comprehension and appreciation of the attractions of male homoeroticism. The object of desire in Shakespeare's cross-dressed heroines is the 'potentially rapeable boy', the young androgyne who, in his 'submissiveness, coyness, dependency, passivity, exquisite whiteness and beauty', echoes feminine attractions.[3] Jardine's account obviates the possibility of a 'feminist' Shakespeare precisely because the boy actor's role is so evidently a role, a representation of 'woman' conceived, inter-preted and acted by males.

However, despite Jardine's contention that 'Wherever Shakespeare's female characters in the comedies draw attention to their own androgyny . . . the resulting eroticism is to be associated with their *maleness* rather than their femaleness', she also argues that the *specific* erotic charge of the boy actor lies in his ability to mimic the attractions of 'femininity'.[4] She thus unwittingly dilutes the specificity of gender involved in *male* homo-eroticism. To argue that the 'erotic interest which hovers somewhere between the heterosexual and the homosexual' finally descends on the boy actor's 'femininity' reconstitutes this interaction as implicitly *hetero-erotic*.[5] Whereas pederasty *may* have been the dominant mode of homo-eroticism among literate men for whom the Greeks were familiar models, and *may* have been the model for aristocratic 'libertines' for whom love of adolescents was merely one among a retinue of risqué behaviours, we have little evidence that it structured the majority of early modern homoerotic encounters. To take pederasty and 'effeminacy' as the primary models of homoerotic desire, to posit all homoerotic desire as organised around poles of activity and passivity, and then to conflate male–male interactions with male–female encounters reduces the complexity of homoerotic identifica-tions, styles and roles – in Shakespeare's time and in ours.

What is happening (rhetorically, theoretically, politically) when the female reader can stand for 'nonheterosexual males' (Waller), when women's same-sex love is equated with comic bestiality (Howard), or when male homoeroticism is modelled on heterosexuality (Jardine)? And what is at stake when gender difference is signified through the sign of heterosexual intercourse, as in the work of feminist Lacanian Jacqueline Rose;[6] or when critics use synonomously such terms as sexual difference and sexual identity, androgyny and bisexuality, femininity/masculinity and heterosexuality? The difficulty most readers will have in even *identifying* a problem is precisely the problem. I hasten to point out that the first term in the above pairings denotes a gender relation and the second an erotic one. In other words, gender and sexuality pose as synonymous in our critical discourse in a way that not only despecifies our analyses but denies and delegitimates erotic difference. Whose interests are served by this denial of difference?

In 'Thinking sex: notes for a radical theory of the politics of sexuality', Gayle Rubin challenges

> the assumption that feminism is or should be the privileged site of a theory of sexuality. Feminism is the theory of gender oppression. To automatically assume that this makes it the theory of sexual oppression is to fail to distinguish between gender, on the one hand, and erotic desire, on the other.[7]

The preceding examples make it clear, I hope, that feminists need to theorise more accurately the specific relations between gender and sexuality, beginning by questioning the assumptions that this relationship is isomorphic and historically constant. For the purposes of dissecting this relationship, we must be willing to place sexuality at the centre, rather than on the implied periphery, of our analyses, and only after that should we:

1. Detail the way *specific* erotic discourses and practices are informed by or associated with gender discourses and practises.
2. Analyse how race, ethnicity and class differences inform the relationship between sexuality and gender at specific moments in time.

To assume that gender *predicates* eroticism is to ignore the contradictions that have historically existed between these two inextricably related yet independent systems. While they are always connected, there is no simple fit between them. Gender is not equal to sexuality.

II

Feminists, materialist feminists, cultural materialists and new historicists implicitly draw on a psychoanalytic construct whenever they pose the question of 'desire'. 'Desire', like 'power', has taken on a certain currency in contemporary critical discourse, in part because the popularisation of Lacanian psychoanalysis has offered so much to two broadly defined readerships: to gender critics, Lacanians offer a reading of the simultaneous construction of gender and sexuality that problematises even as it upholds patriarchal prerogatives; to historical critics, Lacanians offer a theory of the radical contingency of a speaking subject always constructed through social practices. The psychoanalytic construct 'desire' combines these concerns into a tripartite structure of a radically discontinuous subjectivity, gender and sexuality, in which the unruliness of the unconscious undercuts the subject's pretensions to self-identity.

According to the psychoanalytic narrative, subjectivity, gender and sexuality are constituted contemporaneously. I want to argue that it is precisely the capacity of 'desire' to connote this mutual complicity and constitutiveness that has rendered it such a powerful, provocative and perversely hegemonic construct – perversely hegemonic because, despite its disruptive Lacanian valences, 'desire' often works as a totalisation that conceals the dynamic divisions inherent in its construction: rather than holding the specificity of gender and sexuality in mutual tension, it conflates and then collapses them into the supposedly larger matrix of subjectivity. For instance, discussions regarding the meaning of female presence and the possibility of female power in early modern texts often hinge on assumptions about 'feminine desire'. By relying on a Lacanian revision of the Freudian dictate that there is only one 'libido' (a masculine one), in which the structural exigencies of phallocentrism not only delimit but deny the possibility of 'feminine desire', some critics come perilously close to writing women out of representation and history.[8] Or rather, by focusing their analyses on 'woman' as she is representationally positioned within the symbolic order, critics give away far too much – namely, the degree of agency that exists in the schism between 'woman-as-representation' and women themselves, who continually negotiate for power within and against the phallocentric order.[9]

However, merely to reassert the presence of female agency in the form of 'feminine desire' is not an adequate response to the problem of women's subjectivity. First, any assertion of agency must address those constraints placed on women's lives by the conceptual and material demarcations of a phallocentric system. But secondly (and this is my main concern), reinserting 'feminine desire' into discourse reinscribes women's eroticism as always already defined and reified by the gender category 'feminine'. The adjectival link between 'feminine' and 'desire' neutralises the difference between an ascribed gendered subject-position and the erotic experiences and expressions of a female subject. In a move that obscures the constructedness of subjectivity, gender and sexuality, the female subject is defined in terms of a desire that is implicitly passive, heterosexually positioned in relation to man. Generated as an appeal, 'feminine desire' in fact operates as a trick, a double bind for women always already confined by their previous definition. *How* a woman's sexuality is positioned in accordance to gender ascriptions, and the possibility of *resistance* to that positionality, are questions foreclosed by the appeal to 'feminine desire'.

This mutually referential circularity of gender and sexuality in our critical discourse, not surprisingly, can be traced to Freud. In his attempt to advance over late nineteenth-century sexologists by dividing sexuality into three independent variables – physical characteristics, mental characteristics and object choice – Freud implicitly recognised the possibility of conflict between biological inheritance, gender role behaviour and erotic identification.[10] And yet, in spite of this theoretical move towards greater specification, in practice Freud continued to conflate gender and sexuality, and to link both to biological inheritance. Despite his well-known disclaimer that passivity is not the exclusive province of women, nor aggressivity the sole prerogative of men, Freud reproduced precisely these gender determinisms to connote erotic positioning and style.

This becomes most evident when, in his case histories, the signifiers for male homosexuality become 'effeminacy' and 'passivity', and for lesbianism, 'masculinity' and 'activity'.[11] Consider the following statement:

> [I]t is just those girls who in the years before puberty showed a *boyish character and inclinations* who tend to become hysterical at puberty. In a whole series of cases the hysterical neurosis is nothing but an excessive over-accentuation of the typical wave of repression through which *the masculine type of sexuality is removed and the woman emerges.*[12]

In this remark we can see two characteristic moves. First, through a rhetorical sleight-of-hand, the phrase 'masculine type of sexuality' collapses into one construct precisely those components Freud had taken such pains to distinguish. In its relationship to 'boyish character and inclinations', the phrase 'masculine type of sexuality' refers to what Freud called sexual attitude or character (gender role conformity); in its relationship to sexuality, the phrase refers to homoerotic object choice. In the second rhetorical conflation, 'woman' in the final clause becomes the sign, not only of proper gender role behaviour, but of heterosexual object choice. Both gender role conformity and heterosexuality correspond to the essential woman. Likewise, the young boy who expresses a 'feminine attitude' takes on a 'passive role' towards a male object;[13] the desire to be touched on his genitals rather than be the agent of phallic penetration is a 'passive aim'. 'Passive homosexuals', according to Freud, 'play the part of the woman in sexual relations.'[14]

The vocabulary employed by Freud demonstrates that, theoretical protestations to the contrary, his work is caught within a nineteenth-century paradigm of 'inversion' which assumes that 'normal' heterosexuality follows unproblematically from ascribed gender role, and that disruptions in gender role result in deviant object choice. Despite the gender of the persons involved, Freud's concept of homoeroticism (like his concept of heterosexuality) is based on a gender model of 'masculine' activity and 'feminine' passivity.

Whenever critics use 'desire' to refer simultaneously to gender and eroticism, we implicitly reassert this dualistic, patriarchal, normalising history inherent in 'desire's' formulation. Even when no explicit reference to 'desire' is made, critics often unwittingly follow Freud in referring gender conflict (whether between men and women, or within a woman) to bisexuality. Consider, for example, the following statement by Karen Newman, in her otherwise brilliant analysis of the ambivalence towards female power in *The Taming of the Shrew*: 'We might say that this conflict [between female speech and silence] shares the *bisexuality* Freud claims for the hysterical symptom, that the text itself is *sexually ambivalent*.'[15] Newman is arguing that *The Taming of the Shrew* empowers Kate, even as it subordinates her, by putting the power of speech (even if it is an encomium to subordination) in her own mouth. Such an argument is largely persuasive – except when it is led, via Freud, to conflate gender and sexuality. Whatever *gender* ambivalence the text expresses, it is distinct from the text's consistently *non-ambiguous* definition of female erotic desire as the projection and fulfilment of male heterosexual fantasy. In *The Taming of the Shrew*, female desire is encoded as the desire-of-the-man.

While many gender and historical critics remain caught within the circularity of this conflation of gender and eroticism, gay and lesbian culture scholars are asserting a 'counter-discourse' of 'desire'. In this discourse, not only are gender and eroticism explicitly differentiated, but each is given greater specificity, and both are referred back to their cultural origins. As in psychoanalytic literature, gender is conceived as a matter of core gender identity (the persistent experience of oneself as male, female or ambivalent: I am a man, I am a woman, I am both/neither); but gender is viewed as additionally constructed through gender role (the degree to which one complies with the societal expectations of 'appropriate' behaviour) and gender style (the personal choices one makes daily to assert agency within the confines of gender). Generally believed to be in place by the age of three, core gender identity is the least flexible of these constructs. Although it is usually 'consistent' with anatomical sex,[16] transsexuals demonstrate not only the occasional fallibility of this process but also the highly inflexible nature of core gender identity once it is constituted. Gender role, while also ascribed by culture, is open to greater improvisation as each child positions him/herself in relation to activities culturally coded (and historically variable) as 'masculine' or 'feminine'. Gender style is an even more personal matter, and can be complicit with or in contradiction to one's gender role behaviour. The difference between gender role behaviour and individual gender style can be understood by recognising that a woman who identifies as 'feminine' might choose to wear jeans, work boots and a leather jacket without disrupting her own sense of gender role (whatever it might do to others' expectations). Most feminists, it could be argued, are feminists precisely because their core gender identity (woman) does not correspond to many conventional social expectations of the 'feminine'; even so, there is a great deal of variety to our gender styles.

Eroticism, like gender, is also given greater differentiation in this counter-discourse. Most importantly, eroticism is defined as independent of gender identity, behaviour and style. As a recent article in *Outlook* put it: 'Wearing high heels during the day does not mean you're a femme at night, passive in bed, or closeted on the job.'[17] Of course, there are periods in history when wearing high heels is an erotic signifier – indeed, in the 1940s and 1950s North American 'butch-femme' lesbian culture, high heels were erotic signifiers of the first degree (as they were, for that matter, in North American culture generally). But what they signified within that context – passivity, availability, self-confidence, sexual courage – is still a matter of debate.[18] The point is that there is no necessary connection between eroticism and gender role conformity – any connection is a matter of culturally contingent signifying practices.

Eroticism itself is increasingly being defined less as a fixed identity dependent on the gender of one's partner, and more as a dynamic mode based on the sum of one's erotic *practice*. The gender of object choice is only one variable among many, including erotic identification, fantasy and preference for specific activities, and it is not necessarily the most crucial.[19] Erotic identification refers to one's sense of self as an erotic object or subject – the position one takes up at any given moment in any given erotic encounter (initiating, receiving, playful, passionate, bored, etc.). In contrast to psychoanalysis's designation of activity and passivity as rigid states of being, in this counter-discourse one's erotic identification can switch from one moment to the next, one partner to the next, one year to the next; most people do, however, have a general erotic script that provides the degree of safety mixed with excitement necessary for erotic arousal and orgasm.[20] Fantasy, obviously, has two levels, both conscious and unconscious, with conscious fantasy further distinguished by those elements one enacts and those one merely dreams. As Cindy Patton argues, 'fantasy and actual practice are separate and different. . . . Fantasy can retain qualities of ambiguity, impossibility, and a connection with atemporal desire that no experience at any given moment can have.'[21] Preferences for specific activities (scenes and situations, combinations of oral, genital and anal stimulation) and types of partner (male, female, gender-identified 'masculine' or 'feminine', vulnerable, nurturing, aggressive, non-emotional, etc.) further differentiate and individuate each person's erotic mode.

From the perspective of this counter-discourse, psychoanalysis reduces sexuality to one variable – object choice (whether 'latent' or 'manifest') – which is presumed to flow directly from gender identity. The contradiction at the heart of this problem, as well as the alternatives posed by this counter-discourse, can be better understood by imagining oneself in the following voyeuristic scenario: when viewing a love scene on a movie screen, you experience pleasure by watching an interplay of power and erotic desire. Your eye is drawn to particular body zones, and you are aroused not only by body type and position, but also by the 'scene', the pace of interaction, the affective content. But whether you are aroused by watching a woman's body or a man's, two women together or two men, a woman with a man, or any other combination imaginable, the mere fact of your excitement does not explain what is happening on the dual levels of identification and erotic desire. That is, is your arousal dependent upon a process of identification with or desire for an eroticised object? To state it simplistically, do you *want* or do you *want to be* one of the images on the screen? Which one? Can you tell? Does your identification and/or desire shift during the interaction? And are your desire and identification dependent upon the *gender* or any one of many other constituents of the image: power, class, status, age, relative aggressivity, vulnerability, energy level, clothing, skin colour/texture, hair type/length, genital size/shape . . . ? Do specific acts (sucking, penetration, kissing) seem more relevant to your identification and/or desire than the gender of persons involved?

Rather than explain the manifold possibilities inherent in these phenomena – desiring and identifying with the same gender; identifying with one gender and desiring the other; desiring both genders; desiring or identifying on some basis other than gender – psychoanalysis asserts that desire will follow gender identification. Men desire women because their gender role positions them as active; women desire men because their own 'lack' must be filled. Men who desire men do so because they have taken up a 'feminised' passive position in relation to other males; lesbians desire women in imitation of active male desire. All sexuality engages in a structurally heterosexual mode of operation based on the duality of passivity and activity: whatever your biological sex, if you identify as/with a man, then you will desire a woman, and vice versa. That this theory fails to address the presence of 'masculine' gay men and 'feminine' lesbians is only made more evident by post-Freudian efforts to differentiate between the 'true invert' and the seduced, corrupted 'pervert'.[22]

For those persons who actually live the contradictions inadequately addressed by psychoanalysis, the conflation of gender and sexuality is specious at best. Contemporary lesbians and gay men at various moments have constructed their own erotic significations through the use of a deviant vocabulary: 'butch, rough-fluff, and femme', 'top/bottom' and sign systems of hanky codes and key signals. It may seem as though the gender polarities that structure these signifying systems remain within the psychoanalytic frame of reference. Not completely, however: while butch/rough-fluff/femme designations continue to conflate gender and eroticism, they recognise an implicit continuum rather than a dichotomy of identifications, and there are no rigid assumptions structuring who can be involved with whom (that is, a butch can be with another butch, a rough-fluff or a femme). The S/M rhetoric of top/bottom asserts each individual's erotic position as a matter of play, varying with each erotic 'scene'. Similarly, the position of hankies on the hip and keys on the belt can be altered at any time.

And yet, the difficulty of extracting a new erotic vocabulary out of the polarities of gender testifies both to the enduring consequences of a highly gender-inflected language, and to the imaginative limitations of us all; we can barely conceive of an eroticism free from gender constraints. These limitations, as well as the liberations, of contemporary erotic practice indicate the need to push erotic theory towards the recognition that, both within an intra-psychic framework and on a systematic, structural level, the 'sex/gender system' is related to but incommensurate with sexuality. Gender, sexuality and subjectivity are separate but intersecting discourses.

III

To attempt to historicise 'desire', to tease out the mutually implicated but distinct relation between gender and eroticism, is the obvious task. Such a project involves specifying erotic discourses and practices; describing institutional delimitations on erotic practice; detailing the resistance of subjects to the ideological and material constraints upon their erotic lives; and tracing the play of erotic discourses and practices throughout history. Both the congruences and the contradictions between dominant ideology and material practice must undergo thorough analysis. More problematically, insofar as the material and subjective experience of the erotic can also contradict – desire, after all, is experienced not only in the contact between bodies, and between bodies and institutions, but through the experience of subjective need, want, anxiety and fulfilment – the subjec- tive quality of desire's historical formulation must also be approached.

To what extent, it may be asked, is such a task aligned with the goals of materialist feminism? What does it borrow from materialist feminist analysis, and, perhaps more importantly, what can it contribute? I approach the latter question in Section V; first let me describe how this project falls within the scope of concerns shared by the other essays in this volume.

I have implied thus far that sexuality is a domain of power; and to say this is to extend a materialist feminist analysis in three directions. First, the erotic body is a material site for the inscriptions of ideology and power. As Michel Foucault and others have demonstrated, dominant social formations not only manipulate but produce erotic desire through ideological and institutional means.[23] Sexuality thus embodies (in the dual sense of inhering in the body and bodying forth) a power relation, not only for those members of erotic minorities who are positioned so as to feel most overtly the effects of institutionalised oppression, but for all sexual subjects (perhaps most insidiously for those who do not recognise the extent to which they are ideologically incited to act/think/fantasise erotically in prescribed ways). Sexuality as a crux of contemporary women's oppression has long been acknowledged, especially in its more violent or physically intrusive aspects – rape, battering, incest, porno- graphy, advertising, constraints on reproductive rights. But that sexuality in its more benign manifestations – marriage, monogamy, the desire for particular genres of pleasures – is also a matter of ideological and institu- tional investments is an insight more difficult to sustain, perhaps because these practices implicate us where change is most difficult, in our erotic propensities and love relationships.

Secondly, the result of such inscriptions is that erotic practice is mater- ial practice. Not only do physical bodies materially relate to one another, but more to the point, our own erotic choices position us in material (including, but not limited to, economic) ways. The *difference* between erotic choices – the matter of difference, if you will – is thus a palpable determinant of power. Unfortunately, the insertion of minority erotic practice into cultural discussion often results in its annexation – to too many readers, the automatic response is 'Oh, that refers to them, not me.' However, it is precisely my point that insofar as gay theory foregrounds the possibility of erotic agency within a determinant field of constraints, it offers a mode of analysis applicable to all erotic practices.

Precisely because sexuality is socially constructed, erotic practices and ideologies are open, albeit difficult, to change. Therefore, while recognising the hegemony of particular erotic ideologies, I am most interested in high- lighting the contradictions between dominant discourses and subversive practices, the ways individuals negotiate within ideological matrices to satisfy their complex needs and desires. This third materialist feminist premise of limited agency implicitly suggests to me a corollary: to refuse to view individuals as fully subjugated victims of their culture is to recognise the import of subjective, psychic experience as well – for it is within the psyche (conceived itself as a social product) that the possibility of erotic disruption is born.

The contradictions with which I am most concerned – between gender and eroticism; between dominant discourses and subversive practices; between subjective, internal need, and material, institutional pressures – are all foregrounded in the early modern British experience of homoeroticism. By 'experience' I mean to suggest the whole matrix of discourses and practices, the negotiations, interchanges, assertions, withholdings and refusals that occurred in reference to erotic desire between members of the same gender.

Before I proceed, it is perhaps important to acknowledge that by positing the presence of homoerotic desire and anxiety in early modern society and texts, I move against the social constructivist stance that locates the advent of 'homosexuality' in either the eighteenth or nineteenth centuries.[24] I do not mean to dispute the evidence that homosexuality in the modern sense (as a distinct mode of identity) came into being under the auspices of sexological discourse. Nor do I mean to imply, as some 'essentialists' do, that the 'experience of homoeroticism' is unproblematically available to the historically inquiring eye – that it exists in some pure form, unmediated by language, political discourse and the process of historical narrativisation. I *do* mean to contest the assumption that, because of our inevitably skewed apprehension of it, early modern homoerotic experience can be treated as if it never existed.

I thus put into play the following hypothesis: like all forms of desire, homoerotic desire is implicit within all psyches; whether and how it is given cultural expression, whether and how it is manifested as anxiety, is a matter of culturally contingent signifying practices. What is culturally specific is not the fact or presence of desire toward persons of the same gender, but the meanings that are attached to its expression and the attendant anxieties generated from its repression. In this, I reject the dominant constructivist trend that sees specific desires as being *produced* independently by discursive practices, and return to Freud's assertion of the polymorphous perversity and nondifferentiated nature of the infant's earliest desire. However, whereas Freud myopically focuses on the family as site of erotic development, I, like the social constructivists, emphasise the social and ideological character of the process of subjectification, by which the various modalities of desire are manipulated and disciplined: some are, in Foucault's terms, incited by social ideology and institutions;

some are, in the terms of psychoanalysis, displaced or repressed. That cultural forms that could be considered homoerotic have existed in virtually all societies argues for this mode's inherent position as potentiality; that what differs from society to society is whether homoeroticism is ritualised or privatised, gender-encoded or free of gender associations, vilified, tolerated or celebrated, implies the constitutive import of complex and often contradictory discursive practices and social investments.

In order to discuss the signification of homoeroticism in early modern England – its ideological, material and subjective practice – one does well to review the critical approaches that have been employed to address its textual representation. For many years, the dominant critical discourse on homoeroticism in Shakespearean drama has been that of narcissism. Shakespeare's most basic identity configuration, the mirror image, has provided a fertile field for the psychoanalytic rehearsal of Freud's linkage of narcissism, paranoia and homosexuality.[25] Whereas I agree that questions of self and other are often posed through such self-reflexive constructs, and that narcissism, like jealousy and madness, plays an important role in the structure of dramatic conflict, I disagree that such 'identity themes' are necessarily linked to one erotic mode. I therefore question not only this model's normalising pretentions, but also its presupposition about the object of inquiry. That is, it takes as a given what remains more properly a question: *is* there a connection between narcissism and homoerotic desire beyond the rather obvious banality of gender similitude? The common-sense proposition that heterosexual arousal depends on gender difference, while homoerotic excitement depends on gender sameness, obscures both the implication of gender in larger systems of power and the role of difference in erotic arousal. Erotic arousal is preeminently (but not exclusively) a function of power differences – of exchanges, withholdings, struggles, negotiations. Because of the institutionalised character of heterosexuality, gender has appeared as the sole determinant of arousal, but I suspect that gender is only one among many power differentials involved: arousal may be as motivated by the differences *within* each gender as by gender difference itself.[26] How comforting for a dominant ideology predicated on oppositional genders to relegate homoerotic desire to an endless immersion in the self-same, rather than to acknowledge those differences within desire that are not heterosexual.

Currently, the critical trend is to move away from psychoanalytic paradigms in one of two directions. First, in the model of male homosociality brilliantly developed by Eve Sedgwick, male homoerotic desire is situated in relation to male homosocial bonds and the patriarchal traffic in women.[27] This paradigm provides important access to the complex and historically varying relation between erotic and gender systems, as the structural congruity between homo*social* and homo*sexual* desire engenders a thematics at once homophobic and misogynist. However, in Sedgwick's attempt to situate homoeroticism in the context of all social bonds, homosociality tends to supplant homoeroticism, resulting in the unfortunate elision of the specific *sexuality* of homoerotic *practice*. Drawing the social back into the erotic illuminates the desire which sustains patriarchal configurations, but it does little to articulate the meanings of homoerotic sexuality. Structural congruity is not isomorphism. For the purpose of Sedgwick's analysis, the conflation between the social and the erotic seems to serve as a necessary means to foreground the intersection between *women's* oppression and homosociality; but as a methodological problem it becomes more acute in the work of other feminist critics enamoured of the homosocial paradigm, who are less consistently careful than is Sedgwick to assert allegiance to an antihomophobic politics. The uncritical use of this model thus risks reproducing a homophobic discourse in the interest of advancing a particular feminist agenda.[28] That the model also tends to deny the availability of female agency is a related, though separate, problem.

Invigorated by Sedgwick's contribution, a pre-existing 'gay and lesbian' studies criticism of early modern texts has increased in rigor and sophistication.[29] Whereas I view this evolving body of work as refreshingly progressive, and am especially pleased to see critics of various erotic identifications engaged in its formulation, this criticism unfortunately reenacts some of the problems of progressivism in general: that is, it uncritically accepts the polarising structure of its problematic. Within Shakespearean criticism, this method seems to align itself along one of only two axes: either Shakespeare participated in the homophobia that is seen as dominating early modern discourse, or he defied such homophobia in celebrating homoerotic love. (Or, correlatively, Shakespeare was or was not homosexual.) The oppositional structure of this paradigm not only reproduces a false binarism of desire/attraction versus anxiety/phobia, but also employs a reductive account of cultural power – namely, that cultures (and authors) either unequivocally deny or affirm *any* erotic mode.[30]

That neither denial nor affirmation provides an adequate theoretical model to account for the complexity of Shakespearean representations of homoeroticism is suggested, first, by the lack of unitary discourse on homoeroticism in early modern England. Not only did legal, moral, religious and literary discourses understand and evaluate homoeroticism differently, but within each discourse there existed contradictory positions. Officially condemned yet routinely ignored, a sinful potential within all subjects yet also a specific illegal physical act, homoeroticism (or more accurately, sodomy and buggery) was a matter of contradictory social investments. Prosecutions were relatively rare (those that did occur often involved child molestation, rape or some extraneous political motivation), and punishments, despite the fact that sodomy was a capital crime after Henry VIII's statute of 1533, were usually moderate.[31]

In addition, Alan Bray argues persuasively that those institutions which condemned homoerotic activity did so in such absolute, apocalyptic and heretical terms, and within such a broad display of 'unnatural' sins, that men who engaged in homoerotic activities routinely distanced such condemnations from the meanings they attached to their own behaviours.[32] As Jonathan Goldberg notes, sodomy 'always was embedded in other discourses, those delineating anti-social behavior – sedition, demonism, atheism.'[33] Thus, for example, when James I wrote his treatise on kingship, *Basilikon Doron*, he

> listed crimes that were treasonous and warranted death. Among them was sodomy. James, of course, was notorious for his overtly homosexual behavior. Yet, his treatise does not simply dissimulate; rather it shows that sodomy was so fully politicized that no king could possibly apply the term to himself.[34]

A distance inserts itself between the discourse on sodomy and the subject of that discourse, *even as that subject discourses*. Through a kind of selective blindness, the cognitive dissonance of those early moderns participating in homoerotic practices was kept at a minimum.

The contradiction posed here between discourse and practice cannot be neatly described as oppositional: homoerotic activity was not only condemned, but was afforded a social logic, a psychic space, within which it could be pursued. The implication of this ideological configuration is far-reaching; in Goldberg's words, sodomy 'was disseminated throughout society, invisible so long as homosexual acts failed to connect with the much more visible signs of social disruption represented by unorthodox religious or social positions'.[35] Sodomy was not, as in modern times, sexually immoral in and of itself; whatever immorality accrued to it was by virtue of its power of *social* disruption.

If male homoeroticism was officially invisible unless associated with other transgressions, female homoeroticism was even more so. Indeed, how *women* understood their own homoerotic desires is still very much under-investigated and under-theorised. I would like to initiate such theorising now. Two strategies suggest themselves as ways into the female homoerotics of Shakespearean drama: a 're-visioning' of close female friendship in the sense proposed by Adrienne Rich, and enacted by such scholars as Carroll Smith-Rosenberg and Lillian Faderman;[36] and a detailed examination of the erotic predicaments of the cross-dressed heroines of the comedies. We might want to look, for instance, at the relationships between Rosalind and Celia in *As You Like It*, Helena and

Hermia in *A Midsummer Night's Dream*, and Marina and Philoten in *Pericles*, and ask why we assume that the images of 'a double cherry' and of 'Juno's swans . . . coupled and inseparable' are qualitatively different, somehow less erotic, than the 'twinn'd lambs' of Polixenes and Leontes in *The Winter's Tale*.[37] To pose the question in this way is to highlight the fact that, whatever the actual erotic practice of women historically, in terms of critical discourse female homoeroticism must be thought into existence.

For now, however, I must limit myself to the second strategy. Most critics would agree that the device of cross-dressing involves the suggestion of homoeroticism. The problem arises, however, in delineating precisely what kind of homoeroticism is represented. The materialist critic often turns to the theatrical practice of using boy actors to play female parts. From that material practice, it can be argued (as I did in my discussion of Lisa Jardine's work) that the homoeroticism embodied by the cross-dressed heroine is implicitly male: if Olivia is attracted to Viola/Cesario, or Phebe to Rosalind/Ganymede, the presence of boy actors suggests that the homoerotic exchange occurs between the transvestised boy actor playing Olivia or Phebe and the boy actor who (once dramatically transvestised as Viola or Rosalind) is now back in masculine dress.

But before we ratify the maleness inherent in this action too quickly, is it not also possible these exchanges express female desire? If we focus on the text rather than theatrical practice, the desires circulating through the Phebe/Rosalind/Ganymede relation, or the Olivia/Viola/Cesario interaction, represent woman's desire for woman. Indeed, this is the reading Jean Howard implicitly proposes, with Olivia bearing the brunt of an anti-homoerotic humour. In the following section, I will argue that the female (and male) homoeroticism of *As You Like It* is a mutual exchange (though not without anxieties and complications), which the contemporary practice of employing *female* actors for these parts can heighten.

But objections immediately present themselves to this 'feminist formalism'. If Phebe is attracted to the 'feminine' in Rosalind/Ganymede, could this be merely an indication of her preferred erotic style (that is, having a small, lithe lover), and having no reference to object choice (a female)? In other words, is it possible to separate early modern erotic *style* from gender inflections? Is such a separation merely the imposition of late twentieth-century preoccupations upon an earlier era? Or does the foregoing analysis of Freud suggest that the conflation of gender and sexuality is a distinctly *modern* formulation?

In the absence of historical analysis of female homoeroticism, such questions are impossible to answer. Indeed, women's general illiteracy, which prevented first-hand recording of their experience, combined with the relative absence of legal and ecclesiastical documents pertaining to women's erotic investments in one another confounds the very possibility of historical analysis. If the materialist feminist's method is to return to the site of inscription, how does one read the impossibility of such a return? The dearth of materials supports a number of possibly conflicting interpretations: assuming that women *did* engage in homoerotic behaviours, it is possible that the nature of their erotic contacts did not invite sexual interpretation (by themselves? by others?); that such behaviour was unremarkable in so far as it did not threaten the basis of the social contract – the open lineage family; that women's confinement in the household not only privatised their sexual contact but prevented the formation of those wider social networks which provided the embryonic basis of male homoerotic 'subcultures'; that the internal distancing evident in male homoeroticism was even more pronounced in that of female homoeroticism.

What evidence we do have suggests that in early modern England, women were not summoned before courts on accusations of 'sodomy'; according to Louis Crompton, England's 'buggery' statute 'was not interpreted as criminalizing relations between women.'[38] Randolph Trumbach observes that the preeminent judicial scholar, Sir Edward Coke, 'took for granted that a woman's action came under the sodomy statute primarily if she commit buggery with a beast.'[39] Crompton provides evidence, however, that in other Western European countries (France, Spain, Italy, Germany and Switzerland) sexual acts between women 'were regarded as legally equivalent to acts of male sodomy and were, like them, punishable by the death penalty.'[40] The significance of this is at least twofold: first, judicially, England seems to have been uniquely unconcerned with female homoeroticism: thus, it seems important to ask how various differences in social formation affect judicial discourse on erotic practice. Is Catholicism, for instance, less tolerant in this regard than Protestantism? To the extent that female homoeroticism was conflated with doctrinal unorthodoxy in Catholic countries, religion does seem to have played a role in its suppression. In addition, were the English more inclined to define sexuality itself as phallic penetration, and thus unable to envision women-centred activities as sexual? Second, what is interesting about this is that women's impunity from prosecution for homoerotic activity contrasts sharply with their *lack* of impunity in cases of heterosexual transgression. The plethora of cases involving premarital sex, adultery and bastardy (and the drama's obsessive preoccupation with cuckoldry) suggest that the lack of concern about female homoeroticism did not derive from an assumption of women's asexuality. As Katharine Maus makes clear, 'anxiety about female sexual fidelity ran high in English Renaissance culture'; she reports that the majority of defamation suits were prompted by the opprobrious terms whore, whoremaster and cuckold.[41]

Curiously, 'sodomitess' was used synonymously with 'whore' as a generic insult, and yet, unlike 'whore', was not employed as accusation in the courts. The question of why the 'sodomitess' lacked legal culpability when so many other insults (scold, shrew, adulteress, whore) carried the onus of defamation leads only to more questions. Were specific erotic behaviours associated with the legally and socially execrated 'whore', while others were reserved for the socially denegrated but legally unculpable 'sodomitess'? Or was female sodomy defined as a matter of sexual *excess*, of quantity rather than kind? Whereas we have come to believe that early modern ideology regarding women's sexuality was informed by the patriarchal need to control women's reproductive capacities, we do not yet know the extent to which erotic behaviour between women either challenged or existed coextensively with that political mandate.

Not only were the regulatory mechanisms towards heterosexual and homoerotic transgressions asymmetrical; the erotic system was also inconsistent with the gender system – as evidenced by the fact that when women cross-dressed, they did *not* experience impunity. From at least 1580 on, women wearing 'masculine' attire were regularly castigated from pulpits and by pamphlets, and by 1620 were perceived to be such a threat that James I spoke out against the practice.[42] The gender and class infraction of cross-dressing *was* linked to prostitution through words like 'whore' and 'trull', but it does not seem to have occasioned accusations of homoerotic deviancy automatically – not, at least, for women.[43] That the anti-theatricalists regularly, even obsessively, returned to the alleged homoerotic transgressions of the *male* cross-dresser underscores the asymmetry most palpably expressed later on in the eighteenth century: women who not only cross-dressed but *passed* as men were prosecuted for *fraud*, while their male counterparts were prosecuted for sodomy (a rather telling instance of woman's metaphysical positioning – to uphold, indeed embody, the truth).[44] And, notoriously, in the nineteenth century, Queen Victoria refused to sign an anti-sodomy bill until all references to women were deleted – she professed complete disbelief in the possibility of women engaging in such acts.[45]

The official invisibility of early modern female homoeroticism, however, tells us little about its *popular* cultural significations. What does seem clear is that in England, women's sexuality did not derive wholly from gender identity or role ascriptions. That is, deviations in gender role did not automatically implicate women as being 'unnatural' in their sexual tastes; deviations in erotic behaviour were not necessarily coded as gender transgressions. The conflation of gender and eroticism that we so often bring to our critical activity does not adequately address early modern women's homoeroticism.

Whatever its significations, they were not identical to those of male homoeroticism, which had both a greater social and discursive presence and, one would suspect, a greater range of practice. In contrast to the silence surrounding female homoeroticism, many early modern terms specifically denote male homoerotic activity: ganymede, catamite, ingle, androgyne. As terms of disparagement, they were directed toward those persons whose youth, 'effeminacy', and/or transvestism positioned them as vulnerable to social scorn. However, despite the cultural availability of derogatory language, of all the arguably homoerotic moments in Shakespearean drama, snide references to males are limited to those used by such characters as the 'deformed and scurrilous' Thersites.[46] Indeed, the representation of male homoeroticism in Shakespearean drama does not suggest any particular aversion – as I will soon argue, quite the contrary: as long as it did not threaten exclusivity, homoeroticism was most often treated in a relaxed, respectful, even urbane way.

In short, the meanings of homoerotic desire during the early modern period seem to have been remarkably unfixed, with contradictory meanings existing across a complex and fractured field of signification. The discourses of homoeroticism were neither monological nor monovocal. Most importantly, homoerotic activity – for men or women – was not a primary means of identification of the self. Homoeroticism had little to do with any of the social roles, statuses and hierarchies in which an early modern subject might be located and thereby define him/herself. That early moderns did not essentialise homoeroticism in quite the way we do (with our assumption that engaging in homoerotic behaviours confers a gay or lesbian 'identity') becomes increasingly significant as a model for those who theorise sexuality in a contemporary context. Even before the threat of AIDS to gay men, gay and lesbian theorists had begun to move from a paradigm of identity to one of erotic practice. Now, in the global context of AIDS, even conservatives must acknowledge that it is not 'who you are' (gay/straight) but 'what you do' that is the salient factor in identifying risk.[47] As horrifying as is the impact of AIDS on our individual and collective lives – and I do not mean to trivialise that horror by mentioning it in this theoretical context – it also pressures us to re-examine the paradigms within which we conceive our sexual subjectivities.

My use of two seemingly opposed yet not directly antonymic terms – homo/eroticism and hetero/sexuality – is a response to the early modern social configuration. In that period, neither heterosexuality nor homosexuality (nor sexuality itself for that matter) existed in our modern senses of the terms. Yet, despite the absence of both concepts from the early modern consciousness, it is still possible to speak of crucial differences in the social organisation of those activities which we now term 'homo' or 'hetero'. Although neither an originating cause nor organising principle, heterosexual object choice was involved in the social formation both subjectively and institutionally in the following ways: as a subjective state of desire, if not for an object proper, then for the results that union with that object would hopefully insure (family, name, property, rank, lineage – all that is connoted by the early modern term 'house'); as a well-defined and well-investigated erotic act (fornication) organised around the presence or absence of female chastity; and as a dominant ideology which found its teleology in the material institution of marriage.[48] My use of the linguistic root 'sexuality,' despite its historical anachronism, is meant to imply this institutional and political mandate, in which identity was situated in relation to one's sexual congress as a socially ascribed subject-position – as husband, mistress, wife, widow or widower, for instance. To that extent, 'heterosexuality' performed a crucial function of subjectification *vis-à-vis* the dominant social order.

In contrast, homosexuality – as identity, ideology or institution – did not exist. What did exist discursively, in the form of sodomy and buggery, were a number of dispersed acts, organised around penetration: anal intercourse between males or between males and females, intercourse with children, fellatio and bestiality – none of which referred to specific acts between women. Following the implicit lead of the documentary discourses of law, religion and morality, many critics thus focus on early modern homoeroticism as an *act*, defining it in terms of its material practice: sodomy. To do so, however, is to conflate homoeroticism with other forms of 'sexual confusion', to ignore the gender asymmetry of sodomy's definition, and to obviate the subjective motivation for and experience of homoerotic activity. Legal, ecclesiastical and moral discourses positioned homoeroticism as 'Other' and, within that logic, refused the power of speech to those who would speak from the position of their own intentionality. I want to argue that to the extent that material practice did not exhaust homoeroticism's meaning – either for those who experienced it or for those who represented it in literature – what is in excess remains in the amorphous register of erotic *desire*.[49] More accurately, homoeroticism was a position taken in *relation* to desire – a position, however, that was neither socially mandated nor capable of conferring identity or role.

And yet, even as I formulate homoeroticism as a position taken in relation to desire, I am in danger of reifying what is really a relational process – desire or eroticism – and granting it a certain structural autonomy. Such a method risks attributing agency to desire by raising it to the status of ontology or attributing to it a teleology. It represents, at best, an interim strategy, a way to keep the exigencies of materiality and subjectivity poised in mutual tension, while at the same time insisting on the material and subjective asymmetry between hetero/sexuality and homo/eroticism.

The above concerns inform my critical practice in the following ways. In the next section, I attempt to resist fixing erotic identity onto specific characters, and instead argue that the text itself displays a homoerotic circulation of desire; homoerotic energy is elicited, exchanged and displaced as it confronts the pleasures and anxieties of its meanings in early modern culture. As it traverses 'masculine' and 'feminine' sites, this desire challenges the binary language of identity that upholds the modern erotic economy. At the same time, however, homoerotic desire must be located within a matrix of gender and class relations, since its signification, like that of heterosexuality, differs along hierarchical lines. Thus, it is not so much homoeroticism 'itself' that is analysed, as its relation to other modes of power. The issue becomes less a matter of 'proving' the existence of homoerotic desire than of refusing to credit such a request in the first place. Once the hierarchy between homoerotic and heterosexual is dissolved within the critical enterprise, homoerotic significations are everywhere – both in their expansive, inclusive modes, and in their anxious and repressed forms. That this is true seems to me to be less a matter of the critic's own projective desire (although there is certainly an element of that in all of our reading) than of the polymorphous potential of desire itself, which Shakespeare so assiduously evokes and controls.

IV

That homoerotic significations will play a part in *As You Like It* is first intimated by Rosalind's adoption of the name Ganymede when she imagines donning doublet and hose. Of all the male names available to her, she chooses that of the young lover of Zeus, familiar to educated Britons through Greek and Latin literature and European painting, and to less privileged persons as a colloquial term used to describe the male object of male love. As James Saslow, who traces the artistic representation of Ganymede in Western culture from the fifteenth to the seventeenth centuries, argues, 'the very word *ganymede* was used from medieval times well into the seventeenth century to mean an object of homosexual desire.'[50] Both James Saslow and Stephen Orgel agree: 'the name Ganymede [could not] be used in the Renaissance without this connotation.'[51]

That Rosalind-cum-Ganymede becomes the object of another woman's desire is obvious. Consciously, of course, Phebe believes Ganymede to be a man, and is thus merely following the dominant heterosexual course. And yet, what attracts Phebe to Ganymede are precisely those qualities that could be termed 'feminine'. Notice the progression of the following speech:

> It is a pretty youth: not very pretty. . . .
> He'll make a proper man: the best thing in him
> Is his complexion. . . .
> He is not very tall; yet for his years he's tall;
> His leg is but so so; and yet 'tis well;
> There was a pretty redness in his lip,
> A little riper and more lusty red
> Than that mix'd in his cheek; 'twas just the difference
> Betwixt the constant red and mingled damask. (III, v, 113–23)

During the first half of her speech, as she measures Ganymede against common male attributes – height, leg – Phebe fights her attraction (he is; he is not); in the last four lines, as she 'feminises' Ganymede's lip and cheek, she gives in to her desire altogether.

Many critics acknowledge the underlying homoeroticism of Phebe's attraction; however, they tend to undermine its thematic importance by relegating it to the status of a temporary psychosexual stage. C.L. Barber, for instance, remarks:

> She has, in effect, a girlish crush on the femininity which shows through Rosalind's disguise; the aberrant affection is happily got over when Rosalind reveals her identity and makes it manifest that Phebe has been loving a woman.[52]

When Barber says that Phebe's 'aberrant' affection is 'happily got over', he reveals the extent to which homophobic anxiety structures the developmental logic of his response. But if a 'girlish crush' is outgrown or overcome, what are we to make of Rosalind's desire to 'prove a busy actor' in the 'pageant truly play'd' of Phebe and Silvius (III, iv, 50–8)? Although her ostensible motivation is her belief that 'the sight of lovers feedeth those in love' (56), s/he soon interjects in order to correct the literal-mindedness that feeds Phebe's 'proud disdain' (III, iv, 52). And yet, the pleasure Rosalind/Ganymede takes in this task seems in excess of her putative function. Significantly, it is s/he who first mentions the possibility of Phebe's attraction, interpreting and then glorying in Phebe's changed demeanor:

> Why, what means this? Why do you look on me?
> I see no more in you than in the ordinary
> Of nature's sale-work. 'Od's my little life
> I think she means to tangle my eyes too! (III, v, 41–4)

Is there not a sense in which Rosalind/Ganymede *elicits* Phebe's desire, constructing it even as she refuses it? Indeed, s/he delights in her role of the rejecting male:

> Down on your knees,
> And thank heaven, fasting, for a good man's love;
> For I must tell you friendly in your ear,
> Sell when you can, you are not for all markets. (57–60)

And why does s/he put Silvius through the exquisite torment of hearing Phebe's love letter to Ganymede read aloud, if not to aggrandise her own victorious position as male rival (IV, iii, 14–64)? Indeed, as a male, her sense of power is so complete that s/he presumes to tell Silvius to tell Phebe 'that if she love *me*, I charge her to love *thee*' (71–2, my emphasis).

Homoerotic desire in *As You Like It* thus circulates from Phebe's desire for the 'feminine' in Rosalind/Ganymede to Rosalind/Ganymede's desire to be the 'masculine' object of Phebe's desire. Even more suggestive of the text's investment in homoerotic pleasure is Orlando's willingness to engage in love-play with a young shepherd. Throughout his 'courtship' of Ganymede (who is now impersonating Rosalind), Orlando accepts and treats Ganymede as his beloved. To do so requires less his willing suspension of disbelief, than the ability to hold in suspension a dual sexuality that feels no compulsion to make arbitrary distinctions between kinds of objects. That Rosalind-cum-Ganymede takes the lead in their courtship has been noted by countless critics; that there is a certain homoerotic irony in that fact has yet to be noted. As a 'ganymede', Rosalind would be expected to play the part of a younger, more receptive partner in an erotic exchange. S/he thus not only inverts gender roles; s/he disrupts alleged homoerotic roles as well.

What began as a game culminates in the 'mock' marriage, when Orlando takes for his wife the boy he believes to be fictionalising as Rosalind. It is Celia, not Orlando, who hesitates in playing her part in the ceremony – 'I cannot say the words', she responds to Orlando's request that she play the priest (IV, i, 121) – in part because those words possess a ritualistic power to *enact* what is spoken. Insofar as ritual was still popularly believed to be imbued with magical power, the fact that Orlando does not hesitate, but eagerly responds in the precise form of the Anglican marriage ceremony – 'I take thee, Rosalind, for wife' (129) – suggests the degree to which the play legitimates the multiple desires it represents. The point is not that Orlando and Ganymede formalise a homosexual marriage, but rather that as the distance between Rosalind and Ganymede collapses, distinctions between homoerotic and heterosexual collapse as well. As the woman and the shepherd-boy merge, Orlando's words resound with the conviction that, for the moment, he (as much as Rosalind and the audience) is engaged in the ceremony as if it were real. As both a performative speech act and a theatricalisation of desire, the marriage is both true and fictional at once. The subversiveness of this dramatic gesture lies in the dual motion of, first, appropriating the meaning of matrimony for deviant desires; and, secondly, exposing the heterosexual norm of matrimony as a reduction of the plurality of desire into the singularity of monogamy. The 'mock' marriage is not a desecration but a deconstruction of the ritual by which two are made one.

When Hymen in Act V symbolically reintroduces the logic of heterosexual marriage, the text's devotion to simultaneity would appear to be negated. However, contrary to the assumptions of many critics, for whom generic form determines content, the play does not close with a firm reassertion of heterosexuality, but rather with a renewed attack on the pretensions of erotic certitude. In a repetition of her previous gender and erotic mobility, Rosalind-cum-boy-actor, still wearing female attire, leaps the frame of the play in order to address the audience in a distinctly erotic manner: 'If I were a woman I would kiss as many of you as had beards that pleased me, complexions that liked me and breaths that I defied not' (Epil., 16–19). As Orgel, Howard, Phyllis Rackin and Catherine Belsey all intimate, the effect of this statement is to highlight the constructedness of gender and the flexibility of erotic attraction at precisely the point when the formal impulse of comedy would be to essentialise and fix both gender and eroticism.

Throughout the play, what makes erotic contingency possible is a simple conjunction: 'if'. Indeed, Touchstone's discourse on the virtues of 'if' can serve as an index of the play's entire erotic strategy: 'If you said so, then I said so' (V, iv, 99–100). The dependence on the conditional structures the possibility of erotic exploration without necessitating a commitment to it. Orlando can woo and even wed Ganymede as '*if* thou wert indeed my Rosalind' and as *if* the marriage were real (IV, i, 189–90, my emphasis). Through the magic of 'if', the boy actor playing Rosalind can offer and elicit erotic attraction to and from each gender in the audience. 'If' not only creates multiple erotic possibilities and positions, it also conditionally resolves the dramatic confusion that the play cannot sustain. As Rosalind says to Silvius, Phebe and Orlando, respectively: 'I would love you, if I could'; 'I will marry you, if ever I marry a woman, and I'll be married tomorrow'; and, 'I will satisfy you, if ever I satisfied man, and you shall be married tomorrow' (V, ii, 107–72).

My own reliance on 'if' should make it clear that I am not arguing that Rosalind or Orlando or Phebe 'is' 'a' 'homosexual'. Rather, at various moments in the play, these characters temporarily inhabit a homoerotic position of desire. To insist on a mode of desire as a position taken up also differs from formulating these characters as 'bisexual': as Phyllis Rackin reminds us, bisexuality implicitly defines the desiring subject as divided in order to maintain the ideologically motivated categories of homo- and hetero- as inviolate.[53] The entire logic of *As You Like It* works against such categorisation, against fixing upon and reifying any one mode of desire.

Simultaneity and flexibility, however, are not without their costs. In so far as the text circulates homoerotic desire, it displaces the anxieties so generated in the following tableau, described by Oliver, Orlando's brother:

> A wretched ragged man, o'ergrown with hair,
> Lay sleeping on his back. About his neck
> A green and gilded snake had wreath'd itself,
> Who with her head nimble in threats approach'd
> The opening of his mouth. . . .
> A lioness, with udders all drawn dry,
> Lay crouching, head on ground, with catlike watch,
> When that the sleeping man should stir. (IV, iii, 107–17)

The dual dangers to which the sleeping Oliver is susceptible are, on the face of it, female: the lioness an aged maternal figure ('with udders all drawn dry'), the snake seductively encircling Oliver's neck. Let us first give this passage a conventional psychoanalytic reading: the virile and virtuous Orlando banishes the snake and battles the lion while his evil 'emasculated' brother, unconscious of his position as damsel in distress, sleeps on – their sibling rivalry displaced onto and mediated by gender conflict. However, at the same time that the snake encircles her prey, she approaches and almost penetrates the vulnerable opening of Oliver's mouth. Rather than posit the snake, in this aspect, as the representation of the 'phallic mother', I want to argue that in her figure are concentrated the anxieties generated by the text's simultaneous commitment to homo-eroticism and heterosexuality. If Oliver is endangered by the snake's 'feminine' sexual powers, he is equally threatened by her phallic ones. He becomes both the feminised object of male aggression and the *ef*feminised object of female desire. The snake thus represents the erotic 'Other' of the text, the reservoir of the fears elicited by homoerotic exchanges – fears, I want to insist, that are not inherent in the experience of homoerotic desire, but rather produced by homophobic ideology.

Indeed, the relations represented in this tableau suggest that no desire, male or female, heterosexual or homoerotic, is free of anxiety. As Touch-stone says in a lighter vein, 'as all is mortal in nature, so is all nature in love mortal in folly' (II, iv, 52–3). But what is most interesting is that sexual danger is encoded as feminising to the object persistently figured as male. Consistently, the text seems less interested in the threat of a particu-lar mode of desire (hetero/homo) than in the dangers desire *as such* poses to men. It is, in this sense, thoroughly patriarchal, positing man as the centre of, though vulnerable to, desire. That the text marginalise this expression of vulnerability by not dramatising it on stage but reporting it only in retrospect suggests the extent to which the anxiety is repressed in the interests of achieving comic, heterosexual closure.

I do not mean to imply that *As You Like It* represents a paradisiacal erotic economy, a utopian return to a polymorphously perverse body unmediated by cultural restraints. As the penultimate gesture towards the institution of marriage clearly indicates, endless erotic mobility is difficult to sustain. But just as clearly, *As You Like It* registers its lack of commitment to the binary logic that dominates the organisation of desire. If *As You Like It* suggests the 'folly' of desire, part of that folly is the discipline to which it is subject.

V

Several implications evolve from the problems and methodology I have outlined here. First, by arguing that eroticism *is* cultural practice – material, ideological and subjective – I encourage literary and cultural critics to recognise and distinguish the workings of eroticism in the texts and cultures they analyse. If even the most sophisticated feminist materialist analyses misrecognise gender as a signifier in such a way that eroticism is conveniently forgotten, clearly, both gender and historical critics need to rethink their assumptions about the meaning and significance of erotic practice.

Secondly, implicit throughout my essay is the belief that the problems posed by erotic desire demand feminist analysis from two angles simultaneously: historical materialist analysis of ideological and material practice, and psychoanalysis of subjective states of desire. Indeed, the case of early modern homoeroticism(s) demonstrates the extent to which the opposition between the social and the psychic is a false one, and that erotic theory must accommodate both institutional and subjective processes. Despite psychoanalysis' belatedness, its construction within the specific problematics of modernity, and its unfortunate history as a normalising institution, its recognition that eroticism involves several modes of desire is crucial to the possibility of a non-normalising analytic. To investigate homoeroticism only from the standpoint of ascertainable material practice, our understanding of which is limited to the dominant discourses of legal and religious records, is to ignore the subjective erotic dramas of countless early modern persons. We cannot know the content of those subjective dramas, but we can reconstruct partial (that is both incomplete and necessarily biased) approximations of their meaning from the rhetorical strategies employed to describe them. To my mind, this is where a historical, discourse-based model faces its greatest challenge: to delineate not only those statements that circulate throughout the social fabric, but also to 're-vision' and put into play those meanings that have been repressed, lost, or unspoken.

The viability of the kind of critical rapproachment I advocate – feminist-historical-materialist-psycho-analysis – depends on the continuing deconstruction of psychoanalysis's will to mastery. The first move in such a project is the internal displacement of those totalisations that obscure historical and social processes. One such totalisation, I hope to have demonstrated, is 'desire' itself.

The work I have begun here is only a small first step in the much larger project of deconstructing 'sex-desire', in the words of Foucault, in the interests of 'bodies and pleasures'.[54] Insofar as gay men and lesbians are still subject to institutionalised oppression (including the recent revision of the archaic 'sodomy' law specifically to criminalise homosexual acts in the state in which I live, and the revoking of the right to freedom of speech in matters homoerotic in Great Britain), asserting the specificity of homoeroticism is politically progressive.

It is not, however, radically deconstructive, if only because it continues to pay implicit obeisance to the prestige of object choice as the primary criterion of sexuality. A more radical project would move not only beyond the regime of object choice, but also beyond the representational strategy that supports it: the hegemony of the phallus. Both the phallus and object choice depend on a binary system that reifies eroticism by privileging one erotic position over all others. Even in Lacanian psychoanalysis, in which the phallus represents a 'lack-in-being', the recourse to phallus-as-signifier-of-desire defines the problematic of presence/absence as ontologically originating in the male body. Rather than demystifying male sexuality as it exposes subjectivity as a (w)hole, it reproduces male genetalia as transcendental signifier (not of presence but of absence), in an inversion that leaves the privilege of the term undisturbed. Male sexuality remains both the referent and repetition of the problem of subjectivity 'itself'.[55] And the static relations between power and desire remain uncontested, with power always the 'substitute of choice' for what we always already and always will, essentially, lack.

The deconstruction of erotic binarism would involve putting into play more heterogenous and heteronomous representations, by recognising what Jonathan Dollimore has called the 'creative perversity of desire itself'.[56] Persons of all erotic persuasions – and I stress that this is not solely the task of erotic minorities – can renegotiate the terms by which desire is understood, setting into critical motion the various contingencies that structure arousal and foster erotic satisfaction. Beginning to conceptualise desire as the sum of discontinuous and incongruent discourses, practices, identifications, fantasies, preferences for specific activities, as well as object choice(s), we could do worse than adopt as a critical strategy the kind of rhetorical displacement evident on the following political T shirt:

so-do-my
neighbours
parents
friends

Deconstructing 'desire' opens up a field of inquiry to materialist feminists, a way of thinking about bodies, pleasures and history that allows us to ask previously unapproachable questions. Indeed, questions that hitherto seemed ahistorical may be viewed with a new historicity. For instance, what precise intersections of discourses on power, gender, bodies and pleasures produce the possibility of seeing in *Twelfth Night's* Antonio the macho 'Castro clone' encased in leather in San Francisco? Or why does Sebastian seem to prefigure the 'bisexual' who can go either way? Why does Viola and Rosalind's adoption of 'doublet and hose' seem to foreshadow our own taste for androgynous and practical fashions?

And where is Olivia? Perhaps sitting at her computer, wearing high heels.

NOTES

I would like to gratefully acknowledge Valerie Wayne, Phyllis Rackin, Peter Stallybrass, Abbe Blum, Murray Schwartz, Arthur Kinney, Lee Edwards, Peter Erickson and Brenda Marshall for their help with this essay.

1. Marguerite Waller, 'Academic Tootsie: the denial of difference and the difference it makes', *Diacritics*, 17 (1987), pp. 4–5.
2. Jean Howard, 'Crossdressing, the theatre, and gender struggle in early modern England', *Shakespeare Quarterly*, 39 (1988), p. 432.
3. Lisa Jardine, ' "As boys and women are for the most part cattle of this colour": Female roles and Elizabethan eroticism', in her *Still Harping on Daughters: Women and Drama in the Age of Shakespeare* (Hemel Hempstead: Harvester Wheatsheaf, 1983), p. 8.
4. *Ibid.*, p. 20.
5. *Ibid.*, p. 11.
6. See Jacqueline Rose's analysis of Leonardo da Vinci in *Sexuality in the Field of Vision* (London: Verso, 1986), p. 226.
7. Gayle Rubin, 'Thinking sex: notes for a radical theory of the politics of sexuality', in Carole Vance, ed., *Pleasure and Danger* (London: Routledge & Kegan Paul, 1984), p. 307. See also Pat Caplan, *The Cultural Construction of Sexuality* (London: Tavistock, 1987), pp. 1–30, and Jeffrey Weeks, *Sexuality and Its Discontents* (London: Routledge & Kegan Paul, 1985). Eve Sedgwick has taken up precisely this question in 'Across gender, across sexuality: Willa Cather and others', *South Atlantic Quarterly*, 88 (1989), pp. 53–72.
8. In an important passage, Freud writes, 'There is only one libido, which serves both the masculine and the feminine sexual functions. To it itself we cannot

assign any sex; if, following the conventional equation of activity and masculinity, we are inclined to describe it as masculine, we must not forget that it also covers trends with a passive aim. Nevertheless the juxtaposition "feminine libido" is without any justification' ('Femininity', in his *New Introductory Lectures on Psychoanalysis*, ed. James Strachey (New York: W.W. Norton, 1965), p. 116. See also Joel Fineman, 'The turn of the shrew', in Patricia Parker and Geoffrey Hartman, eds., *Shakespeare and the Question of Theory* (New York: Methuen, 1985), pp. 138–60; and Carol Cook, ' "The sign and semblance of her honor": reading gender difference in *Much Ado About Nothing*', *PMLA*, **101** (1986), pp. 186–202, especially p. 190.

9. See Teresa de Lauretis, *Alice Doesn't* (Bloomington: Indiana University Press, 1984); *Technologies of Gender* (Bloomington: Indiana University Press, 1987); and 'Feminist studies/critical studies: issues, terms, and contexts', in her *Feminist Studies/Critical Studies* (Bloomington: Indiana University Press, 1986), pp. 1–19.

10. Sigmund Freud, 'The psychogenesis of a case of homosexuality in a woman' (1920), *Standard Edition*, trans. and ed. James Strachey, *Standard Editions of the Complete Psychological Works of Sigmund Freud* (London: Hogarth Press, 1953–74) 1955, vol. 18, p. 170. 'Physical characteristics' refers to the secondary sex characteristics 'appropriate' to each sex, as well as to anatomical ambiguities; 'mental characteristics' refers to what Freud calls 'masculine or feminine attitude' – in other words, gender role conformity; and 'object choice' refers, as now, to the direction of one's erotic preference: hetero-, homo- or bi-.

11. Freud, 'Psychogenesis', p. 154, and 'Leonardo da Vinci and a memory of his childhood' (1910), *Standard Edition*, vol. 11, pp. 59–106.

12. Sigmund Freud, 'General remarks on hysterical attacks' (1909), in his *Dora: An Analysis of a Case of Hysteria*, ed. Philip Rieff (New York: Macmillan Publishing Co., 1963), p. 157, my emphasis.

13. Sigmund Freud, 'From the history of an infantile neurosis' (1918), in his *Three Case Histories*, ed. Philip Rieff (New York: Macmillan Publishing Co., 1963), p. 305.

14. Freud, 'Leonardo da Vinci', p. 86.

15. Karen Newman, 'Renaissance family politics and Shakespeare's *The Taming of the Shrew*', *ELR*, **16** (1986), p. 99, my emphasis.

16. Nancy Chodorow, *The Reproduction of Mothering* (Berkeley: University of California Press, 1978), p. 150.

17. Arlene Stein, 'All dressed up, but no place to go? Style wars and the new lesbianism', *Outlook: National Lesbian and Gay Quarterly*, **1** (1989), p. 38.

18. See Joan Nestle, 'Butch-fem relationships: sexual courage in the 1950s', *Heresies: A Feminist Publication on Art and Politics*, vol. 3 (1981), pp. 21–4.

19. For an initiating but problematic attempt at this new erotic theory, see Esther Newton and Shirley Walton, 'The misunderstanding: toward a more precise sexual vocabulary', in Carole Vance, ed., *Pleasure and Danger: Exploring Female Sexuality*, pp. 242–50. I am also indebted to Cindy Patton's manuscript, 'Desire in the academy'.

20. Robert Stoller, *Observing the Erotic Imagination* (New Haven: Yale University Press, 1985).

21. Cindy Patton, *Sex and Germs: The Politics of AIDS* (Boston: South End Press), p. 105.

22. See Henry Minton, 'Femininity in men and masculinity in women: American psychiatry and psychology portray homosexuality in the 1930s', *Journal of Homosexuality*, **13** (1986), pp. 1–21; and Kenneth Lewes, *The Psychoanalytic Theory of Male Homosexuality* (New York: Simon & Schuster, 1988).

23. Michel Foucault, *The History of Sexuality*, vol. 1 (New York: Random House, 1978).

24. Actually, within social constructivist theory, there exists considerable disagreement as to the date of emergence of the 'modern homosexual'. Saslow cautiously suggests that 'the Renaissance planted the first seeds of a new identity and social status for homosexuality', 'Homosexuality in the Renaissance: Behaviour, identity, and artistic expression', *Hidden From History*, eds. Martin Duberman, George Chauncey, and Martha Vicinus (New York: NAL Books, 1989), p. 105. See also his *Ganymede in the Renaissance: Homosexuality in Art and Society* (New Haven: Yale U P, 1986); and ' "A Veil of Ice between My Heart and Fire": Michelangelo's sexual identity and early modern constructs of homosexuality', *Genders*, 2 (1988), pp. 77–90. Randolph Trumbach, in 'Birth of the Queen: Sodomy and the emergence of gender equality in modern culture 1660–1750', *Hidden From History*, pp. 129–140; and 'London's Sodomites', *Journal of Social History*, 11 (1977), pp. 1–33 and Alan Bray in *Homosexuality in Renaissance England* (London: Gay Men's Press, 1982) date modern homosexuality from the appearance of London's 'molly houses' and the exclusive adult male sodomite in the early eighteenth century. Michel Foucault, *The History of Sexuality*, vol 1; Jeffrey Weeks, *Sexuality and its Discontents* (London: Routledge & Kegan Paul, 1985); Lillian Faderman, *Surpassing the Love of Men: Romantic Friendship and Love Between Women from the Renaissance to the Present* (New York: William Morrow, 1981); and George Chauncey, 'From sexual inversion to homosexuality: Medicine and the changing conceptualization of female deviance', *Salmagundi* 58/59 (fall 1982/winter 1983), pp. 114–46 argue that not until the sexologists' medicalisation of sexual deviance at the end of the nineteenth century did a homosexual identity emerge. All constructivists agree that urbanisation (and the social networks and anonymity it affords) was a crucial factor; I wonder, however, whether this emphasis on city subcultures is not itself a product of a particularly male perspective. Not only does urbanisation seem to have been far less salient for the formation of lesbian identity, but it does little to account for the erotic practices of those persons living in rural communities. For excellent renditions of the constructivist view, see David Halperin, 'One hundred years of homosexuality', *Diacritics*, 16 (summer, 1986), pp. 34–45 and 'Sex before sexuality: Pederasty, politics, and power in classical Athens', *Hidden from History*, pp. 37–53. For useful accounts of the debate between social constructivists and essentialists, see Steven Epstein, 'Gay politics, ethnic identity: The limits of social constructionism', *Socialist Review*, 93/94 (1987), pp. 9–54; John Boswell, 'Revolutions, universals, and sexual categories', *Salmagundi* 58/59 (1982/1983), pp. 89–113; Robert Padgug, 'Sexual matters: On conceptualizing sexuality in history', *Radical History Review*, 20 (1979), pp. 3–23; Gregory Sprague, 'Male homosexuality in western culture: The dilemma of identity and subculture in historical research', *Journal of Homosexuality*, 10 (1984), pp. 29–43; John De Cecco and Michael Shively, 'From sexual identity to sexual relationships: A contextual shift', *Journal of Homosexuality*, 9 (1982/1983), pp. 1–26; and Diana Fuss, *Essentially Speaking: Feminism, Nature and Difference* (London: Routledge, 1990), pp. 97–112.

25. See, in particular, the way appeals to narcissism work in W. Thomas MacCary, *Friends and Lovers: The phenomenology of desire in Shakespearean comedy* (New York: Columbia University Press, 1985); and Leonard Tennenhouse, 'The counterfeit order of *The Merchant of Venice*', and Joel Fineman, 'Fratricide and Cuckoldry: Shakespeare's doubles', both in Murray Schwartz and

Coppélia Kahn, eds., *Representing Shakespeare* (Baltimore: Johns Hopkins University Press, 1980), pp. 54–109.

26. To my mind, power permeates all aspects of human relations; however, this is not to imply that all relations are based on a sadomasochistic paradigm of dominance and submission. What is important to me is not to *escape* from power (in my view a hopelessly essentialist fantasy), but to increase our awareness of the positions we occupy and to *use* our power as humanely as possible. Paramount in that attempt is the ability to manoeuvre one's position flexibly, to exchange roles and positions. Robert Stoller is helpful in detailing the kinds of roles, positions and tensions that contribute to the construction of erotic excitement: 'I could never list all the polar fields that might make an excitement, but they are such things as: aesthetic/anaesthetic, alive/dead, active/passive, safe/endangered, unmasked/masked, brave/cowardly, loving/hating, loved/hated, kill/be killed, start/not start, move/stop, clever/stupid, strong/weak, secrets kept/secrets exposed, unbound/bound, I/not-I, in control/out of control, free (for example, from deception)/enslaved (by deception), sound/silence, accepted/rejected, broken/whole, triumphant/humiliated, shall I/shan't I, can I/can't I, will I/won't I (refusal), defended/defenseless, familiar/strange, clarity/confusion, movement/paralysis, constancy/inconstancy, time/timelessness, go/stop, permanence/change, knowledge/ignorance, simplicity/ambiguity, tension/relaxation [the list continues]' (*Erotic Imagination*, p. 53).

27. Eve Sedgwick, *Between Men: English Literature and Male Homosocial Desire* (New York: Columbia University Press, 1985).

28. Sedgwick has recently come under attack, most notably by David Van Leer, 'The beast in the closet: homosociality and the pathology of manhood', *Critical Inquiry*, **15** (1989), pp. 587–605. Van Leer identifies 'two problematic moves in Sedgwick's analysis of homosocial bonds: her desire to relate homosexuality to 'larger questions' of society and sexuality, and her attempt to thematize homophobia and the homosexual/homosocial bonds that underwrite it as "homosexual panic" ' (p. 592). Specifically, Van Leer argues that despite Sedgwick's stated project, embedded in her work are homophobic assumptions that foster rather than deconstruct homosexual stereotypes: 'the unintentional result is to banish from her discourse the category of the healthy, well-adjusted male homosexual while reintroducing two chief myths of gay self-contempt – the fag hag and the closet queen' (p. 598). In this and in the subsequent exchange between Sedgwick and Van Leer ('Critical response I: tide and trust', and 'Critical response III: trust and trade', *Critical Inquiry*, **15** (1989), pp. 745–63), what becomes most clear is that the language by which we analyse homoerotic desire is thoroughly permeated with homophobic and misogynistic associations, irrespective of individual intention. That Van Leer sees this not as a problem of available language, but as a problem of Sedgwick's positioning – 'as doubly an outsider [neither gay nor male] she is unlikely to delineate "most authoritatively" a male homosexual tradition' (pp. 600–1) – seems to me a criticism of dubious analytical power. In his efforts to delegitimise Sedgwick, he adopts the untenable position that because she is 'unable to speak from within the minority, Sedgwick must perforce speak from within the majority; denied the language of homosexuality, she necessarily speaks heterosexuality' (p. 603). Surely there are more positions than that! Neither homosexuality nor heterosexuality (nor masculinity nor femininity, for that matter) are oppositional *essences*; precisely as positions, they are available in varying degrees to us all. Finally, that Van Leer adopts an affirmative gay male rhetoric at the expense of women and feminist theorising (he calls Sedgwick's

comparison of gay men and women 'minimally castrating' [p. 601]), seems to me an unfortunate step backward, from the point of view of both feminism and gay theory. At the same time, to the extent that Van Leer argues for the necessity of keeping conceptual categories distinct, and for the reinsertion of the lived experience of homosexuals, their specific erotic identities and practices, into the field of analysis, his project and mine are aligned.

29. See, for instance, Joseph Porter, 'Marlowe, Shakespeare, and the canonization of heterosexuality', *South Atlantic Quarterly*, **88** (1989), pp. 125–47; and *Shakespeare's Mercutio: His History and Drama* (Chapel Hill: University of North Carolina Press, 1988). At the spring 1989 Shakespeare Association of America Conference, at least fifteen seminar papers dealt with homoeroticism in the plays.

30. Joseph Pequigney, for instance, sees his task as securing the 'identity' of both Shakespeare and his characters as 'homosexual'. His impulse to produce 'evidence' of 'classic male homosexual relationships' works against my thesis in multiple ways. See *Such is My Love: A Study of Shakespeare's Sonnets* (Chicago: University of Chicago Press, 1985); and 'The two Antonios and same-sex love in *Twelfth Night* and *The Merchant of Venice*', unpublished manuscript presented to the Shakespeare Association of America, 1989.

31. The most recent and critically sophisticated analyses of early modern legal discourse on homosexuality are Ed Cohen, 'Legislating the norm: from sodomy to gross indecency', *South Atlantic Quarterly*, **88** (1989), pp. 181–217; and Bruce Smith, 'Touching the friendship of Shakespeare's heroes: literary discourse versus moral and legal discourse about homosexual desire', unpublished manuscript presented at the Shakespeare Association of America seminar on Renaissance Sexualities, April 1989. Helpful as more general analyses are Stephen Orgel, 'Nobody's perfect: or why did the English stage take boys for women', *South Atlantic Quarterly*, **88** (1989), pp. 7–29; and Jonathan Goldberg, 'Sodomy and society: the case of Christopher Marlowe', *Southwest Review* (Autumn 1984), pp. 371–8. Each is influenced by Foucault as well as by Alan Bray. See also John Boswell, *Christianity, Social Tolerance and Homosexuality* (Chicago: University of Chicago Press, 1980); Arthur Gilbert, 'Buggery and the British navy, 1700–1861', *Journal of Social History*, **10** (1976), pp. 72–98; Caroline Bingham, 'Seventeenth-century attitudes toward deviant sex', *Journal of Interdisciplinary History*, **1** (1971), pp. 447–68; B.R. Burgh, 'Ho hum, another work of the devil: buggery and sodomy in early Stuart England', in Salvatore Licata and Robert Petersen, eds., *The Gay Past* (New York: Harrington Park Press, 1985) and Guido Ruggiero, *The Boundaries of Eros: Sex crime and sexuality in Renaissance Venice* (Oxford University Press, 1985).

32. Bray, *Homosexuality*, p. 92.

33. Goldberg, 'Sodomy and society', p. 371.

34. *Ibid.*, p. 376.

35. *Ibid.*, p. 372.

36. Adrienne Rich, 'When we dead awaken: writing as re-vision', *College English*, **34** (1972), pp. 18–25; Carroll Smith-Rosenberg, 'The female world of love and ritual: relations between women in nineteenth-century America', *Signs*, **1** (1975), pp. 27–55; Lillian Faderman, *Surpassing the Love of Men*. See also Rich's important, if problematic, essay 'Compulsory heterosexuality and lesbian existence', *Signs*, **5** (1980), pp. 631–60.

37. *A Midsummer Night's Dream*, III, ii, 198–216; *As You Like It*, I, iii, 72–5; *Pericles*, IV, Prol., 15–40; *The Winter's Tale*, I, ii, 62–71. All references to

Shakespeare are from *The Complete Works of Shakespeare*, 3rd edn., ed. David Bevington (Glenview: Scott, Foresman & Co., 1980).

38. Louis Crompton, 'The myth of lesbian impunity', *The Gay Past*, pp. 11–25. See also Brigitte Eriksson, 'A lesbian execution in Germany, 1721: the trial records', in the same volume, pp. 27–40; and Judith Brown, *Immodest Acts: The life of a lesbian nun in Renaissance Italy* (Oxford: Oxford University Press, 1986).

39. Trumbach, 'London's sodomites', p. 13.

40. Crompton, 'Lesbian impunity', p. 11.

41. Katharine Eisaman Maus, 'Horns of dilemma: jealousy, gender, and spectatorship in English Renaissance drama', *ELH*, **54** (1987), p. 562.

42. See Howard's far-reaching analysis of cross-dressing and anti-theatricalist rhetoric; see also Mary Beth Rose, 'Women in men's clothing: apparel and social stability in *The Roaring Girl*', *ELR*, **14** (1984), pp. 367–91; Leah Marcus, 'Shakespeare's comic heroines, Elizabeth I, and the political uses of androgyny', in Mary Beth Rose, ed., *Women in the Middle Ages and the Renaissance* (Syracuse: University of Syracuse Press, 1986), pp. 135–53; and Laura Levine, 'Men in women's clothing: anti-theatricality and effeminization from 1579 to 1642', *Criticism*, **28** (1986), pp. 121–43.

43. Howard suggests that 'In the polemical literature women who cross-dressed were less often accused of sexual perversion than of sexual incontinence, of being whores . . . in part because the discursive construction of women in the Renaissance involved seeing her as a creature of strong sexual appetites needing strict regulation' ('Crossdressing', p. 424). This seems to me to do little to explain the meaning of the charges against women for indulging in homoerotic activity.

44. Lynne Friedli, ' "Passing Women": A study of gender boundaries in the eighteenth century', in G.S. Rousseau and Roy Porter, eds., *Sexual Underworlds of the Enlightenment* (Chapel Hill: University of North Carolina Press, 1988), pp. 234–60.

45. Vera Brittain, *Radclyffe Hall: A Case of Obscenity?* (London: A Femina Book, 1968), p. 21.

46. *Troilus and Cressida*, V, i, 13–24.

47. See, for instance, Steven Seidman, 'Transfiguring sexual identity: AIDS and the contemporary construction of homosexuality', *Social Text* (Fall 1988), pp. 187–203; and the articles collected in 'AIDS: cultural analysis, cultural activism', *October*, **43** (1987), especially Paula Treichler, 'AIDS, homophobia, and biomedical discourse: an epidemic of signification', pp. 31–70.

48. I am indebted to Peter Stallybrass for helping me to clarify my understanding of early modern heterosexuality.

49. In his excellent and nuanced discussion of the transformations of legal discourse over the course of the sixteenth and seventeenth centuries, Bruce Smith distinguishes between the discourses of acts and desires.

50. James Saslow, *Ganymede in the Renaissance*, p. 2.

51. Orgel, 'Nobody's perfect', p. 12. In addition to Orgel, Jardine, Howard, Marcus and Newman, other influential critics have recently addressed the transvestism of Shakespearean comedy: Stephen Greenblatt, 'Fiction and Friction', in his *Shakespearean Negotiations: The circulation of social energy in Renaissance England* (Oxford: Clarendon Press, 1988); Catherine Belsey, 'Disrupting sexual difference: meaning and gender in the comedies', in John Drakakis, ed., *Alternative Shakespeares* (London: Methuen, 1985), pp. 166–90; Phyllis Rackin, 'Androgyny, mimesis, and the marriage of the boy heroine on

the English Renaissance stage', *PMLA*, **102** (1987), pp. 29–41. In so far as these critics have recognised the homoeroticism residing in theatrical transvestism, they have initiated the posibility of a homoerotic analytic. However, for the most part these critics have focused on gender rather than sexuality: after mentioning the erotic complications raised by the boy actor, they more often than not decline to interrogate how homoeroticism works in specific plays, how homoerotic desire is differentiated between plays, and whether homoeroticism is distinguished along gender lines.

52. C.L. Barber, *Shakespeare's Festive Comedy* (New York: Meridian, 1959), p. 231. An extremely interesting lineage can be traced from Barber's treatment of gender in *As You Like It*, through Louis Adrian Montrose's important essay, 'The place of a brother in *As You Like It*: social process and comic form', *Shakespeare Quarterly*, **32** (1981), pp. 23–54, to Howard's analysis in the above cited article.

53. Phyllis Rackin, 'Historical difference/Sexual difference', April 1990, Shakespeare Institute Conference, CUNY Graduate School.

54. Foucault, *Sexuality*, vol. 1, p. 157.

55. See, in this regard, Luce Irigaray, *This Sex Which is Not One*, trans. Catherine Porter (Ithaca, N.Y.: Cornell University Press, 1985): 'We might suspect the *phallus* (Phallus) of being the *contemporary figure of a god jealous* of his prerogatives; we might suspect it of claiming, on this basis, to be the ultimate meaning of all discourse, the standard of truth and propriety, in particular as regards sex, the signifier and/or the ultimate signifier of all desire, in addition to continuing, as emblem and agent of the patriarchal system, to shore up the name of the father (Father)' (p. 67).

56. Jonathan Dollimore, 'Shakespeare, cultural materialism, feminism and marxist humanism', *New Literary History*, **21** (Spring 1990), pp. 471–93.

PART TWO

Shakespearean Tragedy

—4—

Are There any Women in
King Lear?

Ann Thompson

I THE FAMILY QUARREL REVISITED

In recent years, feminist criticism has had an uneasy relationship with various forms of historical and materialist criticism, a fact which has been highly visible at international Shakespeare conferences. At the World Shakespeare Congress in West Berlin in April 1986, for example, considerable tensions emerged between feminist, new historicist and cultural materialist critics at two of the seminars, the one on 'Shakespeare and Ideology' organised by Jean E. Howard and Marion F. O'Connor, and the one on 'Gender and Power in Shakespeare' organised by Carol Thomas Neely and Lisa Jardine. Subsequently at the Shakespeare Association of America conference in Boston in April 1988, there was a plenary session chaired by Madelon Sprengnether entitled 'Feminism *versus* New Historicism' which brought together some leading practitioners – Lynda E. Boose, Peter Erickson, Kathleen McLuskie and Louis Montrose – apparently in the expectation of a showdown.

While the audience in the Oval Room at Boston's Copley Plaza Hotel were in fact disappointed in their hopes of a highly polemical debate – all the participants were keen to focus on areas of common ground rather than on their differences – it cannot be denied that the relationship between feminist criticism and historical/materialist criticism has often been characterised in recent years by anger and fierce polarisation. The nature of this debate, which goes back to at least 1982, has been analysed in some detail by Lynda E. Boose,[1] Jean E. Howard and Marion F. O'Connor[2] and Carol Thomas Neely.[3] It seems significant that all these critics are female and that male critics, especially male new historicist critics whose positions have been most under attack, have not yet responded in print. (Exceptions are Walter Cohen and Don E. Wayne, whose essays on 'Political criticism of Shakespeare' and 'Power, politics, and the Shakespearean text: recent criticism in England and the United States' appear in

Shakespeare Reproduced,[4] the published collection of the Berlin 'Shakespeare and Ideology' papers; but Cohen writes as a Marxist critic and Wayne, writing as a new historicist, adopts a conciliatory line rather like that adopted by Louis Montrose at Boston. An exception of a different kind is Peter Erickson, whose essay 'Rewriting the Renaissance, rewriting ourselves'[5] discusses the debate from the standpoint of a male feminist critic.)

Reconciliation between these approaches ought not to be impossible. Carol Thomas Neely concedes that what she neatly (if rather wickedly) labels 'cult-historicist' forms of criticism have had a 'liberating and regenerative effect on a Renaissance studies complacent in the grip of a worn-out formalism' ('Constructing the subject', p. 6), and Jean E. Howard and Marion F. O'Connor argue that feminists must 'acknowledge the necessity to historicize gender constructions if [they wish] to escape the oppressive notion of a universal human nature, or, worse, of an eternal feminine' (*Shakespeare Reproduced*, p. 3). Only Lynda E. Boose sounds a warning note of scepticism about the valorisation of a conception of 'history' whose authority might be challenged ('Family in Shakespeare studies', pp. 733–5).

But while feminist critics accept the need to pay attention to history, they accuse 'cult-historicist' critics of ignoring the need to pay attention to gender. Observing that, whether consciously or not, the effect of new historical discourses has been 'to oppress women, repress sexuality and subordinate gender issues' (Neely, p. 7), they stress the continuing obligation on feminism to 'lodge a powerful critique of any political mode of cultural analysis, be it Marxist or new historicist, which fails to take account of the central role played by the production of gender difference in the perpetuation of economic and social oppression' (Howard and O'Connor, p. 3).

There are two sites for this struggle: the text and the profession. I shall not have much to say in this paper about the latter issue, but it is clearly significant that the full title of Boose's essay is 'The family in Shakespeare studies; or – studies in the family of Shakespeareans; or – the politics of politics'. Like Howard and O'Connor, she gives an account of the growth of both feminist and 'cult-historicist' modes of criticism out of the social and political activism of the 1960s, commenting on the different experiences of men and women, Americans and British. It is claimed quite explicitly by both Boose and Neely that the marginalisation, displacement and erasure of women in 'cult-historicist' readings of Shakespeare's texts is replicated in the professional situation feminist critics find themselves in today, and that new historicism's preoccupation with institutional forms of absolute male power represents a drive for 'mastery' which goes beyond the text. These professional issues are also discussed by Erickson

118

in 'Rewriting the Renaissance', and by Stephen Foley in his contribution to the present volume.

It is, however, the text with which I am concerned in this paper, and specifically with the text of *King Lear*. How does this quarrel amongst the 'family of Shakespeareans' affect readings of this family-centred tragedy? Is it the case that feminist readings and materialist readings are incompatible or mutually exclusive? Or is a materialist feminist reading attainable?

II HAVE WOMEN BEEN ERASED?

While no one could plausibly accuse feminist Shakespeare criticism of the 1980s of focusing exclusively on readings of female characters, it has done much to stimulate interest in the plays' representations of sexuality, courtship and marriage, leading to a number of stimulating rereadings and revaluations of the comedies and romances. 'Cult-historicism' on the other hand, with its concern for politics and power, has tended to reinforce the traditional preeminence of the tragedies and to offer rereadings of the histories. And within this division of the kingdom there are subdivisions: as Walter Cohen puts it, '[While] *Othello* and *Antony and Cleopatra* are the privileged tragedies for American feminist critics, . . . *King Lear* occupies a similar position for traditional Marxist critics.'[6] But does this imply that readings of *King Lear* which are concerned with class and economics ignore gender, while feminist or gender-conscious readings ignore class and economics? If so, is something sinister going on, or should we simply attribute these omissions to the inevitable fact that critical arguments are selective, that one cannot quote the entire play or attend to every element in it within a single chapter or essay?

I was recently obliged to read a great deal of critical writing on *King Lear* in order to write a book on 'the critics' debate' concerning the play.[7] I did observe a tendency for new historicist and cultural materialist critics to play down gender issues, but did not feel I had the space or the right context to pursue this point. Returning to the same critics in order to write this paper (and reading in addition some work published after my book went to press), I began to observe not just the absence of women but the specific ways in which they were marginalised or displaced. This is something new in the criticism of the 1980s which I did not find in quite the same way in earlier class-conscious readings of *Lear*, such as Rosalie L. Colie's 'Reason and need: *King Lear* and the "crisis" of the aristrocracy', Paul Delaney's '*King Lear* and the decline of feudalism' or Alessandro Serpieri's 'The breakdown of medieval hierarchy in *King Lear*'.[8] In these earlier essays the focus of attention is indeed on male power relationships, class and property, and the authors are particularly interested in the role of Edmund (usually seen as a Hobbesian 'new man') and the tensions between the aristocracy and the bourgeoisie. But they give due weight to the fact that Shakespeare actually chose to represent generational conflict most intensely in the father–daughter relationship, and they do not altogether erase the women from the play.

This is the accusation levelled at 'cult-historicists' by feminists: Carol Thomas Neely, for instance, complains that 'Cordelia virtually disappears from discussions of *King Lear*' ('Constructing the subject', p. 8), citing Stephen Greenblatt's essay on 'Shakespeare and the exorcists' and Jonathan Dollimore's chapter on *Lear* in *Radical Tragedy* as examples.[9] These are perhaps not the worst offenders; Greenblatt is after all specifically discussing the relationship between *Lear* and Harsnett's *Declaration of Egregious Popish Impostures*, an area of 'source-study' which would not necessarily require the mention of Cordelia. Dollimore, who explicitly offers 'a materialist reading', is more vulnerable. Dismissing both Christian and humanist accounts of *Lear* as essentialist readings which mystify suffering and leave justice overly dependent on empathy, he insists that the play is 'above all, about power, property and inheritance' and that 'human values are not antecedent to material realities but are, on the contrary, in-formed by them' (p. 197). Like Colie and other earlier critics he concentrates on Edmund, though he denies that he is a 'new man', pointing out that the nature of his opposition does not in fact liberate him from the values of the older generation – if anything he is even more obsessed with power and property than they are (p. 201). It is true that Dollimore has very little to say about Cordelia or indeed about gender, and it is noticeable that his discussion of the opening scene focuses on the extent to which Cordelia's speech 'threatens to show too clearly how the laws of human kindness operate in the service of property' (p. 198). On the next page, the father–daughter relationship is generalised into a master–slave relationship and the gender component vanishes. Goneril and Regan are mentioned only once by name, in the course of an analysis of the importance of Lear's retainers. Terence Hawkes, who also takes an avowedly materialist approach in his discussion of recent developments in criticism of *King Lear*, 'Lear's maps: a general survey',[10] similarly focuses on male-centred political issues and has almost nothing to say about Cordelia or about feminist criticism.

While these writers seem simply, perhaps unconsciously, to omit women and feminist issues from their readings, two other recent critics are much more explicit and apparently deliberate about displacing and marginalising the feminine in *King Lear*, though both would probably claim that this is an effect of the text, rather than something imposed by a particular mode of reading. Leonard Tennenhouse, in *Power on Display*,[11] is concerned to demonstrate that Shakespeare's version of the story exemplifies a Jacobean attitude to questions of power (and specifically to monarchy) as contrasted with the Elizabethan attitude of the earlier *King Leir* play. The fact that Shakespeare's Lear banishes Cordelia in the opening scene is not as important as that he is 'destroying the whole iconography of nationalism centred in the monarch's body' (p. 135). The argument over the retainers becomes (again) a major element, and their apparent inversion of patriarchal order is made to seem more central than that of Goneril and Regan. Ingratitude is said to be 'characteristically a male crime arising from a patronage relationship in which the ungrateful client mistakes his patron's generosity for a lack of aristocratic largess' – but Shakespeare has 'displaced this crime onto the female' (p. 138), while the punishment for it is displaced onto the male in the blinding of Gloucester:

> This sexual transposition makes pollution and ingratitude into two forms of the same crime against the aristocratic body. Each one is a crime against patriarchy which explicitly challenges the metaphysics of the blood. By undergoing ritual punishment, Gloucester purifies the aristocratic body. (pp. 138–9)

It is essential in this reading that patriarchal authority is restored by the actions of men (Gloucester and Edgar), and that to achieve this Shakespeare 'suddenly removes Regan and Goneril from the sphere of male patronage relations' and 'reinscribes them within more properly female roles where they become monstrous women' – by displaying lust for Edmund (p. 140). Gloucester's homage to Lear in IV, vi, is more significant in 'repairing the metaphysics of patriarchy' than Cordelia's acknowledgement of him as her father in IV, vii (p. 140), and the reason for her death is self-explanatory: 'because the patriarchal principle itself rather than the identity of the monarch's natural body is in question' (p. 141). That principle is emphatically masculine and cannot (despite the audience's memories of Queen Elizabeth) be embodied in a woman. As Tennehouse insists

> the relationship of power to gender is obviously *not* the issue this play asks an audience to consider. Rather, in reestablishing the bond between kinship and kingship, this play wants us to think of them both in male terms. (p. 142)

Exit Cordelia indeed. There would seem to be a considerable difference between this reading which so strenuously *works at* the exclusion of women and earlier readings which, in an apparently more casual and less deliberate way, simply fail to focus on them.

Similar effects can be seen in John Turner's chapter on *King Lear* in *Shakespeare: The play of history*,[12] which I would categorise as a 'cult-historicist' approach despite the reservations he expresses in the book's introduction about the tendency of both new historicism and cultural materialism to 'collapse the cultural artefact into its economic base' and to 'disregard the degree of autonomy that a cultural artefact might achieve, as it struggles to make its own meanings amidst the complex currents of its times' (p. 5). He is, nevertheless, interested in class and power rather than in gender, and especially in the breakdown of the old notions of social reciprocity contained in the complementary relationships of authority and service. Like Dollimore, he rejects the earlier reading of the play as a clash between feudal and bourgeois ideologies, arguing that the old order succumbs, not to a new order, but to its own internal contradictions (p. 101). In so far as Cordelia represents the values of the old order, she is epitomised by her silent tears in IV, vii, which 'seem to express at last her own paradoxical recognition of how little her pity and her service have achieved. . . . The fragmentation already begun in the play's opening scene is here completed with the marginalization of those virtues in which a feudal society had seen its best self' (p. 105). So Cordelia, the 'girl who went about her father's business' (p. 105), is characterised by her impotence.

As for her sisters, their rebellion is discounted: Goneril, we are assured, has 'created nothing new; her oppositional energies have been marginalized and corrupted by the injustices of the system she has opposed' (p. 109). She is contrasted with Edmund who 'most exhilaratingly sets out to create "a new kind of reality and to dethrone God the Father".' His 'adventure in orality' (p. 109) is more sympathetically viewed as a justifiable defiance of his original social marginalisation, and he carries the good will of the modern audience:

> Edmund – the Bastard, the Unwanted, the Marginalized – emblematizes all the injustices of history that we have inherited out of Lear's Britain. He does not bear them away as a scapegoat might; even at his death, he brings them into play. Similarly, the sisters – the Wicked Sisters, the Ugly Sisters – emblematize all the envious malice still at the heart of family life. (p. 111)

Somehow, Edmund's kind of marginalisation is potent and glamorous, while that of the women is either impotent or evil. But who is responsible for this distinction – the author or the critic? Are 'cult-historicists' conspiring to erase women from this play, or are they simply noticing the extent to which Shakespeare has already done so?

III CAN WOMEN BE RESTORED?

Feminist critics of *King Lear* have been rueful (or realistic) in acknowledging the difficulties of the task before them. In particular, they have commented on the way in which the text treats Edmund very differently from the way it treats Goneril and Regan: Marilyn French notes that 'In the rhetoric of the play, no male is condemned as Goneril is condemned',[13] and Marianne L. Novy, while offering something of an apology for the sisters' behaviour – 'the obvious way for a woman to survive is to go along with the social order' – admits that Shakespeare himself does not provide them with any excuses: 'He does not allow them to point out wrongs done to them in the past as eloquently as Shylock does, or to question the fairness of their society's distribution of power as articulately as Edmund.'[14] Kathleen McLuskie, agreeing that 'the representation of patriarchal misogyny is most obvious in the treatment of Goneril and Regan', identifies a sort of impasse for feminists:

> A feminist reading of the text cannot simply assert the countervailing rights of Goneril and Regan, for to do so would simply reverse the emotional structures of the play, associating feminist ideology with atavistic selfishness and the monstrous assertion of individual wills. Feminism cannot simply take 'the women's part' when that part has been so morally loaded and theatrically circumscribed.[15]

Her bleak statement in this essay that, in the case of some plays by Shakespeare, feminist criticism 'is restricted to exposing its own exclusion from the text' (p. 97) evokes dismay in both Boose ('Family in Shakespearean studies', pp. 723–6) and Neely ('Constructing the subject', p. 10), and perhaps marks a distinction between what one might call a sort of 'apologist' feminism, which emphasises the more enlightened side of Shakespeare (and which is associated with American liberalism), and a more 'radical' feminism, which emphasises the limitations of this approach (and which is associated with British Marxism and socialism).

McLuskie makes a similar point to that of Tennenhouse when she notes how the text relates political chaos to evil women: 'The penultimate scene opposes the ordered formality of the resolution of the Gloucester plot with the unseemly disorder of the women's involvement' (p. 102). But on the whole her reading, like other feminist readings, denies his statement that 'the relationship of power to gender is obviously *not* the issue this play asks an audience to consider' (Tennenhouse, *Power on Display*, p. 142). Whether the play asks for it or not, feminists do consider the ending in terms of this relationship and are troubled by it. Stanley Cavell seems to have been the first person to point out that Lear's desire to be alone with his daughter, expressed so touchingly in his 'Come, let's away to prison' speech in V, iii, represents 'not the correction but the repetition of his strategy in the first scene'.[16] Lear simply appropriates Cordelia without taking account of her desires (or indeed her husband). Marianne L. Novy tries to suppress her feminist reaction at this point, saying that 'there is so much sympathy with Lear at the end that it seems cold to turn from feeling to any further analysis of the play in terms of sex-role behaviour', though she then continues 'but it is worth noting that part of the effect of the play is to impress on us the suffering created by these behaviour patterns and then to show how inadequate they are' (*Love's Argumemt*, p. 162). Even the 'hard-line' Kathleen McLuskie finds Lear's situation at the end so moving that 'the most stony-hearted feminist could not withhold her pity even though it is called forth at the expense of her resistance to the patriarchal relations which it endorses' ('The patriarchal bard', p. 102).

Perhaps these are examples of feminist critics being reluctant to indulge in the practice of 'over-reading' or 'reading to excess' advocated by Carol Thomas Neely at the end of her essay, whereby feminists are encouraged to over-read text with history and to concentrate on 'the possibility of human (especially female) gendered subjectivity, identity, and agency, and the possibility of women's resistance or even subversion' ('Constructing the subject', p. 15). A complementary practice is that of 'under-reading', in the sense of unearthing a subtext which indicates that a text is 'really' more concerned with gender issues than it might seem on the surface. Coppélia Kahn's essay on 'The absent mother in *King Lear*' is a case in point, a deliberate attempt to 'excavate . . . the maternal subtext, . . . like an archaeologist, to uncover the hidden mother in the hero's inner world' (p. 35).[17]

Beginning from the acknowledgement that 'there is no literal mother in *King Lear*' (p. 35), Kahn's strategy could be seen as the precise opposite of that of the 'cult-historicists': where they erase the women who are present in the text, she seeks out and reinstates the woman who is absent. In her reading, the opening scene, while ostensibly displaying the omnipotent role of the father as sole parent with total control over his children, in fact reveals much about male anxiety and deficiency. Lear tries to manipulate his ritual division of the kingdom in such a way that he can hold on to his favourite daughter's love even as he gives her to a husband, but 'the renunciation of her as incestuous object awakens a deeper emotional need in Lear: the need for Cordelia as daughter-mother' (p. 40). It is the frustration of Lear's desire to be mothered – to become 'his majesty, the baby' – that provokes his 'oral rage' and his savage verbal assaults against the 'bad mothers', Goneril and Regan, who fail to satisfy his need for 'kind nursery'. In addition to betraying him in this way, they shame him by 'bringing out the woman in him' (p. 45), reducing him to tears ('women's weapons') and to an attack of 'the mother' – hysteria or the 'wandering womb'. For Kahn, Goneril and Regan in fact do Lear a blessing against their wills, since the only progress for him is to admit his vulnerability and to acknowledge the power of his feelings, going against

124

a culture which 'dichotomized power as masculine and feeling as feminine' (p. 47). This is almost achieved in Act IV, when Cordelia becomes the daughter-mother 'in a benign sense' (p. 47) and Lear comes closest to 'a mature acceptance of his human dependency' (p. 48), but 'Cordelia's death prevents Lear from trying to live out his fantasy, and perhaps discover once again that a daughter cannot be a mother' (p. 49). In a footnote on this passage Kahn remarks that in this reading of the play Cordelia dies because Shakespeare 'wanted to confront as starkly as possible the pain of separation from the mother' (p. 328).

Women are clearly present here, but politics and economics are largely absent (as they are from other feminist readings, such as those of French and Novy). Insofar as 'history' enters Kahn's argument, it is social history with reference to the treatment of the elderly in Jacobean England and the practice of farming children out to wet-nurses. So must we accept that feminist readings and materialist readings are indeed incompatible in the case of *King Lear*, that we can attend either to the personal level of the play (which is at least partially female) or to the political level (which is pretty solidly male), but not to both? Interestingly, one reading that attempts to build some bridges between these two 'sides' is that of Peter Erickson, who discusses *Lear* in a chapter called 'Maternal images and male bonds' in his book *Patriarchal Structures in Shakespeare's Drama*.[18] Observing, like Kahn, that notions of mothering and nurturing are important in the play, Erickson is concerned to demonstrate the extent to which it offers comforting images of male bonding and the sympathy of the all-male circle as an alternative to the potentially vulnerable dependence of the male on female nurturance and 'kindness'. Examples of this are the all-male 'chorus', the 'ragged band of brothers' (p. 106), who provide support for Lear on the heath, and the moving moment in IV, vi, when the mad Lear and the blind Gloucester briefly succour each other. At the end of the play, too, the comfort of male bonding is powerfully present in Edgar's account of his reunion with Kent, and 'even Edmund is drawn into this circle of male sympathy', abandoning his (always cynical) alliance with Goneril and Regan and returning to his all-male family (p. 105).

But, while Erickson claims that it is Edgar, rather than the women, who facilitates Lear's openness to vulnerability (p. 108), and even states that 'the motif of the missing mother is only a decoy' (p. 110), he does not, like the 'cult-historicists', go so far as to erase the women altogether and turn *King Lear* into a play exclusively or primarily about male power. If Lear's divesting himself of his authority 'initiates the dismantling of patriarchal order and the reinstatement of maternal power' (p. 111), one of the results is a confusion over the adequacy of male beneficence. The King's attempt to share in the sufferings of the 'poor naked wretches' on the heath and his appeal to 'pomp' to 'shake the superflux to them' are seen as a fantasy of benevolent paternal bounty, which 'cannot serve as a substitute for the absence of maternal generosity' (p. 112). At this point, a gender-conscious reading makes contact with a materialist or economics-conscious reading – a comparatively rare event in recent discussions of the play.

Kathleen McLuskie's reading does also, despite its notoriety as exemplifying some sort of dead-end for feminism, suggest a bridge between feminism and materialism, though in a very different way. This may be because she writes as a cultural materialist rather than as a new historicist. While these approaches are in many ways similar, Louis Montrose has suggested that an important difference between them is that, while new historicism has focused on 'a refiguring of the socio-cultural field in which Renaissance texts were *originally* produced', cultural materialism has had 'a relatively greater emphasis upon the uses to which the *present* has put its versions of the past' – has in fact charted 'the history of ideological appropriations of the Renaissance'.[19] Thus McLuskie can turn from the recalcitrant text of *King Lear* to remark that 'A more fruitful point of entry for feminism is in the process of the text's reproduction' ('The patriarchal bard', p. 103), and go on to argue that

> Feminist criticism need not restrict itself to privileging the woman's part or to special pleading on behalf of female characters. It can be equally well served by making a text reveal the conditions in which a particular ideology of femininity functions and by both revealing and subverting the hold which such an ideology has for readers both female and male. (p. 106)

In analysing the ways in which *King Lear* dramatises the material conditions which lie behind power structures within the family, and understanding the nature of the threat posed to those structures by female insubordination, we can interrogate our own socialisation and recognise the power of resistance, 'subverting rather than co-opting the domination of the patriarchal bard' (p. 106). Citing this passage in his 1987 essay, Peter Erickson points out that 'this feminist criticism does not aim to update Shakespeare by recreating Shakespeare in a feminist image that makes his texts fully compatible with contemporary feminism', but rather insists on 'the dead Shakespeare' and on the need for critics to resist the ideology of femininity that Shakespeare historically represents ('Rewriting the Renaissance', p. 337).

My own feeling is that feminist critics cannot and should not simply give up on *King Lear*. We may well wish to put more time and energy into teaching and writing about tragedies such as *Othello* and *Antony and Cleopatra*, where the gender issues can be confronted more centrally (and this may lead to a revision of the hierarchy within the Shakespearean canon), but we must not be content to turn our backs on such a powerful text. I think it is clear from the evidence I have given above that some male critics are operating on the assumption that historicist or materialist readings can ignore the specific oppression of women within social and political structures, while some female critics are reluctant to allow that men as well as women are ideologically inscribed in the past as well as in the present. This polarisation is understandable but not very constructive. I do not want our profession to conclude that 'feminism' and 'material-ism' are mutually exclusive categories. I hope this book will help to persuade it otherwise.

NOTES

1. Lynda E. Boose, 'The family in Shakespeare studies; or – studies in the family of Shakespeareans; or – the politics of politics', *Renaissance Quarterly*, **40** (1987), pp. 706–42.
2. Jean E. Howard and Marion F. O'Connor, 'Introduction' in their *Shakespeare Reproduced* (New York and London: Methuen, 1987), pp. 1–17.
3. Carol Thomas Neely, 'Constructing the subject: feminist practice and the new Renaissance discourses', *English Literary Renaissance*, **18** (1988), pp. 5–18.
4. Walter Cohen, 'Political criticism of Shakespeare', in Howard and O'Connor, *Shakespeare Reproduced*, pp. 18–46; and Don E. Wayne, 'Power, politics and the Shakespearean text: recent criticism in England and the United States', *ibid.*, pp. 47–67.
5. Peter Erickson, 'Rewriting the Renaissance, rewriting ourselves', *Shakespeare Quarterly*, **38** (1987), pp. 327–37.
6. Cohen, 'Political criticism', p. 28.
7. Ann Thompson, *The Critics' Debate: 'King Lear'* (London: Macmillan, 1988).
8. Rosalie L. Colie, 'Reason and need: *King Lear* and the "crisis" of the aristro-cracy', in Rosalie L. Colie and F. T. Flahiff, eds., *Some Facets of 'King Lear': Essays in prismatic criticism* (Toronto and London: University of Toronto Press, 1974), pp. 185–219; Paul Delaney, '*King Lear* and the decline of feudal-ism', *PMLA*, **92** (1977), pp. 430–1; Alessandro Serpieri, 'The Breakdown of medieval hierarchy in *King Lear*', in Seymour Chatman, Umberto Eco and Jean-Marie Klinkenberg, eds., *A Semiotic Landscape* (The Hague: Mouton, 1979), pp. 1067–72.
9. Stephen Greenblatt, 'Shakespeare and the exorcists', in Patricia Parker and Geoffrey Hartman, eds., *Shakespeare and the Question of Theory* (New York and London: Methuen, 1985), pp. 163–87; and Jonathan Dollimore, *Radical Tragedy* (Hemel Hempstead: Harvester Wheatsheaf, 1984).
10. Terence Hawkes, 'Lear's maps: a general survey', *Shakespeare Jahrbuch* (Heidelberg, 1989), pp. 134–47.
11. Leonard Tennenhouse, *Power on Display* (New York and London: Methuen, 1986).
12. John Turner, '*King Lear*', in Graham Holderness, Nick Potter and John Turner, *Shakespeare: The play of history* (London: Macmillan, 1988), pp. 89–118.
13. Marilyn French, *Shakespeare's Division of Experience* (London: Jonathan Cape, 1982), p. 233.

14. Marianne L. Novy, *Love's Argument: Gender relations in Shakespeare* (Chapel Hill and London: University of North Carolina Press, 1984), pp. 152–3.
15. Kathleen McLuskie, 'The patriarchal bard: feminist criticism and Shakespeare: *King Lear* and *Measure for Measure*', in Jonathan Dollimore and Alan Sinfield, eds., *Political Shakespeare* (Manchester: Manchester University Press, 1985), pp. 88–108. The passage quoted is on p. 102.
16. Stanley Cavell, *Must We Mean What We Say?* (New York: Scribner, 1969), p. 296.
17. Coppélia Kahn, 'The absent mother in *King Lear*', in Margaret W. Ferguson, Maureen Quilligan and Nancy J. Vickers, eds., *Rewriting the Renaissance* (Chicago and London: University of Chicago Press, 1986), pp. 33–49.
18. Peter Erickson, *Patriarchal Structures in Shakespeare's Drama* (Berkeley, Calif., and London: University of California Press, 1985).
19. Louis Montrose, 'Renaissance literary studies and the subject of history', *English Literary Renaissance*, 16 (1986), pp. 5–12.

5

'The Swallowing Womb': Consumed and Consuming Women in *Titus Andronicus*

Marion Wynne-Davies

I

Christine de Pisan, one of the first female authors to write in defence of women, devoted three chapters of *The Book of the City of Ladies* (1404) to rape:

> Then I, Christine, spoke as follows, 'My lady [Rectitude], I truly believe what you are saying, and I am certain that there are plenty of beautiful women who are virtuous and chaste and who know how to protect themselves well from the entrapments of deceitful men. I am therefore troubled and grieved when men argue that many women want to be raped and that it does not bother them at all to be raped by men even when they verbally protest. It would be hard to believe that such great villainy is actually pleasant for them.'[1]

Her comments remain valid today; for example, they could have been usefully addressed to Judge David Wild, who said, in his summing up of a 1986 rape trial:

> Women who say no do not always mean no. It is not just a question of saying no. It is a question of how she says it, how she shows it and makes it clear. If she doesn't want it, she only has to keep her legs shut and there would be marks of force being used.[2]

Not surprisingly, the man was acquitted. The issue of rape appears to be founded upon certain premises about women's sexuality which have remained unchanged for five centuries. This male intransigence, then as now, provokes virulent debate from both sides, cutting across different areas of cultural production and allowing an insidious concoction of social and moral value judgements to infiltrate the supposed 'impartiality' of the law.

Every week our newspapers and televisions carry, in varying combinations of outraged morality and salacious detail, actual or fictional accounts of rape, the court's judgement, the sentence, and the adequacy of the law to police the crime. On the surface they might appear to be simple variations of the tales recounted by Christine de Pisan, of Lucretia, of the Queen of the Galatians and of the Lombard Virgins.[3] But the interest in and the control of rape vary in their intensity depending upon the particular social and cultural value systems of the period which produces them. As Anna Clark writes in *Women's Silence, Men's Violence*:

> Rape is not an unchanging consequence of male biology, for the way sexual violence functions as a means of patriarchal domination, and indeed patriarchy itself, varies historically. Sometimes economic deprivation, or political powerlessness, may be more important features in the repression of women; at other points violence, and sexual violence, come to the foreground as a means of male domination.[4]

Rather than being located within a static position, the issue of rape appears to emerge into the foreground of legal and sexual discourses in relation to a variety of social and cultural forces. These fluctuations can be traced through the spasmodic and infrequent changes in rape legislation. However, as sexual identity, especially feminine identity, is indissolubly bound to the idea of rape, similar shifts of interest occur in other ideological fields of play. It follows that in the first pages of this essay I am able to quote from two recent works on rape, because post-1970s feminism has opened up the whole issue of women's sexual identity and has liberated my own critical discourse. Consequently, I have been able to undertake an analysis of rape in a Shakespearan play, yet this task in its turn is dependent upon the problematising of sexual identity which occurred in the late sixteenth century and upon the ensuing conjunction of legal and literary discourses.

The early history on the law of rape is minimal, since there are very few acts of Parliament to cover, but one of the most significant changes occurred in 1597, about four years after the staging of *Titus Andronicus*, a play which has at its heart one of the most horrific rape scenes in English drama.[5] The 1597 act legislates that:

> Whereas of late times divers women, as well maidens as widows and wives, having substance, some in goods moveable, and some in lands and tenements, and some being heirs apparent to their ancestors, for the lucre of such substance been oftentimes taken by misdoers contrary to their will, and afterward married to such misdoers, or to others by their assent, or defiled, to the great displeasure of God, and contrary to Your Highness laws, and disparagement of the said women, and great heaviness and discomfort of their friends, and ill example of others; which offences, albeit the

same made felony by a certain Act of Parliament made in the third year of
King Henry the seventh, yet for as much as Clergy hath been heretofore
allowed to such offenders, divers persons have attempted and committed
the said offences, in hope of life by the Benefit of Clergy. Be it therefore
enacted . . . that all and every such person and persons, as at any time after
the end of the present session of Parliament . . . shall in every case lose his
and their Benefit of Clergy, and shall suffer pains of death.[6]

The act is primarily concerned with the 'benefit of clergy', which meant
that a man who could claim certain clerical skills had the right to be tried
by an ecclesiastical rather than a civil court. Although this had originally
functioned with a degree of probity, it became open to vast abuse and
particularly favoured the nobility, who were more likely to be literate. By
1576, the only penalty incurred by a rape conviction was imprisonment
for a year or less.[7] When the 1597 act withdrew the benefit of clergy it
gave the state authority to punish, or legally enact vengeance upon, the
perpetrator of the crime, a power hitherto denied. Apart from this
strengthening of retributive powers, the act tacitly accepts that the crime
committed is one against the corporal person of the woman, rather than
one of theft against her family.[8]

In medieval Europe a woman was often abducted and sexually pene-
trated in order to force an unwanted or unsuitable marriage, thereby
enabling her abductor to take possession of her lands and inheritance.
Legally this was seen as the theft of property by one man from another,
and once wedlock occurred very little redress was obtainable; indeed, the
marriage redeemed the offender from any punishment. Henry VII's act of
1486 had removed this matrimonial protection, thereby allowing the
family to reclaim its possessions, but the criminal went unpunished
through benefit of clergy.[9] Elizabeth I's act of 1597 makes the crime
against the woman's person more important, and punishable regardless of
the property element. The simple presence of rape legislation after a
century's inactivity reveals a peak of interest in, and concern about, sexual
assault, but the change enacted suggests a greater signification for the
female identity as a whole in late sixteenth-century England. From this
point on a woman's body in its sexual sense was seen legally to be her
own possession and not that of her nearest male relative. Although this
legal gesture towards female self-determination was hardly adhered to in
practice, its very existence suggests that by the 1590s the idea of women as
independent subjects was sufficiently substantial to be encoded within a
legal text. It is hardly surprising, then, that the fissure which had opened
up between property and independent female subject should be seen on
the public stage as well as in the civil courts of Elizabeth I.

Rape is a crime primarily enacted by men against women, but in all
circumstances it is used to assert the absolute authority of one being over

another.[10] In one of the most influential and pioneering cultural analyses of rape, *Against Our Will: Men, women and rape*, Susan Brownmiller suggests that 'Rape became not only a male prerogative, but man's basic weapon of force against woman, the principal agent of his will and her fear',[11] and she explicitly associates rape with social control, property and the domination of women. Moreover, as sexual identity in the early modern period was inextricably bound to personal identity, the violation of the body became an invasion and domination of the inner subject, an absolute depersonalising. There can hardly be a dramatic scene more redolent of feminine repression and the annulment of the subject than when Lavinia staggers onto the stage, her body violated by rape, her tongue cut out so that she cannot speak and her hands severed so that she may not write. The Empress's sons proceed to taunt their victim:

> Demetrius
> So now go tell, an if thy tongue can speak,
> Who 'twas that cut thy tongue and ravished thee.
>
> Chiron
> Write down thy mind, bewray thy meaning so,
> An if thy stumps will let thee play the scribe . . .
> An 'twere my cause, I should go hang myself.
>
> Demetrius
> If thou hadst hands to help thee knit the cord.
> (II, iv, 1–4, 9–10)[12]

Not only is Lavinia denied the means of self-expression, but her ability to claim death and the absence it creates, with all its purport of deconstructive power, is eliminated. Her function as a meaningful entity appears to end, although her role is immediately metamorphosed in Marcus's subsequent speech. The denial of individual identity is clearly part of the assault on Lavinia, but it is important to bear in mind that the play never once lets us forget the physical horror of rape, even through the grotesque inversion of Ovidian rhetoric.[13]

While provoking our repugnance, however, the play gradually appears to offer the audience a satisfying (only in that it is just) conclusion: when Lavinia participates in the revenge against Chiron and Demetrius. This would have had greater impact on an Elizabethan audience, steeped as it was in the conventions of revenge tragedy. More usually the revenger was a man, and the violated woman, as in the stories of Christine de Pisan, would kill herself for the sake of 'honour'. But by the end of the play Lavinia is no longer 'Rome's rich ornament' (I, i, 52), the idealised feminine beauty possessed by a patriarchal Rome; instead she becomes an active participant in the revenge, who, while her father cuts the throats of Demetrius and Chiron

.. 'tween her stumps doth hold
The basin that receives [their] guilty blood. (V, ii, 182–3)

By accessing the convention of revenge tragedy, normally assigned to
male characters, Lavinia seems to evade containment within the sign of
property and lays claim to an independent self, unrestricted by gender
conventions.[14] Whether this device can successfully undermine the dominant ideological circumscription of female sexuality remains a moot
point, but what is clear is that the play briefly offers up this subversive
possibility as an acceptable, indeed desirable, alternative.

That rape is an essential theme in *Titus Andronicus* cannot be questioned: the word is mentioned fifteen times in the play compared to five
times in all of Shakespeare's other works, including *The Rape of
Lucrece*.[15] Still, the associations between this latter poem and the play are
numerous: their composition dates are, at the most, two years apart; both
deal with a threat to civic order through the political allegory of a Roman
setting; they link rape to revenge; poetically both employ an exaggerated
rhetoric to describe brutal violence; and, most strikingly, the history of
Lucrece is specifically referred to in the play (II, i, 109, and III, i, 297).
Coppélia Kahn, in her intelligent and forthright article 'The rape in
Shakespeare's *Lucrece*', asserts that

> the poem's insistent concern [is] with the relationship between sex and power.
> That relationship is established by the terms of marriage in a partriarchal
> society. The rape is ultimately a means by which Shakespeare can explore the
> nature of marriage in such a society and the role of women in marriage.[16]

Whereas in *Lucrece* female identity is centred exclusively upon marriage,
in *Titus* it is seen in a broader familial context; women are mothers and
daughters first, wives second. The political import of an emphasis on
lineage, rather than matrimony, foregrounds the importance of women in
genealogical terms and raises questions about the validity of inheritance
and descent. When rape occurs it inevitably threatens the values of the
patrilineal society and necessitates a breakdown of its value systems and
laws. Both texts engage in the problem of rape, *Lucrece* within the more
intimate confines of marriage and *Titus* in the glare of lineage and political
accountability.

Titus Andronicus and *The Rape of Lucrece* are not the only works
written in the early 1590s which carry overtones of sexual assault: *Venus
and Adonis* inverts the traditional gender roles and makes Venus the
attacker: 'Her lips are conquerors, his lips obey' and 'her blood doth boil,
/ And careless lust stirs up a desperate courage' (549, 555–6).[17] Like the
paradigmatic rapist, Venus uses force to overcome her victim, while her
powerful sexuality carries a covert threat of castration. Whatever the

vever, Venus cannot rape Adonis biologically, and the
lly sidles into the comic absurdity that this realisation must
seems to me intriguing is that the idea of rape is related to
a powerful, mature woman in an analogous fashion to the rape in *Titus*,
which is condoned and encouraged by Tamora, herself a character of
independent political power and forceful sexuality. Indeed, in Thomas
Nashe's *The Unfortunate Traveller* (1594), which has clear linguistic parallels with *Titus*, the rape victim is Roman and 'a noble and chaste matron'
with grey hair.[18] It almost seems as if we are being offered the well-worn
dichotomy of virgin and whore, the abused and depersonalised maidens –
Lavinia and Lucrece – and the threatening sexuality of a puissant woman
– Tamora and Venus.

The importance of strong, but older, female characters in late sixteenth-
century texts is further evinced by a unique and contemporary representational response to *Titus* by Henry Peacham. The Longleat manuscript
consists of a drawing which illustrates Tamora begging for the lives of her
sons, and several lines from the play. These extracts include the Empress's
plea (I, i, 104–20) and Aaron's catalogue of his crimes (V, i, 125–44).[19] The
two central figures in the cartoon are not dressed in contemporary costume; Titus wears Roman garb, while Tamora appears in stately robes and
wearing a crown, as befits her role as queen of the Goths. The figure of
Aaron is set to the side, and he is outstanding in that Peacham has chosen
to colour his face and limbs a matt black. The two prominent speeches
recorded are by Tamora and Aaron. Peacham's choice of the Moor is
understandable, partly because of the artistic novelty of representing a
negro, and partly because he provides an archetypically villainous
counterpart to Titus on the page. Tamora, however, poses a more intriguing response. She is dressed as a queen and the lines quoted are both
touching and pure; this is not the woman who rejects Lavinia's claims for
pity, or the incarnation of revenge who tries to drive Titus mad. Why,
then, did Peacham choose to depict Tamora as royal and sympathetic?

It is now a critical commonplace that Rome often stands as a mirror of
the Elizabethan world for Shakespeare and his contemporaries, and on
these grounds we can well imagine Tamora as a distantly refracted image
of Elizabeth I.[20] *Titus*, however, is too awkward a play to settle exclusively into close political allegory. This movement towards complexity
rather than neat identifications recurs in the play's rejection of the
common stereotyping of women into virgins and whores. Instead, it
appears both to enact and to confuse these treatments of women: feminine
power and female sexuality are inextricably linked, simultaneously provoking and repressed. *Titus* is about the limits of these identifications and
the point at which woman as subject is confronted with a destructive
depersonalisation. The rape of Lavinia is the physical enactment of a more

pervasive assault in the play on that which is feminine, and on the manifold metaphors drawn from the female body.

II

Since rape is a central theme of *Titus Andronicus*, it seems darkly appropriate that one of the corporal symbols of the play should be the womb.
While Act I is set in the imperial city, Act II offers the alternative world of
a wooded valley, at the heart of which lies a 'detested, dark, blood-
drinking pit', an 'unhallowed and bloodstained hole' 'whose mouth is
covered with rude-growing briers, / Upon whose leaves are drops of new
shed blood' (II, iii, 224, 210 and 199–200). The imagery is blatant, the cave
being the vagina, the all-consuming sexual mouth of the feminine earth,
which remains outside the patriarchal order of Rome. This is the 'swallowing womb' (239) that links female sexuality to death and damnation.
The association is not unique in Shakespeare, the most famous example
being Lear's condemnation of women and his description of their wombs:

> There's hell, there's darkness, there is the sulphurous pit –
> Burning, scalding, stench, consumption. (*King Lear*, IV, vi, 128–9)

An analogous description occurs in *Romeo and Juliet*, when the tomb is
described as 'detestable maw' and a 'womb of death' (V, iii, 45).[21] The
association of hell, death and consumption with the womb clearly evokes
a concept of woman's sexuality that is both dangerous and corrupting.
The identification was not a purely artistic one: the physiological supposi-
tions concerning the uterus in the medieval and Renaissance periods saw
it as something alien. For example, Plato's description of the womb as an
animal in its own right was often cited, and the organ was thought to be
dominated exclusively by external forces, such as the imagination and the
moon. Moreover, since the prevalent ideas on the body were governed by
a theory of humours, it was clear that these physical manifestations had
psychological implications.[22] The first mention of the 'abhorred pit' in
Titus is made by Tamora:

> They told me here at dead time of the night
> A thousand fiends, a thousand hissing snakes,
> Ten thousand swelling toads, as many urchins,
> Would make such fearful and confused cries
> As any mortal body hearing it
> Should straight fall mad. (II, iii, 99–104)

The Empress suggests that it is herself who will fall victim to this fate. The
womb of the ultimate mythic female body – the earth – threatens to make

135

Tamora mad, as in Renaissance beliefs any woman's uterus weakened her mind and made her susceptible to lunacy.[23] But in *Titus* this is not the case; on the contrary, Tamora fabricates the tale of injury and is in no danger of madness. And although Demetrius and Chiron threaten to rape Lavinia in this 'secret hole' (II, iii, 129), they take her offstage rather than incarcerating her in the pit, which remains in full view of the audience. Instead, the cave consumes Bassanius's corpse and the bodies of the doomed Martius and Quintus. The 'swallowing womb' does carry the promise of death, but for men and not women. Its power is to castrate, not to madden.

The womb is not only the centre of female sexuality, but also the repository of familial descent. Michel Foucault, in *The History of Sexuality*, writes that the rules governing sexuality in the early modern society in France and England were determined by blood relations, and that it was through them that the mechanisms of power were able to function.[24] Control of the womb was paramount to determining a direct patrilineal descent, and when this exercise of power failed and women determined their own sexual appetites regardless of procreation, the social structure was threatened with collapse. This is exactly what happens in *Titus* when Tamora seeks amorous gratification with Aaron, and the subsequent presence of the half-caste child menaces 'Our Empress' shame and stately Rome's disgrace' (IV, ii, 60). The 1597 rape legislation, with its suggestion of female self-determination, is a parallel validation of this same independent sexual control. Although it manifestly did not bring about the collapse of Elizabethan society, its very existence suggests a need to answer the same worrying concerns about women's identity as those evinced in *Titus Andronicus*.

The control of the female subject is not achieved only through the policing of her sexuality, since orality too is an important aspect of self-construction.[25] The pit in *Titus* functions as both a womb and a consuming mouth. As the play attempts to repress female sexuality through rape, so it denies female speech when Lavinia has her tongue cut out. Tamora's unheeded plea for her sons is likewise a reminder of women's muted state.[26] Yet it is through the 'consumption' of a pen that Lavinia regains the power of communication, and at the end of the play Tamora will literally eat her children. The play persistently empowers its female characters with a hard-won freedom of self-expression, only to have it rebound in a final reassertion of male dominance.

I have already suggested that the act – rape – and the acted upon – the womb as sign for the female body – pursue, through metaphor, multifarious and often uneasy incarnations. These fields of rhetorical play serve to test the limits of dismemberment and thrust before the audience a series of almost unacceptable collusions. The issues so pinned down are not solely concerned with the female subject, but she penetrates several of them.

III

In one respect, familial, social and political stability in a patrilineal society resides in the policing of a woman's womb. The essentiality of this premise recurs throughout the Shakespearean canon from Gratiano's comic recognition that

> while I live, I'll fear no other thing
> So sore as keeping safe Nerissa's ring. (*The Merchant of Venice*, V, i, 306–7)

to the destructive and ultimately tragic actions of the base-born Edmund in *King Lear*. The pervasive impact which occurs when this control breaks down is traced by Robert Miola who, perhaps rather tellingly, translates the bloody rape of Lavinia into 'a direct assault on the Andronici family and the Roman virtue which it represents [and an expression of] the perversion of normal familial relations and values in Rome's royal household.'[27] The fundamental issue is assurance of blood descent, a point clearly indicated by pre-1597 rape legislation, but in *Titus* the issues are divided. Lavinia, who signifies the blameless victim and eradicated subject, remains barren, whereas Tamora, who acts as a symbol of egressive female sexuality, bears the subversive blackamoor child. By emphasising the illegitimate fruits of female rather than male sexual transgression, the play appears to hold guilty the lust of women rather than of men for any social breakdown.

The extent of Tamora's vitiosity is evident in the metaphoric import of her child's black skin as well as in her displacement of the father in relation to her sons, Demetrius and Chiron. It was the Empress who 'unadvised' gave her sons swords, rather than the more acceptable gift of a book which young Lucius receives from his mother and which is read by his aunt.[28] Military activity is a masculine trait to be passed between father and son, culminating in honourable triumph such as is enjoyed by Titus and his sons at the start of the play. The sword given by Tamora, even as its distorted source prefigures, leads only to the debased dismembering of Lavinia. The privileging of paternal over maternal value systems is most persuasive in the comparison of Tamora's and Titus's pleas for their children. At the beginning of the play the Empress begs Titus not to sacrifice her son:

> Stay, Roman brethren, gracious conqueror,
> Victorious Titus, rue the tears I shed,
> A mother's tears in passion for her son;
> And if thy sons were ever dear to thee,
> O, think my son to be as dear to me.
> Sufficeth not that we are brought to Rome
> To beautify thy triumphs, and return
> Captive to thee and to thy Roman yoke;

But must my sons be slaughtered in the streets
For valiant doings in their country's cause?
O, if to fight for king and commonweal
Were piety in thine, it is in these. (I, i, 104–115)

Titus is forced to make a similar request when his sons are condemned for the murder of Bassianus:

Hear me, grave fathers. Noble tribunes, stay.
For pity of mine age, whose youth was spent
In dangerous wars, whilst you securely slept;
For all my blood in Rome's great quarrel shed,
For all the frosty nights that I have watched,
And for all these bitter tears which now you see,
Filling the aged wrinkles in my cheeks,
Be pitiful to my condemned sons,
Whose souls is not corrupted as 'tis thought. (III, i, 1–9)

The physical actions of mother and father are the same: both prostrate themselves and shed tears. Both begin their speech in a commanding tone with brief phrases, and with a similar call to familial sympathies.[29] Both refer to honourable battle and ask for pity for their offspring. Moreover, Titus's poignant plea for his sons is as vain as that Tamora addressed to him earlier in the play. But the narrative construction appears to deploy the audience's sympathy, even if it leaves those on stage unmoved. Although both sets of progeny are innocent, we have been party to the events of the Andronici's condemnation and are aware that deceit and treachery have been involved, not impersonal militarism. After the Goth is put to death Tamora improves her position and becomes empress, whereas our sympathy for Titus is wrenched still further in our foreknowledge, and then experience, of his meeting with the mutilated Lavinia. The audience seems to be tacitly aligned with a familial discourse which enshrines male power. We are still left, though, with the disconcerting pictorial response of the Peacham manuscript, which depicts the plea of Tamora and not of Titus.

The deconstructive power of this single image is reinforced by the ambiguous elevation of Aaron's love for his son. The Moor, who repudiates all moral standards and stands in the play as an incarnation of evil, will risk everything for the sake of his child:

My mistress is my mistress, this myself,
The vigour and the picture of my youth:
This before all the world do I prefer. (IV, ii, 107–9)

The sympathy aroused by Aaron in this scene can hardly be reconciled with the Moor's demonic role, and it results in a simultaneous humanisation of the indiviudal character and a devaluation of the paternal value systems of the play.[30] The imaginative and ideological shifts required of the audience to encompass both a fatherly and a devilish Aaron fissure the patrilineal dominance irretrievably. Doubts about Titus's function as the archetype of fatherhood lurk around his sacrifice of his own son, Mutius, in the name of imperial loyalty, and about his conference of the kingship on grounds of primogeniture rather than election and individual worth. Both acts are in error and set in motion a series of familial and royal deaths which culminate in his own. When set in a dualism of mother/Tamora and father/ Titus the value of a patrilineal society seems at first unquestionable, but the play slides into unexpected similarities and contrasts which compel a reworking of expected and perhaps accepted gender identities.

IV

Primogeniture not only determined familial inheritance but was the basis of royal descent in the early modern period. Ensuring that there was a male heir to further the line was a persistent concern of the monarch and his/her statesmen. However, in late sixteenth-century England the determining of a successor was a paramount source of disquiet and a promise of, rather than an insurance against, future political turmoil.[31] The first scene of *Titus* opens upon similar political worries, with an ungoverned Rome and the decision of the tribunes, through Marcus, to offer the crown to Titus:

> Marcus
> . . . help to set a head on headless Rome.
>
> Titus
> A better head her glorious body fits
> Than his that shakes for age and feebleness.
> . . . this suit I make,
> That you create our emperor's eldest son,
> Lord Saturnine, whose virtues will, I hope,
> Reflect on Rome as Titan's rays on earth,
> And ripen justice in this commonweal.
> Then if you will elect by my advice,
> Crown him and say, 'Long live our emperor!' (I, i, 186–8, 223–9)

The Roman citadel and state are envisaged as a headless feminine body, a motif which is repeated at the end of the play when the contrasting office of governorship is offered to Lucius (V, iii, 66–75).[32] Nor is the image of a dismembered female body singular within the play. The horrific violence which is enacted upon Lavinia demands by analogy a brutal visualisation of an otherwise common metaphor for the body politic. In *Titus*, as in the

139

best traditions of horror, the figurative tends to become the actual.[33] Apart from forcing a brutal vision of a political future without an assured and worthy ruler, the speech also calls into question the adequacy of public discourses to handle the impending crisis. If Rome begins and ends the play as a mutilated female form, then Titus's resolution of primogeniture can hardly be adequate.

The importance of public and political ideologies to the play is evident from the opening scene, with its panoply of the most renowned physical structures of civic Roman life: the Capitol, the Pantheon, the city walls and gates.[34] The action occurs in a series of ceremonies, public orations and almost pageant-like entries.[35] The females are acted upon within this formal setting, allotted according to the wishes of the patriarchy: Titus gives both Lavinia and Tamora to Saturninus, with as much proprietorial assurance as he gives away Rome. His doctrines are strikingly redolent of the pre-1597 act, when rape was a law of theft against the family, the women being regarded as possessions of their dominant male relations rather than as autonomous beings. Still, his actions in the play will prove misguided, and previously unquestioned ideologies are disrupted within the subsequent lack of moral or social determinants.[36] *Titus* presents us with a conundrum: the civil dismemberment endemic upon a female body politic set against the total inadequacy of the formal patriarchal solution of primogeniture. In contemporary allegory, how can one ensure the inheritance of the throne by a non-existent eldest son of a virgin Queen? This was not a question located solely in literary discourses, and the active public debate which accrued about the succession had far-reaching implications for a more general understanding of what constituted a state.[37]

In his detailed and well-researched account, *The Body Politic*, David Hale traces the arguments around this metaphor, from the organic and hierarchical body to the idea of the 'social contract'.[38] The most commonplace treatment of the image is found in Sir Thomas Elyot's *The Governor*, where he writes that 'A publike weale is a body lyvyng, compacte or made of sondry estates and degrees of men.'[39] The 'sondry estates' begin with the monarch at the head and end with the peasants at the feet; all align in a natural and unchallengable order. Shakespeare uses this organic analogy more than any other playwright.[40] At the beginning of the 1590s, however, a Jesuit argument arose which suggested that a monarch had to keep faith with his/her subjects, as the head must look after the other members of the body. This initiated a series of political pamphlets which utilised the analogy of the body in a debate about the natural or elected state of the monarchy.[41] This same argument is enacted throughout the first scene of *Titus*, where Titus's assertion of inherited status confronts the election of the Roman emperor on grounds of worth:

Marcus
   Princes that strive by factions and by friends
Ambitiously for rule and empery,
Know that the people of Rome, for whom we stand
A special party, have by common voice,
In election for the Roman empery,
Chosen Andronicus, surnamed Pius,
For many good and great deserts to Rome. (I, i, 18–24)

Shakespeare's use of Roman political history to enact the conceptual debate between imperialism and republicanism is commonly accepted. What *Titus* contributes is a disturbing gender dialectic.[42] The metaphor of the body politic here gives us a female state and city governed by a man whose inheritance rests on primogeniture and not on personal worth. This combination fails utterly. By analogy, if Marcus was right in suggesting self-determinism for the state, and indeed it seems he was, then the female body, human rather than civic, also has a valid right to independent choice. It was just such a freedom from the patriarchal ownership of their own sexuality that the 1597 rape legislation gave women, while our own horror at Lavinia's fate subtly nurtures the audience's complicity with this judgement.

The use of Rome in the context of contemporary political discourse also raises the spectre of imperialism. For an Elizabethan audience accustomed to the propagandist panoply of Tudor myth, which claimed dynastic descent from Aeneas, the legendary founder of Rome, the political resonance of empire would have been readily imparted to the sixteenth-century diplomatic arena.[43] When Titus first appears on stage in a triumphal entry bearing with him the conquered royal family of the Goths, he encapsulates an image of military triumph and imperial domination. The contemporary parallels of nationalistic victories are overt; Titus procures for the audience a parallel self-image dependent upon the defeat of the Spanish Armada in 1588, together with the territorial claims of Drake in California in 1579 and Raleigh's in Roanoke in 1585.[44] On stage the terms of conquest would have been transformed into a gender dialectic of Titus and Tamora, male and female. The importance of this association may be seen from its elision in the comparable text, *The Tragical History of Titus Andronicus*, where the Goths are led by their king, Tottilius, who is not even mentioned in Shakespeare's play.[45] Coppélia Kahn draws a similar gender parallel from *The Rape of Lucrece*: 'The heroine becomes an image for two fields of political conquest, the expanding Roman empire and the New World.'[46] Tamora and Lavinia fulfil equivalent functions: Tamora as the conquered Queen of the Goths, a slave 'brought to yoke', and Lavinia as an imperial treasure to be disputed over by rivals for the imperial throne (I, i, 69, 52). Enslaved nations must always act as the identifying 'other' of imperial expansion; Tamora's gender accentuates this difference, while Aaron's race removes the Goths

141

still further from the Roman victors and their signification in contemporary allegory. The interweaving parallels and contrasts which abound in
Titus also occur between Aaron and Tamora, for not only are both cap-
tives of Rome, they are also mutually enslaved in physical passion:

> Aaron
>   So Tamora;
> . . . whom thou in triumph long
> Hast prisoner held, fettered in amorous chains,
> And faster bound to Aaron's charming eyes
> Than is Prometheus tied to Caucasus. (II, i, 9, 14–17)

The use of slavery as a metaphor for binding love in *Titus* belongs to a
romantic discourse, but it must also provoke political associations of
power, even as the hunt scene, while evoking Petrarchan parallels, ends in
rape.[47] Through the forced awareness of jarring affinities, the ownership
and control of women – here Aaron's of Tamora – are seen to permeate
the play. The hell-like associations of the womb and Tamora's bond with
the demonic Moor confirm this identification.[48]

While using the audience's repugnance at, and fascination with, dominance and violence, *Titus* explores the idea of the independent subject, both
corporal and metaphoric, but it never entirely overthrows the patriarchal
values of the political system. Although Lavinia and Rome may be pitied,
Tamora almost stands for a misogynistic stereotype of the scheming
woman perversely taking political power and sexual freedom. Nor is she
alone, for as Lavinia is set against the Empress, so the natural world of the
forest with its 'swallowing womb' may be contrasted with Rome.

V

The concept of the organic body politic with its acceptance of blood
descent carries, in the Elizabethan period, overtones of the feminine, and
this is reinforced in *Titus* by identifying the organic and elemental images
in the play with the quintessentially female earth.[49] The disturbing and
threatening associations of the forest scene, with its 'swallowing womb'
centre stage, are made throughout the play, as for example when Titus
tells Chiron and Demetrius their fate:

> Hark, villains, I will grind your bones to dust,
> And with your blood and it I'll make a paste,
> And of the paste a coffin I will rear,
> And make two pasties of your shameful heads,
> And bid that strumpet, your unhallowed dam,
> Like to the earth swallow her own increase. (V, ii, 186–91)[50]

Titus's metaphor is conventional and refers to the idea of the earth assimilating her children, that is humankind, when they are buried. But although Tamora is once more linked to the powerful otherness of the natural body, both are here perverted so that the consumption is *un*natural; a precipitous doom, rather than humankind's allotted and inevitable return to dust.

The symbolic signification of the forest and its female associations can, however, be read in quite another manner: Albert Tricomi in his article on 'The mutilated garden in *Titus Andronicus*' acknowledges that 'the forest . . . eventually becomes synonymous with barbarism and chaos', but he also points out that it is initially described in pastoral and romantic terminology.[51] More significantly, he shows, through the repetition of lily, deer and fountain motifs, that 'Lavinia and the forest in *Titus Andronicus* are imagined as one or nearly one throughout the play.'[52] The chaste Lavinia cannot easily be reconciled with the overt and intimidating sexuality of the 'swallowing womb' and Tamora, but her close ties to the natural imagery of the forest demand that such an association be made. This fusion of opposite female stereotypes is compounded by Aaron's 'rape' of the earth, thus linking it in turn to the violated Lavinia. Mining for gems and precious metals is often described as rape; and this occurs in *Titus* when the Moor digs for gold in Act II, scene iii.[53] The earth is both castrating and raped, consumed and consuming.

The slippage between nurturing and disordering organic symbols still resides within the feminine, but Titus's famous 'I am the sea' speech to Lavinia, when he has been cruelly deceived by Aaron into sacrificing his hand, self-consciously dissolves all delineations of difference:

> If there were reason for these miseries,
> Then into limits could I bind my woes;
> When heaven doth weep, doth not the earth o'erflow?
> If the winds rage, doth not the sea wax mad,
> Threat'ning the welkin with his big-swoll'n face?
> And wilt thou have a reason for this coil?
> I am the sea. Hark how her sighs doth blow!
> She is the weeping welkin, I the earth;
> Then must my sea be moved with her sighs;
> Then must my earth with her continual tears
> Become a deluge, overflowed and drowned;
> For why my bowels cannot hide her woes,
> But like a drunkard must I vomit them. (III, i, 218–30)

This speech is one of the cruxes of the play, set at a point of narrative crisis where the audience realises Titus has been duped, but where he remains hopeful. Moreover, the mythic language and solemn tone make it one of the most powerful and poignant speeches of the play. When our pity and sympathy become overwhelming this figurehead of patriarchy, whose stubborn adherence to the most conservative ideologies initiates the tragic action of the play, turns to his mutilated daughter and denies difference, elemental and gender. The complexity of Titus's identifications and the rapidity with which he changes them are sufficient to commingle the elements in the audience's imagination. But as the speech moves towards its end, a fatalistic sense of total breakdown becomes apparent. Titus's sea 'must' be affected by Lavinia's wind, but then his earth loses its separate identity and becomes liquid like her tears; he is 'overflowed and drowned'. The stark inevitability of this merging is emphasised by the biblical resonances of 'deluge'; there is no mystical metamorphosis into an idealised hermaphrodite. Instead we are faced with the appalling consequences of tragedy, which perforce takes identity beyond its limit to a point where gender overflows itself into another. Then as Titus returns to the body imagery this excessive unity becomes unbearable, as it must in a material world, and gender returns to otherness. The female is perceived as within and belonging intimately to the male, but only until disgorged.[54] Limits are breached in their connotation of dividing different forms as well as in the sense of containment and control. The overburdening and excessive nature of events – familial and social tragedy figured in the elemental symbolism – collapses the hierarchical and differential structures which retain order. Like the central image of the 'swallowing womb', Titus's speech evokes the utter and unquenchable forces of nature. In its biting evocation of grief it comes to the very brink of allowing the 'deluge' full sway, before retreating behind the sandbags of conventional gender difference. The utter pathos of this speech, which gives authenticity to this desperate immersion in the magnetic power of symbolism, lies in the knowledge of the audience that events will indeed get worse.

VI

The determination to empower the figurative aspects of poetic language that we see so forcefully asserted in Titus's speech is one of the recurrent features of *Titus Andronicus*. It often becomes apparent in inappropriate textual composites, the most famous example being Marcus's display of fine Ovidian rhetoric on seeing the mutilated Lavinia.[55] Similarly, the female body with its sexual threat and violation is expected to stand as a metaphor for organic as well as social forms. Then again, while Titus's elemental speech conflates difference, the contemporary allusions in the play demand precise definition, yet both coexist. I have already indicated several areas of late sixteenth-century allusion, commencing with the focus upon rape, and I have also suggested that Tamora may be partially identified with Elizabeth I. Significantly, this latter correlation is based not only on their similar regal states, but on emblematic repetitions, such as allusions to Phoebe/Diana and to the sun (I, i, 316; II, iii, 57–9; II, i, 1–9), which were commonly used synonyms for Elizabeth herself.[56] A more tenuous political comment may be made in the age difference between the Empress and Saturninus (I, i, 332), which could allude to the similar discrepancy between Elizabeth and Essex.[57] The allegory appears to be almost unacceptable in political terms, but *Titus* does work on the limits of the countenanced. The play deconstructs stereotypes so that the dualism of chaste Lavinia/Lucrece and lustful Tamora/Venus are collapsed into one another, while simultaneously encompassing contemporary allegory.[58] Repeatedly the play confronts its audience with oppositions rather than reconciliations.

This essay has taken as its premise the containment and repression of women, and has dealt with the tensions and challenges to this convention as dramatic appurtenances. Woman as a physical entity to be possessed and controlled within sexual, familial and political discourses, as well as in the metaphoric figures of city, state, empire and the earth itself, is seen to be consumed by the patriarchal ideologies of late sixteenth-century England. Yet at the same time the strain produced by the pathologically strict adherence to these determinants necessitates a modulation of demarcations. Titus's 'I am the sea' speech suggests a way in which this collapse of differentiation may be attained, a way in which division might be unified, the female incorporated into the male. But it would be wrong to assume that the female characters of the play lack self-expression or fail to make claims for independent subjectivity. The play does not rest solely upon the father–daughter relationship of Titus and Lavinia.

The importance of authoritative women is refracted through the character of Tamora. She resembles Venus from *Venus and Adonis*, is related to the all-powerful mother earth, in political allegory recalls Elizabeth I, and it is she whom Peacham depicts at the centre of his drawing. In addition she is compared in the play to Dido, Hecuba and Semiramis (II, iii, 22; I, i, 36; I, i, 22), and Waith traces her name to Tomyris, a Scythian queen.[59] Yet Lavinia does not stand as an unambiguous sign for female repression either; she too is compared to Hecuba (IV, i, 20), and she is the foremost instrument in the initiation of revenge against her rapists.[60] Further links occur between the two women through associations with Virgil's *Aeneid*; Tamora is related to Dido, and Lavinia suggests her own namesake who founds the imperial Roman dynasty. But the most curious textual semblance is drawn from Ovid.[61]

The account of Lavinia's rape and the method of its discovery are taken from the tale of Philomela, a debt which is acknowledged several times in the play. A copy of *Metamorphoses* is even brought on stage in the fourth act.[62] Ovid's story tells of how Philomela is raped by her brother-in-law, Tereus, who tries to conceal the assault by cutting out her tongue. However, she portrays the events in a tapestry and sends it to her sister, Procne. The two sisters are united and revenge themselves upon Tereus by killing his son and serving up the flesh for him to eat. Tereus tries to slay them but all three are metamorphosed into birds. The resemblance to Lavinia's experiences is manifest, but those of Tamora in the last scene of the play also recall the Ovidian text.

The final speech of *Titus* is given to Lucius, who heralds the new age of order and expunges the old. Lavinia is buried in the family tomb, and

> As for that ravenous tiger, Tamora,
> No funeral rite, nor man in mourning weed,
> No mournful bell shall ring her burial;
> But throw her forth to beasts and birds to prey;
> Her life was beastly and devoid of pity,
> And being dead, let birds on her take pity. (V, iii, 194–9)

The threat posed by the Empress is such that she must be expurgated altogether from Rome to the organic and inherently feminine world of the earth, with its 'swallowing womb'. Her fate seems an almost inevitable return to that with which she has been so closely associated, and the method of her expulsion recalls Titus's vomiting up of feminine woes. It is the excess of Tamora's subversive signification which demands that she be finally removed and the breach repaired, while Lavinia is disempowered by being safely interred within the patriarchal vault. A choice of destinies awaits the egressive woman: if she may be reintroduced into the patriarchal value system, then she will be awarded an identity within that structure. But if her irregularities prove too virulent, too ingrained, then she must be ejected from the system altogether. The last speech thus enacts a final circumscriptive locating of women in relation to the dominant male body – corporal and politic; they can either be consumed or, if they prove indigestible, they can be 'disgorged'.

Yet even at the close of the play *Titus* remains ragged and uncontainable, refusing to rest upon such formulaic dialecticisms. The birds are left to consume Tamora's carrion, thereby metamorphosing her body into the creatures which subsequently proceed to pity her; their actions recall for the audience the heavy indebtedness to Ovid. Tamora and all she represents may be eliminated from the public and political voices of Rome, but in the last line she accesses a literary discourse which perforce takes the audience back to one of the most dramatic moments in the play.

The scene where Lavinia takes the staff in her mouth and writes the names of her violators in the sand is the narrative fulcrum of *Titus*

Andronicus (IV, i). From this point the revenge of the Andronici has purpose and the play's conclusion can be foreseen. In a text so redolent with images of eating and sexual penetration the act is startling. She takes in her mouth – that is, she consumes – the means of self-expression, thus encompassing what has been a masculine prerogative of subjectivity, and transmutes it into a feminine rhetorical practice. That she relates herself to the Ovidian text simply affirms our expectations of change and difference. But the action is also threatening, for the female mouth in *Titus* must also signify the womb, and the link between pen and phallus inevitably follows.[63] Lavinia's mouth appears to reenact the swallowing womb of Act II when she consumes the masculine signifier, whether pen or phallus, and takes over the textual discourse, thereby castrating the source of male power.

The action does not convey this simple message of liberated female language, however, for Titus reads what Lavinia has written; he transmits her text to the audience, thereby once again attempting to confuse the issues of gender and production. The words – 'Stuprum. Chiron. Demetrius' (IV, i, 77) – become the location of mutual production and consumption, rebounding between Lavinia, Titus and the audience. The breakdown of traditional actor/audience response is redolent of Titus's elemental speech, where limits likewise collapse under the pressure of personal grief. Yet in this instance the audience wills the rapid pursuance of complicity, the union of minds, so that, when recourse to official channels fails, the injured can enact vengeance for themselves.

This essay began with a discussion of the injustices of rape legislation from the medieval period to the present day and, more particularly, the relevance of the 1597 rape act to the contemporary location of female sexual identity. *Titus Andronicus* participates in a corresponding discourse of disruption and revision; it draws upon the horror of rape and throws into sharp relief the difference between the sexual constraint and sexual self-determination of women. Like the legal encodement, the play at times appears to offer women control over their own corporal identities, but it reaches beyond the confines of the formal document into a multiplicity of interpretations and consequences. At times the play politically empowers Tamora, offers Lavinia a means of self-expression, weights the play with contemporary allegory which privileges an aged queen, allows the audience to focus upon the symbolic centre of the 'swallowing womb' and promises redemption for women through the metamorphosing power of Ovidian rhetoric. Yet at the same time as proffering an independent subject position for women, *Titus* shores the very fissures that it has mined. Moreover, it achieves this retrenchment through its figurative depiction of the violation and destruction of women. What both legal and dramatic discourses open is a distorted image of female sexuality, where its very independence is bound up in the brutal denial of its existence, where women can be both consumed and consuming. While the language of the parliamentary act remains coolly impartial, what the play forces recurrently before our eyes is an evocation of rape so horrific that, while we recognise its ideological location, we cannot help but question the values of a society which allows such a violation to occur.

NOTES

1. Christine de Pisan, *The Book of the City of Ladies* (London: Picador, 1983), pp. 158–64; see especially pp. 160–1.
2. Joan Smith, *Misogynies* (London: Faber and Faber, 1989), p. 3.
3. Christine de Pisan, *City of Ladies*, pp. 159–164.
4. Anna Clark, *Women's Silence, Men's Violence* (London: Pandora Press, 1987), pp. 2–3.
5. Here I am happy to follow the arguments of Eugene M. Waith in the Oxford edition of *Titus* (Oxford: Oxford University Press, 1984), where he suggests a date shortly before 1592 for the original composition, and late 1593 for the revision (pp. 4–11). Stanley Wells, in his review of Deborah Warner's 1986 production of the play, confirmed that it is a part of the Shakespearean canon in need of revaluing: Wells, 'Shakespeare performances in London and Stratford-upon-Avon 1986–7', *Shakespeare Survey*, 41 (1988), pp. 159–81.
6. Elizabeth I, Cap. ix, *The Statutes of the Realm* (London: The Record Commission, 1819).
7. A description of the benefit of clergy may be found in Sir William Holdsworth, *A History of English Law* (London: Methuen, 1935), 4th edn, vol. III, pp. 293–302.
8. Roy Porter, 'Rape – does it have a historical meaning?', in Sylvana Tomaselli and Roy Porter, eds., *Rape: An historical and cultural enquiry* (Oxford: Basil Blackwell, 1986), p. 217. For a discussion of the relationship between revenge and the law see Catherine Belsey, *The Subject of Tragedy* (London: Methuen, 1985), pp. 113–16; for the relationship between revenge and violence see Huston Diehl, 'The iconography of violence in English Renaissance tragedy', *Renaissance Drama*, NS 11 (1980), pp. 27–44.
9. The history of the rape laws is discussed in Susan Brownmiller, *Against Our Will: Men, women and rape* (New York: Bantam Books, 1975), pp. 6–22; and in Barbara Toner, *The Facts of Rape* (London: Arrow Books, 1977). There is a discrepancy over the dating of Henry VII's 1486 or 1487 law, 'The penalty for carrying a woman away against her will that hath lands or goods', between *Statutes of the Realm* and *Statutes at Large* (Henry VIII, cap. ii, *Statutes of the Realm* (London: Dawsons of Pall Mall, 1816), and Henry VII, cap. ii, *The Statutes at Large* (London: Printed for Mark Basket, 1770)).
10. It is important to note that men also rape other men; Brownmiller, *Against Our Will*, pp. 285–97.
11. Brownmiller, *Against Our Will*, p. 5.
12. All quotations are taken from the Oxford edition of *Titus Andronicus*, ed. Waith.

13. The use of Ovidian rhetoric in Marcus's speech is discussed by Albert H. Tricomi in 'The mutilated garden in *Titus Andronicus*', *Shakespeare Studies*, 9 (1976), pp. 89–105.
14. There is a discussion of how women function as signs in an exchange system in Elizabeth Cowie, 'Woman as sign', *M/F*, 1 (1978), pp. 49–63. The masculine confines of revenge tragedy will be discussed more fully later on in relation to Tamora. However, it is worth pointing out here that there are numerous parallels between Lavinia and the Empress, which link them firmly as women despite their other differences.
15. 'Rape': I, i, 404 and 405; II, i, 117; IV, i, 48, 49 and 90; IV, ii, 9; V, ii, 37, 45, 62, 94, 134 and 156. 'Rapes': IV, i, 57; V, i, 63. Rape is also mentioned in *King John*, II, i, 97; *Troilus and Cressida*, II, ii, 148; *All's Well That Ends Well*, IV, iii, 233; and *Lucrece*, 909 and 1369. All references to Shakespeare's works, other than *Titus*, are taken from *William Shakespeare: The Complete Works*, ed. Peter Alexander (London: Collins, 1951).
16. Coppélia Kahn, 'The rape in Shakespeare's *Lucrece*', *Shakespeare Studies*, 9, (1976), pp. 45–72; quotation from p. 45. Kahn also has an interesting section on rape in *Venus and Adonis* in *Man's Estate: Masculine identity in Shakespeare* (Berkeley: University of California Press, 1981), pp. 547–58. See also Katharine Eisaman Maus, 'Taking tropes seriously: language and violence in Shakespeare's *Rape of Lucrece*', *Shakespeare Quarterly*, 37 (1986), pp. 66–82.
17. Tricomi discusses the relationship between *Titus* and *Venus and Adonis* ('Mutilated garden', p. 94).
18. Thomas Nashe, *The Unfortunate Traveller*, ed. J.B. Steane (Harmondsworth: Penguin Books, 1972), pp. 331–41.
19. For a reproduction of Peacham's drawing and a discussion of its authorship, see Waith's edition of *Titus*, pp. 20–7.
20. Kahn, 'The rape in Shakespeare's *Lucrece*', pp. 45–6; Alan Sommers, ' "Wilderness of tigers": structure and symbolism in *Titus Andronicus*', *Essays in Criticism*, 10 (1960), pp. 275–89.
21. Kahn, *Man's Estate*, pp. 101.
22. Ian MacClean, *The Renaissance Notion of Woman* (Cambridge: Cambridge University Press, 1980), *passim*.
23. *ibid.*, p. 42. The uterus was also supposed to predispose women to revenge, as at V, ii, 36.
24. Michel Foucault, *The History of Sexuality*, vol. I, trans. Robert Hurley (London: Allen Lane, 1978), p. 147.
25. Susan Rubin Suleiman, *The Female Body in Western Literature* (Cambridge, Mass: Harvard University Press, 1986), pp. 1–29.
26. An analysis of the theory of women's muted state may be found in Shirley Ardener, *Defining Females: The nature of women in society* (London: Croom Helm, 1978), p. 21.
27. Robert Miola, '*Titus Andronicus* and the mythos of Shakespeare's Rome', *Shakespeare Studies*, 14 (1981), pp. 88; see also Kahn, 'The rape in Shakespeare's *Lucrece*', p. 55.
28. II, i, 38.
29. Although Titus has every reason to refer to the tribunes as kin, Tamora's plea to brotherhood seems markedly inadvisable in such a patriarchal society.
30. The popularity of Aaron as a stage character is traced by Waith in his introduction to the play, pp. 43–58. See also Waith, 'The appeal of the comic deceiver', *Yearbook of English Studies*, 12 (1982), pp. 13–23.

31. For a discussion of civil turmoil in the play see Ronald Broude, 'Roman and Goth in *Titus Andronicus*', *Shakespeare Studies*, 6 (1970), pp. 27–34. Several Elizabethan plays evince similar concerns about civil disruption: *Gorboduc* (1561); George Gascogyne, *Jocasta* (1566); Christopher Marlowe, *Tamburlaine* (1590); Thomas Lodge, *Wounds of Civil War* (1586–7).

32. Elizabeth I can be seen as a representation of the country: Roy Strong, *The Cult of Elizabeth* (Wallop, Hampshire: Thames and Hudson, 1977); and Peter Stallybrass, 'Patriarchal territories', in M. W. Ferguson, M. Quilligan and N. J. Vickers, eds, *Rewriting the Renaissance*. (Chicago: University of Chicago Press, 1986), pp. 123–42; see especially p. 129.

33. Albert H. Tricomi, 'The aesthetics of mutilation in *Titus Andronicus*', *Shakespeare Survey*, 27 (1974), pp. 11–19.

34. Lavinia is herself referred to as a 'ruin' at III, i, 206, and this metaphor is discussed in Bernd Jager, 'Body, house, city, or the intertwinings of embodiment, inhabitation and civilization', in Dreyer Kruger, ed., *The Changing Reality of Modern Man* (Nijerk: Uitgeveriz G.F. Callenbach, 1984), pp. 50–8.

35. The pageant-like entries occur when Titus first enters, at the beginning of II, ii, and at V, ii, 1–3.

36. A.C. Hamilton, *The Early Shakespeare* (San Marino: the Huntington Library, 1967), pp. 63–89; see especially pp. 74–5.

37. A detailed description of the debate on hierarchical and social contract forms of state can be found in David Hale, *The Body Politic* (The Hague: Mouton, 1971).

38. *Ibid.*, pp. 69–81. See also Carolyn Merchant, *The Death of Nature: Women, ecology and the scientific revolution* (London: Willwood House, 1980), p. 73. For a contemporary account see Thomas Floyd, *The Picture of a Perfit Commonwealth* (London: Simon Stafford, 1600), pp. 1, 261–2 and 274.

39. Sir Thomas Elyot, *The Governor* (1531), I, i.

40. Hale, *Body Politic*, p. 70.

41. *Ibid.*, p. 81.

42. Broude, 'Roman and Goth', pp. 27–34.

43. Sidney Anglo, 'The British history in early Tudor propaganda', *The Bulletin of the John Rylands Library*, 44 (1961), pp. 17–48.

44. S.T. Bindoff, *Tudor England* (Harmondsworth: Penguin Books, 1950), pp. 277–307. Similar triumphal scenes may be seen in Thomas Lodge, *The Wounds of Civil War* (1586–7), III, iii.

45. Waith's edition of *Titus* includes both history and ballad on Titus Andronicus, pp. 196–207; the reference here is to pp. 196–9.

46. Kahn, 'The rape in Shakespeare's *Lucrece*', p. 57.

47. Edgar Wind, *Pagan Mysteries in the Renaissance* (Oxford: Oxford University Press, 1958), pp. 89–90 and Figure 77 (Francesco Cossa, 'Mars Enchained by Venus'); and Tricomi, 'Mutilated garden'.

48. The significance of Aaron's blackness is worthy of another essay in itself. It must suffice here to point out that black men were seen as demonic (Aaron as Pluto: IV, iii, 13), partly because of their colour but also, in the late sixteenth century, because of the merciless exploits of an actual Moor, Abd-el-Malek; these permutations are discussed by Elred Jones, *Othello's Countrymen* (London: Oxford University Press, 1965). Evil Moors became stage commonplaces, as with Barabas in Marlowe's *The Jew of Malta* and Muly Mahamet in George Peele's *The Battle of Alcazar* (1588).

49. Merchant, *Death of Nature*, pp. 1–27.

50. Similar images occur at II, iii, 194, 232, and V, ii, 191.
51. Tricomi, 'Mutilated garden', p. 92.
52. *ibid.*, p. 91.
53. II, iii, 280; Miola, 'Mythos of Shakespeare's Rome', p. 92.
54. See Suleiman, *Female Body*, pp. 1–2, 262–87.
55. Ben Jonson's criticism at the beginning of *Bartholomew Fair* (Introduction, 96) must be the most famous record of this. See also Hamilton, *The Early Shakespeare*, pp. 65–7; Richard T. Brucher, ' "Tragedy, laugh on": Comic violence in *Titus Andronicus*', *Renaissance Drama*, 10 (1979), pp. 71–91; Tricomi, 'Mutilated garden'; and Maus, 'Taking tropes seriously'.
56. Edmund Spenser, *The Faerie Queene* (1590), I Proem, 4. For an analysis of Tamora's royal ascendency see Judith M. Karr, 'The pleas in *Titus Andronicus*', *Shakespeare Quarterly*, 14 (1963), pp. 278–9.
57. Bindoff, *Tudor England*, pp. 297–304.
58. Stephen Orgel, 'Making greatness familiar', *Genre*, 15 (1982), pp. 41–8.
59. Waith's edn, note to I, i, 69.
60. Tamora becomes a personification of revenge in V, ii.
61. See Waith's edn, p. 36.
62. References to Philomela: II, iii, 43; II, iv, 26–7, 38–9; IV, i, 47–8, 56; V, ii, 194–5. *Metamorphoses* is brought on stage in IV, i.
63. This recalls the famous opening line of Sandra Gilbert and Susan Gubar, *The Madwoman in the Attic* (New Haven: Yale University Press, 1979).

6

Historical Differences: Misogyny and *Othello*

Valerie Wayne

I

Among all the critiques of the new historicism that are currently available, Carolyn Porter's remarkable essay, 'Are we being historical yet?', seems to me to explain most fully the process by which subversive elements are contained and marginal elements subordinated, dominated and othered in some new historicist practices. 'The problem lies . . . in being limited to one set of discourses – those which form the site of a dominant ideology – and then reifying that limit as if it were coterminous with the limits of discourse in general. It is this issue of framing the discursive field which new historicists most urgently need to address.'[1] I would like to approach this problem by examining the text of *Othello* as presenting a range of ideologies on women and marriage that interact with one another, on the assumption, which I have illustrated elsewhere, that there were also multiple discourses on those subjects available within English Renaissance culture.[2] An obvious place to look within the text for at least one alternative discourse is where it is hardest to find in recent productions – in the scene that has so troubled modern editors and directors that it has been complained about and cut in performances of the play. That is the conversation about women between Iago and Desdemona in Act II, scene i.

No one has objected to the scene more than M.R. Ridley, who calls it 'one of the most unsatisfactory passages in Shakespeare' because it is 'unnatural' to Desdemona's 'instinct' and 'distasteful to watch her engaged in a long piece of cheap backchat with Iago'.[3] Ridley's comments show that he is offended by Desdemona's 'vulgarity', as Lisa Jardine has already pointed out;[4] his own critical discourse also attempts to establish an interpretive purity for which objection becomes 'backchat' and backchat is always 'cheap'. Reading Shakespeare apart from other texts of the period, including those in the debate about women that Jardine connects briefly to the play, he is a critic who objects to the bad bits in the bard from the safety of his editorial sanctuary. There is a drive to ideological tidiness in this approach that functions much like Ridley's impulse 'to wash an Ethiop white' in his treatment of Othello, a subject that Karen Newman has explored in her essay on the play. Jardine and Newman object to Ridley's sexism and racism and also address what Newman terms the 'historical contingency' of the Renaissance text.[5]

Yet while asserting the claims of history and showing how Othello figures monstrosity in the play, Newman creates her own totalising gesture by describing 'the white male norms' of the play encoded through Iago, Roderigo and Brabantio.[6] This gesture, made in an important essay that expands our knowledge of the racism in western culture, also occurs with disturbing frequency in less sophisticated feminist criticism – in uses of patriarchy as a monolithic and unvarying phenomenon, in assumptions that the forms by which men dominate women are the same across cultures, and in the compatible assumption that women's oppression is similarly felt and repressed at various historical moments. If very different totalising moves have marginalised women in the texts of new historicists, as feminist critics we need to be wary of comparable gestures that totalise and reify men, in order to free our own critical practices from complicity in the operations we seek to criticise and resist. 'What we do not need', Porter points out, and her 'we' applies to feminist as well as historical critics, 'is a criticism which re-others those voices which were and are marginalised and disempowered by dominant discourses.'[7] Nor do we need a criticism that essentialises white men.

Porter's caution applies whether marginal voices arise from persons of other races or classes, from women, or from men as malevolent as Iago. So rather than seeking alternative discourses only through the differences of race, class or sex in *Othello*, I want to consider Iago not as an archetype of patriarchy or of evil,[8] but as one who articulates a marginal discourse in English Renaissance culture, a discourse that was and is in a particularly unstable relation with the dominant discourses available both then and now. I will argue that Iago's conversation with Desdemona in Act II, scene i, associates him quite specifically with the residual Renaissance discourse of misogyny. Through Iago's influence on Othello, the misogynist text of the Renaissance is written onto Desdemona's body after the woman's text that marks her as chaste has been displaced. While my focus will be on the play's allusions to the writing of texts in the Renaissance debate about women, and on the historically specific ideological positions and gender differences arising from it and from discourses on marriage, I want also to comment on how the discourses we privilege in relation to Renaissance texts inscribe the criticism we produce about them.

Misogyny is especially effective as an ideology when it masquerades or is taken for something else, and it has been taken for much besides misogyny in discussions of this play, as if Shakespeare could not possibly have understood what he was writing. Thomas Rymer confused it with ' "Jack-pudding farce . . . that runs with all the little plays, jingle, and trash below the patience of any Country Kitchenmaid with her Sweetheart" '. Ridley quotes him and comments: 'It is difficult not to sympathise for once with Rymer, who, for all his regrettably crude ebullience of expression, does sometimes hit the nail on the head.'[9] But which (gendered) head? In Rymer's remark Iago's discourse on gender is effaced as the discourse of class, too low even for the kitchen-maid; and in Ridley's, the critic also becomes 'crude'. Peter Stallybrass, in his essay addressing *Othello*, observes that members of oppressed groups some-times deny class boundaries by 'collapsing . . . women into a single un-differentiated group' through the articulation of 'misogynist discourse'.[10] What happens in this critical discourse on the play is a related, although reverse, move: Ridley affirms Rymer's displacement of the concerns of gen-der onto class, thereby muting issues in the play relating to women, and simultaneously condemns Rymer's remarks as evincing a lower-class style like its subject matter, thereby reasserting the class boundaries of critical discourse that Rymer supposedly violated. In this way an elitist critical dis-course maintains the marginalisation of gender while asserting the primacy of class in style and content. Since displacements such as these occur frequently in Renaissance drama and its criticism, effecting a double silencing of gender issues, misogyny has often not been addressed as a discourse that articulates the distrust and hatred of women. Yet in its undisplaced form it was pre-valent in medieval and Renaissance literature.

The Middle Ages was so known for it that Howard Bloch remarks in 'Medieval misogyny' that the title of his essay may seem redundant,

> because the topic of misogyny . . . participates in a vestigial horror prac-tically synonymous with the term *medieval,* and because one of the as-sumptions governing our perception of the Middle Ages is the viral presence of antifeminism. . . . The discourse of misogyny runs like a rich vein throughout the breadth of medieval literature.[11]

Christine de Pisan was so angered to find it in Matheolus that she wrote *The Book of the City of Ladies* in response, and incited the *querelle des femmes* in French literature. Chaucer provides a good bibliography of medieval misogyny through the texts listed in Jankyn's 'boke of wikked wives' from *The Wife of Bath's Prologue.* Jean de Meun's portions of *The Romance of the Rose* made Le Jaloux's tirades against women widely available to medieval and Renaissance readers, but they could also find misogyny in the Bible, in writings of the church fathers, in books on courtly love and in countless proverbs.[12] While these texts raise interpre-tive complexities, there was still nothing subtle about their denunciation of women. It was blatant:

All you women are, will be, and have been whores, in fact or in desire, for, whoever could eliminate the deed, no man can constrain desire. All women have the advantage of being mistresses of their desires. For no amount of beating or upgrading can one change your hearts, but the man who could change them would have lordship over your bodies.[13]

Such passages are designed to persuade as fully against marriage as against women, and Bloch identifies 'the defining rhetorical context of all misogynistic literature' as that 'which seeks to dissuade from marriage'.[14]

During the Renaissance, misogyny does not disappear but is seemingly contained through an association with specific characters. Lord Gasper in Castiglione's *Courtier*, Master Gualter in Tilney's *Flower of Friendshippe*, the eponymous characters of the anonymous play, *Misogonous*, or Beaumont and Fletcher's *The Woman Hater*: these figures articulate a misogyny that is directed against marriage as well as women but is condemned by other participants in the fictions. There is also a misogynist in Shakespeare's source for *Othello*, Cinthio's *Gli Hecatommithi*, a fellow named Ponzio who rejects Fabio's praise of marriage in the debate that opens the collection of tales on the grounds that 'women are dangerous beings'. Ponzio quotes from Menander, ' "Better bury a woman than marry her" ', from King Alfonso of Naples, ' "For there to be peace between husband and wife the husband must be deaf and the wife blind' ", and from other authors to support his position.[15] In *Women and the English Renaissance*, Linda Woodbridge discusses over three dozen stage misogynists, Iago among them, and she describes their 'antimasque function' as embodying all doubts, fears and hatred of women, so that when the misogynist is converted, banished or killed, those responses to women appear to be, too.[16] By the time William Gouge published his *Domesticall Duties* in 1612, it was even possible to charge a Puritan clergyman who discussed marital duties with misogyny. Although Gouge advocates the subjection of wives, he also resists husbands' abuse of their authority, so he protests that wives have no cause to complain about his advice: 'This just Apologie I have beene forced to make, that I might not ever be judged (as some have censured me) *an hater of women*.'[17] Gouge did not carry the badge of misogynist proudly, especially since that criticism could have implied that he advocated a Catholic, rather than Protestant or Puritan, position on marriage. Through its frequent use as a charge, the term came to function as a threat, much as the charge of 'shrew' functioned for insubordinate wives.

The illusion that misogyny was contained or destroyed by these Renaissance texts is important to a character who was nearly always recuperated, for attributing misogynist attitudes only to him obscured similar assumptions within other characters and the defences they offered on behalf of women. Gasper and Gualter are both threatened with being thrown out of the restricted aristocratic worlds that they inhabit by the female participants in their dialogues, and their continued presence within courtly society depends upon their containment. The existence of the misogynist in a text does not, therefore, guarantee its position on women from a modern perspective, for as an identifiable ideology, misogyny was overdetermined during the Renaissance. While it was presented as a residual ideology that the dominant discourse had put aside, the debate about women in sixteenth- and seventeenth-century texts was one means by which misogyny was fully sustained in the culture. It was residual in the sense that Raymond Williams uses that term to identify an ideology that 'has been effectively formed in the past, but . . . is still active in the cultural process.'[18] During the Renaissance, misogynist discourse had a history and continued to make history.

The frequent identification of misogyny in Renaissance texts distinguishes it from the dominant ideology, usually with the implication that the later writers are superior for having spurned such outmoded ways of thinking. But literary misogyny was still being produced. In 1596, for example, C.M. (perhaps Christopher Middleton), the author of a very conventional romance, defended the title of his text by remarking on misogyny's residual position in the culture. *The Nature of a Woman* tells of twin brothers who are 'blessed in all worldly wealth, except the unfortunate choyse of two wicked wives, . . . both wicked, because both women'. These women become the occasion for discord between the brothers and their children, and after many fabulous episodes in the woods, everyone is reconciled when the two wives admit their guilt. For the reader who is wondering why such a story has this title, C.M. explains in his preface to the second part that he was 'loath to breake square' with his real purpose, so he used the present title, 'which though therein it answer not everie mans privat expectation in what they meane, yet could not I fit it better to the matter, containing indeede nothing but the envious practises of two wicked women.' His title is admittedly misleading, but it has a kind of validity given his misogynist text. Then he explains the cause: 'wherein if any take offence, let him for this time winke at my fault, as rather affecting to frame my selfe to the new fashion, that it should be accounted new stuffe, then following the old be esteemed as too stale.'[19] The old fashion here referred to is literary misogyny, which is C.M.'s mode within a romance genre; the new stuff is the more positive presentation of women that would have been signalled by the apparently neutral phrase, 'the nature of a woman'. We can now read that phrase as naturalising yet another, hardly neutral, construct of woman; but in 1596, at least in C.M.'s opinion, the most blatant form of misogyny that associated women with evil was clearly old hat. Yet it was not so outmoded or irrelevant that he felt obliged to apologise for producing a misogynist text: he merely asks pardon for the disjunction between text and title.

In 'Discourse in life and discourse in art', Vološinov/Bakhtin makes a distinction that explains why a residual ideology such as misogyny would appear even more visible in a culture than one that was dominant:

> If a value judgment is in actual fact conditioned by the being of a given community, it becomes a matter of dogmatic belief, something taken for granted and not subject to discussion. On the contrary, whenever some basic value judgment is verbalized and justified, we may be certain that i[t] has already become dubious, has separated from its referent, has ceased to organize life, and, consequently, has lost its connection with the existential conditions of the given group.[20]

The very presence of misogynist discourse in the Renaissance suggests the instability of that view of women. It was not that no one any longer associated women with evil, but that the ideology was at issue and not an unquestioned presupposition or a given of the culture. Many texts in the Renaissance debate position themselves against that ideology. Thomas Elyot's *Defence of Good Women* places a character named Candidus against Caninius, who 'lyke a curre, at womennes condicions is alwaye barkynge': Candidus is not unambiguously feminist,[21] but Caninius is clearly antifeminist and is prompting a humanist defence of women's worth. The misogynists in Renaissance texts engender controversy over that ideology rather than belief: they keep misogyny alive at the same time that they call it into question.

What this discourse also diverts attention *from* are the misogynist assumptions about women's inferiority and inadequacies that patriarchal structures often assert in historically different forms and modes. Less explicit forms of misogyny or sexism were not frequently contested during the Renaissance, so the observation that Candidus's domesticated and idealised prescriptions for women in *The Defence of Good Women* also restrict women's agency, or that Cassio treats women as others in a way similar to Iago, requires working against the distinctions between discourses available at that time, since the rhetoric that both characters use is markedly different from Iago's. Gouge's resistance to being identified as a woman-hater is similarly justified on rhetorical grounds, since he does not associate women with evil. Yet the women who charged him with misogyny may have felt that his justifications for wives' subjection to their husbands were based not on an articulated hatred, but on a structural requirement of the subordination of women in theology and in social formations that also assumes a deep distrust of women. By what means can we distinguish more pervasive and less explicit forms of misogyny, which are still with us, from the local version so readily identified by its rhetoric? During the Renaissance, the very presence of a separate discourse made the latter form of misogyny more easy to see, while it also obscured the visibility of other 'misogynies'[22] that operated in that culture and continue to operate in ours. The charges made against Gouge suggest the possibility that some persons in his culture saw through the screen of rhetorical misogyny to some other means of condemning or confining women that functioned in many personal and institutional contexts.

The different forms that misogyny can assume within cultures therefore require some modified application of Vološinov/Bakhtin's axiom in relation to this problem, because misogyny as a structural principle governing power-relations has not 'ceased to organize life' or 'lost its connection with the existential conditions of the given group'. Patriarchal structures create numerous and varied opportunities for reinforcing misogyny, so there is an uneasy relation between misogynist discourse and other forms of patriarchal oppression. The localised, residual misogyny available in the sixteenth and seventeenth centuries could therefore be remobilised by the dominant discourse: the ideology of marriage that valorised chastity as yet another means of containing women's desire was its complement, not its opposite. Because both ideologies were still active in the cultural process, the dominant discourse could simultaneously reject and promulgate residual misogyny in order to enforce women's continued subordination within the culture.

We do need a way of identifying discursive misogyny, especially in medieval and Renaissance texts, because its very visibility made it function as a literary device during those periods. Yet if we are presently spared some of that rhetoric, various other means of subordinating and discrediting women that have very material consequences affect us daily. Literary theories and critical practices often marginalise and degrade issues relating to women. Forces within the academy effectively establish a male elite and simultaneously demean the work of women. As feminist critics, we address these problems by resisting the marginalisation of women in texts and in other material practices and by calling attention to issues of gender that other critics either do not see or prefer to ignore. To interpret from our present moment meanings in *Othello* that have been effaced through time, for example, we can consider the play's association of Iago with the misogynist and its use of Renaissance discourses on women. It is not historical accident that has obscured our knowledge of those controversies: it is the historical oppression of women that marginalises those controversies and continues to do so within contemporary critical practice. So in this analysis I want to look at two kinds of difference in the play – the historical difference of positions for and against women as they were constructed by the Renaissance debate and texts on marriage, and the gender differences that were mapped out by those discourses.

159

II

In Act II, scene i, the audience hears divergent constructions of women by Cassio and Iago that parallel the praise and blame accorded to women in the Renaissance debate. Even before Desdemona comes on stage, Cassio celebrates her as one who surpasses all other *textual* constructions of exemplary women: she is a maid

> That paragons description and wild fame;
> One that excels the quirks of blazoning pens
> And in th'essential vesture of creation
> Does tire the ingener.[23]

The passage says less about Desdemona than about the effort of an ingenious artist to pen her praise, drawing attention to the verbal constructions of women that will be a concern of the next one hundred lines. When she does arrive in Cyprus, Desdemona is greeted with a proud flourish from Cassio:

> Hail to thee, lady! And the grace of heaven
> Before, behind thee, and on every hand,
> Enwheel thee round. (85–7)

This salutation is adventitious, given Desdemona's more material concern for her husband's safety, and perhaps repetitious of the wheeling round she received during her sea voyage; but Cassio's enthusiasms extend beyond rhetorical praise of Desdemona to a kiss for Emilia.

Such 'courtesy' prompts Iago's first remark:

> Sir, would she give you so much of her lips
> As of her tongue she oft bestows on me
> You would have enough. (100–2)

Here the misogynist charges his wife with being a shrew, which was a common, not an ingenious, assertion. Although Desdemona observes that Emilia has not yet spoken and may have been stunned into silence by his attack – 'Alas, she has no speech' (103), Iago replies that his wife speaks 'too much . . . when I have list to sleep' (104). He is referring to the 'curtain lecture', when wives were said to complain to their husbands while they were both within the curtains of their bed.[24] Since even an absence of woman's speech is described by Iago as 'too much', he revises his complaint: 'she chides with thinking' (106). Yet he is the one who thinks of chiding as he projects his own dissatisfaction onto her. Emilia then defends herself – 'You have little cause to say so' (107) – and Iago reveals the 'cause' through generalised charges against women:

Come on, come on; you are pictures out of doors, bells in your parlours,
wild-cats in your kitchens, saints in your injuries, devils being offended,
players in your housewifery, and housewives in your beds. (108–11)

Again Iago says nothing new: these charges were proverbial assaults.[25]
Yet the speech makes it clear Emilia's fault is simply that she is a woman.
In this catalogue of vices, women are vain, talkative, vengeful, idle and
wanton.

When Desdemona hears these remarks, she replies, 'O fie upon thee,
slanderer!', and however playfully she delivers the line, it can imply a
serious charge, one with more far-reaching consequences than the generalised charge of 'misogynist'. The two words were related because misogynists frequently slandered women: Linda Woodbridge explains that
'misogynists libel womankind; slanderers blacken one woman's reputation.'[26] The more localised abuse was also an actionable offence during the
Renaissance if it occurred in a public context. On this subject, Lisa Jardine's
relation of defamation suits in ecclesiastical courts to the events in *Othello*
is especially informative. Jardine sets out the consequences of the public
event of calling someone a whore, for example: the offended party made a
deposition that, 'if substantiated in court, led to the offender's doing public
penance, paying a fine, or (in extreme cases) being excommunicated.'[27] In
addition to the cases Jardine cites from the Durham records, there is the
instance of Shakespeare's own daughter, Susanna, who, like her biblical
antecedent, also suffered the abuse of slander.[28]

On 15 July 1613, Susanna Shakespeare Hall sued John Lane, Jr., for
slander in the consistory court of Worcester Cathedral. ' "[A]bout 5
weeks past the defendant [Lane] reported that the plaintiff [Susanna] had
the running of the reins and had been naught with Rafe Smith at John
Palmer." ' Schoenbaum glosses 'the running of the reins' as 'to suffer
from gonorrhoea ("reins" = kidneys or loins).'[29] Lane had charged that
Susanna had a venereal disease and had been wicked or 'naughty' with
Rafe Smith: and the phrase 'to have been naught with' suggests how
immediately a woman could become naught through the charge of adultery.[30] Lane did not appear for the court proceedings, and less than a
fortnight later he was excommunicated. Schoenbaum infers the need for
Susanna's suit from the community she inhabited: 'Stratford was a closely
knit society, in which scandal – quick to circulate – had to be quicky
quashed.' In her more general account of such suits, Jardine points out
'the defamation, if it went unchallenged could become an "actuality" ',
not only through gossip but through charges brought in the courts if the
defamation were allowed to stand.[31] For personal and for legal reasons, it
was important that Susanna act to defend herself.

Othello also conveys the need for a woman to defend herself from
slander, because it calls attention to the relation between verbal abuses

and their 'eventful' consequences, whether in defamation suits or in the murder of one's wife. Slander is the offence that Emilia suspects 'some eternal villain' to have committed when Othello accuses Desdemona of being a whore – that 'some busy and insinuating rogue' has 'devis'd this slander' of Desdemona in order 'to get some office' (IV, ii, 129–32). The act is consistent with Iago's earlier intent 'to abuse Othello's [ear] / That he [Cassio] is too familiar with his wife' (I, iii, 377–8), and with Othello's threat that Iago should 'abandon all remorse' if he 'doest slander her and torture me' (III, iii, 369–70). It is a major crime committed in the play and the only one committed by Iago against Desdemona: we see and hear it committed, and objected to, as early as II, i. In these instances, too, it deserves to be treated as a serious offence: Madeleine Doran observed that 'in Shakespeare slander is one of the worst of evils; it is a vice that I do not recall ever being excused.'[32] When Iago declares at the end of the play that 'From this time forth I never will speak word' (V, ii, 301), the very means by which he avoids self-incrimination becomes an assurance that he will not repeat his offence.

Emilia's response to Iago's generalisations about women specifically relates his slander to the misogynist position against women that formed one side in the Renaissance debate, for she denies her husband the opportunity to construct her as a text by saying, 'You shall not write my praise' (II, i, 115). The statement forbids Iago's inscriptions, but he easily agrees – he certainly will not be the one to praise his own wife. Yet the remark also implies a rejection of any praise that he might attempt to write. Emilia suggests that even the praise of women can convey blame when constructed by someone like Iago, so she refuses him the opportunity. Desdemona, who has less experience of this man, understands less the risk of being the object of Iago's pen, so she sets him to the task of using words in praise rather than blame of herself: 'What wouldst thou write of me, if thou shouldst praise me?' She is requesting that he assume the opposite side in the Renaissance debate. Although her request seems unwise and self-congratulatory, it does coerce Iago into trying to speak well of women. At the same time, her engagement in this banter reveals that she is not the perfect creation Cassio described her as being, or Ridley wished she were.

Iago is so unsure that he can meet Desdemona's challenge that he at first declines to try; even when he begins, he admits his own insufficiency in this kind of discourse:

> I am about it, but indeed my invention
> Comes from my pate as birdlime does from frieze –
> It plucks out brains and all. But my muse labours,
> And thus she is delivered. (124–7)

Stephen Greenblatt reads these lines as a 'covert celebration of Iago's power to ensnare others', associating birdlime, the sticky substance used to catch birds, with Iago's own invention,[33] but they can also be read as an overt admission that Iago sees himself unfit for this kind of creative activity. When birdlime is removed from coarse wool, it takes the nap off; when Iago tries to praise women, he has to work so hard that the task plucks his brains out. It is the project of praising women that is like the birdlime – a project that might have caught women as well as birds; and Iago's mental activity is like the wool losing its nap. Iago's worry that he cannot do what Desdemona asks implies that his dispraise of women was candid and easily produced, while the praise requires labour and inspiration from a source beyond himself. His insufficiency is more surprising because elsewhere in the play Iago appears as a master rhetorician, but as Bloch explains, 'the misogynistic writer uses rhetoric as a means of renouncing it, and, by extension, woman.'[34] To be asked to produce the economiastic flourishes of Cassio exposes Iago's ruse *against* rhetoric. It is to ask him not to speak 'home', which is Cassio's own word for plain speech (II, i, 161), one that evokes the domestic nature of Iago's crabbed complaints.

While he tries to praise women or at least gives some appearance of trying, Iago's muse at first only delivers standard misogynist fare: approaching women through four categories and showing their insufficiency in each derived from Theophrastus's famously misogynist *Golden Book on Marriage*, as that text was cited in Jerome's *Epistle Against Jovinian, The Romance of the Rose* and *The Wife of Bath's Prologue*.[35] Each account presented wives as inconvenient and troublesome whether they were rich or poor, fair or ugly. Iago instead claims that four different kinds of women are sexually wanton: either their beauty or intelligence help them to bed, or their ugliness or foolishness get them there anyway. Fair or foul, wise or foolish, women are all whores to him. Desdemona dismisses this 'miserable praise' as 'old fond paradoxes to make fools laugh i'th'alehouse' (136–7), but it is a particularly rank form of such mockery that dilates in every instance upon women as objects for sexual use and then blames them, as whores, for a use constructed by that discourse. Shakespeare adapts misogynist rhetoric with such precision and in a context so relevant to the debate and the events of the play that it is not an 'unsatisfactory' version of that discourse. The talk was cheap and it is represented as such. It suits this uneasy moment in the play and aligns Iago with an ideological position that is consistent with, and anticipates, his future actions and those of Othello. It specifically identifies Iago's slander as an act of verbal violence against women, one that will lead to the physical violence against one woman later in the play. So the scene establishes the gendered character of the crimes of both men by evoking positions in the written texts about women available in Renaissance culture. If we cut it or ignore it because we cannot understand it, we are effacing the concerns of gender that the play, as written, raises.[36]

Desdemona does collude in this activity, and she persists in asking for a third time: 'But what praise couldst thou bestow on a deserving woman indeed? One that in the authority of her merit did justly put on the vouch of very malice itself?' (II, i, 141–2), a malice very like that Iago has just displayed. Her insistence is finally rewarded, because what follows might, but for the last line, have been written by the most devoted humanist in praise of women:

Iago	She that was ever fair, and never proud,
	Had tongue at will, and yet was never loud;
	Never lacked gold, and yet went never gay;
	Fled from her wish, and yet said, 'Now I may';
	She that being angered, her revenge being nigh,
	Bade her wrong stay, and her displeasure fly;
	She that in wisdom never was so frail
	To change the cod's head for the salmon's tail;
	She that could think, and ne'er disclose her mind,
	See suitors following, and not look behind;
	She was a wight, if ever such wight were –
Desdemona	To do what?
Iago	To suckle fools and chronicle small beer. (145–57)

Iago does achieve some eloquence here. In this catalogue, a woman may be beautiful without being vain, able to speak without being loud, wealthy without showing her riches off, restrained but consenting where appropriate. She is not vengeful; she would not commit adultery – that is, she would not exchange her sexual partner for one who is more attractive;[37] she can keep confidences; suitors do not turn her head. The same categories that appeared in Iago's attack on women appear here but are inverted. That is why the description is so often framed in the negative, since it is in large part what women do *not* do, given men's charges against them, that makes them good. To constitute that goodness primarily through restricted activity, Shakespeare puts six 'nevers' in this passage. The last line then undercuts the entire construction by positing only the hypothetical existence of such a woman – which reasserts Iago's doubt and also suggests how difficult it would be to affirm anyone's identity through a catalogue of prohibited behaviours.

Yet if such a woman does exist, the problem is not one of nature, but of culture: what is she permitted to do – generally and sexually – ever? Iago's answer to Desdemona's question is appropriate given the rigid restrictions placed upon women's lives by those who *praised* them – by the humanists and Protestant reformers. Lines 61–162 in this scene present the problems on both sides of the controversy: it was not just that mis-ogynists condemned all women, but that even their advocates, like Elyot's Candidus and William Gouge, described a severely restricted life for them. They show that the sport of debates about women was suspect from the start, since it assumed positions of attack or defence that defined women as uncomplicated others who could be catalogued for their virtues and vices because they were inferior to and far less complex than men. Only a woman who admits men's restrictions on her behaviour deserves to be a person, a 'wight', which is a term that suggests, especially when heard, how different from 'whites' both women and Moors could be. Yet Desdemona refuses to acknowledge just *any* man's right to direct his wife: after Iago's 'praise' she contradicts humanist advice by remarking, 'Do not learn of him, Emilia, though he be thy husband' (159–60). She notes too the 'most lame and impotent conclusion' (159) of Iago's last speech, implying that he who cannot praise women cannot relate genitally with them. Again, the words of the debate are interpreted as more than rhetorical display, more than writing, by their relation to feelings and actions: Desdemona reads them on Iago's body.[38]

The entire project of the debate depended on a perception of women that Emilia calls into question later in the play:

> What is it that they do
> When they change us for others? Is it sport?
> I think it is. And doth affection breed it?
> I think it doth. Is't frailty that thus errs?
> It is so too. And have we not affections,
> Desires for sport, and frailty, as men have? (IV, iii, 92–7)

When men 'change us for others', the double standard that permits men's adultery and forbids a woman's depends upon constituting women's sexuality as different from their own. The debate about women was one way of constructing that difference. In it, as outside of it, the otherness of heterosexual attraction became a basis for inferring differences in sexual desire: women were seen as either less or more desiring, less or more chaste, because they were different in other ways, in the ways of the other. When Emilia affirms women's similar desire, she questions the presuppositions of many inscriptions of women and constructs us differently from anyone else in the play.

Even Desdemona, who in Act I had affirmed the 'downright violence' (iii, 245) of her love for Othello, had asserted her desire only when the man who became her husband had provoked it. While the degree of her arousal might have made humanist and Protestant writers on marriage uneasy, even as Othello has been interpreted as uneasy at her assertion, the conduct books harnessed women's devotion to their husbands through valorising acts of self-sacrifice in loving wives. As long as a woman's affection was directed to her husband, the authors of conduct books did not object to it: when the misogynist in Tilney's text remarks that Julia should advise women to 'bring your mayred women unto a meane', the latter responds, 'Not so . . . I will have no meane in love.' Destructive acts such as wives jumping off cliffs with their husbands or slitting their wrists after their husbands had died were celebrated as proving the exemplary love of women. Female masochism in the interests of marital harmony was not only tolerated but actively encouraged by some Renaissance discourses on marriage.[39]

When Stephen Greenblatt claims that Protestant as well as Catholic approaches to marriage assert a 'constant fear of excess' of sexual desire in marriage,[40] he is eliding important differences between Catholic and Protestant ideologies as well as different treatments of desire set forth for women as compared to men. The former difference did not even begin as a Protestant protest: it was Erasmus who first naturalised sexual relations in marriage by claiming that bodily pleasure, although the least of all pleasures in marriage, was not unworthy of 'man':

> Neither do I here utter unto you those pleasures of the body, the which, whereas nature hath made to be moste pleasaunt unto man, yet these greate witted men, rather hide them, and dissemble them (I cannot tel how) then utterly contempne them. And yet what is he that is so sower of witte, and so drowpyng of braine (I will not saie) blockheded, or insensate, that is not moved with suche pleasure, namely if he maie have his desire, without offence either of God or man, and without hynderaunce of his estimacion. Truely I would take such a one, not to be a man, but rather to bee a very stone. Although this pleasure of the body, is the least parte of all those good thynges, that are in wedlocke. But bee it that you passe not upon this pleasure, and thinke it unworthy for man to use, although in deede we deserve not the name of manne without it, but compte it emong the least and uttermoste profites, that wedlock hath.[41]

It was this humanist view that, with all the other writings of Erasmus, was placed on the *Index of Prohibited Books* in the 'highest category of heterodoxy' in 1559 and condemned by the Council of Trent. At its session in November 1563, the Council declared as anathema anyone who claimed that the married state excelled the state of virginity or celibacy. After Trent, the humanist position on marriage was primarily associated with Protestants and Puritans.[42] In *Christian Oeconomie*, for example, which was written in the 1590s and first published in English in 1609, William Perkins objects to the results of the Counter-Reformation in the Catholic church by saying that 'whereas it opposeth mariage and chastitie; it plainely determineth that in marriage there is no chastitie.' Perkins aligns these Catholic retrenchments with Rome's earlier view of sexual relations in marriage as acts of 'filthines' and 'uncleannesse of the flesh', adding that through such condemnations of sexuality, 'some beganne to detest and hate women.'[43] He asserts a relation between post-Tridentine Catholicism, misogyny and the condemnation of sexual pleasure in marriage, in order to resist it from his Puritan position. While Protestants of any sort did not sanction unrestrained sexual play in marriage, and while they, too, were not free of the fear of desire, the valorisation of marital chastity offered them an alternative to the position of Rome that seemingly contained desire.

When he elides this difference between Catholic and Protestant positions on marriage, Greenblatt blames Desdemona for what he terms her 'erotic submission': 'this frank acceptance of pleasure and submission to her spouse's pleasure is, I would argue, as much as Iago's slander the cause of Desdemona's death, for it awakens the deep current of sexual anxiety in Othello.'[44] The danger of erotic pleasure in marriage has been heightened to the degree that it accords with medieval misogyny, leading Greenblatt to displace considerable blame for the words and actions of Iago and Othello onto Desdemona. He has presented a residual discourse as if it were the dominant one and, from this alignment, has produced a construction of Desdemona's role in her own death that is consistent with the misogynist view of her. In other words, the displacement of blame for Iago's slander results in a critic's collusion with that slander in his estimate of Desdemona. While I am not asserting that this interpretation results from a conscious or willed desire on Greenblatt's part, it does result from his reluctance to distinguish between a residual and a dominant discourse, his inattention to historical differences in advice to women and men, and his use of 'arbitrary connectedness' to relate literary and extra-literary texts.[45] The result of this procedure is that Desdemona has been slandered yet once more by a fine critic who is refashioning our approach to the Renaissance. Residual misogyny remains at risk of being remobilised by the dominant discourse.

Emilia's alternative claims for women's desire are made through asserting not a difference but a likeness between the 'affections, / Desires for sport, and frailty' of men and women, and those claims constituted an emergent ideology during the period. While the dominant discourse asserted difference and inequality (yet, as Gouge would have it, a 'small inequalitie . . . for of all degrees wherein there is any difference betwixt person and person, there is the least disparitie betwixt man and wife'),[46] the emergent discourse on women's behalf argued for equality on the grounds of a similarity between the sexes. Tilney's Isabella contends, 'For women have soules as wel as men, they have wit as wel as men, and more apt for procreation of children than men. What reason is it then, that they should be bound, whom nature hath made free?'[47] Shakespeare's Emilia reasons on the same principle of likeness, but her questions were even more threatening to those who championed marriage, because the dominant discourses presented marriage as a relation that would contain women's desire. While an antimatrimonial misogyny is the residual ideology articulated in this play through Iago and, eventually, Othello, and a general advocacy for marriage is projected as dominant through Desdemona, Emilia's emergent position calls the constitution of woman as other into question by claiming that woman's desire can no more be harnessed than man's can. Her position challenged the double standard implicit in some (though not all) descriptions of monogamy and questioned the objectification of the other that occurs in many manifestations of desire. Instead of affirming an opposition between women and men, Emilia proposes that women, like men, are not so constituted as to permit sexual control by their spouses. The emergent character of her approach is especially difficult for us to read now because our own emergent discourses ask us to be alert to gender differences and to differences within genders; yet during the Renaissance, asserting a likeness with men was an important means by which women justified some of their claims to power. The position most fundamentally opposed to Emilia's in the play is that which asserts identity as absolutely different from and opposite to an other.

Iago constructs his own identity on this principle in Act II, scene i. After Desdemona calls him a slanderer for his generalisations against women, he replies,

> Nay, it is true, or else I am a Turk:
> You rise to play, and go to bed to work. (113–14)

Iago's projections on women ensure his own identity as a Venetian, but if women are not objects or whores, then the alternative is that he is the other, the Turk, because someone has to play the other in his world. When Othello finally kills himself and says he is killing the 'turbaned Turk' who 'beat a Venetian and traduced the state' (V, ii, 349–50), he is killing the monster he became through Iago's mental poison, but he is also killing the only ethnic and racial other of the play. To be more precise, he is killing that self who is the other, the Turk or the Moor, as an act of Venetian patriotism. Just as one woman was praised by Iago for becoming a 'wight' through restricting her behaviour to the requirements of men, so Othello becomes white – both virtuous and Venetian – through annihilating his alien self. This is one way in which the coherent self is established in some forms of discourse, by defining itself off against internal and external selves, asserting its own freedom by denying 'theirs'. Critical discourse can also engage in this practice through the monolithic construction of others. Shakespeare's Venice looks like some accounts of his plays, since it is not a place that can tolerate difference: the only characters left alive on stage are white men.

But all of the white men left on stage are not the same, and it is important that Iago's misogynist discourse is specific to his character and then spreads, through a kind of oral/aural abuse, to Othello. In Act IV, scene ii, Othello's focus is on Desdemona's body, specifically 'there' on her body:

> But there where I have garnered up my heart,
> Where either I must live or bear no life,
> The fountain from the which my current runs
> Or else dries up – to be discarded thence
> Or keep it as a cistern for foul toads
> To knot and gender in! (56–61)

Norman Sanders notes the origin of the vocabulary of this passage in Proverbs 5:15–18. The biblical chapter advises against whoredom and compares the wife of a man's youth to 'thine owne well' or a 'fountaine blessed'. A woman's womb sustains her husband with life-giving water, and to be discarded from it is to die of thirst. Yet the waters offered there are not for everyone: 'But let them be thine, even thine onely, and not the strangers with thee.'[48] It is this verse that prompts Othello's alternative image of the womb as a site for engendering foul creatures when it is not exclusive property. The womb is either a place of privileged ownership or a common pond breeding bestiality. In both instances its nurturant and procreative function gives wives the power of phallic mothers, who can turn each husband into a 'young and rose-lipped cherubin' (IV, ii, 62).[49]

Having constructed Desdemona as a pre-Oedipal and powerful whore, Othello then sees her as capable of having authored her own identity:

> Was this fair paper, this most goodly book,
> Made to write 'whore' upon? What committed?
> Committed? O thou public commoner. (70–2)

Desdemona's body before her supposed adultery is here likened to a paper-book, one of the books of blank paper that Renaissance students used for practice in writing, translation and copying. Othello imagines she has written 'whore' there through committing adulterous deeds. But Desdemona does no writing in this play and hence no 'committing' in word or deed. The activities of writing are always associated there with men; it is women's speech that Iago worries about. So Othello is confusing the agency of the discourse: he does not notice who does the writing, who commits it.[50] In this scene it is Othello who is writing the body of misogynist discourse onto Desdemona's 'book'.

The act is so clear to Emilia that she makes it a verb:

> Alas, Iago, my lord hath so bewhored her,
> Thrown such despite and heavy terms upon her
> As true hearts cannot bear. (IV, ii, 114–16)

The word 'bewhored' marks the connection between this discourse and Desdemona's body, for in being termed a whore, Desdemona becomes one. Three more times in the scene Emilia objects to his applying the word to her (119, 126, 136). When Desdemona begs Iago to tell her husband that she did not 'trespass 'gainst his love / Either in discourse of thought or actual deed' (151–2), something Iago is not likely to do, her request asserts the relation between thoughts, words and deeds. For her the connection is intolerably close, and she admits, while contradicting herself as she says so, 'I cannot say "whore": / It does abhor me now I speak the word' (160–1). She cannot separate the language from her own body – 'abhor' again affirms the connection – and Stallybrass reminds us that 'there is no simple opposition between language and body because the body maps out the cultural terrain and is in turn mapped out by it.'[51] For Desdemona there is no difference at all, because she is unable to resist this rhetoric when it comes from her own husband. Instead she thinks he may be right:

> 'Tis meet I should be used so, very meet!
> How have I been behav'd, that he might stick
> The smallest opinion on my least misuse? (106–8)

When she does not oppose misogynist discourse, Othello's words 'stick' on Desdemona's body and become a part of her mind. Her response shows how misogyny spreads within a text and a culture, for as it works through language, it constructs the very thoughts and deeds that Desdemona did not do.

The other signifier that moves through the play in a complementary way is the handkerchief. Newman remarks that 'as it passes from hand to hand, both literal and critical, it accumulates myriad associations and meanings.'[52] I want to link some of those associations with the dominant ideology concerning women in the Renaissance, in order to suggest why its loss is an important precedent to the bewhoring of Desdemona and how it figures women's activity, their work. Edward Snow observes two genealogies for the handkerchief in the play: the matrilineal account of its passage from an Egyptian charmer to Othello's mother to Desdemona, where the three women merge into one another; and the patrilineal descent of the token from Othello's father to his mother. He sees the first story as narrating the gap in the second concerning how the son received from his mother the emblem of his father's sexual power and the means by which he establishes authority over his wife. Then he adds, 'although it would be missing the point to try to distinguish the true version of the story from the false, the first version clearly engages Othello's imagination more deeply, and his psychic investment in it appears much greater.'[53] The matrilineal origin of the handkerchief also extends to its embroidered inscription: to the sibyl who 'sewed the work' in a 'prophetic fury', to the hallowed worms that bred the silk thread, and the 'mummy' or embalming fluid taken from 'maidens' hearts', which was thought to have healing properties and provided its red dye (III, iv, 66–71).[54] I think Lynda Boose is right to see in the handkerchief spotted with strawberries 'visual proof of [Desdemona and Othello's] consummated marriage' through its evidence of Desdemona's virginity, like wedding sheets spotted with blood:[55] the dye 'conserved of maidens' hearts' used to colour the embroidery thread even seems applied to the handkerchief itself, since the 'it' of line 70 might refer to 'the work' (168) and the entire piece, as if the dye had bled from the pattern through to the cloth. The handkerchief becomes both metaphor and metonymy to prove the state of Desdemona's body before and after their marriage.[56] And in serving this function it remains also a symbol for the woman's *text* – for the work that women do, since in the play they do not write books but serve as bodies to be written upon.

In Cinthio's *Gli Hecatommithi*, the handkerchief has no genealogy and no specific pattern, although it had been 'embroidered most delicately in the Moorish fashion'. A woman in the house of the captain, Cassio's counterpart, 'worked the most wonderful embroidery on lawn' (a sheer linen or cotton), and she 'began to make a similar one before it went back'.[57] Shakespeare heightens this emphasis on copying the pattern in the handkerchief: Emilia remarks, 'I'll have the work tane out' (III, iii, 298) when she finds it; Cassio says to Bianca, 'Take me this work out' (III, iv, 174) and

I like the work well. Ere it be demanded –
As like enough it will – I'd have it copied.
Take it and do't, and leave me for this time (183–5)

Bianca returns later with objections to the task: 'I must take out the work? . . . This is some minx's token, and I must take out the work? There, give it your hobby-horse, wheresoever you had it. I'll take out no work on't' (IV, i, 145–9). These passages shift the emphasis from making a handkerchief *like* the one Desdemona had to copying the pattern itself. The phrase used so consistently for this activity, 'taking the work out', which may have come from the French translation of *Hecatommithi*,[58] conveys in its ambiguity a threat that when the pattern is copied, it is also taken away. Neither Emilia nor Bianca does copy the work as the woman did in the source: Emilia seems unable to take it out herself and gives the handkerchief to Iago before she can have it copied, and Bianca refuses to perform the task. So with all this emphasis on copying the handkerchief, it remains a single and original piece of work.

The handkerchief serves as a woman's text in that women alone are associated with the work and copying of it. During the Renaissance embroidery was women's work because they did it; but it was also an activity they were enjoined to do rather than reading or writing, for it kept them busy without allowing their minds to become too active. The pen and the sword were associated with men, while the counterparts for women were the distaff and the needle. In *The Subversive Stitch*, Rozsika Parker explains that 'Needlework was designated a frontline position in the defense of women's chastity. . . . No other activity so successfully promoted the qualities that Renaissance man, anxious to define sexual difference, wanted in a wife.'[59] This emblem of Desdemona's body that is made by women is made *for* women's apparent well-being: the Egyptian charmer told Othello's mother "Twould make her amiable and subdue my father / Entirely to her love' (III, iv, 55–6). It reassures a husband that his wife is doing her work by engaging in the domestic activities proper to her – by day and by night – for Iago was not alone in claiming that women 'go to bed to work', too (II, i, 14).

Because the handkerchief serves as proof of married chastity, it cannot be copied by Emilia and Bianca. It is an emblem of Desdemona's body that does not circulate because her body is not supposed to circulate: the regulated passage of the handkerchief is along family lines, not elsewhere. This restriction usually applied as well to the woman's text, for her work was private, performed for her family and produced primarily for their consumption. In Cinthio's narrative, the mere appearance of the woman in the window doing her work of embroidery, since she 'could be seen by whoever passed by on the street', convinced the Moor of her adultery.[60] The value of married chastity, which is figured in the handkerchief, asserts a worth and purpose for women that contradict the assertions of misogyny by requiring the sexual control of women in marriage. Chastity was a charm. The Egyptian charmer knew that 'if she lost it / Or made a gift of it', Othello's father and any husband would lapse into misogyny – he 'should hold her loathed, and his spirits should hunt / After new fancies' (III, iv, 56–9). When Desdemona loses the handkerchief, she loses the means of presenting herself as amiable, the proof that she is doing her private, domestic, bed-work. She loses her own text, as the Renaissance constructed it for her.

Marriage was, then, the historical response to misogyny in the Renaissance: those who praised marriage worked in concert with those who defended women to claim that marriage was a holy and chaste state and women were sufficiently virtuous to be suitable as marital partners. But the shift from a valorisation of virginity to married chastity still depended on women's sexual control. It was haunted by the very question that Emilia asks about women's desire and that Othello raises earlier in the play:

> O curse of marriage,
> That we can call these delicate creatures ours
> And not their appetites! (III, iii, 270–2)

Othello's lines are uncomfortably close to Le Jaloux's charge that 'all you women are, will be, and have been whores, in fact or in desire, for whoever could eliminate the deed, no man can constrain desire.' They are preceded by Othello's harrassed question, 'Why did I marry?' (III, iii, 244). By the middle of the play, Othello has absorbed Iago's misogyny and a residual discourse has infected the dominant ideology. However, this transference was not due smply to the brilliant exercise of Iago's own malice: it was made easier by a contradiction that obtained within the dominant discourse.[61] The ideology of marriage permitted husbands to call their wives 'ours' and to write upon their bodies, but it could not control women's desire. Since men's appropriation of women was never entire, jealousy arose from the contradictory claims of possession and desire. In this play Renaissance marriage produced what Kenneth Burke has called 'a tragic trinity of ownership in the profoundest sense of ownership, the property in human affections, as fetishistically localized in the object of possession, while the possessor is himself possessed by his very engrossment'.[62] The handkerchief becomes a fetishised sign of Desdemona's commodification through marital exchange, yet for her jealous husband the curse of marriage is that she, like it, cannot be fully possessed. Desdemona and Othello are no phoenix and turtle: their relation collapses when property is *not* appalled but marriage permits a partial and appalling assertion of property rights.

The woman's text as it appears in this play colluded with this ideology: instead of interrogating it, it was intent only upon proving wives' chastity in order to keep their husbands' good opinion. There was no way of copying or passing the text from woman to woman because it depended upon men for its production: the staining of the wedding sheets required men's agency, the embroidery women wrought did not sustain them, and the only safe passage of the text was within the line of the patriarchal family. However, the presence of that emblem in the play and its association with the historical response to misogyny does not signify women as complete lack, as some contemporary criticism does: this is not a blank handkerchief, for women have inscribed it. It is the historical antidote to the blank page of Desdemona's body where Othello inscribed 'whore'. Instead of constructing women as an absence, it figures chastity as their charm that they must keep and treasure, lest it be lost. When it is lost, the handkerchief comes to signify Renaissance women's painful contingency, for their reputations were as easily displaced through some of the texts of men.

Hence the gender differences that were mapped out by discourses on women and marriage and that are refigured in this play represent men as writers and women as bodies that are written upon. Women assert themselves more actively through speech and through sewing (Marina in *Pericles* says that instead of being a prostitute, 'I can sing, weave, sew, and dance',[63] and even as Othello curses Desdemona, he claims she is 'so delicate with her needle' [IV, i, 177]), but these activities do not create texts with a discursive content that is widely recognised as contributing to history. Feminist critics have claimed the importance of listening to 'the voice of the shuttle', and that voice can be heard through the story of Philomela, who gave evidence through her weaving that Tereus had raped her.[64] In Chaucer's version in *The Legend of Good Women*, Philomela does 'endyte' her own story in 'letters' as she weaves her tapestry, since in prison she is denied use of a pen: 'She coude eek rede and wel ynow endyte, / But with a penne coude she nat wryte.'[65] Because women's hands manage to tell the story of their oppression in Ovid and Chaucer, Shakespeare's Lavinia must lose hers when she is raped: the words she writes with a stick in the sand produce an even more transient text that soon disappears. The ephemeral nature of speech and the silent status of sewn or woven characters are in some ways like Lavinia's letters: given their impermanency and the difference of their form, they are not often recognised as texts producing history. Like texts in the debate about women, those by women are washed away on the next high tide of historical reproduction.

Yet becoming alert to alternative discourses that are present at a particular historical moment and the variety of textual forms associated with them may enlarge our notion of what is available to us as we reconstruct history and politics in our own present. The male text in *Othello* shows that men have the power to appropriate women for their own purposes and to write women out, annihilate them or make them 'naught'. The female texts often collude with those projects rather than resisting them. The risks of appropriative writing were high in the Renaissance when women were enjoined to silence and compliance; they are high now as we write about a silent past that cannot talk back. Approaching the past through dominant discourses only doubles the risk of that appropriation and prevents our being able to distinguish among available ideologies. It is in this sense, among others, that 'knowledge is made possible and is sustained by irreducible difference, not identity',[66] for one cannot grasp what is or is not dominant without examining the range of positions occurring within a given culture. Instead of treating the Renaissance as a passive body at the mercy of our own inscriptions, we might address its texts for the play of their diversity – permitting their dissonances, giving them voice – as still another way of remaking the past into a palpable presence.

NOTES

I am grateful to Margaret W. Ferguson, Lisa Jardine, Cristina Malcolmson and John Rieder for their knowledgeable and helpful comments on this essay.

1. Carolyn Porter, 'Are we being historical yet?' *South Atlantic Quarterly*, **87** (1988), pp. 769–70. See also Carolyn Porter's 'reprise' and extension of this argument in 'History and literature: "after the new historicism" ', *New Literary History*, (Winter, 1990), pp. 253–72.
2. See the introduction to my edition of Edmund Tilney's *'The Flower of Friendshippe': A Renaissance Dialogue Contesting Marriage*, forthcoming from Cornell University Press. An earlier version of this essay on *Othello* was prepared for a seminar on 'Shakespearean Tragedy and Gender' at the Shakespeare Association of America meetings in 1987.
3. M.R. Ridley, ed., *Othello* (London: Methuen, 1958), note to II, i, 109–66. Stanley Cavell also refers to 'that difficult and dirty banter between [Desdemona] and Iago' in 'Othello and the stake of the other', in his *Disowning Knowledge in Six Plays of Shakespeare* (Cambridge: Cambridge University Press, 1987), p. 136. He cites the play from Ridley's Arden edition.
4. Lisa Jardine, *Still Harping on Daughters* (Hemel Hempstead: Harvester Wheatsheaf, 1982), p. 120.
5. Karen Newman, ' "And wash the Ethiop white": femininity and the monstrous in *Othello*', in Jean E. Howard and Marion F. O'Connor, eds., *Shakespeare Reproduced* (London: Methuen, 1987), pp. 141–62, quotation from p. 153.
6. Newman, 'And wash the Ethiop white', p. 153.
7. Porter, 'Are we being historical yet?', pp. 780–1.
8. Bernard Spivack's *Shakespeare and the Allegory of Evil* (New York: Columbia University Press, 1958) explores another side to Iago's character that also connects him to medieval traditions. When the figure of medieval vice is combined with the misogynist, misogyny becomes more recognisable *as* a vice rather than a slight character flaw or conversational habit.
9. Ridley's edn, note to II, i, 109–66.
10. Peter Stallybrass, 'Patriarchal territories: the body enclosed', in Margaret W. Ferguson, Maureen Quilligan and Nancy J. Vickers, eds., *Rewriting the Renaissance* (Chicago: University of Chicago Press, 1986), p. 133.
11. R. Howard Bloch, 'Medieval misogyny', *Representations*, **20** (Fall, 1987), p. 1.
12. For a good collection of medieval misogyny in these texts, see 'The antifeminist tradition' in R.P. Miller, ed., *Chaucer: Sources and Backgrounds* (Oxford and New York: Oxford University Press, 1977), pp. 399–473. See also Katharine M. Rogers, *The Troublesome Helpmate: A history of misogyny in literature* (Seattle and London: University of Washington Press, 1966); and Eleanor Commo McLaughlin, 'Equality of souls, inequality of sexes: woman in medieval theology', in Rosemary Radford Ruether, ed., *Religion and Sexism: Images of woman in the Jewish and Christian traditions* (New York: Simon & Schuster, 1974), pp. 213–66.

13. Guillaume de Lorris and Jean de Meun, *The Romance of the Rose*, trans. Charles Dahlberg (Princeton, N.J.: Princeton University Press, 1971), pp. 165–6.
14. Bloch, 'Medieval misogyny', p. 18. His reference to 'all misogynist literature' as situated against marriage is in conflict with his earlier discussion of a passage from Theophrastus as 'less a true example of misogyny, a denunciation of the essential evil of woman, than a subgeneric topos known as the *molestiae nuptiarum* or antimarriage literature' (p. 2). Miller remarks that 'it has been soundly suggested that this tradition should not be labeled "antifeminist", but rather "antimatrimonial", directed primarily at clerks tempted to search out the "mixed love" of the world' (*Chaucer: Sources*, p. 402). While the term 'anti-marriage' is more descriptive of some types of misogyny, it is also important to distinguish, when possible, between places where women and where marriage are being denounced. If we do not, we contribute to the invisibility of misogyny, which I believe has a much wider field than antimatrimonial texts.
15. Geoffrey Bullough ed., *Narrative and Dramatic Sources of Shakespeare*, vol. 7 (London: Routledge and Kegan Paul; New York: Columbia University Press, 1978), p. 239.
16. Linda Woodbridge, *Women and the English Renaissance: Literature and the nature of womankind, 1540–1620* (Urbana: University of Illinois Press, 1984), p. 290. See also Rogers, *Troublesome Helpmate*, pp. 118–33.
17 William Gouge, *Of Domesticall Duties* (1622; reprint edn Amsterdam: Theatrum Orbis Terrarum, 1972), dedicatory epistle, sig. ¶4.
18. Raymond Williams, *Marxism and Literature* (Oxford: Oxford University Press, 1977), p. 113.
19. C.M., *The First Part of the Nature of a Woman*, 1596 (Ann Arbor: University Microfilms, Pollard Reel 995), sig. F1; *The Second Part of the Historie called the Nature of a Woman*, 1596 (Ann Arbor: University Microfilms, Pollard Reel 477), sigs. A2–A2^v.
20. V.N. Vološinov, 'Discourse in life and discourse in art', in Vološinov's *Freudianism: A Marxist critique*, trans. I.R. Titunik (New York: Academic Press, 1976), p. 101. This essay from 1926 is usually attributed to Mikhail Bakhtin. For a full discussion of the issues surrounding the attribution, see 'The disputed texts' in Katerina Clark and Michael Holquist's *Mikhail Bakhtin* (Cambridge, Mass. and London: Belknap Press of Harvard University), pp. 146–70.
21. I have discussed the problems of interpreting Elyot's *Defence* and other humanist texts on women as feminist in 'Zenobia in medieval and Renaissance literature', in Carole Levin and Jeanie Watson, eds., *Ambiguous Realities: Women in the Middle Ages and Renaissance* (Detroit: Wayne State University Press, 1987), pp. 48–65 and in my introduction to *The Flower of Friendshippe*. An alternative approach informs Constance Jordan's *Renaissance Feminism: Literary Texts and Political Models* (Ithaca, N.Y.: Cornell University Press, 1990).
22. See Joan Smith's *Misogynies* (London: Faber and Faber, 1989), for an account of the discrimination, denigration and violence that women have suffered recently in Britain. I am grateful to Marion Wynne-Davies for this reference.
23. *Othello*, ed. Norman Sanders (Cambridge: Cambridge University Press, 1984), II, i, 61–4. All subsequent references to the text of the play will be to this edition.
24. See Carroll Camden, *The Elizabethan Woman*, rev. edn. (Mamaroneck, New York: Paul P. Appel, 1975), pp. 126–8, who discusses Thomas Heywood's *Curtain Lecture*, Swetnam's *Arraignment, The Proud Wives Paternoster* and other texts, including Desdemona's threat of shrewishness in *Othello* at III, iii, 22–6.

25. Sanders's note to II, i, 108–11, cites Tilley W702: 'Women are in church saints, abroad angels, at home devils.'
26. Woodbridge, *Women and the English Renaissance*, p. 288.
27. Lisa Jardine, ' "Why should he call her whore?": defamation and Desdemona's case', in M. Tudeau-Clayton and M. Warner, eds., *Addressing Frank Kermode: Essays in Criticism and Interpretation* (Oxford: Blackwell, forthcoming).
28. For discussion of another Susanna and parallels with Shakespeare, see Joyce Hengerer Sexton, 'The theme of slander in *Much Ado about Nothing* and Garter's *Susanna*', *Philological Quarterly*, **54** (Spring 1975), pp. 419–33. The biblical story of Susanna that appears in the Apocrypha was included in the Geneva Bible.
29. Samuel Schoenbaum, *William Shakespeare: A compact documentary life* (New York: Oxford University Press, 1977), p. 289.
30. *OED* 'naught', adj., 2.c. 'Const. *with* (one of the other sex)'. See also *Richard III*, I, i, 99, for the implication of adultery:

    Naught to do with Mistress Shore? I tell thee, fellow,
    He that doth naught with her (excepting one)
    Were best to do it secretly alone.

31. Schoenbaum, *Shakespeare*, p. 290; Jardine, ' "Why should he call her whore?" ', forthcoming.
32. Madeleine Doran, 'Good name in *Othello*', *Studies in English Literature, 1500–1900*, **7** (Spring 1967), p. 203.
33. Stephen Greenblatt, *Renaissance Self-Fashioning: From More to Shakespeare* (Chicago: University of Chicago Press, 1980), p. 233.
34. Bloch, 'Medieval misogynyy', p. 19.
35. The portion of Theophrastus that is quoted in Jerome appears in Miller, *Chaucer: Sources*, pp. 412–13, and that from *The Romance of the Rose* is also cited by Miller on p. 456. In the Dahlberg translation it is ll. 8561–607, pp. 157–8, and in *The Wife of Bath's Prologue* it is ll. 248–75 in *The Riverside Chaucer*, 3rd edn, ed. Larry D. Benson (Boston: Houghton Mifflin, 1987). Adaptations of the joke also appear in Vives's *Instruction of a Christian Woman*, Pedro di Luxan's *Coloquios Matrimoniales* and Tilney's *Flower of Friendshippe*.
36. The production of *Othello* by Sir Laurence Olivier, which was first staged in 1963 and filmed shortly thereafter, eliminates lines 115–62 of Act II, scene i, including Iago's comments on four kinds of woman and the passage of 'praise'. Jonathan Miller's more recent production for the BBC Shakespeare series cuts the fourth kind of woman and the entire 'praise' passage, ll. 137–59.
37. Iago's admirable woman is one who is sexually confined, so she refuses to exchange one penis for another, however desirable the latter or undesirable the former. One who would do so would be, to him, weak in wisdom. Hence Iago explicitly forbids good women from exchanging men as men do women. Sanders's note to l. 152 in his edition glosses 'to change the cod's head for the salmon's tail' as ' "to exchange something worthless for something more valuable" ', noting the sexual innuendos in 'cod's head' for 'penis' and 'tail' for 'pudendum'. See also Eric Partridge in *Shakespeare's Bawdy*, rev. edn (New York: E.P. Dutton, 1969), pp. 77–8, who glosses 'tail' as 'penis' at p. 196. The *OED* defines 'change, v.' with 'for' as 'taken in exchange' at 1.b and 'cod's head' as 'blockhead' at meaning 2. For an alternate reading, see Balz Engler,

'*Othello*, II, i, 155: to change the cod's head for the salmon's tail', *Shakespeare Quarterly*, 35 (1984), pp. 202–3.

38. Since misogynist discourse was sustained during the Middle Ages in order to justify and support a celibate clergy, the connection that Desdemona asserts between its rhetoric and sexual impotence might have been happily received – as a kind of insurance – in some quarters, although restraining desire for women risked its being redirected towards men.

39. *The Flower of Friendshippe* (London: Henry Denham, 1568), sig. D7. I have discussed this issue more fully in Part II of my introduction to Tilney's text.

40. Greenblatt, *Renaissance Self-Fashioning*, p. 249. In Richard Strier's review of *Renaissance Self-Fashioning* called 'Identity and Power in Tudor England', *Boundary 2* (1982), pp. 383–94, Strier also takes issue with Greenblatt on this point. See especially p. 393.

41. The quotation is from the English text of Erasmus's *Encomium Matrimonii* that appeared in Thomas Wilson's *Arte of Rhetorique*, ed. Thomas J. Derrick (New York and London: Garland, 1982), pp. 126–7, since Erasmus's text was published most frequently in this translation.

42. Margo Todd, *Christian Humanism and the Puritan Social Order* (Cambridge: Cambridge University Press, 1987), pp. 206–10; *Canons and Decrees of the Council of Trent*, ed. and trans. H.J. Schroeder (St Louis, Mo.: Herder Book Co., 1941), p. 182; also Part I of my introduction to *The Flower of Friendshippe*.

43. William Perkins, *Christian Oeconomie*, in *Works*, vol. 3 (Cambridge: Cantrell, Legge, 1618), p. 689. Although Pickering's translation was first published in 1609, Ian Breward, who is the editor of *The Works of William Perkins*, vol. 3 (Appleford, England: Sutton Courtenay Press, 1970), says 'it was probably written in the early 1590s' (p. 414). See also C.S. Lewis, who remarks in *English Literature in the Sixteenth Century* (Oxford: Oxford University Press, 1954) that 'so far as there was any difference about sexual morality, the Old Religion was the more austere. The exaltation of virginity is a Roman, that of marriage, a Protestant, trait' (p. 35).

44. Greenblatt, *Renaissance Self-Fashioning*, p. 250.

45. 'Arbitrary connectedness' is Walter Cohen's phrase for the relation new historicists assume between diverse cultural texts. See his 'Political Criticism of Shakespeare', in Howard and O'Connor, eds., *Shakespeare Reproduced*, esp. pp. 34–8. The assumption 'seems to preclude a systematic survey of the available evidence, leading instead to a kind of synecdoche in which a single text or group of texts stands in for all texts and thus exhausts the discursive field. . . . Thus in the extreme case women cease to be historical actors or subjects. They can be victims or objects, but it is not, however complexly, their experience that matters' (p. 38).

46. Gouge, *Of Domesticall Duties*, p. 271.

47. *The Flower of Friendshippe* (1568), sig. D8. I have discussed another emergent aspect of Emilia's words as a positive adaptation of shrewish speech in 'Refashioning the shrew', *Shakespeare Studies*, 17 (1985), pp. 159–87.

48. *The Geneva Bible: A Facsimile of the 1560 Edition* (Madison: University of Wisconsin Press, 1969), p. 268; and Sanders's edn, note to IV, ii, 58–61. Since the biblical passages uses 'cistern' to mean a reservoir or pond, and toads breed in such places, I have departed from Sanders's gloss of the word as 'cesspool' at I.60, although it does begin to take on those associations. See *OED*, 'cistern', 1–3.

49. Edward Snow finds in this passage Othello's 'primitive fantasies of a more

ancient maternal betrayal', in 'Sexual anxiety and the male order of things in *Othello*', *English Literary Renaissance*, 10 (1980), pp. 404–5.

50. The *OED* defines sixteenth-century meanings of the verb 'commit' as 'to commit to writing, to put in writing, write down for preservation', etc.
51. Stallybrass, 'Patriarchal territories', p. 138.
52. Newman, p. 156.
53. Snow, 'Sexual anxiety', p. 404.
54. E.A. Wallis Budge discusses the medicinal use of 'mummy' in *The Mummy: A handbook of Egyptian funerary archaeology* (1893; 2nd edn 1925; rpt. London: Routledge & Kegan Paul, 1987), pp. 201–9, explaining that the fluid was sometimes taken out of previously mummified bodies for its healing properties. 'Abd al-Latif mentioned that he saw *mumia*, or bitumen, which had been taken out of the skulls and stomachs of mummies sold in the towns, and he adds, "I bought three heads filled with it for half an Egyptian dirham." ' Budge continues, 'About three or four hundred years ago [from 1893] Egyptian mummy formed one of the ordinary drugs in apothecaries' shops. The trade in mummy was carried on chiefly by Jews, and as early as the XIIth century a physician called Al-Magar was in the habit of prescribing mummy to his patients. It was said to be good for bruises and wounds' (p. 202).
55. Lynda Boose, 'Othello's handkerchief: the recognizance and pledge of love', *English Literary Renaissance*, 5 (1975), p. 363. See also Carol Thomas Neely, 'Women and men in *Othello*', in her book, *Broken Nuptials in Shakespeare's Plays* (New Haven: Yale University Press, 1985), p. 128 ff., and Cavell, *Disowning Knowledge*, p. 135. My students Carmen Wickramagamage and Carina Chotiware say that the custom of displaying the wedding sheets is still sometimes observed in Sri Lanka and India.
56. Stallybrass, 'Patriarchal territories', p. 138.
57. Bullough, *Narrative and Dramatic Sources*, p. 249.
58. See Sanders's introduction to the play, p. 3.
59. Rozsika Parker, *The Subversive Stitch: Embroidery and the making of the feminine* (New York: Routledge, 1984), pp. 74, 64.
60. Bullough, *Narrative and Dramatic Sources*, p. 249.
61. In *The Expense of Spirit: Love and sexuality in English Renaissance drama* (Ithaca, N.Y.: Cornell University Press, 1988), Mary Beth Rose shows that in *Othello*, 'the heroics of marriage also collapses from within, dissolving inevitably from its own unresolved contradictions' (p. 131). I agree generally with her conclusions and especially like pp. 144–53, where she discusses Desdemona's three lies, although I have described the discursive field of the play differently to include its evocations of the Renaissance debate about women and conflicting religious positions.
62. Kenneth Burke, '*Othello*: an essay to illustrate a method', *The Hudson Review*, 4 (Summer 1951), pp. 166–7.
63. *Pericles* in *The Riverside Shakespeare*, ed. G. Blakemore Evans (Boston: Houghton Mifflin, 1974), IV, vi, 183.
64. Patricia Klindienst Joplin, 'The voice of the shuttle is ours', *Stanford Literature Review*, 1 (1984), pp. 25–53. I am grateful to Tina Malcolmson for this reference.
65. In *The Riverside Chaucer*, 3rd edn, ll. 2356–8.
66. This Derridean observation is from Gayatri Chakravorty Spivak, 'A literary representation of the subaltern: a woman's text from the third world', in her book, *In Other Worlds: Essays in cultural politics* (New York and London: Routledge, 1988), p. 254.

—7—

Defacing the Feminine in Renaissance Tragedy

Sara Eaton

'The theatre, that tragic scaffold, was a place for self-knowledge precisely because it mirrored the state, because its re-presentations duplicated public life. It is there that Renaissance man went to know himself.' Goldberg collapses what are conventionally perceived as real differences between the tragic stage and the scaffold – after all, on the latter, dramatically, someone really dies – to point to the spectacular, the representational aspects of both scenes of suffering (as Aristotle would put it) in early modern English life. In a subsequent discussion of Chapman's *Bussy D'Ambois* concerning the play's dislocation of language and gesture, Goldberg observes that the collapse of the real and the imaginary in the play re-enacts from the spectators' point of view James's staging of similar political scenes. For spectators, both scenes assume the same degree of 'reality', but Chapman and James were deliberately obfuscating, Goldberg argues, and he concludes, 'It would mean that we could not see what was going on, even when it was before our eyes, and that what we could see was likely not to be what was really happening.'[1]

Goldberg's argument echoes T.S. Eliot's conclusions long ago concerning the function of the Stoic character in Renaissance drama. The Stoic character, Eliot says, 'takes in the spectator, but the human motive is primarily to take in himself . . . [to] expose this *bovarysme*, the human will to see things as they are not . . . Stoicism is the refuge for the individual in an indifferent or hostile world too big for him; it is the permanent substratum of a number of versions of cheering oneself up.'[2] A theatrically induced self-knowledge, a self-deception, a 'cheering oneself up', both critics agree, all seem to result from a mimetic experience, specifically a scene of suffering, and are realised when the spectator sees what is (not) really happening.

My point is to make unlikely bedfellows of Goldberg and Eliot here and to emphasise what seems obvious – that since Aristotle it has been assumed that what spectators see in a play, in particular a scene of suffering, is central

181

to their subsequent understanding of the tragic experience. Put another way, what spectators see confirms *their* subjectivity, their ability *really* to 'know' themselves.[3] This formulation designates the drama a humanist endeavour in our time, as one which inspires self-consciousness as a product of the production, and, as both Goldberg's and Eliot's pronouns reveal, the recipient, the spectator, is assumed 'universal' and male. The critical gaze is a patriarchal one, to borrow a phrase from recent feminist film criticism.[4]

Film theory, with its emphasis on the visual experience, has appropriate applications for theatre criticism of early modern England, if only because literary critics of the latter have traditionally relied on their experience of the written text and literary methodology for its explication. A camera in a movie, of course, focuses and manipulates the spectator's gaze more efficiently than any staged production could, but a writer's critical gaze may counter theatric distanciation by reconstructing the dramatic text as though the eyes were a camera, thus recreating a mental performance of the text in as voyeuristic a manner as any film director would.[5] The alignment of a (male) critical reader's gaze with the imagined spectator's and the play text creates the conditions for what Roland Barthes called 'the pleasure of the text', perhaps, and what Laura Mulvey has termed 'visual pleasure' and critiqued as scopophilia when turned on the female image. Mulvey argues that the 'fictional drama cannot achieve reality, obviousness and truth' without this kind of seeing, but she also suggests that

> The camera becomes the mechanism for producing an illusion of Renaissance space, flowing movements compatible with the human eye, an ideology of representation that revolves around the perception of the subject; the camera's look is disavowed in order to create a convincing world in which the spectator's surrogate [the character] can perform with versimilitude. Simultaneously, the look of the audience is denied an intrinsic force: as soon as fetishistic representation of the female image threatens to break the spell of illusion, and the erotic image on the screen appears directly (without mediation) to the spectator, the fact of fetishisation, concealing as it does castration fear, freezes the look, fixates the spectator and prevents him from achieving any distance from the image in front of him.[6]

A dramatic experience is reified (or becomes what it is not) *because* the camera – or critic – situates the spectator as a privileged 'invisible guest' (p. 26) at a very subjective performance of the text.

Mulvey's psychoanalytic analysis of how spectral seeing participates in an 'ideology of representation' is useful for understanding how women's roles on the Renaissance stage are reconstructed critically. In spite of evidence that women were really spectators in both private and public theatres and were really writing plays,[7] the canonised dramatists in early modern England we teach are male, and the spectators for those plays have been imagined male. Using Mulvey's perspective, we can say that in the plays most widely read, anthologised, staged and subsequently taught, women, acted by boys, are fetishised and represent constructs of desire. These women are part of a dramatic spectacle imagined by male dramatists, reflecting dominant ideologies even as their plays might subvert them. Perhaps we can take Goldberg quite literally – 'what we could see was likely not to be what was happening' – because, as Annette Kuhn puts it, 'the gendered subjectivity of spectators may inform these relations of looking.'[8] Put simply, spectators, including the critical audience, may be seeing what they would like to believe is true about male–female relationships.

Mulvey's essay on 'visual pleasure' appeared in 1975, and in a later essay, 'Myth, narrative and historical experience',[9] written in 1983, she analyses her methodology:[9]

> There is a sense in which this argument, important as it is for analysing the existing state of things, hinders the possibility of change and remains caught ultimately within its own dualistic terms. The polarisation only allows an 'either/or'. As the two terms (masculine/feminine, voyeuristic/ exhibitionist, active/passive) remain dependent on each other for meaning, their only possible movement is into inversion. They cannot be shifted easily into a new phase or new significance. There can be no space in between or space outside such a pairing. . . . Is it possible that the way in which ideas are visualised can, at a certain point, block the process that brings thought into a dialectical relationship with history? . . . This is the question of *how* ideas are formulated in relation to *when*. (p. 163)

Mulvey is questioning the impact of her feminist analyses of 1950 Hollywood movies. She is concerned that her methodology has repeated the dominant ideologies of these films rather than 'suggest[ing] an alternative theory of spectatorship' (p. 162). Again, her questions are useful in understanding our own literary practice as readers, critics, teachers – as spectators – of Renaissance plays. As Jean Howard has argued in an essay surveying what is 'new' in Renaissance historical studies:

> I am not suggesting that it is desirable to look at the past with the willful intention of seeing one's own prejudices and concerns. Nonetheless, since objectivity is not in any pure form a possibility, let us acknowledge that fact and acknowledge as well that any move into history is an *intervention*, an attempt to reach from the present moment into the past to rescue both from meaningless banality.[10]

Most of us would prefer avoiding endless repetitions and banality. It is only by accounting psychologicaly and sociologically for as much as we can that we are able to disassociate ourselves as postmodern readers and teachers from repeating Renaissance ideologies, casting ourselves as characters and spectators in their plays.[11]

But if critical practice has too often avoided theatric distanciation and indulged itself as an 'invisible guest' of the dramatic text, re-fetishising and repeating the plays' representations of women as 'truthful' expressions of our culture, participating in a spectator sport of sorts, we should notice that the plays themselves ask us to do this. They often focus our attention as spectators on the physical conditions of a woman's body as part of how a scene of suffering is enacted. For example, Anne Frankford, caught in her infidelity by her husband in Thomas Heywood's *A Woman Killed with Kindness* (1607), desires first insensibility, then an unmarked body at her death, as she says:

> I would I had no tongue, no ears, no eyes,
> No apprehension, no capacity.
> When do you spurn me like a dog? When tread me
> Under your feet? When drag me by the hair?
> Though I deserve a thousand thousand fold
> More than you can inflict, yet, once my husband,
> For womanhood – to which I am a shame,
> Though once an ornament – even for His sake
> That hath redeemed our souls, mark not my face
> Nor hack me with your sword, but let me go
> Perfect and undeformed to my tomb.[12]

Expressing a like desire for the 'perfect' female death when he explains his decision to strangle Desdemona, Othello (1604) says:

> Yet I'll not shed her blood,
> Nor scar that whiter skin of hers than snow,
> And smooth as monumental alabaster . . .
> Be thus when thou art dead, and I will kill thee,
> And love thee after.[13]

Similarly wishing to appear in death 'perfect and undeformed', Webster's 'alabaster' statue, the Duchess of Malfi (1613), when she 'would fain put off my last woman's fault',[14] asks of Bosola: 'Dispose my breath how please you, but my body / Bestow upon my women' (IV, ii, 228–9) so that when 'laid out', her brothers 'then may feed in quiet' (IV, ii, 236–7). The attention paid to the condition of the fetishised female body is curious here. The construction of a 'visual pleasure' much like that which Mulvey isolated in 1950s Hollywood movies would seem to be operating, even though, generally, in these plays women's actual bodies are perceived by the male characters through the conventional prism of courtly love and revenge. Part of each play's dramatic action reveals women's physicality and shows how they fall from their idealised positions into lustful ones.

Only when dead do these heroines recover their original 'perfect' and 'undeformed' condition in the male characters' minds. How can their vital bodies – and when these lines are spoken in each play the woman is still alive – signify this imagining?

Are their bodies 'real'? When Leontes, in *The Winter's Tale* (1611), is 'mocked with art' of the dead,[15] and when he moves to kiss the statuesque Hermione, Paulina stops him with:

> The ruddiness upon her lip is wet;
> You'll mar it if you kiss it; stain your own
> With oily painting. (V, iii, 81–3)[16]

Kissing the oily poisoned paint on the Lady's dead lips kills the Tyrant in *The Second Maiden's Tragedy* (1611), for she is 'winter / And kills with unkind coldness'.[17] The action of this play revolves around her ghostly attempts to reclaim her dead body from the court, where it has been installed as queen, and the Tyrant, she complains, 'folds me with his arms and often sets / A sinful kiss upon my senseless lips' (IV, iv, 71–2). These women's 'ornamental' physical role in men's lives is emphasised by their imagistic appearances. The result is that they 'live' in a strange ontological space, both inside and outside of their dramatic worlds, alive, as artifice, *and* as dead things.[18] Their essence, defined as their sexual honour, is comprised of how they are seen and the uses to which those perceptions can be put.

Along with these 'cold' and 'perfect' portrayals of 'ornamental' heroines, we should note scenes like Tamyra's torture in Chapman's *Bussy D'Ambois* (1607), which focus on the production of those perceptions. Montsurry will monstrously 'write in wounds, my wrong's fit characters' on his wife's body.[19] Tamyra says first that he breaks 'all the bounds / Of manhood, noblesse, and religion' (V, i, 119–20) and then pleads 'Oh, kill me, kill me! / Dear husband, be not crueler than death' (V, i, 127). This violation of her body renders them both 'images' of horror for the other – he of 'all tyranny', she of 'adultery' (V, i, 131–2) – because he literally inscribes or sculpts her body. Doubling this dramatic action, Tamyra then writes with *her* wounds to her lover, revealing and hoping to conceal, or save, him with her bloody 'characters'. Less ambiguously drawn, Lavinia becomes an extraordinary image of violated, inscribed and inscribing chastity in *Titus Andronicus* (1592?). Wishing to be dead rather than be seen after her rape and mutilation, she becomes the praiseworthy emblem of shame, sorrow and revenge, haunting the play even before her death. Both of these women's bodies reveal in their mutilations their presence as 'alphabets'[20] in a patriarchal script. Written on by violence, they write and are read.

In all these plays the persistent image of an idealised, cold, chaste, often dead, female body is placed in juxtaposition to that same body's fleshy failures, whether or not the inhabitant is sexually guilty. The transformation of feminine physicality into the chaste realm of the imaginary seems to motivate the action of a great number of plays for at least twenty years, from roughly 1590 to 1615. Again, what is curious is the attention given to the desire to 'go perfect and undeformed to my tomb', to quote Anne Frankford once more, along with her subsequent declaration that 'to redeem my honor / I would have this hand cut off, these breasts seared' (xiii, 134–5). Deadly perfection is juxtaposed to honourable mutilation in this play as though it makes sense, and numerous variations on this binary opposition of perfection and mutilation, or more generally the imagistic with the physical, occur, in plays as different as *The Duchess of Malfi* and *Titus Andronicus*.[21] How do we 'rescue' these plays from 'banality', as Jean Howard puts it, and account for the persistence of these visions in the drama? If the staged transformation of the 'real' flesh to the imagistic mimes on a metadramatic level the process of (re)fetishising or understanding which the (male) spectator undergoes – converting what is seen into what is imagined, both characters and spectators demonstrating what Eliot called 'the will to see things as they are not' – what, or whose, social construct is being duplicated? Does the way in which these female characters are visualised 'block the process that brings thought into a dialectical relationship with history' (to recall Mulvey's formulations)?

The first part of an answer to these questions is the recognition, much as we would like it otherwise, that female characters in this period give us little evidence of being physically in their bodies as the males are. Their expressions of desire, of will, of being, their explanations for their actions, rarely add up to the complicated declarations of interiority common to male characters by the 1590s.[22] If given to reflection at all, female characters tend to be puzzled about why they are acting as they are. Frequently, their sense of identity, their ontological status, is at issue – usually shortly before the scenes of suffering cited above. Anne Frankford's and Desdemona's confusions, Malfi's famous statements, Tamyra's self-justifications and Lavinia's attempts to be understood, Hermione's and the Lady's doubled selves, all are commentaries on their status as characters whose subjectivity can be doubted – by themselves, by the male characters, by the audience.[23]

The treatment of women's suffering, then, presents the dramatist with a problem. Presumably, all these dramatists wish the audience to respond in terms of the pathos (bathos?) represented by these women's fates in these scenes of suffering. They must elicit audience empathy with characters who need 'fleshing out' with characters not fully and pathetically developed within the plot. In this context following Elaine Scarry's work on *The Body in Pain* we can argue that the infliction of pain is an attempt by the torturer to project, or inscribe, self-perceptions onto the other, seemingly inert, body of the tortured. In the process of torturing, the body is 'substantiated', becomes as the torturer would perceive it, because it expresses pain. Pain validates perceptions as the victim's body is 'read' and seems to acquire 'all the sturdiness and vibrancy of presence of the natural world'.[24] Tortured women on the stage are substantiated and acquire presence in a 'natural' body if we apply Scarry's formulations, because the male characters and the audience see them hurt. These women assume 'a materiality that is fully and unashamedly involved in the process of domination and resistance which are the inner substance of life', as Francis Barker puts it.[25] In this sense, embodiment demystifies and demythologises these women, and their bodies are thus reinscribed as intelligible social texts.

Scarry's and Barker's explanations of the psychology and sociology of pain get us closer to understanding the 'nature' of the fetish, the desire for deadly perfection, as a projection expressed by violent mutilation, in, for example, Tamyra's and Montsurry's self-inscribing practices. But Scarry also insists that a demonstration of pain endured verifies the existence of the torturer's subjectivity, what she terms 'an obsessive, self-conscious display of agency' (p. 27), and renders the victim an object of desire. Torture verifies self-consciousness in one body and constructs it in another. The tortured body becomes 'a material or verbal artifact' reflecting its objectification as 'nothing' become 'something' (p. 280); the body is finally transformed into 'the structure of a perception' (p. 289) which is 'visibly enacted' (p. 290), in this case, I would argue, on the stage. In fact, Scarry's conclusions here on the product of torture coincide oddly with Nicholas Breton's discussion of rhetorical practices when he describes the consequences of seeing women as images in his 1606 *Praise of Vertuous Ladies and Gentlewomen*:

> Some have a delight to term women by nick-names; as in the door she is an image. But how wise is the man that hath his wits so cozened, to take one thing for another. They be lunatic, or in love, that worship such idols. And this I will say further, if she be an image she is like nothing than a man.[26]

Pain, paint, or ink can mark women's bodies whether they are tortured or framed (in the door) by art. And both Scarry and Breton suggest a 'cozening', a willingness to believe that things are as they are not, 'to take one thing for another', on the part of the 'maker'. 'Nothing' can become 'something' if the perceiver wishes it so.

It is the function of images to mirror their makers. If female characters signify they are perceptual, imagistic or iconic structures of a perception in these plays, Scarry's and Breton's conclusions are useful for understanding these characters' desires for a 'perfect' death in an 'undeformed' body. But while Scarry's formulations reflect on the construction of a 'real' tortured body when it is viewed by spectators, Breton's invokes 'nothing' but masculinity. His glance at the pun 'no thing' (slang for female genitalia) in his comparison of the female image and man also elides their difference. His woman is simultaneously (un)like a man, a signifier of moonlight madness, a verbal artifact. Because these bodies are perceived as potentially 'something' *and* 'nothing', they are 'both sacred and profane, tortured and celebrated in the same gesture',[27] marked both by their physicality in the 'real' world of the play and the desires projected on them by other characters and – if Mulvey's sense that characters and spectators 'see' the same thing is correct – by critics. Visible mutilation is potentially symbolic of the men's fallible and 'profane' perceptions, while a perfect death symbolises men's projection of 'sacred' agency, of self-hood – and the reverse of these symbolic oppositions is also true.

This oscillation of meanings in what is 'sacred' and 'profane', of the ways in which the female body and projected desire can alternate to define a fallible or infallible world, results from their binary opposition in a neo-Platonic world view generally (and loosely) organised on the cognitive level around 'contrarieties'. In effect, what is seen cannot be trusted as a sign of 'the true and the beautiful', a construction which returns us to the fetishised need to turn 'nothing' into 'something'. And depicting this tension between the 'profane' and the 'sacred' inherent in perceptions was the goal of the artist, according to Lucy Gent in her work on the relationship between literature and the visible arts in early modern England: 'The eye has to accept deceptions to record accurately what it sees, just as the eye can only depict an unfallen, purely natural world by recourse to "Nice Art" '.[28]

'Nice Art' was produced by painting, a generic term applied to rhetoric, the visible arts and make-up, and an activity viewed with suspicion. Gent notes that 'image' can be found meaning 'statue' at least up to the 1620s, 'while "counterfeit" is often used instead of "portrait" ' (p. 14). The same collapsing of terms, she suggests, applies to Puttenham's understandings of the uses of rhetorical ornamentation in the *Arte* when he writes that *figures* 'deceive the eare and also the minde, drawing it from plainesse and simplicitie to a certain doublenesse, whereby our talk is the more guilefull and abusing'.[29] Thus women in the plays, once embodied, exist in a fallen state because they are visual or rhetorical images, or both. For example, Hermione and the Lady are transformed into images of 'Nice Art' – by paint in these plays. Hermione's ageing and the Lady's decomposing body, however, remind the audience that these images deceive and are mortal in their imperfection.

As Francis Junius wrote in 1638, in *The Painting of the Ancients*, 'They make us in such an astonishment of wonder to stare upon the limitation of things naturall, as if we saw the true things themselves.'[30] A dramatist's embodying the naturally mortal and perfectly artificial in the female figure replicates artistic and cultural understandings of the nature of 'true things', things which Elaine Scarry and Francis Barker insist link political power with projection, or the 'power of self-description'.[31]

In this sense, representations of women must be fetishised by viewers if self-consciousness, or perception of 'true things', in the spectator is to result, and this process is supported then and now as part of a humanist agenda for documenting emerging subjectivity in a variety of spectators. For example, Roy Strong and Leonard Tennenhouse have recently argued that the same correlation between political power and self-description suggested by Scarry and Barker obtained in Elizabeth's and the Stuarts' courts. Strong details how from 1538 (with Henry VIII's separation from Rome), 'everything that could be construed as an image' shows the effects of being 'hacked to pieces'.[32] These attacks, often inspired by anti-Catholic sentiment and conducted by mobs, were repeated in 1559 and 1560, and resulted in *A Proclamation Against breakying or defacing monuments or antiquities* in 1560, which forbade 'the breaking or defacing of any parcel of any Monument, or tomb, or grave, or other inscription . . . or to break any image of Kings, princes or nobles estates of this realm, or any other' (p. 16). The generalised problem of mutilation of images as an expression of, in this case, religious and political autonomy is also gendered. Queen Elizabeth's own sensitivity to self-description as representing both her 'naturall' body and her political power is documented as late as 1596 by contemporaries, and resulted in commands that a half-dozen face patterns only be used in her formal portraits (p. 11). What is more, these portraits, often displayed in churches, were attacked: Strong writes that 'throughout the reign efforts were made to dispose of the Queen by stabbing, burning, or otherwise destroying her image'.[33] Imagistic perfection is opposed through mutilation.

Strong's explanation here stresses how spectators reacted as though one thing could be taken for another (to paraphrase Breton) in the expression of religious and political desires, if they were acted out as a kind of torture. In *Power on Display* Tennenhouse expands on Strong's findings concerning the queen's self-displays, to explain how scenes of suffering on the stage represent life in the aristocracy. From his point of view, the meanings in the queen's image and body extend to include aristocratic females generally. Before 1603, he argues, 'these representations – perhaps any representation – of the aristocratic female provided the substance of a political iconography which enhanced the power of the Elizabethan state'.[34] After Elizabeth's death, the emphasis shifts to depictions of aristocratic women as sources of social corruption to reflect James's and his court's more ambiguous attitudes about the role of women in aristocratic life: 'The women on the Jacobean stage are tortured, hung, smothered, strangled, stabbed, poisoned or dismembered for one of two reasons: either they are the subject of clandestine desire or else they have become the object of desire which threatens the aristocratic community's self-enclosure' (p. 116). Violence towards them, an act of 'sexual disfigure-ment' (p. 119), he argues, 'subordinate[s] the female body to male authority, for this renews the symbolic power of the sexual body to authorize patriarchy' (p. 120).

Whether Tennenhouse is right or wrong in his conclusions is not of as much importance here as the way in which he sees it: in his construction, the mutilated and fallible female body signifies the infallibility or historical sta-bility of political structures before and after 1603, symbolising shifts in his-torical 'facts' in an aristocracy whose subjectivity is gendered male. Repeating Breton's rhetorical moves in much the same ways as those discussed earlier in this essay, by the end of his argument the woman's mutilated body in scenes of suffering is 'simply the other side of the same cultural coin whose positive image is the generous patron' (p. 120). His refetishised images of femininity (the negative image?) are 'like nothing than a man'.

Tennenhouse is not alone in repeating what we might call the history of sexualised oppositions in the pursuit of 'true things'. Others' arguments extend even farther the meanings of masculine aristocratic life in its expe-rience of women. The sexual body authorising patriarchy *and* the positive image of the generous patron is, according to Jonathan Goldberg and David Bergeron, James I, who displayed himself as *Parens Patriae*. Both Goldberg and Bergeron analyse the Stuarts' formal family portraits and find that these portraits, like Elizabeth's, form a political iconography, which 'mirror[s] the language of domestic life converted to state use'.[35] Bergeron notes that this formulation, which created a spectacle of the family, presupposed a limited – but modern – understanding of 'privacy' and reflected James's desires for a 'retired' life style as well as his defini-tion of a king as 'one set on a stage, whose smallest action and gestures, all the people gazinglie doe beholde'.[36] James's representations of a 'public' and 'private' patriarchy reflected contemporary understandings of the family as one which 'functioned . . . to reproduce society' in its every gesture.[37] James's representation of his authority as a 'private' man open to the 'public' gaze is perhaps not so different from Elizabeth's displays of her invisible virginity, or her own sense that she was 'on stage' from this point of view;[38] both become 'public figures that create the private as that which is displayed but cannot be seen'.[39] The 'private' becomes the object of intense scrutiny, the site of a spectator's voyeuristic 'pleasure' in what is imagined as seen.

Goldberg and Bergeron see the privatised and politicised spectacle of the family in an aristocratic medium, just as Tennenhouse saw a shift in the dramatic treatment of women in a change of monarchs. Tennenhouse, in particular, has been widely criticised for doing so, since these studies of the monarchs' imagistic bodies are complemented by other equally compelling historical and political studies suggesting a shift in English sensibilities in how 'true things' are seen, especially in relation to public and private representations of the self and the family. The dramatic, and necessarily critical, paradox I have been describing which juxtaposes the 'sacred', deadly, idealised body with a 'profane', mutilated, natural one in all of its transformations, reflects a change taking place in the social sphere, the other spectators suggest, a change in which punishment for sexual crimes becomes privatised at the same time that women's lives are redefined as domestic. Those spectators, in this case historians, supply a 'new' opposition for the plays' viewers, creating scenarios in which the 'facts' of history seem juxtaposed to dramatic representations. Wife-beating, in the home, rather than 'hacking to pieces' in a public display, seems to have been the more usual remedy for cuckoldry, according to these writers.

For instance, Susan Amussen's recent study of defamation cases registered between 1590 and 1660 in Norfolk supports the literary critics' conflation of the sexualised body with the political one, but she relocates that body in the bourgeoisie. She documents in *An Ordered Society* how non-aristocratic women's increasing sensitivity to attacks on their reputations was in a direct correlation to changes in their social roles in the community caused by changes in the structure of cottage industries and agricultural practices.[40] As women's lives became more circumscribed by their domestic roles as wives and mothers, their 'honesty was determined and judged by their sexual behavior; men's honesty was judged in a wide variety of contexts with their neighbors, and bore a closer relation to our notion of honesty as "truthful". Reputation was a gendered concept in early modern England.'[41] Amussen emphasises that women's reputations were constructed out of communal perceptions of their behaviour, and that both were contested in the courts and in the women's communities.

Amussen's sense that the domestic worth of non-aristocratic women's lives came to be measured by their perceived sexual purity is supported by other studies focusing on the rise of the 'middling sort' during this period, which reveal this class's conflation of moral values with material ones. What David Underdown terms a 'preoccupation with social discipline' led to a flurry of bills in Parliament aimed at managing the unruly: 'In the sessions of 1601 1604, and 1606, for example, twenty-five bills for the regulating of alehouses were introduced (in no other three consecutive sessions between 1576 and 1629 were there anything like half as many), and there was a similar increase in the number of bills to enforce sabbath observance.'[42] But if, in what sounds like a parallel to our own times, the control of the subordinate classes became more and more a matter of public legislation and 'management', a term applied to the gentry's attitudes by Fletcher and Stevenson,[43] women's sexual transgressions, while described as an attack on property, 'a form of theft as well as a consumer of goods, a waster of bodies, and a destroyer of reputations' by one Puritan reformer,[44] were hardly addressed in the Parliament. A bill in the 1601 Parliament to strip property from adulterers met with no success. According to Richard Greaves, 'the episode reflects the unwillingness of the propertied classes to sanction severe punishment for a moral offense that was enmeshed in ecclesiastical jurisdiction. White sheets, public acknowledgements, and even excommunication were safe enough to trust to church courts: life and property were not' (p. 236).

And these were the ecclesiastical punishments for adultery, employed rarely, since most offences, unless they were repeated, never reached the church courts. Even if, as Fletcher and Stevenson report, 'the assertive, quarrelsome, scolding, extravagant or immodest woman was perceived as a threat to the social order', the preferred corrective was 'supervision at home, and, if necessary, . . . intervention and correction by the community in which she lived' (p. 32, my emphasis) in rituals such as the skimmington.[45] In their sentence structure, Fletcher and Stevenson seem to conflate the quarrelsome and garrulous woman with the 'immodest' one, collapsing distinctions we should not be so quick to repeat, perhaps; but their study suggests that, already defined by her sexual reputation and domesticity, an adulterous woman was usually punished, not by extravagant mutilations and death, but by enclosing her at home and making explicit her vulnerability to others' perceptions of her behaviour.[46]

These historians' assertions that women's private lives were marked by visualised and visible social enclosures, especially in the case of sexual offences, correspond with Pieter Spierenburg's findings in The Spectacle of Suffering, which document 'the long term process of hiding the physical and visible aspects of punishment' in the Low Countries and England.[47] Between 1550 and 1650, he argues, physical mutilation as a 'sign' of punishment (frequently used by the Tudors) slowly disappeared, because the public was revolted by the resulting disability of the punished, who then could not maintain themselves (p. 77). Public scaffolds appeared as 'concretely visible' signs of a government's appropriation of the power to punish in the early seventeenth century (p. 201), but adulterers rarely appeared there (p. 121).[48] Spierenburg explicitly links this slow transformation of punishment for sexual and social transgressions to ideas related to the emergence of a 'modern' subjectivity and an enclosed 'private' life:

> Aspects of human existence such as violence, sexuality, death, bodily functions generally came to be hidden behind the scenes of family life. The 'area behind these scenes' was not a space which had always been there and simply needed to be 'filled up'. It developed along with the hiding process

itself and the domesticated nuclear family [by the eighteenth century] became one such enclosed space. (p. 97)

'Official' punishment could occur in the Fleet, but even that was a matter of class (or family) and increasingly more circumspect in its applications.[49] Queen Elizabeth jailed and heavily fined the alderman involved in the imprisonment and whipping of two gentlewomen for adultery and prostitution, for example.[50] These historians would argue that punishment for sexual transgressions as well as reputation was a gendered concept irrevocably tied to class identity in early modern England, their studies verifying that configurations of power, violence, punishment and social change were engaged in a process of 'hiding' the 'realities' of women's lives.

While these spectators' histories would seem to be in counterpoint to literary spectators' interpretations in their accounts of what 'really' was happening in early modern England, we should notice that women function in both as part of an ideology of representation. Functioning as the other half of the binary in a male–female social construction, women's presence in the text validates the critical perceptions of them. From this point of view, the plays and the studies of them and their culture support Michel Foucault's contention that 'what is peculiar to modern societies, in fact, is not that they consigned sex to a shadow existence, but that they dedicated themselves to speaking of it *ad infinitum*, while exploiting it as *the* secret.'[51] The 'fact' of feminine sexuality in the plays and in the academic studies is submerged in social structures which are 'uncovered' and then transformed into talk about sexuality. 'Nothing' is still transformed into 'something'. Woman as a sign of visual pleasure functions to allow for the makings of 'Renaissance' ideologies of meanings.

Perhaps women's sexual misbehaviour had become something of a family matter for the bourgeoisie and aristocrats by the time the plays displaying their punishment began to be produced. But what social changes had rendered private, the theatric space publicised. As female sexual miscreants were less and less physically marked by the legal system – and less and less seen if they were punished at home – the theatre created their mutilated and idealised images for public consumption, and played out the contradictions inherent in a system comprised of gendered concepts of order. Thus on the stage the appearance of feminine fidelity, of honest reputation, is invariably the male protagonist's chief concern, and punishments are enacted 'privately', in homes, often in 'closets' or bedrooms. Men's power to punish is made visible by their actions, and is rarely questioned, demonstrating the power of the patriarchy to construct the 'realities' of women's lives. Still, the patriarchy's articulations of its political power in this period must be rendered invisible, internalised as moral codes, to be 'perfect'. Scenes of sexualised suffering depict this desire.

It is a good story, but the female images in these scenes require fetishising to achieve significance inside of oscillating binary oppositions. As 'signs' they are 'nothing', but they 'legitimate and constitute social support for an ideological construction of women as objects of *evaluation* in terms of socially *visible* criteria.'[52] As images, as artistic constructions meant to convey perceptual structures of meaning, their scenes of suffering can signify the precariousness of those constructions, the desire for certain kinds of social order rather than its achievement. As Stephen Greenblatt so emphatically put it, *'power over sexuality produces inwardness'* in characters, in critics.[53] But the cost, the vision of a mutilated 'natural' feminine body, should make the social, political and aesthetic failures of such ideologies apparent.

NOTES

1. Jonathan Goldberg, *James I and the Politics of Literature: Jonson, Shakespeare, Donne and their contemporaries* (Baltimore: Johns Hopkins University Press, 1983), p. 158.
2. T.S. Eliot, *Elizabethan Essays* (London: Faber and Faber, 1934) pp. 40–1.
3. Contexts determine whether Goldberg and Eliot use 'see' to mean the visual experience, understanding, or both. The *OED* shows that both meanings were interchangeable as early as 1200, and I am interested in when these critics intend both meanings, as Shakespeare did in *Lear*, for example.
4. E. Ann Kaplan uses this phrase in *Woman and Film: Both sides of the camera* (New York: Methuen, 1983), and discusses how the camera creates the conditions for fetishising an object (p. 30ff.). Annette Kuhn, in *Women's Pictures: Feminism and the cinema* (London: Routledge & Kegan Paul, 1982), suggests that if the spectator is imagined a 'gendered object', 'masculine subjectivity [is] the only subjectivity available' (p. 63) and the film, 'as a condition of being meaningful, must in effect defeminize the female spectator' (p. 64).
5. My intention here is not to exclude performance criticism of any kind from this formulation, but rather to encourage more use of it in conventional 'literary' studies for reasons discussed in the text; emphasis on a dramatic text more than its performance may account for a persistent point of view in the works considered in this essay.
6. Laura Mulvey, *Visual and Other Pleasures* (Bloomington: Indiana University Press, 1989), pp. 25, 26. I quote from Mulvey's controversial and influential essay, 'Visual pleasure and narrative cinema', which is reprinted in this book but was first published in 1975 in *Screen*.
7. Richard Levin, 'Women in the Renaissance theatre audience', *Shakespeare Quarterly*, 40 (1989), pp. 165–74, has culled many of the available dramatic sources, concluding that since women were in the audience, 'it is therefore not unreasonable to look . . . for sympathetic treatments of the nature of women and of woman's side in conflicts between the sexes' (p. 174). The nature of those treatments is what is in question. Mary Sidney, the Countess of Pembroke, and Elizabeth Cary are just two examples of women writing during this period whose dramatic work, until recently, received little critical attention.

8. Kuhn, *Women's Pictures*, p. 80.
9. This essay was published in *Discourse* in 1985 and *History Workshop Journal* in 1987, and then anthologised in the collection cited above.
10. Jean E. Howard, 'The new historicism in Renaissance studies', in Arthur F. Kinney and Don S. Collins, eds., *Renaissance Historicism* (Amherst: Massachusetts University Press, 1987), p. 33. Recently, in a discussion of feminist readings of the period, Lisa Jardine argued that 'what we each subsequently chose to read out of the library texts that we considered depended rather strictly on this initial "positioning" of our reading attention. This is only one example of the pressure on the textual critic to embrace the fiction that there exists a reliable body of social and cultural historical "fact," to be "tested" somehow against the "fiction" of the literary representation. It ignores the fact (as the social historian frequently does) that in practice social historians' evidence on which these studies draw – evidence concerning women's "independence," "assertiveness," and so forth – is as much in need of scrutiny and deconstruction as is the literary critic's' ('Cultural confusion and Shakespeare's learned heroines: "These are old paradoxes" ', *Shakespeare Quarterly*, **38** (1987), p. 4). My argument begins such a 'scrutiny and deconstruction' in relation to one textual convention, I think, but the fuller treatment of the sources Jardine indicates as necessary (and I agree) is beyond the scope of this essay.
11. Bertolt Brecht's remarks in 'A short organum for the theatre', *Brecht on Theatre*, ed. and trans. John Willett (New York: Hill and Wang, 1964) influence my argument here, particularly his assertions in numbers 36 and 37: '[W]e must drop our habit of taking the different social structures of past periods, then stripping them of everything that makes them different. . . . And if we play works dealing with our own time as though they were historical, then perhaps the circumstances under which [the spectator] himself acts will strike him as equally odd; and this is where the critical attitude begins' (p. 190). Margot Heinemann, in 'How Brecht read Shakespeare', in Jonathan Dollimore and Alan Sinfield, eds., *Political Shakespeare: New essays in cultural materialism* (Ithaca, N.Y.: Cornell University Press, 1985), pp. 202–30, has analysed Brecht's ideas on historicity in relation to Shakespeare specifically. Kathleen McLuskie, in 'The patriarchal bard: feminist criticsm and Shakespeare: *King Lear* and *Measure for Measure*', also in *Political Shakespeare*, has written an influential essay showing how feminist readings can be 'co-opted' by 'the domination of the patriarchal bard' (p. 106). For broader discussions of the politics of reading Renaissance drama, see Walter Cohen's 'Political criticism of Shakespeare', and Don E. Wayne's 'Power, politics, and the Shakespearean text: recent criticism in England and the United States'. Both essays are published in Jean E. Howard and Marion F. O'Connor, eds., *Shakespeare Reproduced: The text in history and ideology* (New York: Methuen, 1987), pp. 18–46 and 47–67 respectively. For an analysis of historical methodologies since the Greeks and their purposes, see Joel Fineman's "The history of the anecdote: fiction and fiction', in H. Aram Veeser, ed., *The New Historicism* (New York: Routledge, 1989), pp. 49–76.
12. Thomas Heywood, *A Woman Killed with Kindness*, *Drama of the English Renaissance II: The Stuart period*, eds. Russell A. Fraser and Norman Rabkin (New York: Macmillan 1976), xiii, 90–100.
13. William Shakespeare, *Othello*, *The Complete Signet Classic Shakespeare*, ed. Sylvan Barnet (New York: Harcourt Brace Jovanovich, 1972), V, v, 3–5, 18–19.

14. John Webster, *The Duchess of Malfi, Drama of the English Renaissance II: The Stuart Period*, eds. Russell A. Fraser and Norman Rabkin (New York: Macmillan, 1976). I, i, 458; IV, ii, 226.
15. William Shakespeare, *The Winter's Tale, The Complete Signet Classic Shakespeare*, ed. Sylvan Barnet (New York: Harcourt Brace Jovanovich, 1972), V, ii, 68.
16. The similarities between Hermione in *The Winter's Tale* and the Lady in *The Second Maiden's Tragedy* lead me to include *Winter's Tale* in this discussion; technically, *Winter's Tale* is a tragi-comedy, of course, but I would argue it is more tragic than comic in its treatment of Hermione.
17. Thomas Middleton, *The Second Maiden's Tragedy*, ed. Anne Lancashire (Baltimore: Johns Hopkins University Press, 1978), V, ii, 119.
18. See also Valerie Traub's essay, 'Jewels, statues, and corpses: containment of female erotic power', *Shakespeare Studies,* **XX** (1988), pp. 215–38, which argues that Shakespeare's transformation of female characters into 'dead' sexual objects in *Hamlet, Othello* and *Winter's Tale* reveals much about Shakespeare's development as an artist.
19. George Chapman, *Bussy D'Ambois, Drama of the English Renaissance II: The Stuart period*, eds. Russell A. Fraser and Norman Rabkin (New York: Macmillan, 1976), V, i, 125.
20. William Shakespeare, *Titus Andronicus, The Complete Signet Classic Shakespeare*, ed. Sylvan Barnet (New York: Harcourt Brace Jovanovich, 1972), III, ii, 44.
21. Christine Brooke-Rose, in her analysis of 'Woman as a semiotic object', in Susan Rubin Suleiman, ed., *The Female Body in Western Culture* (Cambridge, Mass.: Harvard University Press, 1986) suggests that oppositions like this are 'purposely confusing values and signs': 'The whole problem is that the confusion is inherent to the system, allowing the necessary circulation of women as "essential values" to degenerate into a negotiated exchange of women as value-objects, in other words, tokens, signs' (p. 308). See also Gayle Rubin's influential essay, 'The traffic in women: notes on the "political economy" of sex', in Rayna R. Reiter, ed., *Toward an Anthropology of Women* (New York: Monthly Review Press, 1975), pp. 157–210, for an anthropological and Marxist, rather than linguistic, analysis of the same phenomena. Jane Tibbetts Schulenberg discusses similar attitudes towards women's bodies which were at work in medieval Europe, in 'The heroics of virginity: brides of Christ and sacrificial mutilation', in Mary Beth Rose, ed., *Women in the Middle Ages and the Renaissance* (Syracuse: Syracuse University Press, 1986), pp. 29–72.
    Binary thinking collapses, even as it creates, categories. Early modern English uses of binary oppositions, or 'contrarieties', have been analysed by Walter Ong in *Ramus, Method, and the Decay of Dialogue* (Cambridge, Mass.: Harvard University Press, 1958), Charles O. McDonald in *The Rhetoric of Tragedy* (Amherst: Massachusetts University Press, 1966) and Joel Altman in *The Tudor Play of Mind: Rhetorical inquiry and the development of Elizabethan drama* (Berkeley, Calif.: California University Press, 1978), to name a few, as habits of mind influenced by Ramist logic and Sophist philosophy. Recently, Stuart Clark, in 'Inversion, misrule, and the meaning of witchcraft', *Past and Present,* **87** (1980), pp. 98–127, has demonstrated the period's psychological and political investment in such systems of thought: he argues that 'what ever Christian men might do or say presupposed the relation of contrariety' (p. 110).
22. Madelon (Gohlke) Sprengnether, in ' "All that is spoke is marred": Language and Consciousness in *Othello,*' *Women's Studies,* 9 (1982), pp. 157–176, argues this point.

23. Catherine Belsey, in *The Subject of Tragedy: Identity and difference in Renaissance drama* (London: Methuen, 1985), writes that 'in the family, as in the state, women had no single, unified, fixed position from which to speak' (p. 160).

24. Elaine Scarry, *The Body in Pain: The making and unmaking of the world* (New York: Oxford University Press, 1985), p. 280.

25. Francis Barker, *The Tremulous Private Body: Essays on subjection* (London: Methuen, 1984), p. 25.

26. Nicholas Breton, *Praise of Virtuous Ladies and Gentlewomen* (London, 1606). ed. Sir Egerton Brydges (Kent: Press of Lee Priory by Johnson and Warwick, 1815), p. 19.

27. Barker, *Tremulous Private Body*, p. 24.

28. Lucy Gent, *Picture and Poetry 1560–1620: Relations between literature and the visual arts in the English Renaissance* (Leamington Spa: James Hall, 1981), p. 54.

29. George Puttenham, *The Arts of English Poesie*, eds. Gladys Doidge Willcock and Alice Walker (Cambridge: Cambridge University Press, 1936; reprinted 1970), p. 154; as reprinted in Gent, p. 49.

30. As quoted in Gent, p. 61.

31. Scarry, *Body in Pain*, p. 279. In an influential essay, Louis A. Montrose has argued this linkage of power with projection by analysing Elizabeth's imaginative presence in *Midsummer Night's Dream*, in 'A Midsummer Night's Dream and the shaping fantasies of Elizabethan culture: gender, power, form', in Margaret W. Ferguson, Maureen Quilligan, and Nancy J. Vickers, eds., *Rewriting the Renaissance: The Discourses of Sexual Differences in Early Modern Europe* (Chicago: University of Chicago Press, 1986), pp. 65–87.

32. Roy Strong, *The Elizabethan Image: Painting in England 1540–1562* (London: Tate Gallery, 1969), p. 14.

33. As quoted in Leonard Tennenhouse's *Power on Display: The politics of Shakespeare's genres* (New York: Methuen, 1986), p. 104.

34. Tennenhouse, *Power on Display*, p. 112.

35. Goldberg, *James I*, p. 89.

36. David Bergeron, *Shakespeare's Romances and the Royal Family* (Lawrence: Kansas University Press, 1985), p. 43. Bergeron quotes from the *Basilikon Doron*, p. 163.

37. Goldberg, *James I*, p. 87.

38. Elizabeth said in reference to Mary, Queen of Scots, 'Wee princes, I tell you are set on stages, in the sight and view of al[l] the world duly obserued, the eyes of many behold our actions, a spott is sone spied in our garments, a blemish quickly noted in our doings' (as quoted in Allison Heisch's 'Queen Elizabeth I: parliamentary rhetoric and the exercise of power,' *Signs*, 1 (1975), p. 53). For a discussion of how contemporaries viewed Elizabeth, see Carole Levin's 'Power, politics, and sexuality: images of Elizabeth I', in Jean R. Brink, Allison P. Coudert and Maryanne C. Horowitz, eds., *The Politics of Gender in Early Modern Europe*, Sixteenth Century Studies and Essays, 12 (1989), pp. 95–110.

39. Goldberg, *James I* p. 153.

40. Merry Wiesner, 'Women's defense of their public role', in Mary Beth Rose, ed. *Women in the Middle Ages and the Renaissance* (Syracuse: Syracuse University Press, 1986), pp. 1–28, suggests much the same in her study of German women's written responses to attacks on their 'public' lives; she shows how restrictions and redefinitions of what constituted a 'public' role increased during this period.

41. Susan Dwyer Amussen, *An Ordered Society: Gender and class in early modern England* (Oxford: Basil Blackwell, 1988), pp. 103–4.
42. David Underdown, *Revel, Riot and Rebellion: Popular politics and culture in England 1603–1660* (Oxford: Clarendon Press, 1985), p. 48.
43. Anthony Fletcher and John Stevenson, eds., 'Introduction', *Order and Disorder in Early Modern England* (Cambridge: Cambridge University Press, 1985), p. 11.
44. As quoted in Richard Greaves, *Society and Religion in Elizabethan England* (Minneapolis: Minnesota University Press, 1981), p. 230.
45. Recent studies of the unruly woman, primarily the talkative one, in the drama have been written by Jean Howard, 'Crossdressing, the theatre, and gender struggle in early modern England', *Shakespeare Quarterly*, 39 (1988), pp. 418–40, by Karen Newman, 'Portia's ring: unruly women and structures of exchange in *The Merchant of Venice*', *Shakespeare Quarterly*, 38 (1987), pp. 19–33; by Mary Beth Rose, 'Women in men's clothing: apparel and social stability in *The Roaring Girl*', in Kinney and Collins, eds., *Renaissance Historicism*, pp. 233–47, and by David Underdown, 'The taming of the scold: the enforcement of patriarchal authority in early modern England,' in Fletcher and Stevenson, *Order and Disorder in Early Modern England*, pp. 116–36.
46. Peter Stallybrass analyses this vulnerability in relation to *Othello* in 'Patriarchal Territories: The Body Enclosed', *Rewriting the Renaissance: The Discourses of Sexual Difference in Early Modern Europe*, pp. 123–142. His arguments have influenced mine, especially his assertion that 'there can be no simple opposition between language and body because the body maps out the cultural terrain and is in turn mapped out by it' (p. 138).
47. Pieter Spierenburg, *The Spectacle of Suffering: Executions and the evolution of repression from a preindustrial metropolis to the European experience* (Cambridge: Cambridge University Press, 1984), p. 45. Spierenburg applies Foucault's methodology in *Discipline and Punish* to study historical records in the Netherlands and England. For a discussion of executions of (mostly) men and their impact on Marlowe's plays, see Karen Cunningham's 'Renaissance execution and Marlovian elocution: the drama of death', *PMLA*, 105 (1990), pp. 209–22.
48. Perhaps Marston's *The Insatiate Countess* needs to read as a play positioning itself on this shift of sensibilities; a play rarely read, produced or taught, it is the only play I am aware of that has the aristocratic heroine killed on the 'tragic scaffold' for her sexual transgressions.
49. Spierenburg discusses the shift or relocation of sites for punishment as one in which the severity of the crime corresponded to the severity of the punishment, both of which determined whether the punishment was applied 'inside' and 'privately' or 'outside', 'publicly' (p. 67, my quotation marks).
50. Greaves, *Society and Religion*, p. 235.
51. Michel Foucault, *The History of Sexuality*, vol. 1, trans. Robert Hurley (New York: Pantheon, 1978), p. 35.
52. Kuhn, *Women's Pictures*, p. 6, my emphasis.
53. Stephen Greenblatt, *Renaissance Self-Fashioning: From More to Shakespeare* (Chicago: University of Chicago Press, 1980), p. 125, his emphasis.

I am grateful to the National Endowment of the Humanities and the Folger Shakespeare Library for funding which allowed me to attend the 1988 Summer Institute there, discuss some of the ideas for this essay with other participants; and do the research for it.

PART THREE

English Renaissance Culture

—8—

The World Turned Upside Down: Inversion, Gender and the State

Peter Stallybrass

I

In this essay, I attempt like Polonius 'by indirections [to] find directions out'. Rather than proceeding from a definition of materialist feminism, I try to explore how particular languages of class and gender were formed in the Renaissance and the ways in which class and gender were articulated in relation to each other. The essay, indeed, is an attempt to work my way out of an assumption that I had taken for granted: that oppressed groups, oppressed on the grounds of class, gender, ethnicity or race, 'naturally' had common interests. My assumption developed out of one way of reading Marx. On this reading, class and gender positions, for instance, were determined by the subject's relation to the means of production and of reproduction. The resistance of subjects to their subjugation, then, depended upon the recognition of where their 'interests' lay. And their interests followed from their position as exploited and oppressed. Politics, in other words, reflected social experience: it depended upon recognising one's interests and acting upon them. Moreover, the interests of the exploited would lead them to unite in political action.

This unification was, I believed, symbolically inscribed in the language of 'the world turned upside down', where inversions of status, gender, age and animal hierarchy often mirrored each other. In this language, status and gender were intertwined, neither being of merely 'secondary' importance. Thus, the language of the world turned upside down seemed to provide a way of understanding what I believed, and still believe, to be our own pressing political concerns: the question of how to articulate political struggles over class, gender and sexuality, ethnicity and race without subsuming one struggle under another. Such a language seemed to imply the 'unity' of oppressed groups. The problem, though, when one turned to Renaissance texts was that such a 'unity' emerged as a precarious alliance, as often honoured in the breach as the observance. Interrogations of class were shaped by attacks upon the supposed gender 'corruptions' of the court, interrogations of gender were formulated against the supposed vices of 'foreigners'. Portia's power is sustained by its ideological opposition to a Jew and a usurer; Shylock's power is mapped out in his attempted control of his daughter; Iago's struggle for power is shaped by the languages of racism and misogyny. This essay is mainly concerned with such moments of political disarticulation. But I do not believe that the conclusions which follow from it are necessarily pessimistic. For such a study suggests, I believe, that political languages, if not free-floating, nevertheless construct both how oppression is imagined and the 'interests' which challenge that oppression. Politics does not reflect social experience; it is itself the struggle to define what counts as experience.[1] In looking at the ways in which political languages articulate and disarticulate the relations between class and gender, we may get some sense, however indirectly, of how our own alliances fail, are re-formed, continue.

II

In 1948, Ernst Curtius published *European Literature and the Latin Middle Ages*, and amongst the topoi which he studied he included a section on 'The world upsidedown'.[2] He traced what he called the 'stringing together of impossibilities' (in Latin, *impossibilia*, in Greek, *adynata*) from the *Carmina Burana* back through Virgil's eighth eclogue to Archilochus writing about the eclipse of the sun on 6 April 648 BC. In the fragment of Archilocus, beasts of the field eat dolphins' food; in Virgil, the wolf flees the sheep, the oak bears golden apples, owls compete with swans, and the shepherd Tityrus becomes Orpheus; in the *Carmina Burana*, 'the ass plays the lute, oxen dance . . . , the Fathers Gregory, Jerome, Augustine, and the Father of Monks, Benedict, are to be found in the alehouse, in court, or in the meat market.'[3] The topoi of the world turned upside down, in other words, constitute a systematic language of inversion. But the very persistence of these topoi has perhaps led us to naturalise and take for granted the relations between one topos and another, as if there were some *inevitable* connection between, for example, inversions of status, inversions of gender, inversions of age and inversions of human and animal.

This sense of a *natural* connection between one inversion and another is encouraged by the way in which, as Curtius noted, the impossibilities are so often 'strung together'. In a Dutch woodcut of the world turned upside down from the sixteenth century, for instance, the very format

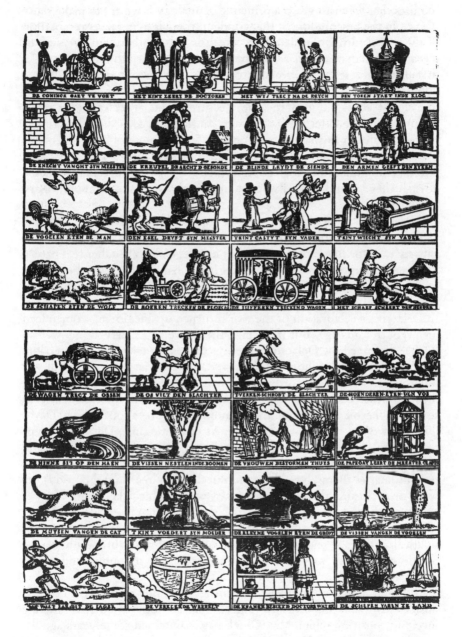

Source: C.F. van Veen, *Dutch Catchpenny Prints: Three Centuries of Pictorial Broadsides for Children* (The Hague: van Hoeve, 1971).

requires that we must grasp a principle of analogy if we are to make sense of it.[4] On the bottom line of the woodcut, there is a literal representation of the world turned upside down, and it is undoubtedly an inversion of hierarchy which characterises all the images. If we turn to the top line, the first picture presents an inversion of status (the servant rides on a horse while the king walks behind); the second, an inversion of age and status (the child teaches old men, the pupil lectures to his professors); the third, an inversion of gender (the wife, with musket and sword, has become a soldier, while her husband sits spinning). The *meaning* of such inversions is not, of course, a given. If they could, indeed, be read as *impossibilia*, farcical and implausible aberrations which reaffirm through antithesis the norm, they could equally be mobilised within a revolutionary iconography.

Delacroix's 'Liberty leading the people at the barricades', painted in 1830, condenses into a single image inversions of status, age and gender. Liberty is a working-class woman, her clothes dishevelled, her feet bare, a Phrygian cap upon her head, a musket in her hand, who leads the revolution. Beside her is a young boy, a pistol in each hand, and behind them, their followers – adult males, whether bourgeois citizens or sans-culottes. In Delacroix's celebration of the world turned upside down, women lead men, youth leads age. But if we take the figure of Liberty alone, we can further examine how Delacroix employs the festive language of inversion. For, as Maurice Agulhon has observed, Liberty is a woman with her mouth open – in other words, she is an affirmative version of that figure through which classical iconography allegorised anarchy.[5] She can also be read as a heroic version of the demonised figure about which David Underdown has written – the scold.[6] At the same time, Delacroix's representation of Liberty rewrites the relation between public (male) and private (female) space. If the barricades were in reality erected by the revolutionaries themselves, iconographically they recall (and parody) the fence or enclosure, the *hortus conclusus*, within which the Virgin Mary is so often depicted. In Delacroix's painting, as so often in enclosure riots in early modern England, the tearing down of boundaries, the overthrow of political and legal enclosure, is figured by the transformation of the female body from private and passive enclosure to public and active transgressor.[7]

My point here is not to insist that the iconography of the world turned upside down was intrinsically radical. Such a view would itself merely invert the position which Max Gluckman maintained some years ago – a position which David Underdown sums up and supports when he writes: 'on the stage, as in carnival, gender inversion temporarily turns the world upside-down – but to reinforce, not subvert, the traditional order.'[8] But I would want to argue against *both* the subversion *and* the containment models of inversion, for in my view they both tend to take the *language* of inversion as a given rather than as a problematic construction. I can perhaps clarify my point by turning to the Dutch woodcut again. For if it is true that the images of inversion can only be understood within a system of analogy, that system is not as cut and dried as I first suggested. I want to look again at the first three pictures on the top line. Now I certainly *do* believe that there is an implicit analogy being made between inversions of status, of age and of gender. But the figuring of that analogy is by no means transparent. For in the first picture, inversion depends not only upon the servant riding a horse and being in front of the king, but also upon the fact that he is literally *higher* than the king. Similarly, in the third picture, the standing position puts the woman in a superior position to the seated man. But in the second picture, it is, on the contrary, the *seated* position which is that of power. The high/low opposition, in other words, can only be understood contextually. We have already moved away from a fixed iconographic hierarchy in which the high would be privileged over the low, the front over the back, the right over the left. The *production* of the system of analogies, then, is not as unproblematic as it first appears.

But perhaps more troubling is the fact that some of these images seem to be confined to the domain of the comically or grotesquely impossible (for example, the ox butchering the butcher, the ass whipping his master, the sheep shearing the shepherd), whereas others are not only possible but even culturally sanctioned. Despite the deliberately repeated framing which implies the equality of the images, the pictures conjure up conflicting discursive frameworks. The second picture, for instance, is iconographically similar to biblical woodcuts depicting Christ preaching in the temple. And that resemblance suggests at least the possibility of rereading the first picture as a version of the *sanctioned* topos: 'the first shall be last, and the last shall be first.' I certainly do not want to press such a reading. But what I do want to argue is that there is a kind of 'discursive unevenness' between the pictures which testifies to a certain resistance in the stringing of them together. To put it another way, the 'naturalness' of these analogues can only be sustained if we temporarily forget the cultural process by which they are put together.

But the extent to which the analogues were themselves a precarious construction is suggested by the ease with which they could be disjoined. The series of analogues which compose the Dutch woodcut were again and again disarticulated in literary narrative, artistic representation and political practice. If, for instance, Delacroix articulates the identity of inversions of status and gender, the Jacobins had previously moved rapidly to undo that identity, replacing the figures of Marianne with that of Hercules. As Lynn Hunt argues, 'the Convention had outlawed all women's clubs at the end of October 1793', because, they claimed, 'women's active participation in politics would lead to "the kinds of disruption and disorder that hysteria can produce" ':

> In the eyes of the Jacobin leadership, women were threatening to take Marianne as a metaphor for their own active participation; in this situation, no female figure, however fierce and radical, could possibly appeal to them. Hercules put the women back into perspective, in their place and relationship of dependency. The monumental male was now the only active figure.[9]

In an engraving entitled 'The people, eater of kings', Hercules is depicted as a sans-culotte, a Phrygian cap upon his head, his trousers rolled up, hair upon his chest; he throws a 'pygmy' king into the fire.[10] But as the male Hercules came to the foreground, women not only ceased to be perceived as allies to the revolution but came to be reinscribed as the potential enemies of civic virtue. Prostitutes, it was claimed, not only corrupted the morality of the *citoyens* but were also the agents of despotism, and they were sentenced to death in 'exemplary numbers'.[11] As Dorinda Outram argues, '[t]o the degree that power in the Old Regime was ascribed to women [and above all to the 'boudoir politics' of Marie-Antoinette], that meant that the discourse of the Revolution was committed to an anti-feminine rhetoric.'[12] There was, of course, nothing new to the analogy between female sexuality and court corruption. And the fact that in the Renaissance it was a staple of republican and proto-republican discourse, as well as of theatrical representation, suggests that we need to be cautious about assuming a *natural* connection between inversions of status and inversions of gender. Yet it was virtually impossible in early modern Europe to conceptualise the redistribution of political power without figuring it in an explicitly gendered language.

What we need to investigate, though, is not the givenness of the language of the world turned upside down, but rather the variety of articulations between different elements within it. In England, for instance, it certainly became a staple of royalist propaganda and satire to represent Puritanism as a political and religious overturning which would subvert the hierarchy of the household. In *Hudibras*, Samuel Butler's satiric attack upon Puritanism published in 1663, we can note the curiously contradictory articulations between Puritan radicalism, popular festivity and sexual inversion. In Part I, Canto 2, the Presbyterian Hudibras and the Independent Ralph confront a crowd of bear-baiters who are *also* portrayed as radical dissenters. Among the bear-baiters is Trulla:

> A bold virago, stout and tall,
> As Joan of France, or English Mall.[13]

Butler's depiction of her as fighting 'more busily, / Than th' Amazonian dame Penthesile' (I, 2, 377–8) is demonstrated in Canto 3, where Trulla overthrows Hudibras, forces him to beg for mercy and exchanges clothes with him (I, 3, 915–28). Here, the festive and the anti-festive are portrayed alike as disorders of the body politic, disorders which are figured in the enforced transvestism of Hudibras.

But in Part II, Canto 2, the relation between the politics of gender and carnival inversion is articulated quite differently. For here the skimmington clearly has no relation to dissent. On the contrary, the 'antique show' (II, 2, 592), with its deafening music of 'horns, and pans, and dogs, and boys, / And kettle drums' (II, 2, 588–9), is now represented as the kind of festivity antithetical to all Puritans. This is, in Butler's construction, not merely because the skimmington is 'ethnique and idolatrous', 'an Antichristian opera, / Much us'd in midnight times of Popery' (II, 2, 761, 769–70)[14] but also because it is directed against the unruly *woman*. Behind a man who dispenses to the crowd grain mixed with excrement rides a man 'mounted on a horned horse', a standard-bearer carrying '[a] petticoat display'd, and rampant', and finally 'the Amazon triumphant' sitting 'face to tail', while her husband is '[a]rm'd with a spindle and distaff' (II, 2, 633, 640, 641, 645). The rough music, in other words, is here an inversion directed *against* an inversion – against the 'greedy women' who fight 'to extend their vast dominion', shifting their sex 'like hares' (II, 2, 699–700, 705). It is the kind of repressive ceremony which Marvell celebrates in 'The Last Instructions to a Painter', where he reports

> news of Pastime, Martial and old:
> A Punishment invented first to awe
> Masculine Wives, transgressing Natures Law.
> Where when the brawny Female disobeys,
> And beats the Husband till for peace he prays:
> No concern'd Jury for him Damage finds,
> Nor partial Justice her Behaviour binds;
> But the just Street does the next House invade,
> Mounting the neighbour Couple on lean Jade.
> The Distaff knocks, the Grains from Kettle fly,
> And Boys and Girls in Troops run houting by.[15]

Festive inversion attacks gender subversion. But it is precisely because of this that Hudibras is offended. For the saints, according to Hudibras, are above all indebted to women. It is they who have supported the revolution, giving up their children's toys to purchase 'swords, carbines, and pistols'; it is they who have raised the defences around London; it is they who 'judge what officers are fit' (II, 2, 780, 803, 814). So Hudibras, in this attack upon popular festivity, is not rejecting inversion as such: rather he is attempting to displace the repressive festivity which Butler himself celebrates.[16]

If Butler attacks radical Protestantism for the power it gives to ordinary women, Cowley suggests that such an inversion is implicit in the historical figuring of nationalism as the triumph of Elizabeth I over the pope. In 'The Character of an Holy-Sister', Cowley jeers:

> She that can sigh and cry, Queen *Elizabeth*,
> Rail at the *Pope*, and scratch out sudden death.
> And for all this can give no reason why,
> This is an holy sister verily.[17]

The implication that there was a connection between the gender inversion of a female monarch and radical Protestantism was not without some substance. Foxe's *Actes and Monumentes*, published in 1563 and chained beside the Bible in churches throughout England, begins with the word 'Constantine', and the initial letter 'C' is a woodcut in the middle of which Elizabeth is seated upon the throne, the sword of justice in one hand, the orb in the other.[18] The top of the 'C' is composed of a cornucopia which includes Tudor roses; the bottom shows the pope, his tiara askew, the broken keys of St Peter in his hand. The triumph of pure religion over papal duplicity is figured as the triumph of female over male. A ballad written 'Upon the Death of Queen Elizabeth' gives a vigorous reinterpretation of this image, and one that draws attention to the problematics of gender:

> I tell ye all both great and small
> And I tell you all truly
> That we have now a very great cause
> For to lament and cry
> O fye, O fye, O fye, O fye, O fye thou cruell death
> For thou hast taken away from us
> Our good Queen Elizabeth
>
> It might have taken other folkes
> That better might have been mist
> And let us alone with our good Queene
> That lov'd not a Popish Priest
> She ruld this Nation by her selfe
> And was beholden to no man
> O shee bore the Sway, and of all affaires
> And yet she was but a woman . . .
>
> And now if I had Argus eyes
> They were one too few to weep
> For our good Queene Elizabeth
> That here lyes fast asleep
> Asleep she lyes, and so shee must lye
> Untill the day of Doome
> But then shee'l arise and pisse out the Eyes
> Of the proud Pope of Rome.[19]

The ending of the ballad celebrates a grotesque version of the iconography of the woodcut: the triumphant female monarch stamps down or pisses upon the papacy.

Yet it was not only royalists like Butler who feared and derided the political power of women. As with the Convention after the French Revolution, so with many Renaissance republicans, the virtue of the male citizen was insistently contrasted with the supposed 'feminisation' of courtier and monarch. The *relation* between gender and state was thus not a given but the effect of specific political articulations. And there seems to have been a disturbing tendency within republican discourse to slide from a critique of the royal patriarch to a celebration of the patriarchal husband and father. That slide was facilitated by the gendering of corruption, a gendering which is present in the work of Tacitus, to whom republicans turned again and again. In *Germania*, Tacitus contrasts 'the sober, innocent and freedom-loving Germans on the one hand, and the worldly, corrupt and exploitative Italians on the other', a contrast which is already figured as that between male and female.[20]

In Renaissance attacks upon the tyrant, as Rebecca Bushnell has finely shown, tyranny, theatricality and effeminacy were conjoined as the very markers of absolutism.[21] Bushnell notes how Sir Edmund Bolton, in *Nero Caesar*, attacks the tyrant for staging plays which 'properly tended to effemination, or rather were effeminacies self', and how in the *Mirror of Policie* La Perrière reviles the tyrant Sardanapulus as 'a monstrous Hermaphrodite, who was neither true man nor true woman, being in sexe a man, and in heart a woman'.[22] And the attack upon absolutism in the English Revolution was often phrased as an attack upon effeminacy and the rule of women. In 1650, Henry Neville, a republican politician, published *The Commonwealth of Ladies*, in which he attacked the 'natural' corruption of women and satirically represented them as having taken over the reigns of government. 'There was a time in England', he writes, 'when men wore the breeches . . . which brought many grievances and oppressions upon the weaker vessels; for they were constrained to converse only with their homes and closets, and now and then with the Gentleman-usher, or the Footman (when they could catch him) for variety.' But under the weak government of the cavaliers, Neville claims, women had 'voted themselves the supreme authority both at home and abroad'.[23]

Neville's mockery of female rule as antithetical to republican virtue may be compared to Milton's more violent attacks. Along with Norman tyranny, claimed Milton, came 'Vices which effeminate mens minds'.[24] And he asserted that Charles I's slavery to his wife engendered his inability to rule. Charles's reign, Milton argued, exemplified

209

how great mischief and dishonour hath befall'n to Nations under the Government of effeminate and Uxorious Magistrates, who being themselves govern'd and overswaid at home under a Feminine usurpation, cannot but be farr short of spirit and authority without dores, to govern a whole nation'.[25]

Milton, like many other English republicans, drew upon a Protestant rhetoric which, since Luther, had tended to idealise the *gemeiner Mann* (common man) as 'the community's representative and the Reformation's hero', in opposition both to the *gemeine Frau* or prostitute and to the Whore of Babylon, 'holding aloft the Cup of Abominations [and] dressed in the garb of a sixteenth-century prostitute'.[26] (The distance between *gemeiner Mann* and *gemeiner Frau* was further marked by the fact that 'civic prostitutes had to be foreign women, not locals, so that they were literally exotic, outsiders to the commune.')[27]

If Tacitus provided a model of the ideal state as insistently masculine, other classical texts challenged such a myth of origin. One might find in the very foundation of the state the inscription of rebellion. Did not the endlessly repeated story of Rome transmit the tale of a conquering civility which was from the first shadowed by discord and division? Hence the disturbing image of Rome's founding which we find recorded in the fifteenth-century *Libellus de deorum imaginibus*:

> since the Romans claimed that the twin brothers, Romulus and Remus, who founded the city, were the sons of Mars, and since Romulus killed Remus, under the chariot of the god [Mars] they depicted Romulus in the act of killing Remus.[28]

The originary moment of the state is stained with fratricide, when the god of war is turned back upon himself, when son destroys son in male rivalry.

And then there was the myth of the she-wolf that suckled and protected Romulus. How was that to be read? Was it an emblem of the wolf lying down with the lamb, the submission of the savage to the civil? Or was it the inscription of barbarism at the birth of the state? Certainly, the wolf was associated with Mars: in Petrarch's *Africa*, Mars stands on a bloody chariot, 'on this side a wolf, on the other the hoarse Furies with their shrill and mournful cries', and in Chaucer's *The Knight's Tale*, the 'god of armes' appears with a wolf 'biforn him at his feet'.[29] But the wolf which suckles Romulus is insistently gendered. And, as Plutarch observed, 'the Latines doe call with one selfe name shee woulfes *Lupas*, and women that geve their bodyes to all commers.'[30] Did the Roman state, then, emerge from what was most antithetical to it: from a femininity inscribed as bestiality and prostitution, from all that stood over against what the state came to define as civic virtue?

However one reads these myths of origin, they inscribe the possibility of rebellion within the intimacy of domestic bonds. What is implicit in them is that, at best, the state is the balancing of discordant elements, at worst, the formation of internecine strife. Yet the contrast between the two myths is also striking: in the first, the image revolves entirely around the male figures of Mars and his two sons, as if origins, however traumatic and divided, could only be a question of paternity and filiality; in the second, the defenceless child is juxtaposed to a figure of power, fear and comfort – *lupa*, the she-wolf. But if there could be no single, stable point of origin, we can witness the repeated and problematic attempt to articulate the relation between gender and the state.

What I want to suggest is that, despite the iconography of the world turned upside down, in which inversions of status mirrored inversions of gender, inversions of gender mirrored inversions of the 'natural hierarchy', and so on, in extended fictions of the sixteenth and seventeenth centuries, whether poetic or dramatic, such mirrorings were usually only *local*. There are, of course, exceptions like Richard Brome's *The Antipodes*, but such exceptions only serve to highlight the more frequent structural pattern whereby an inversion in one sphere is legitimated as a critique of an inversion in another sphere. We have already noted this in the tendency for republicans to legitimate their attack upon the state's hierarchy by representing the state as itself an inverted world, a world of 'boudoir politics' controlled by women. Again and again, we can witness how one inversion is played off against another, how one 'low' group defends itself either by asserting its claims to uphold hierarchical values or by demonising another low group. Allon White and I have called this latter process one of *displaced abjection* and we have argued that, in the inversions of carnival, abuse is often directed against weaker, not stronger, social groups – against women, ethnic and religious minorities, and animals (notably animals which are feminised, like cats, or which are associated with low social groups, like pigs).[31] The riots of apprentices in sixteenth-century London, for instance, were frequently directed against foreigners and against brothels.

It is one such riot, on the Evil May Day of 1517, which is figured in the opening scenes of *Sir Thomas More*, a collaborative play probably written in the early to mid-1590s, another period of apprentice riots.[32] In June 1592, for instance, there was a 'tumult' in Southwark, apparently arising out of resentment against foreign artisans, and the Privy Council, 'apprehensive of further outbreaks, ordered that all servants be kept indoors on Midsummer Eve and Midsummer Night, and that no play nor public pastimes be allowed which might "draw together the baser sort of people" '.[3] In *Sir Thomas More*, though, the foreigners are no longer artisans; on the contrary, they appear as courtiers who are above the law and can treat the native Londoners as they please.

The opening stage direction of the play reads: 'Enter, at one end, John

Lincolne, with [the two Bettses] together; at the other ende, enters Fraunce de [Barde and Doll] a lustie woman, he haling her by the arme' (I, i, s.d.). But the subjection of Doll is a prelude to a reversal in which she will herself become a leader of rebellion. If the 'foreigners', Fraunce de Bard and Caveler, are unconstrained by the law, seizing London women and then forcing their husbands to pay for their board and lodging at their assailants' houses, Doll asserts the right of 'freeborne Englishmen' (I, i, 93) to take the law into their own hands. Defying Fraunce de Bard, Doll cries: 'Hands off, proude stranger! or, [by] him that boughte me, if mens milkie harts dare not strike a stranger, yet women will beate them downe.' And, demanding the return of the pigeons which he has taken from her husband Williamson, she says:

> deliver them back to my husband again, or Ile call so many women to myne assistance as weele not leave one inch untorne of thee: if our husbands must be brideled by lawe, and forced to beare your wrongs, their wives will be a little lawlesse, and soundly beate ye.

And in Act II, scene ii, Doll appears as a leader of the rebels, dressed in 'a shirt of maile, a headpiece, sword and buckler'.

Yet this gender inversion is legitimated because it is directed against a supposed ethnic inversion, in which foreigners rule over 'freeborne Englishmen'. Doll's denunciation of 'mens milkie harts', her assertions of lawlessness and her appropriation of masculine arms are imagined as at least partially justifiable responses to the prior inversions of 'aliens'. In a quite fantastic reworking of the 1517 riots, the dramatists of *Sir Thomas More* clearly suggest that the 'straungers' (as they are called) of Henrician England are legally entitled to dispossess English citizens of their property, including their wives. In other words, London is portrayed as if it was already a world turned upside down, one in which 'aliens' rule with the tacit consent of the court.

But this is not simply a case of one low group being represented as turning against another. After all, if it was in reality predominantly foreign *artisans* whom the London apprentices turned against, in the play those artisans have been transformed into powerful figures protected by the court. Under the guise of xenophobia, then, the rebels are able to interrogate the abuses of the elite. It is, indeed, as if the 'straungers' of the play are a condensation of both the foreign artisans and the London elite. And it was against that elite that the London riots of 1595 were directed. In June, as Penry Williams notes:

> When a silk-weaver went to the Lord Mayor's house and criticized his government, the Mayor, evidently astounded at such presumption, decided that he was mad and ordered him to be committed to Bedlam. On the way,

he was rescued by a crowd of two or three hundred apprentices. In the next week there were riots about butter and fish, followed by another rescue of a prisoner. On this occasion a serving-man, angered by his brother's ill treatment by his master, attacked the master and broke open his head. After he had been arrested and sent to the Counter, he was forcibly released by a crowd of apprentices. The man was again arrested together with some of his rescuers and put in irons. After the Mayor had gone to the prison to order their close confinement, he was passed on his return by an apprentice who refused to take off his cap; he too was sent to the Counter for insubordination. Next day a report came in that some apprentices had conspired with disbanded soldiers, who said to them 'you know not your own strength'.[34]

But in the play, it is only when the rebellion is directed against what are called 'outlandish fugetives' that it can be represented fully sympathetically. In other words it is the presence of the 'fugetives' which acts as the discursive support for inversions of status and gender.

Once that support is removed (and the foreigners do not appear after the first scene), popular rebellion is reconceived as 'this most dangerous insurrection' against the 'natural' rulers, incarnated in Sir Thomas More (II, iii, 29). But the play does not end with More's intercession first against, and then on behalf of, the rebels. For once the rebels are suppressed, his own role as governor loses its discursive antithesis, and he himself is split into the contradictory figures of ruler and rebel. Yet the play can never quite name him as rebel, so that in this portrayal of him as protector of the poor, jester and victim, there is an astonishing silence about what he is the victim *of*. In quelling the rebels, More declares:

> to the king God hath his office lent
> Of dread, of justyce, power and commaund,
> Hath bid him rule, and willd you to obay;
> And, to add ampler majestie to this,
> He hath not only lent the king his figure,
> His throne and sword, but gyven him his owne name,
> Calls him a god on earth.

Yet it is this 'god on earth' whom More himself refuses to obey, when he will not subscribe to the 'articles' presented to him. What these articles are, the play will not, or perhaps cannot, say. The manuscript of *Sir Thomas More* notoriously retains the marks of censorship by Edmund Tilney, the Master of the Revels. On the rebellion scene, he wrote: 'Leave out ye insurrection wholy and ye Cause theroff and begin with Sir Tho. Moore att ye mayers sessions, with a reportt afterwardes off his good servic don.'[35]

But if the insurrection against outsiders was perceived as dangerous, equally dangerous is More's understated refusal to subscribe. In erasing the articles themselves, the play effectively suppresses the names of three women: Catherine of Aragon, Anne Boleyn, and Elizabeth I. To name the articles would be to inscribe More's act of conscience as the bastardisation of Elizabeth, for to reject the annulment of Henry's marriage to Catherine was to deny the validity of Henry's marriage to Anne, Elizabeth's mother. The play, then, stages a series of displacements: the triumph of London women over 'illegitimate' foreigners is displaced by the triumph of authority over rebellion, which is in turn displaced by an act of rebellion that, if it is not disowned, can scarcely be owned. For to own it would be to find not just a woman but illegitimacy at the centre of power, to find, in the very origins of the state, *lupa* – a she-wolf.

We can trace a similar ambivalence toward the complex interactions between rebellion and the figure of woman in *Locrine*. That ambivalence leads to the curiously obscure, almost unreadable, epilogue, spoken by Ate, the goddess of revenge:

> And as a woman was the onely cause
> That civill discord was then stirred up,
> So let us pray for that renowned mayd,
> That eight and thirtie yeares the scepter swayd,
> In quiet peace and sweet felicitie.[36]

The syntax of this passage is curiously at odds with what one might expect to be a conventional passage of praise for Elizabeth. For if praise is the intent, then the emphasis should fall upon the *contrast* between the Scythian Estrild, the 'onely cause' of 'civil discord', and Elizabeth, who brings 'quiet peace and sweet felicitie'. Yet the syntax suggests not antithesis but analogy:

> And *as* a woman was the onely cause
> That civill discord was then stirred up,
> *So* let us pray for that renowned mayd.

It is as if the 'renowned mayd', merely by being a woman, foreshadows 'civill discord'. The syntax, indeed, seems to parallel the papal view that Elizabeth (the daughter of a woman accused of witchcraft and whoredom) was herself the cause of rebellion.

The full title of *Locrine*, though, as it appeared when the play was printed in 1595, gives no suggestion of the connection between woman and rebellion: it reads, 'The Lamentable Tragedie of Locrine, the eldest sonne of King Brutus, discoursing the warres of the Britaines, and Hunnes, with their discomfiture: The Britaines victorie with their Accidents, and the death of Albanact'. The title, in other words, addresses only the first three acts of the play, in which the Trojan origins of England are rehearsed, followed by Locrine's successful defence of Britain against the invasion of the Scythian Humber and his son Hubba. The first scene of the play stages the death of the Trojan Brutus, his division of the kingdom between his three sons (Locrine, Camber and Albanact), and the betrothal of Locrine to his cousin, Gwendoline. But, in contrast to *Lear*, danger comes not from the division of the kingdom, but from outside, in the form of the Scythians who are compared to 'sun-burnt *Aethiopians*' (1.445). And after the Scythians are defeated, Albion is said to repel all 'foreign elements': 'the brave nation of the *Troglodites*', 'the coleblacke *Aethiopians*', 'the forces of the *Amazons*' (11. 1409–11).

Yet the dumbshow which Ate stages at the beginning of Act IV represents not the defeat but the triumph of Amazonian rule. The stage direction reads:

> Then let there follow Omphale daughter to the king of Lydia, having a club in her hand, and a lions skinne on her back, Hercules following with a distaffe. Then let Omphale turn about, and taking off her pantofle, strike Hercules on the head.

The dumbshow foreshadows the displacement of an external threat by a threat which follows upon victory. Having defeated Humber, Locrine captures Humber's wife, Estrild, and falls in love with her. And what Ate calls 'their private amours' (1. 2271) in turn legitimate the gender inversion of Locrine's wife, Gwendoline, rebelling against her husband. Yet the victory of Gwendoline over her husband does not erase that taint of foreignness and exogamy. The culminating death in the play is that of Sabren, the illegitimate daughter of Locrine and the Scythian Estrild. When she drowns herself, Sabren's name is inscribed as that of the river Sabrina, just as her grandfather had given his name to the river Humber.

But if the Scythian can be inscribed upon a British landscape, what is curiously erased in the play's celebration of Brutus and the founding of Troynovant is the uncanny repetition of the Trojan myth, a myth which has at its centre not the celebration of patrilinearity but the figure of woman as the origin of civil discord. It was precisely because of that figure that John Speed argued against the Trojan origins of Britain in his *History of Great Britaine*, published in 1614 and dedicated to James I as 'Inlarger and Uniter of the British Empire, Restorer of the British name'. In the *History*, Speed wrote that true Britons should

> disclaime their Brute, that bringeth no honour to so renowned a Nation, but rather cloudeth their glorie in the murders of his parents, and imbaseth their descents, as sprung from Venus that lascivious Adulteresse: of whom saith du Plessis, I am ashamed that the heathen were not ashamed of this shamefulnesse; but much more that Christians blush not to name her in their verses.[37]

At stake in this interpretation of Venus is a rewriting of the origins of conflict, tracing them not to the conquests of invaders (whether Trojan or

Scythian) but to rebellion inscribed within the domestic. Plutarch in the *Moralia* saw harmony as the taming of Mars by Venus, she 'generous and pleasing', he 'fierce and contentious'. This harmony is celebrated in what Edgar Wind calls 'the many and famous idylls in which the victorious Venus, having subdued the fearful Mars by love, is seen playing with his armor'.[38] But in a more discordant version of this idyll, while Mars slept, Venus appropriated the martial weapons as her own. Dressed in armour, she became the *Venus victrix*. This fantasy of female rule, of rebellion at the heart of family and state alike, is what is figured in *Locrine*, where the tale of Scythian invaders is displaced by the inversions of Locrine's love for Estrild and of Gwendoline's military triumph over her husband. But in *Locrine*, if it is a woman, Estrild, who is named the 'onely cause' of 'civil discord', it is equally a woman, Gwendoline, who is the *cure* for that discord. One inversion is acted out against another inversion. Yet it can scarcely be said that equilibrium has been restored. The very discourses through which the resolution is constructed open up a politics of gender which was unimaginable in the opening scene, in which Brutus divided the kingdom amongst his male heirs. If, then, the inversions of the world turned upside down are not intrinsically radical, neither can they simply be read as the topoi of containment.

III

I want to conclude by trying to clarify the relation between the argument I am trying to make and previous analyses of the world turned upside down. Since the 1950s, I see three dominant 'waves' of interpretation. The first, which might be represented by Max Gluckman's *Custom and Conflict in Africa*, first published in 1956, argued for a safety-valve theory of inversion. Inversion, on this view, was a temporary licence which helped to re-establish the norm.[39] The second wave, which might be represented by the 1968 translation of Bakhtin's *Rabelais and His World*, argued that, on the contrary, inversion was part of the feast of becoming, a celebration of the destruction of settled norms and regulations.[40] Carnival, Bakhtin claimed, subverted all that was socially limited and fixed. The third wave rightly criticised Bakhtin's uncritical populism, and argued that 'subversion', far from constituting a space free from social regulation, was itself a form of play which constituted power in the very moment of its negation. In this view, expansionist forms of power *required* the overthrow of settled norms, but only so as to establish more pervasive forms of domination. But does not this third model, however brilliant its local analyses, reinscribe the stuctural functionalism which has for so long characterised American sociology, even if that functionalism now wears the guise of

Michel Foucault? It is indeed true for Talcott Parsons, although *not* for Foucault, that every discourse is always-already contained, because Parsons (like many other scientists, including, sadly, a Marxist like Gluckman) sees 'social control' as implicitly the key concept for understanding society.[41]

Against this third view, I would want to argue for Gramsci's model of social practices, a model in which conflict and contestation are endemic features, and 'social control' is understood as a local manoeuvre rather than posited as an all-embracing explanation.[42] For Gramsci, hegemony is never achieved once and for all; on the contrary, he sees the hegemonic process as a 'moving equilibrium', a process in which the dominant groups have to negotiate with and respond to both each other and the subaltern classes, and in which the discourses and practices through which alliances are formed are never given in advance. On such a view, there is no *intrinsic* connection between inversions of class, inversions of gender and inversions of ethnic hierarchies. Politics is precisely the work of *making* such connections, not the reflection of a social order that is already known.[43] What I have attempted to explore in this paper is a particular kind of political failure: the failure to articulate a relation between different forms of inversion, and the use of one form of inversion against another. But here too, I have argued, the playing with inversion opens up the very category of the political, showing the labour through which categories of class and gender are formed and articulated in relation to each other.

NOTES

1. On Marxism and the question of the 'political', I am particularly indebted to Ernesto Laclau, *Politics and Ideology in Marxist Theory* (London: Verso, 1979); Ernesto Laclau and Chantal Mouffe, *Hegemony and Socialist Strategy: Towards a radical democratic politics* (London: Verso, 1985); and Gareth Stedman Jones, *Languages of Class: Studies in English working class history 1832–1982* (Cambridge: Cambridge University Press, 1983). For a critique of their work, see Ellen Meiksins Wood, *The Retreat from Class: A new 'true' socialism* (London: Verso, 1986); and Norman Geras, 'Post-Marxism?', *New Left Review*, **166** (1987), pp. 79–106. For my understanding of the relation between Marxism and feminism, I am particularly indebted to Michèle Barrett, *Women's Oppression Today: Problems in Marxist-Feminist analysis* (London: Verso, 1980); Ann Rosalind Jones, 'Writing the body: toward an understanding of *l'écriture feminine*', in Elaine Showalter, ed., *The New Feminist Criticism* (New York: Pantheon, 1985), pp. 361–77; Cora Kaplan, *Sea Changes: Culture and feminism* (London: Verso, 1986); and Jacqueline Rose, *Sexuality in the Field of Vision* (London: Verso, 1986).
2. Ernst R. Curtius, *European Literature and the Latin Middle Ages*, trans. W. R. Trask (Princeton, N.J.: Princeton University Press, rpt. 1973).

3. Curtius, *European Literature*, pp. 94–5.
4. I am indebted to David Kunzle, who prints this woodcut in his important article, 'World upside down: the iconography of a European broadsheet type', in Barbara A. Babcock, ed., *The Reversible World: Symbolic inversion in art and society* (Ithaca, N.Y., and London: Cornell University Press, 1978), pp. 46–7.
5. See Maurice Agulhon, *Marianne into Battle: Republican imagery and symbolism in France, 1789–1880*, trans. Janet Lloyd (Cambridge: Cambridge University Press, 1981), pp. 38–61.
6. David E. Underdown, 'The taming of the scold: the enforcement of patriarchal authority in early modern England', in Anthony Fletcher and John Stevenson, eds., *Order and Disorder in Early Modern England* (Cambridge: Cambridge University Press, 1985), pp. 116–36.
7. See Natalie Zemon Davis, 'Women on top: symbolic and sexual inversion and political disorder in early modern Europe', in Babcock, *Reversible World*, pp. 147–90; and Charles Tilly, 'Charivaris, repertoires, and politics', Center for Research on Social Organization Working Paper no. 214, University of Michigan (1980).
8. Max Gluckman, *Customs and Conflict in Africa* (Oxford: Blackwell, 1956); Underdown, 'Scold', p. 117.
9. Lynn Hunt, *Politics, Culture, and Class in the French Revolution* (Berkeley, Calif.: University of California Press, 1984), p. 104.
10. Hunt, *Politics*, p. 108.
11. Dorinda Outram, '*Le langage mâle de la vertu*: Women and the discourse of the French Revolution', in Peter Burke and Roy Porter, eds., *The Social History of Language*, Cambridge Studies in Oral and Literate Culture 12 (Cambridge: Cambridge University Press, 1987), p. 133.
12. Outram, '*Le Langage mâle*', p. 125.
13. Samuel Butler, *Hudibras* (1663), ed. Zachary Grey (Cambridge: Cambridge University Press, 1744), vol. 1, I, 2, 367–8. 'English Mall' refers to the notorious Moll Cutpurse, who was featured as the heroine of Middleton and Dekker's *The Roaring Girl*.
14. Protestant attacks upon popular festivity tended to focus both upon their idolatrous, and therefore papist, aspects and upon their symbolism of metamorphosis. In *The Popish Kingdome*, for instance, Naogeorgus sees Shrovetide as the privileged season of metamorphoses which 'best beseeme these Papistes'. The people, he writes, change themselves into monks, kings, bears, wolves, lions, bulls, cranes, apes and fools; gender is also inverted:

> Both men and women chaunge their weede, the men in maydes aray,
> And wanton wenches drest like men, doe travell by the way.

See Naogeorgus [Kirchmeyer], *The Popish Kingdome, or Reigne of Antichrist*, trans. Barnaby Googe (London, 1570), p. 48.
15. *The Poems and Letters of Andrew Marvell*, ed. H.M. Margoliouth (Oxford: Clarendon Press, 1952), vol. I, p. 150, 11. 376–86.
16. Butler is a particularly interesting case because it would seem that his attack upon Puritanism was motivated less by a reverence for royalty and for 'traditional' ways than by a Hobbesian emphasis upon order at any cost. In *Characters and Passages from Note-Books* (ed. A.R. Waller (Cambridge: Cambridge University Press, 1908)), Butler emphasises the amoral manipulations which are necessary to sustain that order. Wise princes, he writes, 'have ever used to instill into their People, a Contempt, and Hatred of Forraine Nations, to

render them the more united among themselves' (p. 386), and the prince should work upon the people not 'by telling them Truth and Reason, or using any direct meanes; but by little Tricks and Divises (as they cure Mad men) that worke upon their Hopes and Feares to which their Ignorance naturally inclines them' (p. 391). Similarly, 'Princes ought to give their Subjects as much of the Shadow of Liberty as they can for their lives, but as little of the Reality of it, if they regard the Safety of themselves or their People' (p. 383). And viewing politics as cynical manipulation, Butler declares: 'Publique Actions are like watches that have fine Cases of Gold, or Silver, with a windore of Christall to see the Pretences, but the Movement is of Baser Mettle, and the Original of all (the Spring) a Crooked piece of Steel: So in the Affaires of State, The solemn Professions of Religion, Justice, and Liberty are but Pretences, to conceale Ambition, Rapine, and useful Cheate' (p. 389). I am indebted to E.A. Richards, *Hudibras and the Burlesque Tradition* (New York: Columbia University Press, 1937), for drawing my attention to Butler's notebooks.

17. *The Complete Works of Abraham Cowley*, ed. Alexander B. Grosart (Edinburgh: Edinburgh University Press, 1881), vol. 1, p. cxxvi.
18. Roy Strong, *Portraits of Queen Elizabeth I* (Oxford: Oxford University Press, 1963), p. 119; and Frances A. Yates, *Astraea: The Imperial Theme in the Sixteenth Century* (London: Routledge & Kegan Paul, 1975), pp. 48–51.
19. Bodleian Library, mss. Ashmole 36, 37, fol. 296.
20. Tacitus, *Germania*, trans. H. Mattingly and S. A. Handford (Harmondsworth: Penguin, 1970), pp. 104, 115–20; and Quentin Skinner, *The Foundations of Modern Political Thought*, vol. II, 'The Age of Reformation' (Cambridge: Cambridge University Press 1978), p. 54.
21. Rebecca W. Bushnell, *Tragedies of Tyrants: Political thought and theater in the English renaissance* (Ithaca, N.Y., and London: Cornell University Press, 1990).
22. Quoted in Bushnell, *Tragedies of Tyrants*, pp. 100, 105.
23. Quoted in Antonia Fraser, *The Weaker Vessel: Woman's lot in seventeenth-century England* (London: Weidenfeld and Nicolson, 1984), pp. 222–3.
24. John Milton, *The History of Britain* [1670], ed. George Philip Krapp, in *The Works of John Milton*, vol. X (New York: Columbia University Press, 1932), p. 316.
25. Milton, *Eikonoklastes* [1649], ed. William Haller, in *The Works*, vol. V, pp. 139–40.
26. Lyndal Roper, ' "The common man", "the common good", "common women": gender and meaning in the German Reformation commune', *Social History*, 12 (1987), p. 2.
27. Roper, 'Gender and meaning', p. 2.
28. Quoted in Jean Seznec, *The Survival of the Pagan Gods: The mythological tradition and its place in Renaissance humanism and art*, Bollingen Series XXXVIII (Princeton, N.J.: Princeton University Press, 1953), p. 194.
29. Seznec, *Pagan Gods*, pp. 190–2.
30. Quoted in Robert N. Watson, *Shakespeare and the Hazards of Ambition* (Cambridge, Mass.: Harvard University Press, 1984), p. 152. See also Ann Lake Prescott, '*Translatio lupae*: Du Bellay's Roman whore goes north', *Renaissance Quarterly*, 42 (1989), pp. 397–419; and Agnes Kirsopp Michels, 'The topography and interpretation of the Lupercalia', *Transactions and Proceedings of the American Philological Association*, LXXXIV (1953), pp. 35–59.
31. Peter Stallybrass and Allon White, *The Politics and Poetics of Transgression* (Ithaca, N.Y.: Cornell University Press, 1986), pp. 18–25.

32. Anon., *The Book of Sir Thomas More* (New York: AMS, 1970). Two important recent books on *Sir Thomas More* are: Scott McMillin, *The Elizabethan Theater and 'The Book of Sir Thomas More'* (Ithaca, N.Y. and London: Cornell University Press, 1987) and T.H. Howard-Hill, ed., *Shakespeare and 'Sir Thomas More'* (Cambridge: Cambridge University Press, 1989).
33. Craig Bernthal, 'Treason in the family: Thump *v.* Horner', paper delivered at the Shakespeare Association of America, Boston, 1987. I am indebted to Bernthal's fine paper for my understanding of the relation between drama and apprentice riots in the 1590s.
34. Penry Williams, *The Tudor Regime* (Oxford: Clarendon Press, 1979), p. 329. I am indebted to Craig Bernthal for the reference.
35. For an account more sympathetic to the censor than my own, see William B. Long, 'The occasion of *The Book of Sir Thomas More*', in Howard-Hill, ed. *Shakespeare and 'Sir Thomas More'*, pp. 45–56.
36. Anon., *The Tragedy of Locrine* (1595), ed. Ronald B. McKerrow (Oxford: Malone Society, 1908), ll, 2274–8.
37. John Speed, *The Historie of Great Britaine* (London, 1632).
38. Edgar Wind, *Pagan Mysteries of the Renaissance* (New York: Norton, 1968), pp. 86–9.
39. Gluckman, *Custom and Conflict*.
40. Mikhail Bakhtin, *Rabelais and His World*, trans. Helene Iswolsky (Cambridge, Mass.: MIT Press, 1968).
41. See, for example, Talcott Parsons, *The Social System* (Glencoe, Ill.: Free Press, 1951); his *Essays in Sociological Theory* (Glencoe, Ill.: Free Press, 1954); and his *Politics and Social Structure* (New York: Free Press, 1969).
42. Antonio Gramsci, *Selections from the Prison Notebooks*, ed. and trans. Quintin Hoare and Geoffrey Nowell-Smith (New York: International Publishers, 1971); and his *Selections from Cultural Writings*, eds. David Forgacs and Geoffrey Nowell-Smith (London: Lawrence and Wishart, 1985). See also Perry Anderson, 'The antinomies of Antonio Gramsci', *New Left Review,* 100 (Nov. 1976–Jan. 1977), pp. 5–78; and Chantal Mouffe, ed., *Gramsci and Marxist Theory* (London: Routledge & Kegan Paul, 1979). For a devastating critique of the functionalist notion of 'social control', see Stedman Jones, *Languages of Class*, Chapter 2.
43. See Laclau, *Politics and Ideology;* and Laclau and Mouffe, *Hegemony*.

9

Scripts and/versus Playhouses: Ideological Production and the Renaissance Public Stage

Jean E. Howard

In the 'Documents of Control' section of *The Elizabethan Stage*, E.K. Chambers records a 1574 Act of the Common Council of London which represents an attempt to restrain and regulate public playing within the Liberties. The reasons cited for such restraint are numerous and familiar: the gathering together of playgoers in inns and yards spreads the plague; it creates opportunities for illicit sexual encounters; and it provides the occasion for the dissemination, from the stage, of 'unchaste, uncomelye, and unshamefaste speeches and doynges'.[1] The document is long, and it contains little that would surprise anyone familiar with Renaissance polemic against the public stage or with the numerous petitions sent by the City to the queen and her council urging the restraint of playing during the next thirty years. I was particularly interested, however, in the way the document concludes, which is thus:

> this Act (otherwise than towchinge the publishinge of unchaste, sedycious, and unmete matters:) shall not extend to anie plaies, Enterludes, Comodies, Tragidies, or shewes to be played or shewed in the pryvate hous, dwellinge, or lodginge of anie nobleman, Citizen, or gentleman, which shall or will then have the same thear so played or shewed in his presence for the festyvitie of anie marriage, Assemblye of ffrendes, or otherlyke cawse withowte publique or Commen Collection of money of the Auditorie or behoulders theareof, reservinge alwaie to the Lorde Maior and Aldermen for the tyme beinge the Judgement and construction Accordinge to equitie what shalbe Counted suche a playenge or shewing in a pryvate place, anie things in this Acte to the Contrarie notwithstanding. (p. 276)

What is striking to me here is the absolutely clear demarcation between the dangers of public playing, involving the 'Commen Collection of money of the Auditorie,' and the acceptability of playing within a 'pryvate hous, dwellinge, or lodginge' where presumably no money was collected and where the audience had therefore not been transformed by a commercial transaction from guests to customers. As was to be true in a number of antitheatrical tracts and petitions from the city, what is specified here as objectionable about certain kinds of theatrical activity is less the matter of content of plays *per se*, and more the practices surrounding public playing: specifically, the removal of the scene of playing from the controlled space of the nobleman's house to a public venue; the dailiness of public playing versus its occasional use, for example, as part of a wedding festivity; the transformation of those who attend the play from guests or clients of a great man or wealthy citizen into paying customers; and, implicitly, the transformation of dramatists from straightforward servants of the nobility into something more akin to artisan entrepreneurs. In short, in this document public playing is presented as altering social relations by the emergent material practices attendant upon play production and attendance, quite apart from any consideration of the ideological import of the fictions enacted on the stage.

Another document written a few years later, when amphitheatre playhouses were an established fact, underscores a similar point. In *The Schoole of Abuse* (1579) Stephen Gosson, drawing on Ovid and classical attacks on the theatre, rehearses a number of objections to the public theatre that were to become standard tropes of English antitheatrical polemic: theatre teaches immorality; it allures the senses rather than improves the mind; it encourages flouting of the sumptuary laws; it serves as a meeting place for whores and their customers.[2] While Gosson certainly raises objections to the *content* of plays, he too is keenly alert to the disruptive potential embedded in the very activity of going to a play. It provides occasion, for example, for the conspicuous display of ornate attire and for the promiscuous mixing together of social groups.The money that allowed an upstart crow to ape the clothes of his betters and to display them at the theatre also allowed him to purchase a seat in the galleries. While the public theatres were hierarchically designed to reflect older status categories (common men in the pit, gentlemen in the galleries, lords on the very top), in actuality one's place there was determined less by one's rank than by one's ability or willingness to pay for choice or less choice places. Money thus stratified the audience in ways at least potentially at odds with older modes of stratification, a fact with which Ben Jonson was still ruefully coming to terms several decades later, when, in the preface to *Bartholomew Fair*, he satirically enjoins various members of the audience at the Hope Theatre to offer criticism of his play strictly in proportion to the amount of money they had laid out at the theatre door:

> It is further agreed that every person here have his or their free-will of censure, to like or dislike at their own charge, the author having now

departed with his right: it shall be lawful for any man to judge his six pen'orth, his twelve pen'orth, so to his eighteen pence, two shillings, half a crown, to the value of his place; provided alway his place get not above his wit. And if he pay for half a dozen, he may censure for all them too, so that he will undertake that they shall be silent. He shall put in for censures here as they do for lots at the lottery; marry, if he drop but sixpence at the door, and will censure a crown's worth, it is thought there is no conscience or justice in that. (Induction, 76–86)[3]

At court, as Jonson's epilogue to the same play suggests, he can count on a spectator, the king, whose judgements are absolute and whose position is fixed, unaffected by the fluidity of market relations. In the public theatre things are different. Much to Jonson's dismay, his art has become rather too much like a Bartholomew Fair commodity, liable to judgement by those who can and will pay to see it, whatever their rank, education and taste.

I wish to suggest that in such a context the ideological consequences of playgoing might be quite different for different social groups. Gosson indirectly broaches this issue in what is for me the most interesting part of his tract, namely the concluding epistle, which is addressed to 'the Gentlewomen, Citizens of London', a category of playgoer apparently significant enough to warrant Gosson's specific attention.[4] From Andrew Gurr's important study, *Playgoing in Shakespeare's London*, we now know that women were in the public theatre in significant numbers and that the women who attended the theatre were neither simply courtesans nor aristocratic ladies; many seem to have been citizens' wives, part of that emergent group, 'the middling sort', whom Gosson most explicitly addresses.[5] The presence of such women at the theatre clearly worries Gosson, and he voices his worries in a typically paternalistic form: that is, as a concern for woman's safety and good reputation. What Gosson argues is that the safest place for woman to be is at home, busy with household management, with neighbourhood gossips and, for recreation, with books. As he says, 'The best councel I can give you, is to keepe home, and shun all occasion of ill speech.'[6] The dangerous place for woman to be is the theatre. The interesting question is why.

Ostensibly, the threat is to woman's sexual purity. In the body of his tract Gosson argues that the theatre is a place for sexual assignations; it is a 'market of bawdrie'.[7] Various wantons and paramours, knaves and queens, 'cheapen the merchandise in that place, which they pay for elsewhere as they can agree'.[8] Presumably, any woman – and not just a prostitute – could fall prey to passion if inflamed by the allegedly lewd behaviour of the actors or by the amorous addresses of her male companions at the theatre. Yet in his concluding epistle, Gosson dwells less on the possibility that the gentlewoman citizen may go off to sleep with a fellow playgoer and more on the danger posed to her by being gazed at by many men in the public space of the theatre. As Gosson says: 'Thought is free; you can forbidd no man, that vieweth you, to noute you and that noateth you, to judge you, for entring to places of suspition.'9 The threat is not so much to woman's bodily purity as to her reputation. In Gosson's account the female playgoer is symbolically whored by the gaze of many men, each woman a potential Cressida in the camp of the Greeks, vulnerable, alone and open to whatever imputations men might cast upon her. She becomes what we might call the object of promiscuous gazing. Gosson presents the situation entirely paternalistically. For the 'good' of women he warns them to stay at home, to shut themselves away from all dangers, and to find pleasure in reading or in the gossip of other women.

Yet who is endangered, really, by women's theatregoing? The intensity of Gosson's scrutiny of the woman playgoer indicates to me that her presence in the theatre may have been felt to threaten more than her own purity, that in some way it put her 'into circulation' in the public world of Elizabethan England in ways threatening to the larger patriarchal economy, within which her circulation was in theory a highly structured process, involving her passage from the house and surveillance of the father to the house and surveillance of the husband. This process was more complicated and class specific than I am indicating here, and it is also true that men, at least in the elite classes, often had their marriage choices determined by the father and were in no absolute sense free agents. But it was as the privileged sex that men circulated through the structures of Elizabethan society, and it was they to whom women were by and large accountable, and not vice versa. The threat the theatre seems to hold for Gosson in regard to ordinary gentlewomen is that, in that public space, such women have become unanchored from the structures of surveillance and control 'normal' to the culture and useful in securing the boundary between 'good women' and 'whores'. Not literally passed, like Cressida, from hand to hand, lip to lip, the female spectator passes instead from eye to eye, her value as the exclusive possession of one man cheapened, put at risk, by the gazing of many eyes. To whom, in such a context, does woman belong? Are her meaning and value fixed, or fluctuating? How does one classify a woman who is not literally a whore and yet who is not, as good women were supposed to be, at home? To handle the ambiguity, the potential blurring of ideological categories, Gosson would send the gentlewoman citizen out of the theatre and back to her house, husband, father, books and gossips, where such questions admit of easier answers.

Yet I suspect the threat to the patriarchal order is even more complex than I have so far indicated. By drawing on the Cressida analogy, I have seemed to assent to Gosson's most fundamental premise, namely that women in the theatre were simply objects of scrutiny and desire, and that in that position they were in danger of being read as whores or otherwise becoming commodities outside the control of one man. But what if one reads the situation less within the horizons of masculinist ideology and asks whether women might have been empowered, and not simply victimised, by their novel position within the theatre? In the theatrical economy of gazes, could men have done all the looking, held all the power? Joel Steinberg could not bear the thought that Hedda Nussbaum was looking at him, and he beat her eyes until artificial tearducts had to be inserted in one of them.[10] Is it possible that in the theatre women were licensed to look – and in a larger sense to judge what they saw and to exercise autonomy – in ways that problematised women's status as object within patriarchy?

I have no definitive answer to my own question yet, but what I tentatively suggest is that Gosson's prescriptive rhetoric may be a response, not only to a fear *for* woman, but also to a fear *of* woman, as she takes up a place in an institution which, as Steven Mullaney has argued, existed at least symbolically on the margins of authorised culture, opening space for the transformation, as much as the simple reproduction, of that culture.[11] At the theatre door, money changed hands in a way which gave women access to the pleasure and privilege of gazing, certainly at the stage, and probably at the audience as well. They were therefore, as Jonson ruefully acknowledges, among those authorised to exercise their sixpenceworth, or their penny'sworth, of judgement. Whether or not they were accompanied by husbands or fathers, women at the theatre were not 'at home', but in public, where they could become objects of desire, certainly, but also desiring subjects, stimulated to want what was on display at the theatre, which must have been not just sexual opportunity, but all the trappings of a commodifying culture worn upon the very backs of those attending the theatre, and making it increasingly difficult to discern 'who one really was' in terms of the categories of a status system based on fixed and unchanging social hierarchies. As Jean-Christophe Agnew has argued, the Renaissance stage made the liquidity of social relations in a commercialising culture its theme.[12] I would simply argue that the practice of playgoing may have embodied that liquidity, not simply thematised it. For Gosson, good wives who took up a place at the public theatre were dangerously out of their true and appropriate place, and he clearly meant to return them to that proper place by threatening those who remained in the place of danger with the name of whore. The question is, when is a person out of her place *in* danger and when is she *a* danger to those whom, by her new placement, she is displacing?

I am going to return to the question of women at the public theatre and how their presence may have altered social relations in Elizabethan England, but I want to do so by way of two brief detours: one into the contemporary scene of ideological analyses of Renaissance drama, one into Thomas Heywood's little studied play *The Wise Woman of Hogsdon*, a work which invites thematisation of the question of woman as spectacle and spectator, object and agent within a culture both patriarchal and theatrical, and which invites us to speculate about the potential gap, for certain groups, between the ideological implications of a given play and the ideological consequences of playgoing.

I am interested in the question of what it meant that women attended the Renaissance public theatre in part because I, and a cohort of others from whom I am constantly learning, have for a while been considering the question of the ideological work done by the theatre in English Renaissance culture.[13] By ideological work, I mean simply how this institution and the plays put on there contributed to that larger ensemble of beliefs and practices comprising Elizabethan subjects' lived relations to the real. Ideology in my understanding is the obviousness of culture, what goes without saying, what is lived as true. It is therefore precisely not a set of beliefs known to be 'false' but cynically sold to others to hold them in an inferior position, nor does it originate from a conspiratorial power group (or author) bent on dominating or deceiving others. This does not mean, however, that ideology does not function to produce unequal social relations within social formations stratified by race, gender and class. It simply means that ideology does not lie in anyone's conscious control, nor can it be opposed to 'truth', simply to other ideological modalities of knowing. Traces of Althusserian rhetoric appear in my prose because, despite all that must be rejected and modified in the Althusserian problematic, I still find his one of the most strenuous and fruitful theorisations of ideology we have, valuable enough to warrant modification, rather than outright rejection.[14] For Althusser the work of ideology in general is to reproduce the relations of production necessary to the survival and perpetuation of particular modes of production. It is the work of ideology to call people, interpellate them, into their positions as workers, managers, owners, rulers and ruled, and to provide them with the subjectivities which hold them in these places with a minimum of force or coercion. Ideology thus makes people willing subjects of the dominant order.

Clearly, one of the major elements of Althusser's thought needing modification is his overly deterministic view of the operations of ideology. As many have noted, elegant and therefore powerful as is Althusser's account of the operations of ideology, it gives adequate attention not to explaining change, but only to cultural reproduction. And it gives primacy to struggles between social classes in a way that leaves little room for the independent analysis of other modes of oppression, such as those ing race and gender.[15] Anyone continuing to work with Althusser has to take account of these and other problems, partly by recognising, with Göran Therborn, that interpellation is a process which not only subjects the subject but qualifies him or her for manoeuvre within the terrain of ideology;[16] partly because no subject ever occupies only one subject position, but rather is entangled in a network of competing and contestatory ideologies. This is particularly true for complex societies in which change at different levels of the social formation occurs in a non-homologous fashion. Contradictions among the multiple positionings of the subject can therefore lead to his or her politicisation, to the abandon-ment of particular ideological positions and to the creation of shifting horizons of resistance.[17]

Such ideas become increasingly important in the ideological study of Renaissance drama in this country, as the emphasis in the early moments of new historicism on the stage as the simple agent of state power has come under pressure.[18] Now it seems more adequate to speak of the stage, neither as a site simply for the dissemination of aristocratic and masculinist ideology, nor, in the mirror image of this position, as a site for a simple subversion of a social order statically and monolithically con-ceived as a homologous totality. Instead, a number of scholars are trying to understand how the stage could have functioned in a more complex and contradictory fashion within the interstices of a social formation which was not static, and in which the process of ideological domination is probably best understood as one of constant negotiation with, rather than simple containment of, emergent or oppositional positions.

This new direction in the ideological study of Renaissance theatre is not, I think, simply an attempt to impose a liberationist paradigm on the stage in order to displace or replace a paradigm of containment. It indi-cates instead a recognition both of the possibilities for contradiction in the operations of the stage and of the differential ways it could have impacted on various social groups. Richard Burt, for example, has stressed how the reception of productions in the public theatre could not be controlled in the same way and to the same extent as productions in more explicitly courtly venues,[19] a fact that seems acknowledged by the Act of the Common Council of London with which I began this paper, in which the Council registered a fear that public playing removed the sta-bilising contexts for reception provided by the nobleman's house or the official occasion of the wedding ceremony. Exploring similar issues, Ste-ven Mullaney has recently suggested that the Renaissance stage, in an era when literacy was still not widespread, served to expand, for the urban populace of London, the parameters of the symbolic economy within which it moved; he further argues that such an expansion had potentially unsettling social consequences, simply because the circulation of rep-resentations had moved beyond the control of an elite.[20]

Central to much of this work is the implicit recognition that if one wishes to speak of the ideological consequences of the theatre, one needs to attend not just to theatrical representations *qua* representations, but also to the material practices and conventions of the stage and of theatre going. As Althusser has stressed, the domain of the ideological involves more than just 'ideas'; the materiality of ideology consists precisely in its embodiment in material practices.[21] In terms of the Renaissance theatre, an emphasis upon the materiality of ideology means that it is not sufficient to talk about representations of monarchy without talking about the consequences of having those representations daily enacted by men of low estate in public amphitheatres for commercial gain;[22] not sufficient to talk about the consequences of fables of cross-dressing without considering the fact that they were enacted by men in women's clothing;[23] not sufficient to talk about the interpellation of theatrical subjects by playscripts without talking about their interpellation by the material practices of playgoing in which all people, whatever their rank or gender, were transformed into the paying customers of the emerging mercantile economy. The simplest way to put the point I wish to make is that one can not assume that theatrical representations have an ideological significance that is fixed and unchanging, or that is unaffected by the conditions in which the representations are produced and consumed. It has sometimes been tempting to me to think that the material practices surrounding playgoing in urban London were destabilising to aristocratic and masculinist hegemony while the dramatic scripts themselves mostly were not. This formulation, however, is too simple. It is necessary, I think, to see that the scripts themselves embody social struggle, that they enact a contest between and a negotiation among competing ideological positions; and that a further level of analysis is also necessary, as one tries to take account of the potential consonance or conflict between the ideological import of a dramatic fable and that of the material conditions of its production. As my title awkwardly states the problem: do we assume that scripts and playhouse-practice ideologically reinforce one another, or that, at least potentially, they can be in conflict? That is, can they interpellate subjects in contradictory ways? Because Renaissance discourse about the theatre focuses as much on the scene of playing as on what is performed at that scene, I believe the awkward duality with which I am wrestling is not my own invention, but a problem at some level recognised in the period itself.

Which leads me to *The Wise Woman of Hogsdon*, a play I want to examine briefly with a particular group of spectators in mind, namely Gosson's gentlewomen citizens of London. I chose this play partly because it is not by Shakespeare, and so allows a freshness of address, and partly because it raises in interesting ways the question of what *were* the ideological consequences, for women, of theatregoing. The work is unusual in that it plays out both class and gender conflict around the issue of who will control the power to manipulate the world through theatrical means. The title character, the cunning woman, is a lower-class figure who makes her living by using her 'special powers' to perform services for her neighbours, services such as finding a missing or lost object, diagnosing illness, telling the future. As Keith Thomas reports, such figures were not uncommon in English village life well into the seventeenth century. They not only performed vital physical services, such as helping women in childbirth, but they also filled a psychological gap left when the Reformation led to the abolition of certain practices, such as exorcism and confession, by which the Roman church had allayed the common man or woman's guilt about sin and his or her fears of demonic possession.[24] Cunning people, with their charms and medicines and prophetic powers, seemed in possession of powerful, if forbidden, knowledges, which made them anathema to the church and to medical men, but not necessarily to ordinary people.

Often, in the polemical literature of the time, cunning people, along with witches, were presented as agents of Satan. Sometimes, as in Reginald Scot's treatise, *The Discoverie of Witchcraft*, cunning women, conjurers, exorcists, witches and other 'jugglers' were simply presented as charlatans who gained their power by tricks, illusions and the artful leading on of their clients.[25] Heywood's wise woman is certainly a first-class swindler and charlatan. For example, when her neighbours come to her for advice, she asks leading questions to get them to tell her the details of their troubles, which she then pretends to have known in advance.

Wisewoman	And who distill'd this water?
Countryman	My wives Limbeck, if it please you.
Wisewoman	And where doth the paine hold her most?
Countryman	Marry at her heart forsooth.
Wisewoman	Ey, at her heart, shee hath a griping at her heart.
Countryman	You have hit it right.
Wisewoman	Nay, I can see so much in the Urine.
Luce 2	Just so much as is told her.
Wisewoman	Shee hath no paine in her head, hath shee?
Countryman	No indeed, I never heard her complaine of her head,
Wisewoman	I told you so, her paine lyes all at her heart;
	Alas good heart! but how feeles shee her stomacke?
Countryman	O queasie, and sicke at stomacke.
Wisewoman	Ey, I warrant you, I think I can see as farre into a Millstone as another. (II, i, 7–21)[26]

Alternatively, she conceals herself in a closet by her front door, listening while her servant asks a client her business, and then pretends to have divined that business. Essentially unlettered, she drops Latin tags and pretends to read in deep books of magical lore.

She is, then, a charlatan, and also something of a bawd. Her house is where women come to have their illegitimate babies, which the wise woman then disposes of by leaving them on the doorsteps of the wealthy. And the walls of this house contain the pictures of young women with whom a man can spend the night. Hardly the patron of the chaste, silent and obedient, this lower-class woman traffics in flesh. This makes her house a transgressive space where deceptive and illicit activities are carried on, and which seems to put Heywood's play, ideologically, on the side of Reginald Scot and his debunking demystification of such charlatans.

Yet the class and gender politics of this play are more complicated than I have indicated. For all that the wise woman is a charlatan and her house a house of assignations, it is also the place where all members of the community come, the virtuous and the less than virtuous, and it is the place where the community's problems get solved, thanks largely to the theatrical skills of the wise woman herself. Her house becomes the site where the community's sexual and social economy is regulated; where, in essence, the predatory theatricality of Chartley, the young gallant who is the play's male protagonist, is defeated by the cleverness of a group of women.

The plot, despite some Byzantine overtones, is a simple one. Chartley was once contracted to marry a woman, Luce 2, whom he abandoned practically on her marriage night. This woman, disguised as a man, tracks Chartley down and schemes to win him back by contracting herself as a servant to the wise woman and joining with her in manipulating this rogue. He, after leaving Luce 2, contracts himself to a second woman, Luce 1, virtuous daughter of a London goldsmith, whom he also abandons as he goes off in pursuit of yet a third woman, Gratiana, daughter of a wealthy knight. Chartley acts out what is presented as a dangerous instability in aristocratic male desire. He moves from woman to woman, lying each, and ends up staging an elaborate fiction by which, on the night before his marriage to Gratiana, the knight's daughter, he goes off to sleep with Luce 1 at the wise woman's house, pretending he has been urgently called away by a dying father.

What keeps his predatory desire from ruining the lives of all these prospective brides is the cunning woman, who is presented as his antagonist from the first time they meet. These two knaves are presented as natural enemies. He calls her every sort of name – blackness, witch, hag, she-devil, sorceress, Lady Proserpine, Madam Hecate – and tries to beat her; she, in turn, vows to do anything to frustrate his desires. Twice, using highly theatrical ruses, she deceives him. The first time, when he comes to her house to marry Luce 1, she puts everyone in disguise and fools him into marrying Luce 2, and Luce 1 into marrying an earnest young suitor named Boyster, thus joining Chartley to the first object of his desire and the goldsmith's daughter to a suitably sober mate. When, still deceived into believing he has wed Luce 1, he comes to sleep with her at the wise woman's house, the women stage a trick which exposes his chicanery to all those – his father, Gratiana's father, Luce 1 and Luce 2 – whom he has attempted to deceive. When he appears at her house, the wise woman puts him in a room surrounded by a circle of adjoining rooms from which he is observed by all his gulls, who one by one come forward to confront him. He is left a sputtering mass of jelly, the libertine plots and deceptions of the aristocratic male exposed to everyone's gaze.

The house of the wise woman thus becomes a world upside down where women temporarily have control of men, the lower classes of the upper. Only the stigmatised lower-class figure, the cunning woman, seems to have the power to right the social world threatened by gentle-manly profligacy and theatricality. Fire drives out fire. Yet the role of the two Luces deserves further attention. Significantly, Luce 1, while some-what inexplicably the wise woman's friend, is kept in ignorance by her throughout the play. Luce 1 has all the respectability the wise woman lacks and none of her power. She is chaste, fairly silent and obedient. An early scene finds her lamenting to an apprentice the fact she must sit in public to mind her father's shop, a position which exposes her to the gaze of many men, a position she abhors.

> I doe not love to sit thus publikely:
> And yet upon the traffique of our Wares,
> Our provident Eyes and presence must still wayte.
> Doe you attend the shop, Ile ply my worke.
> I see my father is not jelous of me,
> That trusts mee to the open view of all.
> The reason is, hee knowes my thoughts are chaste,
> And my care such, as that it needes the awe
> Of no strict Overseer. (I, ii, 4–12)

This good daughter of the patriarchy speaks at once to every suitor of marriage; and her marriage choice, Chartley, is directly referred by her to her father to ask his permission. Unlike the stereotypical merchants found in many city comedies, Luce and her father are not rich. They are, simply, virtuous citizens devoid of guile. They are also, importantly, powerless in the face both of Chartley's manipulations and of the wise woman's. Sig-nificantly, Luce 1 does not even know that because of the disguises worn at her wedding she has married not Chartley, but Boyster, the mate she finds herself wedded to at play's end.

That compliance with dominant codes of feminine virtue results in powerlessness and domination is strikingly revealed by the presence in the play of Luce 1's double, the aggressively different Luce 2. Of this woman we know little but that she is a 'gentlewoman', left her father's house when abandoned by Chartley and is absolutely tenacious in her pursuit of this feckless gallant. For most of the play, she dresses as a male page – a theatrical disguise she uses to achieve power over Chartley. In fact, she wears women's clothing only when participating in the plot to trick him into marrying her instead of Luce 1. The power she symbolically assumes by adopting male dress is further indicated by the fact that she is the instigator of much of the plotting that goes on at the wise woman's. She and the cunning woman are the primary architects of the two great scenes of theatrical cozenage: the double wedding where the Jacks get only the Jills that Luce 2 and the wise woman have assigned to them, and the climactic scene in which, before one audience after another, Chartley has his lying ways exposed. As is so often true in this period, power is shown to lie with the theatrically skilful. If the wise woman outsmarts and outdeceives Chartley, lower-class feminine theatricality outstripping his entrepreneurial shapeshifting, the wise woman is in turn outsmarted by the chaste, if hardly silent and compliant, Luce 2, who does not reveal her female sex to the wise woman until the last deception has been played out and Luce 2 claims Chartley for her own, her desire gratified as Luce 1's was not. In the hierarchy of power and knowledge which emerges in the play, Luce 2 is at the very top, and she is the transgressive figure of the woman in man's attire seemingly free from the control of a father or husband.

Of course, it is easy to see a reining in of the subversive impulses of the play in its denouement. This is particularly true concerning Luce 2 who, having spent much of the play in breeches and free of overt patriarchal control, at play's end willingly enters what will in all likelihood be a patriarchal marriage and doffs her breeches, and with them, perhaps, her power. Moreover, her being a gentlewoman affirms class privilege even as she subverts gender hierarchy. It is, after all, the gentlewoman whose desire is gratified, and not the goldsmith's daughter. Moreover, the play ends up affirming patriarchal marriage three times over, and concludes with a utopian image of class reconciliation, rather than class antagonism, as Chartley blesses his enemy the wise woman, and the union of Luce 1 and Boyster marks the non-predatory alliance of citizen and gentleman classes.

Despite these obviously recuperative elements, the play reveals the constructed and interested nature of the social order by showing subordinated groups successfully occupying the positions and clothing and wielding the powers of the dominators, including their use of theatrical practices to control the world. While it is difficult to construe the play as advocating the dismantling of either the patriarchal system or the class system, in several ways it invites disidentification with both. This is not only because it shows men, and gentlemen, as no more inherently and naturally capable of wielding power than women and lower-class figures, thus undermining the 'natural' justification for their privileges; the play is also traversed by competing understandings of the same phenomena, which show the implicit contest between ideological positions. For example, while the wise woman is inscribed within a discourse of the charlatan – even by Luce 2 – she is also clearly inscribed within a discourse of Rabelaisian carnal materiality and associated with the homeostatic regulation of the social and sexual economy of the play. Likewise, while Luce 1 is inscribed within the discourse of the good woman familiar from the conduct books, Luce 2 is her transgressive double, embodying an alternative to, and demystification of, her sister. This play's climactic scene presents the highly entertaining spectacle of a man observed, manipulated and humiliated by the women he has tried to wrong. And this male is ultimately made subject to the desire of the woman who has most aggressively and transgressively sought him. Moreover, that woman has attained her desire, chastely, within the house of a bawd, cooperating with but distancing herself from the wise woman, manoeuvring between the powerlessness of Luce 1 and the victimisation of those nameless women whose babies the cunning woman left on the doorsteps of the rich. The play is thus a site for ideological contestation and negotiation and not merely for the reproduction of dominant ideologies. While it concludes with an image of harmony and utopian resolution of class and gender struggle, it has recorded traces of that struggle.

And what of the female spectator to this fiction? Her experience must have been complicated. Though invited by cultural discourses such as Gosson's to take herself off, like a good Luce 1, to her father's house, to flee the promiscuous gazing of men and to wait for a husband to be delivered to her, the female playgoer nonetheless *was* in the theatre, in this instance watching a fiction that walks a fine line between returning women to their 'proper places' and validating them as desiring, active subjects. If Heywood's text in part enacts in order to allay masculine anxiety about women who exercise control over themselves and over men, it is not clear that female spectators would focus only on the recuperative dimensions of that fiction. Moreover, the female playgoer watching this fiction was herself, in Gosson's terms, within 'the market of bawdrie'; that is, within the commercial theatre, a site, I would argue, every bit as complicated for women as the wise woman's house. In this place of licensed gazing, where men and women alike were both spectacles and spectators, desired and desiring, I doubt that only women's chastity or women's reputations were at risk, despite Gosson's polemic to that effect. Even when this theatre, through its fictions, invited women to take up the subordinate positions masculine ideology defined as proper for them (and Heywood's play, as I have argued, is more transgressive in its gender ideology than such a description would warrant), the very practice of playgoing put women in positions potentially unsettling to patriarchal control. To be part of urban public life as spectator, consumer and judge moved the gentlewoman citizen outside of that domestic enclosure to which Gosson would return her.

While it does no good to exaggerate the powers of women in such a situation, I think the antitheatrical polemicists were right to worry about female theatregoing, though not only for the reasons they were able to articulate. Reading Gosson, I wonder about the unsaid of his text. Focusing on the danger *to* women, did he also feel endangered *by* them? Did he at some level sense that the gentlewomen citizens' attendance at the theatre was part of a process of cultural change, which could help to unsettle the gender positions and definitions upon which masculine dominance rested? In short, was Gosson's unspoken fear that the practice of female theatregoing, the entry of the middle-class woman into the house of Proteus, would spur her transformation from the compliant and powerless object, Luce 1, into the transgressive, desiring subject whose name could only be Luce 2, identical, but oh so different?[27]

NOTES

1. E.K. Chambers, *The Elizabethan Stage*, vol. IV (Oxford: Clarendon Press, 1923), pp. 273–4.
2. Stephen Gosson, *The Schoole of Abuse* (1579), STC 12097.
3. Ben Jonson, *Bartholomew Fair*, ed. Eugene M. Waith (New Haven: Yale University Press, 1963), pp. 30–1.
4. S.P. Zitner in 'Gosson, Ovid, and the Elizabethan audience', *Shakespeare Quarterly*, 9 (1958), pp. 206–8, explores the extent to which Gosson's account of the Elizabethan playgoing audience in the body of *The Schoole of Abuse* draws upon passages in Ovid's *Art of Love*. He concludes that Gosson's descriptions should not be taken as an unmediated eyewitness report of Elizabethan theatregoing. Gosson's debt to Ovid, as well as his polemical intentions, must be taken into account before one accepts his treatise as description of objective fact. In this essay I am more interested in the concluding epistle to the gentlewomen of London than in the body of the tract. More importantly, however, I assume that all of Gosson's tract is ideological and interested, rather than dispassionately objective. I am concerned with why Gosson and his fellow antitheatricalists circulated certain narratives (whatever their source) about women at the theatre; and I wish to offer a counter-account of what the middle-class woman's presence in that cultural space may have signified in terms of changing social relations in early modern England.
5. Andrew Gurr, *Playgoing in Shakespeare's London* (Cambridge: Cambridge University Press, 1987), esp. pp. 56–60.
6. Gosson, Sig. F4.
7. *ibid.*, Sig. C2.
8. *ibid.*, Sig. C2.

9. *ibid.*, Sig. F2.
10. On Nov. 1. 1987, responding to a call from Hedda Nussbaum, police removed 6-year-old Lisa and 16-month-old Mitchell Steinberg from the apartment Nussbaum shared with Joel Steinberg. Both Lisa and Nussbaum had been severely beaten, and when Lisa died four days later, Joel Steinberg was charged with murder and manslaughter. In treating Nussbaum for her many injuries, doctors had to insert a silicon tube to allow one of her eyes to drain properly; she reported that Steinberg had 'a fear of being stared at and repeatedly poked her in the eyes for this offense' (*NY Times*, Dec. 1, 1988). Neighbours reported that Nussbaum had been subjected to continual beating during the previous ten years. The children were subsequently shown to have been adopted illegally. Joel Steinberg was eventually convicted of the manslaughter charge and received the maximum sentence of 8⅓ to 25 years in prison.
11. Steven Mullaney, *The Place of the Stage: License, play, and power in Renaissance England* (Chicago: University of Chicago Press, 1988), esp. pp. 26–59.
12. Jean-Christophe Agnew, *Worlds Apart: The market and the theater in Anglo-American thought, 1550–1750* (Cambridge: Cambridge University Press. 1986), esp. pp. 111–14.
13. The list of those engaged in this enterprise is a long one. I have been especially helped by the work of Catherine Belsey, Lynda Boose, Richard Burt, Walter Cohen, Jonathan Dollimore, Jonathan Goldberg, Stephen Greenblatt, Coppélia Kahn, David Kastan, Kathleen McLuskie, Steven Mullaney, Carol Neely, Karen Newman, Mary Beth Rose, Peter Stallybrass and Leonard Tennenhouse.
14. See especially Louis Althusser, 'Ideology and ideological state apparatuses (notes towards an investigation)', in his *Lenin and Philosophy and Other Essays* (New York: Monthly Review Press, 1971), pp. 127–86.
15. For a useful summary of critiques and extensions of Althusser's work see Terry E. Boswell, Edgar V. Kiser and Kathryn A. Baker, 'Recent developments in Marxist theories of ideology', *Insurgent Sociologist*, **13** (Summer 1986), pp. 5–22.
16. Göran Therborn, *The Ideology of Power and the Power of Ideology* (London: Verso, 1980), pp. 17–18.
17. For the idea of disidentification see Michel Pecheux, *Language, Semantics, and Ideology* (New York: St Martin's Press, 1982), pp. 158–63. For a discussion of the multiple positioning of subjects in complex societies, and of the multiple axes of social struggle, see Chantal Mouffe, 'Radical democracy: modern or postmodern?', in Andrew Ross, ed., *Universal Abandon: The Politics of postmodernism* (Minneapolis: University of Minnesota Press, 1988), pp. 31–45.
18. This critique has by now become a commonplace. It is an indication of changes within new historicism itself that in *Shakespearean Negotiations: The circulation of social energy in Renaissance England* (Berkeley, Calif.: University of California Press, 1988), Stephen Greenblatt writes that 'the circulation of social energy by and through the stage was not part of a single coherent, totalizing system. Rather, it was partial, fragmentary, conflictual; elements were crossed, torn apart, recombined, set against each other; particular social practices were magnified by the stage, others diminished, exalted, evacuated' (p. 19).
19. Richard Burt, ' "Tis writ by me": Massinger's *The Roman Actor* and the politics of reception in the English Renaissance stage', *Theatre Journal*, **40** (1988), pp. 332–46, esp. 343–5.

20. Steven Mullaney, 'The work of culture in an age of theatrical reproduction', unpublished paper delivered at the conference on New Languages for the Stage at the University of Kansas, October 1988.
21. Althusser, 'Ideology', pp. 165–70.
22. David Scott Kastan, 'Proud majesty made a subject: Shakespeare and the spectacle of rule', *Shakespeare Quarterly*, 37 (1986), pp. 459–75, esp. 472–5.
23. A number of scholars have dealt with this issue. For an overview of the debates see my essay 'Crossdressing, the theater and gender struggle in early modern England', *Shakespeare Quarterly*, 39 (Winter 1988), pp. 418–40.
24. Keith Thomas, *Religion and the Decline of Magic: Studies in popular culture in sixteenth and seventeenth century England* (London: Weidenfeld and Nicolson, 1971), pp. 177–279, esp. 265.
25. Reginald Scot, *The Discoverie of Witchcraft* (1584; rpt., ed. Brinsley Nicolson, London: Elliot Stock, 1886).
26. Thomas Heywood, *The Wise Woman of Hogsdon*, in *The Dramatic Works of Thomas Heywood*, vol. 5 (London: Russell and Russell, 1964), pp. 275–353.
27. It has long been debated whether women lost or gained power during the Renaissance. This paper cannot begin to address that question adequately, in part because to do so one must pay careful attention to differences in the positions of women in various class and status groups. Certainly, as the work of Catherine Belsey (*The Subject of Tragedy: Identity and difference in Renaissance drama* (London: Methuen, 1985)), Carole Pateman (*The Sexual Contract* (Stanford: Stanford University Press, 1988)), and others has suggested, it would be naive to assume that in the seventeenth century even middle-class women ceased to be the objects of patriarchal oppression, though the forms of patriarchy were certainly in flux. In this essay I am suggesting, however, that at a period of cultural change such as the seventeenth century certainly was, patriarchal control of female subjects was – in some places, for some women – less than absolute; that in the very display of patriarchal anxiety one can read traces of a social struggle whose outcome could not be known in advance, any more than can the outcome of social struggles in our own time.

10

Nostalgia and the 'Rise of English': Rhetorical Questions

Stephen Foley

'I loathe nostalgia.' So declares Diana Vreeland in the first sentence of her best-selling memoir, *D.V.*[1] Vreeland goes on to recount how she punched Swifty Lazar in the nose and pommelled his chest after he dared to suggest that she revelled in nostalgia. These are unlikely words for the genius of cultural marketing whose costume shows at the Metropolitan Museum of New York discovered in snobbish revivals of aristocratic fashion and decorative femininity the perfect vehicle for promoting consumerist narcissism and elitist ideology. Vreeland was one of the prime movers and profiteers of the recent flirtation of upscale popular culture with its imaginary forebears of the turn of the century. From *Upstairs/Downstairs* to the *Jewel in the Crown*, from the passing cult of the preppie to the flowered chintz of the country-house look and the horsey-set line of Polo fashion (marketed *par excellence* in Ralph Lauren's robber-baron mansion cum boutique on Madison Avenue), consumers have sponged up the opulent decor of elite culture.

But as Debora Silverman argues in *Selling Culture: Bloomingdale's, Diana Vreeland, and the new aristocracy of taste in Reagan's America*,[2] Vreeland's defensive contempt for nostalgia and her stylised personal violence are indeed appropriate to her enterprise in cultural history, which, paradoxically, 'celebrates the destruction of time and money.' 'Nostalgia', Silverman comments:

> presupposes the differentiation of a prior historical world from an experienced present condition. Vreeland's *D.V.* motto, 'Fake it, Fake it', banishes nostalgia for fabrication; in a world where reality is what 'you wish it to be, as you wish it into being', nostalgia dissolves amidst successive moments of vigorous self-invention. (p. 108)

The line Vreeland gleefully draws between nostalgia and historical fabrication is an ironic reinscription of the distinction between nostalgia and historical truth, and it is no less moralistic than the positivism it mocks: it celebrates will rather than truth. But I use the Vreeland story as a preface here because it loosens 'nostalgia' from common sense and convention. Nostalgia involves the complex affective relations to the 'past' that engage us as readers and writers appropriating the past through history. Vreeland loathes nostalgia not because it falsifies 'facts', but because it can master the will of the historian producing it.

In the eighteenth and nineteenth centuries, the word 'nostalgia' suggested homesickness (from the Greek *nostos*, 'return home', and *algia*, 'pain'), a sentimental longing for home that mingled pleasure and pain. In contemporary usage, 'nostalgia' almost always suggests the longing for a lost, idealised past, whether that longing is viewed as the object of scorn ('naive, sentimental, and nostalgic') or admiration ('a warm and nostalgic reminiscence'). Nostalgia has a labile affective range. Just as homesickness can be bittersweet, so too can nostalgia evoke the many feelings generated by imagining the 'past', the pleasure of producing it, the pain of having 'lost' it, or the contempt one feels for its faults, traversing and confusing categories of praise and blame.[3]

As a form of desire, a 'longing for the past', nostalgia is always at work in the writing of history. The interest of an historicist enterprise in nostalgia, then, lies not in the naive attempt to deny or exclude it, but in exploring the many and complex ways nostalgia works in historical rhetoric. What are the uses of nostalgia? My particular concern for the moment is with the complex operations of nostalgia in the 'liveliness' of historiography. 'Liveliness' is produced through an affective rhetoric of nostalgic identification – through received categories of 'life' – that may be at odds with the argument the 'lively' narrative is mounted to demonstrate. To look back for a moment to consumer culture, consider how, even in such thoughtful series as *Upstairs/Downstairs* or the *Jewel in the Crown*, the 'lifelike' cinematic realism of the decor often displaces the social analysis of power, gender, race and class. What bourgeois household would not envy the splendid array of copper pots, the well-honed cutlery, the polished oak, the cast-iron cookstove of the Bellamy kitchen, not to mention the silver combs and brushes of the dressing room or the supple leather on the Chesterfield sofa in the morning room upstairs?

'Liveliness' allows historians to enjoy the 'past', to savour it, to smile at it – even as they critique it. I enjoy my Vreeland story, for example, for the sassy irreverence Vreeland deploys against common sense as much as I deplore the uncritical cultural market and the unchecked opportunism it depicts. What valence does my nostalgic celebration of D.V. obtain? Is the violence of the punch contained in the humour of the anecdote, or reproduced? Am I telling the story for the 'punch'? To what degree can someone who recounts a 'lively' story about the past distance himself from the values displayed in the material he recapitulates or the affective rhetorical structures he deploys? What are the uses of nostalgia in the 'liveliness' of historical narrative? What are the contradictions? Could 'liveliness' as a nostalgic rhetorical operation initiate an unchecked and untheorised counter-movement from within the context of an historicist argument?

I SHAKESPEARE STUDIES ON THE MAKE

The late twentieth-century fascination with the twilight of imperialism and high capitalism is represented in scholarship as well as in popular culture. And I should like to shift now to the current interest among Shakespeare scholars in 'lively' stories about imperial Britain presiding over the origins of English studies in the nineteenth and early twentieth centuries. Variants of the stories may be found, for example, in the opening chapter, 'The rise of English', in Terry Eagleton's influential textbook *Literary Theory*, in Marjorie Garber's elegant allusions to the Baconian and Oxfordian controversies in *Shakespeare's Ghost Writers*, in Marion O'Connor's painstaking survey of William Poel's sumptuous theatrical productions and, most pointedly, in the studied irreverence of Terence Hawkes's *That Shakespeherian Rag*.[4]

One of the most charming and persuasive elements of Hawkes's savvy, casual style is the way he splices stories together in unexpected order, thus eliding cultural categories and suggesting the implication of the present and the past, the beautiful and the ugly, literary appreciation, imperialism, class and patriarchy. Hawkes begins his book from a fast-food joint, 'I am eating fish and chips in Stratord-upon-Avon' (p. 1), leaning upon a canal lock looking down upon the river Avon while the fish-and-chip shop lies to his left and the Royal Shakespeare Theatre to his right. The opening scenario thus foregrounds the full historical implication both of Shakespeare's theatrical enterprise and of the continuing cultural appropriation of 'Shakespeare' in national culture, with their social and cultural economies.

It is on Hawkes's lively stories, then, that I shall linger at the beginning of this essay, because the very strengths of Hawkes's book – above all the 'liveliness' with which he tells his stories and splices them together – seem to provide a fascinating opportunity to study the contradictory rhetorical operation of nostalgia in historical narrative.

In one particularly well-circulated chapter, ' "Swisser Swatter": the making of a man of English letters' – published separately in the liminal anthology *Alternative Shakespeares*[5] – Hawkes interweaves his continuing rereading of *The Tempest* with an account of the career of Sir Walter Alexander Raleigh, the first professor of English literature at Oxford, and the man chosen to write the Shakespeare volume for the English Men of Letters series. If Caliban, as Hawkes suggests, is a dangerous site for the play of competing discourses of 'what makes a man', the English Men of Letters series is an attempt to regulate English culture by 'making a man' along imperialist and patriarchal lines; it supplements other totalising enterprises like the *OED*, the Victoria County Histories, the *DNB* and the establishment of compulsory primary education. As Hawkes puts it: 'The monumentalizing, coherence-generating, sense- and history-making activity of the English Men of Letters simply constitutes the truth: the truth that the true heritage of British culture is written down, and in English, and by men' (p. 56).

In his critique of Raleigh's imperialist and patriarchal industry, Hawkes depicts a Raleigh who comes close to parodying himself and his ideology, a point that Hawkes emphasises by selectively quoting and exposing the most transparent examples of Raleigh's patriarchal pride:

> Finally, the English writer of Letters must be seen to be a Man. I have already discussed the notoriously complex issues this raises for most cultures, not the least the one of which Shakespeare himself was (if you'll pardon the expression) a male member. But I'm happy to report that Raleigh's highly potent critical art proves able to cut through these with the dispatch of one to whom maleness is evidently a crucial touchstone of manliness. Shakespeare's standing as an English Man of Letters is vested . . . in a much more assertive, even aggressive mode of existence where a horny-handed Bard who is 'the greatest of artisans' manifests the starkest kind of maleness not to say membership, 'when he collects his might and stands dilated, his imagination aflame, the thick-coming central thoughts and fantasies shaping themselves, under the stress of his central will, into a thing of life.' Shakespeare as Phallus of the Golden Age – Phallus in Wonderland – is of course no more peculiar a formulation than many. (pp. 59–60)

No more peculiar, perhaps, than Hawkes's comic interest in phallic figuration. Hawkes goes on to demonstrate how Raleigh in a British Academy lecture deployed his considerable skills as an allegorist to bring *The Tempest* into play in the war effort ('A small British expeditionary force, bound on an international mission, finds itself stranded in an unknown country . . .'), celebrating in the Bard the Anglo-Saxon unity of England and the United States in their common language and turning Caliban into a low creature, 'the monster, the mooncalf, as who should say Fritz or the Boche'.[6]

Hawkes's reading of Raleigh's appropriation is meant not to demonstrate that Raleigh was misinterpreting the play but that his reading, like all readings, was ideologically engaged, and in alluding to the outlines of Hawkes's argument I am scarcely doing it justice. But the prominence of the lively anecdote in Hawkes's narrative indeed draws the reader to the outlines. Hawkes's method is, as he puts it, to present only 'the slightest series of sketches'. But these 'barest' sketches allude to an historical argument. What is displaced or covered over in this historical argument as the male member is enlarged in caricature? What is the ideological function of gender in the affective rhetorical structures of Hawkes's nostalgic caricature?

Hawkes cuts off his discussion of Raleigh at the close of the chapter with a neat play of anachronistic name and namesake, turning to another phallic story about making a man of letters, a story related by John Aubrey about the Elizabethan Sir Walter Raleigh:

> He loved a wench well; and one time getting one of the Maids of Honour up against a tree in a wood ('twas his first lady) who seemed at first boarding to be something fearful of her honour, and modest, she cried 'Sweet Sir Walter, what do you me ask: Will you undo me? Nay, sweet Sir Walter! Sweet Sir Walter! Sweet Sir Walter!' At last, as the danger and the pleasure at the same time grew higher, she cried in the ecstasy, 'Swisser Swatter, Swisser Swatter'.[7]

Hawkes's final comments are laconic: 'It remains only a manner of minor interest to record that the wench turned out eventually to be with child, that she was subsequently delivered of a son, and that a man was thus "made" to the sound of this creative deconstruction of English letters' (p. 71).

The phallic humour that was somewhat ironised earlier in the discussion of the 'membership' of Sir Walter Alexander Raleigh is not entirely mitigated here. Hawkes offers the anecdote 'as a perfect instance of how, under the pressures of "making", any use of language proves capable of disintegration' (p. 70). The anecdote stands, I suppose, for the cultural making and unmaking Hawkes observes in the 'making' of Caliban, the 'making' of 'Shakespeare', the 'making' of Sir Walter Alexander Raleigh's career, and 'swisser swatter' stands for the arbitrary reshaping of the difference between sense and nonsense, English and pidgin, along ideological lines. But the anecdote is hardly a 'perfect instance'. Indeed, I find it confusing rhetorically. What precisely is 'of minor interest' in the anecdote? That the victim of the rape was impregnated? That the offspring of the rape happened to be male? It cannot be that the making of a man to the sound of this 'creative deconstruction of English letters' is 'of minor interest' because this is precisely the phenomenon of which the anecdote is a 'perfect instance'. And what accounts for this linguistic disintegration? Who is making (it) here and who is being made? The lascivious masculine wit of the anecdote is played into Hawkes's argument unabashedly, the penetration of an unwilling woman by a man on the make imagined as pleasure and danger, turning a woman's denial into an ecstasy, the undoing of her language the imagined effect of a man undoing her. Perhaps 'creative deconstruction' is dangerously close to a fantasy of imaginative deflowering or rape with flair or the grateful victim. Does the rhetorical structure of the anecdote equate Hawkes's 'creative deconstruction' with Raleigh's?

All I am suggesting is that for the purposes of bringing an argument to a sassy conclusion, a responsible historian and critic of patriarchy has momentarily regressed into a distasteful joke, an incisive and insolent moment of critical reprise that rhetorically works against the position it argues, for the masculinist affective rhetoric of this lively anecdote nostalgically reproduces the patriarchal order it critiques. And the bad joke is perhaps also the marker of a lapse in historiographical practice. For just as Hawkes's rehearsal of Aubrey's anecdote fails to account for the position of the woman, the caricature of the modern Sir Walter Raleigh and the sketch of the rise of English at Oxford leaves out precisely the full range of the material conditions that historicism seeks to invoke, and one of these conditions is the sustained and growing demand from many sectors of British society – labour, evangelical, socialist, liberal, middle-class – to provide education for working-class men and for women. English studies were first institutionalised not at Oxford but in women's cooperative societies and working-men's institutes. As Brian Doyle remarks in 'The hidden history of English studies' (published in his *Re-reading English*, an excellent anthology in an influential series edited by Terence Hawkes): 'The accepted focus upon Oxbridge also misses the key fact that institutional initiatives there were responses to a "well founded national demand" for English in education.' And this demand, Doyle argues, was gendered, and English studies arose as a subject for women and children, 'a key element in a more general demand to school the "nation's children", predominantly using personnel of a certain kind (the mother–teacher)'.[8]

Hawkes's 'revisionist' history of the rise of English studies, like others, replicates some of the gendered structures it discovers in the origins of its discipline. As Lisa Jardine has suggested in ' "Girl talk" (for boys on the left) or marginalizing feminist critical praxis',

> the version of the story which says that traditional Lit. Crit. is a conservative power-base ... depends upon ignoring English's 'suitability' for women – when was a women's subject ever a power-base for anything? Then, the 'progressive' version which says that ideally Eng. Lit. is 'a critical cultural study, bound up with the analysis of forms of writing in their historical conditions of emergence and effect, of conventions and determinations of reading, of the construction and transmission of culture' also appears crucially to involve making women invisible. . . . For here again, such a study is contrasted with obviously subjective (feminine?) approaches to texts, which are not theory-based.[9]

Theoretically, Hawkes's historical narrative opens up the circulation of gendered and class-based discourses of power in the institution of English education. But the rhetorical effect of Hawkes's stylised history through caricature – Raleigh, A.C. Bradley, Dover Wilson – is also reductive, suggesting English as a conspiracy successfully foisted upon a docile populace by avuncular professors. The jocular style of Hawkes's anecdotal history allows it to get away with the professional fallacy of listening only to the teacher. Merely attending to who is the teacher and making fun of what he says does not take into account the full material conditions of ideological production, among those conditions who is present or absent in class, who is listening, and what she accepts, rejects and changes in the lesson.

II VIRGINIA DISCOVERS RALEIGH

As a young writer, Virginia Woolf reviewed two of Professor Raleigh's books; he is mentioned ominously in *A Room of One's Own*; and after his death she used the occasion of a review of a posthumous collection of his letters (edited by Lady Raleigh) to write a satiric essay on his career. In the 11 August 1906 issue of *The Speaker, the Liberal Review* appears a brief unsigned review ('Trafficks and discoveries') of Raleigh's *English Voyages of the Sixteenth Century*, one of his few scholarly endeavours.[10] Woolf professes gratefulness to Raleigh for providing the intellectual guidance that makes the voyage literature previously available only in an early nineteenth-century Hakluyt (she had read Hakluyt voraciously since she was fifteen) historically intelligible:

> To know that it was all founded on hard truth, that the voyagers were substantial Elizabethan seamen, and that the whole makes a consecutive chapter of English history checks the tendency which we feel towards a vague enthusiasm, but founds it on a real and permanent basis. And the more detailed our knowledge of the men and their adventures, the more potently they touch our imaginations. (p. 121)

Woolf is fascinated, above all, by the rough-hewn and authentic style of these rich and strange documents:

> The charm of Hakluyt's great book, indeed, does not lie in any mediated felicity so much as in its air of rough and unsophisticated simplicity, so often made a matter of apology for the writers themselves. They have neither learning nor leisure to 'vary or multiply words'. But their laborious pens, dipping into the stately vocabulary which was common to seamen and poet, build up such a noble structure of words in the end that the effect is as rich and more authentic than that got by more artistic processes. The frequent lists of 'commodities' even have a strange charm . . . In these long lists, moreover, little landscapes are let in, all the more romantic because they have been observed with the same sober and veracious eyes and inscribed with the same stiff pen. (pp. 121–2)

Woolf, following Raleigh, is fully attendant to the various motives of the explorers, to the 'carnival of plunder' (Raleigh's phrase) that they casually enjoyed and to their infinite credulity, 'the largeness of their imaginations, stretched to hold any miracle undoubtingly' (p. 121). But she is fascinated – as she was in her later essay on Hakluyt, 'The Elizabethan lumber room' – with the rough referentiality of their style and the material engagement of the imagination with landscape; and with the way the 'noble structure of words' is gendered 'by the same stiff pen' that 'potently . . . touches our imagination'.

It is precisely this gendered engagement – the manly style that allows the voyagers to see the landscape as they do – that draws Woolf's reading of the voyagers into the figuration of her much revised first novel, *The Voyage Out*, in which a young woman, Rachel Vinrace, accompanying her shipping-merchant father (mother dead, of course) on a trip to South America, voyages – in as much as she can – out of her status as the dutiful daughter of a late Victorian father into a new, partial understanding of herself (cut off by her death by fever). This awakening – and its tragic inadequacy – is in part figured by her identification with the Elizabethan voyagers (as well as with Shakespeare's Miranda). The Elizabethan voyage references, as Alice Fox has proposed, suggest 'the impossibility of a young woman's coming of age when society itself was arrested at an early stage of development and incapable of change.'[11] Rachel, Woolf states, 'had been educated as the majority of well-to-do girls in the last part of the nineteenth century were educated . . . there was no subject in the world which she knew accurately. Her mind was in the state of an intelligent man's in the beginning of the reign of Queen Elizabeth; she would believe practically anything she was told.'[12]

Woolf's playful inversion of gender provides a reminder that Rachel's 'ignorance' is constructed socially, not naturally, and that men could be ignorant too. And the restaging of the 'discovery of the virgin land' suggests how the patriarchal exclusion of women from access to education inscribes itself upon language. The male voyagers enjoy a richer identification with the power and 'imagination' of their Elizabethan predecessors. When the ship *Euphrosyne* arrives in port in South America, one of the passengers, a scholarly and talkative gentleman, borrows from Hakluyt a passage that celebrates the male conquest of the virgin land:

> Half-drawn up upon the beach lay an equal number of Spanish galleons, unmanned for the country was still a virgin land behind a veil. Slipping across the water, the English sailors bore away bars of silver, bales of linen, timbers of cedar wood, golden crucifixes knobbed with emeralds. When the Spaniards came down from their drinking, a fight ensued, the two parties churning up the sand and driving each other into the surf. The Spaniards, bloated with fine living upon the fruits of the miraculous land, fell in heaps; but the hardy Englishmen, tawny with sea-voyaging, hairy for lack of

razors, tawny fingers itching for gold, despatched the wounded, drove the dying into the sea, and soon reduced the natives to a state of superstitious wonderment. (p. 101)

Woolf's irony in this use of Hakluyt is palpable. Violence, discovery, bravery, greed, lust and (not least) the scholarly self-confidence and poise of the paraphrasing gentleman – all figured together with manly style in the story of male rivals fighting over the possession of a virgin land. To the male characters in the book – more and more so in each subsequent revision, according to Fox[13] – belongs the engagement of the imagination with the experience of the new world, for the 'literary' language of the imagination, like the language of exploration and discovery, has been gendered male, shaped by the professional structures of knowledge available to the educated man.

In the published version of the novel, Hewet, Rachel's 'literary' fiancé, exclaims when he looks up from the poem he is composing as the party glides up the river through the forest, 'That's where the Elizabethans got their style . . . staring into the profusion of leaves and blossoms and prodigious fruits.' But Mrs Flushing, an emblem of the woman written out of the 'letters' men 'make', immediately interjects: ' "Shakespeare, I hate Shakespeare" . . . and Wilfred returned admiringly, "I believe you're the only person who dares to say that, Alice" ' (p. 328). A cancelled passage in an earlier draft is particularly revealing of Woolf's scene of reading and writing here. In the earlier draft the passage names one of Woolf's sources: ' "Lord!" Hirst exclaimed, looking up from his sheet of paper. "I feel just like the late Sir Walter Raleigh. I see now where the Elizabethans got their style. Isn't it superb?" he asked Helen.'[14] The late Sir Walter Raleigh, Fox notes, is not the Elizabethan but the contemporary, a late *Sir*, having been recently knighted. Hirst, his own pen on the page, 'discovers' the lush landscape through the empowerment of 'style'. What makes 'it' (the landscape? the experience?) 'superb' to him is not simply the object in his view but the pride of rediscovering the cultural empowerment of 'style', the momentary pleasure of 'feeling just like Sir Walter Raleigh'.

Woolf's satiric review of Raleigh's letters in *Vogue* in 1926 gives full expression to her contempt for the macho professional rhetoric that had won the knighthood for *Sir* Walter Raleigh. Woolf sees in Raleigh's success the danger of the new, safe, unreflected professionalism of university instruction in English, where Raleigh's jocularity and bravado efface the difference of literature and blend it seamlessly into the hearty male banter of the boardroom, the club, the chambers of the law:

There is necessarily a great deal of talk about the profession of teaching literature, and the profession of writing literary textbooks, of 'doing

Chaucer in six chapters and Wordsworth, better known as Daddy, also in six chapters.' But when one looks for the unprofessional talk, the talk which is talked among friends when business hours are over, one is bewildered and disappointed. Is this all the Professor of English literature has to say? 'Scott to-morrow – not a poet I think but a fine old man. Good old Scott.' . . . 'As for old Bill Wordsworth he is the same stick-in-the-mud as ever . . .' Any clever man at a dinner party anxious not to scare the rowing blue or the city magnate who happens to be within earshot would have talked about books exactly as Raleigh wrote about them at his leisure.[15]

Raleigh was a brilliant professor of literature, Woolf writes, because he professed enthusiasm rather than facts, entertainment rather than books, turning his lectures into a vehicle for self-promotion:

> He talked his lectures almost out of his head. He joked, he told stories. He made undergraduates rock with laughter. He drew them in crowds to his lecture room. And they went away loving something or other. Perhaps it was Keats. Perhaps it was the British Empire. Certainly it was Walter Raleigh. But we should be much surprised if anybody went away loving poetry, loving the art of letters. (pp. 315–16)

Raleigh's brusque style at the podium made the study of literature safe for the modern man by deflecting the suspiciously feminine 'love' of letters onto more appropriate objects of desire. The lecture, as a form of univocal authority, was his forte. 'Lecturing', Woolf wrote elsewhere, 'incites the most debased of human passions – vanity, ostentation, self-assertion, and the desire to convert.'[16]

The crisis for Raleigh came, Woolf surmises, when he followed out the logic of his own lectures. 'Soon, therefore', she writes,

> for he was by temperament highly adventurous, he began to find literature a little dull. He began to separate literature from life. He began to cry out upon 'culture' and 'culture bugs'. He began to despise critics and criticism. 'I can't help feeling that critical admiration for what another man has written is an emotion for spinsters,' he wrote. He really believed, he said, 'not in refinement and scholarly elegance, those are only a game; but in blood feuds, and the chase of wild beasts, and marriage by capture'. (p. 317)

Woolf's final paragraphs are devastating. In suppressing identification with spinsters and 'admiration for . . . another man', Raleigh's literary machismo found its final satisfaction in a wilful yearning for change and thoughtless martial pride:

> When the guns fired in August 1914, no one saluted them more rapturously than the Professor of English Literature at Oxford. 'The air is better to breathe than it has been for years,' he exclaimed. 'I'm glad I lived to see it, and sick that I'm not in it.'

It seemed indeed as if his chance of life had come too late. He still seemed fated to praise fighting but not to fight, to lecture about life, but not to live. He did what a man of his age could do. He drilled. He marched. He wrote pamphlets. He lectured more frequently than ever; he practically ceased to read. At length he was made historian of the Air Force. To his infinite satisfaction he consorted with soldiers. To his immense delight he flew to Baghdad. He died within a week or two after his return. But what did that matter? The Professor of English Literature had lived at last. (pp. 317–18)

From the insecurity of a professor appropriating 'women's work' arises a dangerous modern manhood. For Woolf, Raleigh is not a quaint relic of waning imperialism, an effete bearded Victorian patriarch, but the adumbration of a new era. Raleigh despised the Victorians. It was in part at his urging that his former pupil Lytton Strachey wrote *Eminent Victorians*. Raleigh is not so much a Victorian patriarch as a modern man whose patriarchy is suffused by the neutral demeanour of an efficient, above all, and agreeable professionalism. In Raleigh's brusque, manly style, in the jocular style of the boardroom or the club, Woolf found ominous signs of a dark future. As Woolf states in *A Room of One's Own*, written as a parody of the lecture form in which Raleigh and other male professors excelled: 'I began to envisage an era of pure, self-assertive virility, such as the letters of professors (take Sir Walter Raleigh's letters, for instance) seem to forebode, and the rulers of Italy have already brought into being.'[17]

III FEMINISM AND HISTORICISM: RHETORICAL QUESTIONS

I do not hate nostalgia. Nor am I particularly fond of seeing people punched in the nose. And when people *are* being punched in the nose, or shot at across trenches, or even called names across a conference table or from a lecturer's podium, I think it is important to reflect upon the structure of the conflict. Sometimes it helps to theorise. But in the case of the conflict we have recently seen staged in Shakespeare studies between 'feminism' and 'historicism', questions raised on theoretical grounds seem to produce an illusory suspension of disagreement, for the issues generating the conflict are in part untheorised matters of gendered institutional practice and gendered professional decorum.

I have suggested a critique of *That Shakespeherian Rag* because I believe that the affective rhetorical structures of the work return us nostalgically to an uncriticised patriarchal order. And, in an alternative, nostalgic, rhetorical move of my own, I introduce Virginia Woolf. I introduce her not simply as a means of filling in Hawkes's sketch by suggesting how such works as Raleigh's anthology were appropriated by

English-speaking readers (male and female, working class and privileged, British and colonial), but because Woolf insists upon the importance of professional rhetoric and its historical function in elite academic professional culture as a critical issue in feminist historiography (conveniently, my own interest). I am saying the obvious here. But is not the obvious what needs most to be examined? Is not the obvious, to go back to its Latin etymology (*ob via*), what is in the way?

If I were writing the history of the rise of English (would I use the word 'rise'?) I should like to fill in the humorous sketch. I should like to know more about the 'pre-professional', about the women's institutes of nineteenth-century England, about the history of women's journalism, about the affairs of literary and historical societies, about the structures of gender in aestheticism. I should like to know more about the careers of female actors, about the transformations of Ellen Terry on the lecture circuit, where, as Nina Auerbach's rich biography suggests, 'the ruminating actress turns herself into a female Shakespeare'[18] with moving brilliance and at great personal cost. I should like to know more about characters like the generous and violent Frederick Furnival, in whose manifold projects feminism, imperialism, Christian socialism, teetotalling, racism, uxoriousness, pantocracy, sculling, Shakespeare and workingmen's and women's education intersect and challenge one another. I should like to know more about nineteenth-century liberalism, whose complicities should offer useful moments of comparison to our own.

A figure like Joseph Wright, the editor of the *English Dialect Dictionary*, would provide an interesting contrast to Raleigh. First educated as a teenage millworker in evening classes and at the Mechanic's Institute at Bradford, Wright studied for a degree at the University of London and ultimately received a PhD from Heidelberg. In 1888 he was appointed lecturer to the Association for the Higher Education of Women at Oxford, and he also taught for the Taylor Institute. In 1891 he was named deputy to the professor of comparative philology at Oxford, where he worked for fourteen years to complete the Dictionary. In 1901 he was named Corpus Christi professor of comparative philology.

Even looking to pedigreed members of the Oxford clerisy like Sir Edmund Kerchever Chambers might provide subtler shading in the sketch of the story of English studies. It would be easy to caricature Chambers as the Edwardian gentleman-bureaucrat (a first in Greats, failure to win a fellowship, successful career at the Board of Education, brilliant scholarship on the side, knighthood) and to expose the paternalism of his commitment to developing wider access to a national system of education. Even his friends attest to his arch and austere demeanour. The 'forbidding manner' of this intellectual elitist may, his colleague Dover Wilson suggests, have stood in the way of his advancement to permanent secretary of the Board.[19] Indeed, a joke circulated that Madame Tussaud's has a chamber of horrors, but the Board has a horror of Chambers.[20]

But one might also attend to Wilson's caution that 'the sardonic mask he habitually wore concealed a genuine enthusiasm for education and more liberal notions on that subject than those held by many other officials of the Board' (p. 275). For four terms while staying on at Oxford after taking his degree he lectured on Elizabethan literature for the Association for the Education of Women, his only professional teaching appointment. His major commitments and accomplishment at the Board were programmes in 'continuation schools' for adolescents past the leaving age and in winning government funding for the university tutorial classes.

Chambers's broad liberalism, as well as his assiduous research, give his work as a Shakespearean a far different cast from Raleigh's. He was not embarrassed to be a scholar in the field of English literature, and his works, from *The Medieval Stage* and *The Elizabethan Stage* to *Shakespeare* and *Shakespearean Gleanings*, painstakingly 'make' the life of Shakespeare by historicising, by figuring the social, economic, political and cultural conditions of Shakespeare's work. To be sure, Chambers was a patriot, and he revered Shakespeare as a national poet. Chambers's principal popular work, his 'common reader' introductions to the plays (originally prepared for the Red Letter Shakespeare (1904–8) and collected in 1925 as *Shakespeare: A Survey*), are prefaced in that collection by a sonnet written in 1916, imploring Shakespeare for 'solace' – not for the bugle's call to battle, or for the women who bravely conceal their sorrow, but for the 'babbling tongues' and 'fretful pens shod with an egoist's gold'[21]: that is, for the resistance (socialist and pacifist) to the mobilisation for the First World War. But these essays never rise to the imperialist jingoism and phallic, bardolatrous rhetoric Raleigh exhibits.

One might, for example, consider Chambers's parting words on Caliban: 'And is it upon Caliban or upon the missionaries of European civilisation that the irony falls, in his complaint against Prospero – "You taught me language, and my profit on it/Is, I know how to curse" ' (p. 315). Or one might look at his guarded remarks on *Henry V*:

> And with the virtues of nationalism go its defects. To our modern thinking the lust of conquest is at once base and terrible. A spirited foreign policy has its reaction in the ineradicable tendency to regard mere matters of domestic concern as not worth taking thought for. The king tells the French ambassador how – 'We never valued this poor seat of England,' and one recognizes the prototype of the blatant modern imperialist, with his insolent talk of 'little England'. (pp. 142–3)

One might well linger over the circumspectness with which Chambers confronts *The Taming of the Shrew*. Chambers's argument ends with a complex yet indecisive appeal to the historical conditions and generic codes that gave rise to Elizabethan farce, to bourgeois comedy or comedy of the marketplace, a form that confronts entrenched social problems with an outlook 'definitely brutal or cynical', mitigated by shared laughter (p. 43). But he does not skirt the definition of the feminist issues raised for the contemporary critic by the play. He begins by acknowledging with deft irony (as we might today), the dangers of what one might call generational pride or the chauvinism of 'progress':

> An age which flatters itself, so far at least as its formal professions of faith are concerned, that it has rounded Cape Turk, must needs make it a point of honour to take offence at the theme and temper of *The Taming of the Shrew*. The Odyssey of the fair lady of Padua is certainly conceived in a spirit which suggests the author of *The First Blast of the Trumpet against the Monstrous Regiment of Women* rather than the author of *The Subjection of Women*. And if you have wept for the hunted Diana, you can hardly refuse to shed a tear for the humiliation of Katherina. . . . [S]he, no less than her nineteenth-century sister, stands for all time as a type for the wrongs done to her much-enduring sex. You do not need her final sermon, with the symbolical placing of her head beneath the foot of the genial ruffian who has subdued her, to point the obsolete and degrading moral: 'such duty as the subject owes the prince, / Even such a woman oweth to her husband.' (p. 40)

Chambers observes that passing the blame off on Shakespeare's source, miraculously transformed by 'Shakespeare's immortal humour triumphant', is an inadequate argument, for Shakespeare was responsible for the ways in which he appropriated and adapted his sources, and thus 'laid himself open to any ethical criticism which they may entail' (pp. 42–3). Chambers likewise dismisses the appeal to universality or to historical difference, for although 'the saying that Shakespeare "was not of an age, but for all time" is about as true as every mortuary phrase . . . and his ethical standpoint is in many respects incomprehensible to those who come after him' (pp. 42–3), this argument is only true 'so far as it goes' (p. 43).

A final eminent Shakespearean I should mention is Caroline Spurgeon, Hildred Carlisle Professor of English at the University of London, president of Bedford College,[22] whose address on 'Shakespeare's iterative imagery', presented to the British Academy in 1931 (she was the first woman to deliver the annual Shakespeare lecture), grew into an influential book, *Shakespeare's Imagery and What It Tells Us*,[23] which went through six printings between 1935 and 1968. Spurgeon, no less than Raleigh, sought to 'make' a portrait of Shakespeare in her book. But her methods are different. She begins with an epigraph from Virginia Woolf's *Orlando*: 'Every secret of a writer's soul, every experience of his life, every quality of his mind, is written large in his works, yet we require critics to explain the one and biographers to explain the other.' Spurgeon's method is to construct a biography though criticism, pursuing the indirect method of writing a life through images used by Shakespeare:

> like the man who under stress of emotion will show no sign of it in eye or face, but will reveal it in some muscular tension, the poet unwittingly lays bare his own innermost likes and dislikes, observations and interests, associations of thought, attitudes of mind and beliefs, in and through images, the verbal pictures he draws to illuminate something quite different in the speech and thought of his characters. (p. 4)

Spurgeon is looking for the authentic Shakespeare, and she finds what she is looking for, perhaps most memorably when she confirms the source for Shakespeare's image of the current circling back under the arch of a flooded bridge through a chance encounter in a bookstore in Stratford. There Captain Jaggard, the proprietor, a descendant of William Jaggard, the printer of the first folio, described 'in prose, in minute detail, exactly what a Stratford man had thus set down in verse three hundred and fifty years ago'. She immediately went down to the river bank and stood looking at the eighteenth arch, composing the pen-and-ink sketch that appears as the frontispiece to her book: 'There is a sort of little hook or bend in the bank just below where the current strikes it after coming under the arch, which produces the eddy and helps send the water back again (see sketch)' (pp. 97–8).

The breach of 'professional' or 'professorial' decorum here – is it not travel-writers and (lady?) journalists and sentimental lovers of letters who begin their works with sketches from their own hands? – suggests how the origins of Spurgeon's 'making' of Shakespeare differ from Raleigh's or Chambers's. Her style is digressive, sentimental, disarmingly confessional. And the Shakespeare she 'makes' is a man of exquisite feeling:

> These, then, are the five outstanding qualities of Shakespeare's nature – sensitiveness, poise, courage, humour, and wholesomeness – balancing, complementing and supporting one another. . . . The intense sensitiveness, the vividness of his imagination, make the courage the more remarkable. . . . What rouses most his anger is hypocrisy and injustice, what he values supremely is kindliness and mercy.
>   He is indeed himself in many ways in character what one can only describe as Christ-like . . .
>   There is one thought . . . which we find recurring in his work in many forms all through his career, and it would seem, quite simply, to be this: that by, in and for ourselves, we are as nothing; we exist only just in so far as we touch our fellows, and receive back from them the warmth or light we have ourselves sent out. (p. 207)

Spurgeon's Shakespeare recalls the model for English studies as it was constructed for women in the late nineteenth century. This model too, is focused upon 'making' a man, with the critical difference being the affective structures opened up by the charitable intervention of nurturing woman, or, as Raleigh put it, 'emotion for spinsters'. In the words of Charles Kingsley, proposing the suitability of an English course for women:

> Such a course – would quicken women's inborn personal interest in the actors of this life-drama, and be quickened by it in return, as indeed it ought: for it is thus that God intended woman to look instinctively at the world. Would to God that she would in these days claim and fulfil to the uttermost her vocation as the priestess of charity![24]

Spurgeon, in the role of the Christian priestess of charity, is not embarrassed to examine her own feelings and Shakespeare's down to the domestic and intimate detail, an enterprise she defends against the professorial charge of triviality: 'not that we want to know necessarily, or only, as Professor Raleigh scoffingly says, how he wore his hat.' She simply craves knowledge 'of the more significant small things about him which we know and love in those who are dear to us' (p. 201). I too like to find my history in small things, in 'lived relations', and I believe that the rhetorical movements that are licensed by this model in Spurgeon's work are far more complex than her normative preaching about a Christ-like Shakespeare suggests. For in examining the images and the affective structures that will produce Shakespeare the man, Spurgeon's method of indirections – she had considered the title 'Assays of Bias' – in effect takes apart the Christian wholeness and evangelical humanity she seeks.

The book's informal style and the indefiniteness of its title – especially the additive 'and what it tells us', not 'who' it tells us about – suggest the fascinating randomness, accretion and slippage of the words and images struggling against Spurgeon's attempt to marshal them into organic shape. While Spurgeon's intention is to argue for personal wholeness, her relentless citations – sunshine and rain at once, the plumed estridges, lilies that fester, the bowl against the bias, meal and bran together, the caves and womby vaultages of France – exceed the categories she provides to define the human. In seeking the 'revelation of the man', I should contend, Spurgeon's interest in the affective powers of rhetoric, licensed in part by the gendered (female) structures of English education, has enabled what one might call the 'creative deconstruction' of the patriarchal Shakespeare that Raleigh and others had 'made'. The Shakespeare that Spurgeon produces is ultimately not a man but a text whose many competing discourses – politics, the household, smell, sports, landscape, class – are anatomised in the continuing catalogue of images, a complex tissue of quotations and commentary. H.B. Charlton calls *Shakespeare's Imagery* 'the most significant book on Shakespeare since Bradley's *Shakespearean*

Tragedy'. Its importance lies precisely in the way it breaks down Bradleyan notions of organic character, exposing characters – Shakespeare's own and those he creates – as the shifting sites of hetero-geneous cultural discourses. Indeed, the second half of her book, which shifts the argument to readings of the ways recurrent images work in individual plays, open up the texts of Shakespeare's play as fields of meaning that operate independent of problems of character.

Hawkes comments: 'Shakespeare's texts always yield to, though they can never be reduced to, the readings we give them; their plurality makes Walter Raleighs of us all.' In some respects, I am sure that Hawkes is right; any text subject as Shakespeare is to continued appropriation makes us as readers the unwitting victims of our own claims to authority. And yet Hawkes's use of Raleigh as exemplum makes me cautious. I do not want to be his Sir Walter Raleigh. My response would be from a tele-phone prank I learned from my mother: you call a tobacconist and ask 'Do you have Sir Walter Raleigh in a can?' When the tobacconist answers 'Yes', you respond 'Well, let him out'. The Sir Walter Raleigh that each of us lets out of the can as we write and rewrite Sir Walter Raleigh in cultural history is not necessarily the same sweet Sir Walter.

Another Walter, Walter Pater, let one out of the can when he rudely reacted to a dropped glove. Pater had gone to a 'gaudy' at a woman's college. When the lady head of the house dropped her white kid glove in front of Pater, he thought she did it on purpose, and instead of picking it up, he walked on it. 'Didn't you see that?', asked a friend of Pater's who saw the exchange. 'Didn't you see how I rewarded the action?', Pater replied:

> If I had not remembered how, in spite of the honours heaped upon him by Queen Elizabeth, Sir Walter Raleigh was in the end led out to execution, perhaps I, too, might have made a fool of myself. Believe me, sir, it was an insinuation of the devil that caused this woman to drop her glove.[25]

Pater resists the construction of the 'man', resentful of the woman holding power. And, as Jane Marcus suggests in a book that has shaped my reading of Woolf in this essay,[26] Woolf parodies Pater's inversion of the Elizabethan example in her short story, 'The Introduction'.[27] Lily, the young woman who is being 'introduced' in this story, is pleased at how her just completed essay on 'the character of Dean Swift' has been re-ceived well by her professor, who gave it three stars. As she is introduced socially to the patriarchal world of the professional intellectual establish-ment, she loses confidence in her essay, in her ability to write as a woman, and lapses into playing the 'lady', wearing her beauty like a uniform and thinking 'how if she dropped a handkerchief (this had happened) a man would stoop precipitately and give it her' (p. 180). But when she is finally introduced to Bob Brinsley, who has just come down from Oxford, she again summons her pride and courage, insisting that her words too have the power to write the world:

> What had she to oppose to this massive masculine achievement? An essay on the character of Dean Swift! And as she came up to the group, which Bob Brinsley dominated (with his heel on the fender, and his head back), with his great honest forehead, and his self-assurance, and his delicacy, and his honour and robust physical well being, and airiness and direct descent from Shakespeare, what could she do but lay her essay, oh and the whole of her being, on the floor as a cloak for him to trample, as a rose for him to rifle. Which she did, emphatically, when Mrs Dalloway said, still holding her hand as if she would run away from this introduction, 'Mr Brinsley – Miss Everit. Both of you love Shelley.' But hers was not love compared with his. (pp. 180–1)

In insisting that her writing, her being, her body of writing, be displayed like a cloak, even if in sacrifice to the culture that will crush it, Lily comes of age. She has refused to play the 'lady' to the 'gallant'; she emphatically makes a Sir Walter Raleigh of herself on her own terms, using Raleigh in her consciousness as a figure for her internal resistance to the structures of power that she is ineluctably submitting to. Her way of writing Shelley, or Shakespeare, will be different from Bob Brinsley's or Professor Raleigh's. This momentary mental identification with Raleigh paradoxically figures, as Marcus suggests, 'chivalry and misogyny as two sides of the same patriarchal coin' (p. 3). As she listens to Brinsley talk about himself, she watches him tear the wings off a fly, and sees herself and her essay as victims who will continue to struggle, her essay becoming increasingly 'obtrusive' and burning 'with a terrible lustre, no longer clear and brilliant but troubled and bloodstained' (p. 182). Raped figuratively merely in being 'introduced' to her patriarchal culture and seeing it and herself clearly for the first time, she has more to say than 'swisser swatter', for she recognises with a lasting clarity that the civilisation that she has so admired, coming in direct descent from Shakespeare, depends upon her oppression:

> – no, that there are no sanctuaries, or butterflies, in this world, and this civilisation, churches, parliaments, and flats – this civilisation, said Lily Everit to herself, as she accepted the kind compliments of old Mrs Bromley on her appearance, depends upon me, and Mrs Bromley said later that like all the Everits, Lily looked 'as if she had the weight of the world upon her shoulders.' (p. 182)

NOTES

1. Diana Vreeland, *D.V.*, eds., George Plimpton and Christopher Hemphill (New York: Alfred A. Knopf, 1984).

2. Debora Silverman, *Selling Culture: Bloomingdale's, Diana Vreeland, and the new aristocracy of taste in Reagan's America* (New York: Pantheon Books, 1986).
3. For a recent account of nostalgic rhetoric in the work of contemporary male writers, see Janice Doane and Devon Hodges, *Nostalgia and Sexual Difference: The resistance to contemporary feminism* (London: Methuen, 1987).
4. Terry Eagleton, *Literary Theory: An introduction* (London: Oxford University Press, 1983); Marjorie Garber, *Shakespeare's Ghost Writers* (London: Methuen, 1987); Marion O'Connor, 'Theatre of the empire: "Shakespeare's England"' at the Earl's Court', in Marion O'Connor and Jean Howard, eds., *Shakespeare Reproduced* (London: Methuen, 1987), pp. 68–98; Terence Hawkes, *That Shakespeherian Rag: Essays on a critical process* (London: Methuen, 1986).
5. John Drakakis, ed., *Alternative Shakespeares* (London: Methuen, 1985).
6. *Proceedings of the British Academy*, **13** (1917–18), pp. 407–11, as quoted by Hawkes, pp. 63–4.
7. Hawkes, pp. 70–1, citing MS Aubrey 6, fol. 77, as cited by Norman Lloyd Williams, *Sir Walter Raleigh* (London: Eyre and Spottiswoode, 1962), pp. 88–9.
8. Brian Doyle, *Re-reading English* (London: Methuen, 1982), pp. 18–19.
9. Lisa Jardine, ' "Girl talk" (for boys on the left) or marginalizing feminist critical praxis', *Oxford Literary Review*, 9 (1986), pp. 212–13.
10. *The Essays of Virginia Woolf*, ed. Andrew McNeillie, vol. 1 (New York and London: Harcourt, Brace, Jovanovich, 1986), pp. 120–3.
11. Alice Fox, 'Virginia Woolf at work: the Elizabethan voyage out', *Bulletin of Research in the Humanities*, **84** (1981), pp. 65–84.
12. Virginia Woolf, *The Voyage Out* (London: Hogarth Press, 1975), p. 31.
13. Fox, 'Woolf at work', p. 72.
14. *ibid.*, p. 72.
15. Virginia Woolf, *Collected Essays*, vol. I (New York: Harcourt, Brace, and World, 1967), pp. 314–15.
16. Virginia Woolf, *Death of the Moth and other Essays* (London: Hogarth Press, 1942), p. 227.
17. Virginia Woolf, *A Room of One's Own* (New York: Harcourt, Brace, Jovanovich, 1929), p. 106.
18. Nina Anerbach, *Ellen Terry: A Player in Her Time* (New York: Norton, 1987), p. 407.
19. F.P. Wilson (and J. Dover Wilson), 'Sir Edmund Kerchever Chambers, 1866–1954', *Proceedings of the British Academy*, **42** (1956), pp. 267–85.
20. Stephen Hobhouse, *Forty Years and an Epilogue* (London: J. Clarke 1951), p. 97.
21. E.K. Chambers, *Shakespeare: A Survey* (New York: Hill and Wang, 1958), p. x.
22. See her obituary in the *New York Times* (25 October 1942), p. 44.
23. Caroline Spurgeon, *Shakespeare's Imagery and What It Tells Us* (Cambridge: Cambridge University Press, 1935).
24. Cited by Christopher Baldick, *The Social Mission of English Criticism* (Oxford: Oxford University Press), p. 69; the same quotation is also cited by Jardine, ' "Girl talk" ' p. 212 and by Doyle, 'Re-reading English', p. 24.
25. Thomas Wright, *The Life of Walter Pater*, vol. 2 (New York: G.P. Putnam, 1907) pp. 130–1. Woolf quotes the passage in *The Pargiters*, ed. Mitchell A. Leaska (New York: New York Public Library and Readex Books, 1977), p. 126.
26. Jane Marcus, *Virginia Woolf and the Languages of Patriarchy* (Bloomington: Indiana University Press, 1987), pp. 1–5.
27. Susan Dick, ed., *The Complete Shorter Fiction of Virginia Woolf* (New York: Harcourt, Brace, Jovanovich, 1985), pp. 178–82.

— AFTERWORD —

A Future for Materialist Feminist Criticism?

Catherine Belsey

I

I am delighted, if slightly unnerved, to find myself classified as a materialist feminist critic. This new identity seems more significant, more challenging and above all more collective than being a feminist critic with materialist inclinations or, worse, what I feared I was, a feminist fumbling with and puzzled by questions about the materiality of culture and cultural history. But the readiness with which we reach for categories can be worrying: classification is dangerous to the degree that it creates an illusion of clarity, and seems at a stroke to do away with the fumbling and the puzzles. For that reason, it seems important to explore the implications of my new-found identity and feminism's latest political category.

What, in other words, to reiterate the question that this volume consistently addresses, is materialist feminism? What is materialist feminist criticism? Or, more politically, less essentially, what might they be? What might we make them, make out of them?

The now classic essay by Judith Newton and Deborah Rosenfelt emphasises the repudiation of idealism that characterises materialist feminism. Not quite conceding that 'materialist' is a euphemism for the unacceptable, unspeakable 'Marxist', but not quite denying it either, Newton and Rosenfelt emphasise materialist feminism's concern with the social and the economic, as opposed to the purely psychological, and with historical difference, as opposed to the universal and essential categories of 'woman' or 'patriarchy'.[1] Idealism fails to take account of the power of social class and social institutions to determine differences between women, as well as between women and men. It fails to do justice to the different forms of oppression which exist at specific historical moments. Middle-class feminism has had to come to terms with its own idealist tendencies, evident in its failure to engage the commitment of working-class women; white, western feminism is gradually learning to listen to

257

black women and women of colour, whose oppressions are also culturally, historically and economically specific. Materialism stresses the
specificity of struggle because it attends to the social and economic conditions which both permit and promote conflicts of interest.

And in Shakespeare criticism, too, have we perhaps done less than
justice, in the past, to the class positions of Shakespeare's female figures,
in our efforts to stress the gender relations the plays depict? Have we
shared the idealist tendency to analyse love and ignore money? And have
we paid insufficient attention to the specific economic and social instabilities that constitute the context of Shakespeare's plays? One of the
things that materialist feminist criticism means, Newton and Rosenfelt
state firmly, is 'more work than one is used to',[2] and for Shakespeareans,
as this book suggests, that includes more work on the class relations in the
plays, among the audience and in Elizabethan society at large.

II

But materialism as Newton and Rosenfelt define it is not concerned
exclusively with the economy. In Marxism, too, since Althusser, 'economism' – the belief that the economy is the sole or final determinant of
history – has been regarded as unduly limiting. Althusser's famous concept of 'determination in the last instance', however precarious, was an
effort to overcome the reductiveness of some Marxist readings of history,
a reductiveness that Marx himself did not share. In the end Althusser's
work probably generated more questions than answers, but the incisive-
ness of the questions he posed made it impossible to return to an econo-
mistic innocence. In Marxist criticism, the days when the truth of the text
could be read off from the author's class position had gone for good. The
lived experience of individuals was no longer seen as directly determined
by their place in the relations of production. On the contrary, individual
experience was understood to be the complex effect of a number of
interacting forces, among them culture, in the broadest sense of that term.
Culture, itself a complex phenomenon, was not independent of the economy, but it was not merely an expression of it either. Resident in what
was thinkable at a specific historical moment, culture was now a material
practice. And it followed that from now on the categories of 'experience'
and 'meaning' and 'mode of address' would be understood to be within
the range of concerns of a materialist analysis.

Materialist feminism takes advantage of this theoretical development,
and in consequence makes possible a *rapprochement* in theory that feminists have surely never doubted in practice. Much work in feminism has
been concerned with the role of language in reinforcing patriarchy and

keeping women in their (sexual, domestic, subordinate) place. Studies of he-man vocabulary, of gender-differentiated forms of address, and differential terms of abuse and praise, revealed consistent asymmetries which reproduced the inequalities of power between the sexes. The prevalence of this work in the seventies in particular made it possible for hardline Marxists to sneer at the illusion that power was purely discursive or that oppression was merely a matter of language. But those words, 'purely' and 'merely', give the whole game away. To privilege the material-as-economic over meaning and culture is simply to reaffirm, by reversing it, the conventional idealist opposition between consciousness and the 'real' world.

At least since the seventeenth century, women who have written in protest about the injustices of a male-dominated society have recognised the social construction of gender difference. How else, after all, can we account for our continued subordination? If it is not natural, and therefore inevitable, it must be cultural, an effect of visual images, of social and educational processes, of differential ways of talking to little girls and little boys, of definitions internalised and *lived*. We have all learned to read these signifying practices from the earliest age. Culture exists, in a word, as meanings. But the cultural meanings of man and woman, experienced at the level of consciousness, have also been lived precisely as material practices; not only as rape and violence, but as the slower, more tedious and more insidious oppression of women's bodies by regimes of beauty, by corsetry and crippling footwear, by marital availability, domestic labour and continual childbirth.

These differential cultural meanings, and the modes of address which naturalise the power relations between men and women, are learned, but learned so young that they seem transparent. They seem so, that is, until they come into contradiction with other cultural meanings; the 'rights', for instance, of the individual, regardless of sex, to life, liberty and the pursuit of happiness. Feminism is born of the anger which is a consequence of those contradictions lived materially as women's experience.

The proposition that 'experience' is an effect and not an origin, a cultural construct and not the source of truth, could presumably only be doubted by women whose commitment to feminism has never wavered for a moment, or who have simply not yet lived very long. To have lived long enough to have been an adolescent in the fifties is for many of us to have experienced in the deepest areas of our identity a yearning to wear circular skirts, tight, wide belts and three-inch heels (however inappropriate any of this might have been in our own specific instances). For my part it is also to have experienced fantasies of myself as an earth-mother, working at a trestle table to produce apple pies that would gratify hordes of rosy-cheeked and smiling children. Mercifully, in my case it is at the same time to have been sent to a girls' school that firmly regarded such notions as unmitigated nonsense, and to a women's college where it had apparently never occurred to anyone that a rational human being could think of higher education as the prerogative of men. If these contradictions led to difficulties in later life, they did at least allow me to account in theoretical terms for my experiential transition from flared jeans as the only imaginable clothing to flared jeans as the most hideous garment ever devised. And if, to complete the list of contradictions, I invoke my experience to provide evidence that experience is not reliable as a source of knowledge, I do so only in order to suggest that whether we can learn from experience depends on what we make of it, on what theories we bring to bear on it in order to make it make sense, on how we make it produce a knowledge for us.

III

If materialist feminism treats experience as the location of cultural meanings, and if it regards meaning as a material practice, it necessarily acknowledges the importance of literary criticism in the production of feminist analysis and feminist cultural history. Fiction is a crucial site of cultural meaning in its political and historical difference. If the meaning of woman is not an unchanging and universal essence but a cultural construct, feminism moves and alters with and between cultures. Most of the societies we know about have been decisively (though in diverse ways) patriarchal, and in consequence woman has been the difference that specifies the limits – and the limitations – of man. Shakespeare's culture is no exception, and Shakespeare's plays reveal with great subtlety the shifts that language is put to in defence of a Renaissance masculinity which so engrosses meaning to itself that it constantly risks the exclusion of its defining other.

It is the figure of Hamlet who so insistently worries at the question, 'What is a man?' (IV, iv, 33),[3] but perhaps *Macbeth* is the play that struggles most resolutely to produce an answer. In *Macbeth* a man is at various moments daring, not a coward (I, vii, 47–51), humane and not a regicide (I, vii, 46–7); he is human, a part of nature, properly daunted by the supernatural (III, iv, 99–103, 107–8); he is violent (IV, iii, 220); he is also capable of human feeling, tears (IV, iii, 221). The definitions and redefinitions lay claim to include nearly all human-kindness in their scope, so that only a tiny, domestic corner is left for the proper, admissible, socially acceptable meaning of woman.

Woman means mother. It means Lady Macduff playing innocently with her son, engaging and vulnerable, and only marginally less naive than the child she is unable to protect (IV, ii, 30–85). It means breasts and milk (I, v, 44–5) and giving suck (I, vii, 54–5), all of them inevitably and hideously repudiated by a woman who wants to intervene in the public world of history. And the play lays bare the tragic consequences of this system of differences – in the figure of Lady Macbeth unsexed and driven mad, in Macbeth manly and ultimately despairing, and finally in Macduff fulfilling the requirements of *his* manhood, by ominously reiterating Macbeth's own initial display of masculinity, as he too presents the state with the severed head of a traitor.

Macbeth charts the disintegration of a culture which is haunted by images of women who will not stay in place: women with beards, in possession of forbidden knowledge, who vanish into air, and who refuse to confine themselves to the single, narrow meaning that difference allots to them at a specific cultural and historical moment. It displays a world where no earthly power can hold the meaning of woman in its patriarchally legitimated place, where the signified breaks free of its moorings and shows itself unfixed, differed and deferred by a signifier which cannot master it. The play magnificently demonstrates the instabilities of a patriarchy which confines woman to motherhood and promises to man everything else that it means to be human.

IV

Since culture is a material practice, and since literary criticism is a component part of culture, it follows that feminist criticism is itself a cultural phenomenon. Feminist criticism cannot in these circumstances be defined in advance, identified in its essential nature eternally and universally, sought out in earlier epochs and recognised in its unchanging correctness. Feminist criticism takes a position at and in relation to a specific cultural and historical moment. And in that sense it is necessarily a product of its own present. At the same time, it is also an intervention in the power relations which prevail at that present, and in that sense feminist criticism is inevitably political.

Our present is postmodern. That is to say, it participates in the crisis of epistemology which has informed western culture since the aftermath of the Second World War.[4] Both the Holocaust and Hiroshima produced a crisis of confidence in the Enlightenment version of history as a single narrative of the progressive enfranchisement of reason and truth. Where in these hideous episodes, and where in the subsequent squaring up of the superpowers, equipped with their apocalyptic arsenals, were reason and truth to be found? Instead, two hundred years after the Enlightenment prevailed in the West, history was seen to be an effect of conflicting interests after all, but interests defined on all sides as absolute certainties.

The postmodern condition is characterised in consequence by a deep distrust of absolutes, a scepticism about truth, and what Lyotard calls 'incredulity toward metanarratives'.[5] Postmodernity calls into question the knowledges and the histories produced by the Enlightenment. It doubts those humanist ways of interpreting the world and the past which have promoted Man as the hero of history, and thus served to legitimate existing forms of domination. The postmodern undermines rationalist and empiricist modes of knowing, and therefore denaturalises the supremacy of the free West. And, most important for feminists, on all those accounts it dethrones masculinity.

It would appear, therefore, that the postmodern is precisely the condition of the most recent flowering of feminist analysis, that feminism and postmodernism share a scepticism which is both epistemological and political. The Enlightenment commitment to truth and reason, we can now recognise, has meant historically a single truth and a single rationality, which have conspired in practice to legitimate the subordination of black people, the non-Western world, women: liberal Enlightenment history, a story of the emancipation of the people, has in practice neglected the emancipation of black people, the non-western world, women. None of these groups has any political interest in clinging to the values which have consistently undervalued *them*. The plurality of the postmodern, by contrast, discredits supremacism on the part of any single group. It celebrates difference of all kinds, but divorces difference from power. Postmodernism is in all these senses the ally of feminism.

Nevertheless, it has been argued that feminism and postmodernism are inevitable enemies, that feminism itself is precisely an impossibility in our postmodern condition. In *Gynesis*, her brilliant discussion of the discursive allocation of the feminine, the putting into discourse of woman, Alice Jardine makes a strong case for the incompatibility of feminism and the postmodern. Her argument is that insofar as feminism is a commitment to Woman, to the discovery of the truth about Woman, the uncovering of her real, authentic self, feminism refuses to take account of the postmodern problematisation of universal truth. It merely reproduces the founding humanist move, replacing Man with Woman, as humanism crucially replaced God with Man. And in so far as feminist criticism is about women characters in fiction, or about women writers, the postmodern undermines its deepest commitments. When postmodern writing calls into question the whole concept of character, and poststructuralist criticism proclaims the death of the author, what tasks remain for feminist critics? What can we do with our denunciations of female stereotypes in fiction, when the truth about women with which we contrast them no longer seems to hold? And what becomes of feminist history in a world where we have lost our faith in the grand historical narrative, complete with virtuous and heroic protagonists who carry forward a single struggle towards a defined and shared ideal which is also a closure, the end, in every sense, of history?[6]

I do not believe that feminism is incompatible with the postmodern. There are forms of feminism that attribute to unchanging Woman a single history, which is one of unremitting struggle to break or to evade the oppressions of patriarchy. There are modes of feminist criticism that are wholly Woman-centred, which isolate women writers, are content to discuss female characters or depend on a contrast between fictional stereotypes and the truth about women. And it is important to recognise that we may be able to learn something from all of them. But a materialist feminism might, I believe, differentiate itself from them, is indeed compelled to do so by the logic of its own recognition of the materiality, which is to say in this instance the historicity, of culture. Feminism is above all about relations of difference. Its concern is with gender relations which are also power relations. Feminism is a politics, and its modes of resistance are as protean as the patriarchal practices it contests. Resistance is always a relation of difference, a differentiating relation, and the politics of feminism works in the gaps difference produces, in the interstices between specific operations of power and submission.

Woman in patriarchy is a difference and feminism is a commitment to that difference – and at the same time to a separation of difference from power. Woman is no more a transcultural essence than Man: the two terms are interlinked and interdependent. The feminist protest is about power, not anatomy; it is about specific struggles, not a universal human condition. Materialist feminism points out that historically difference has implied domination, and that the subordination of women has no grounding in nature, or indeed in anything other than patriarchal appropriations of control in the service of self-interest.

Patriarchal power is not an essence either: it is not singular or constant or unalterable.[7] Feminist histories tell of changes in gender relations, not all of them either advances or retreats, losses or victories. On the contrary, feminism records a series of specific stories (the *petits récits* of Lyotard's *Postmodern Condition*), which recount false starts, duplicities and betrayals, as well as gains which turn out to present more problems than they solve. I think, for example, and in no particular order, of witchcraft, the advent of the contraceptive pill and the sexual revolution of the sixties, the reign of Queen Elizabeth I, and early psychoanalysis, with its preeminent attention to women. Are these episodes gains or losses in the feminist struggle? How could we classify them in a single grand narrative of emancipation, complete with heroic conquests and specified goals? Do they not each in their turn incur resistances? And how would we classify these? Feminism at any specific moment invades and occupies the terrain between domination and subordination, but the terrain itself is constantly shifting and is often uncertainly defined. Many of the stories feminism recounts lack the happy *obviousness* which would characterise history as one grand romance, with a single virtuous figure at its centre, remorselessly confronting dangers and defeating dragons.

Feminism is first and foremost a politics: and that means taking up a position. But feminism in its current mode is also a constitutive element of our postmodern condition: and that means recognising plurality, acknowledging that there are many ways to be a feminist. A materialist feminism, acknowledging its own historical specificity, recognises its postmodern location and in consequence endorses and incites heterogeneity. Feminist politics may take different forms, may be implemented in a range of different practices, and this difference can be perceived as a strength and not a weakness. Unlike some other kinds of radical politics, feminism has no need to be forever defining and delimiting its territory, purifying its doctrines, policing the edges of truth and denouncing heresy. Feminism is a commitment, but not in my view a commitment to an essence; it tells stories, but not a single history of vice and virtue locked in perpetual opposition. Materialist feminist history is supple, subtle and complex: it has no place for a unitary and univocal metanarrative.

Equally, our readings of texts are supple, subtle and complex. The postmodern attends not only to the plurality of possible practices, including reading practices, but also to the heterogeneity of the text itself. Within the *Macbeth* I have already outlined there resides a second, related but distinct, network of meanings, which offers another signified for Renaissance patriarchy, and links it with Renaissance humanism, to display something of the oppression inscribed in that ostensibly liberating moment. In *Macbeth* it is the difference within the term *man*, and the corresponding difference within the text, which generate the tragedy. If *woman* means mother and giving suck, as I have suggested, it is nonetheless Macbeth himself who is too full of the milk of human kindness (I, v, 14). In that concession, Lady Macbeth identifies her husband's weakness and the audience recognises his humanity. Human kindness, humane as well as generically human, metaphorically includes milk, incorporating the difference that specifies woman and so defines man. Macbeth, we are to understand at this moment, is everything a human being might be, allowing after all no place, no specificity of any kind, for woman. The murder of the unresisting, unprotesting, unoffending Lady Macduff might almost be read as an emblem of that encroachment, as manhood expands to fill all the available human space, leaving no room for her.

By contrast the resisting, protesting, offending Lady Macbeth demands a place, an identity and a specificity which is not masculinity, but an unsexing that takes her altogether outside the realm of the human, beyond all visitings of nature (I, v, 42). It is from there, from a place outside the natural, that she seduces her husband to his own destruction by exploiting the plurality of manhood.

In the event, Lady Macbeth cannot survive in this extra-human realm, and there is finally little to choose between her destiny and Lady Macduff's. Only the witches, whose identity is neither clearly gendered nor unequivocally human (I, iii, 41–3, 45–7, 53), can flourish in a culture which places the meaning of woman at once outside man, as his silent and submissive difference, and inside man as his humane and humanising kindness. On this reading, the villainous Lady Macbeth is at the same time the victim of a humanism which makes humanity synonymous with man, and which cannot in consequence afford to let women live.

The heterogeneous text is one which is not readily coopted on behalf of either subversion or containment. Materialist feminists, I believe, have no need to take sides in the debates between new historicists and cultural materialists on that issue. All texts exceed their own unitary projects; all texts release new interpretations as we bring to bear on them different – and differential – reading practices. That is not to say that they mean whatever we like, but that in the first place, a debate about whether a play 'really' supports or challenges the monarchy is, from a feminist perspective, neither here nor there. And in the second place, that debate only reiterates, with whatever elegance and subtlety, the proposition that meaning is single and univocal, and available to be pinned down by 'correct' reading.[8] The concerns of materialist feminist criticism, I have suggested, are elsewhere.

V

Acknowledging the materiality of culture, and its own identity as an intervention in its cultural moment, materialist feminist criticism also implies a self-consciousness about style. In one sense, this attention to the signifier is itself a postmodern gesture: the empiricism familiar since the Enlightenment to most of the English-speaking world famously repudiates rhetoric and proclaims the plain style as adequate and appropriate to its purpose of speaking out the unvarnished, extra-textual, extra-linguistic truth. Postmodernism, by contrast, is unable to find a place for meaning independent of representation, or presentation, as Lyotard more exactly calls it, since the 're' of representation precisely proposes the autonomy of the signified, affirms a state of pure intelligibility, of untrammelled conceptuality, anterior to signification.[9] It is in France, therefore, where this understanding of language has a stronger hold, that feminism has most insistently posed the question, 'how should women write?' And, of course, the answers French feminists have offered have not always seemed persuasive to their English-speaking readers.

At the same time, however, we know now that the plain style was never as plain as it pretended, and that it was always a good deal more stylish than its adherents acknowledge. Locke, who distrusts the duplicity of metaphor, is full of metaphors, and is more persuasive in consequence. But then Locke never really believed in the existence of pure conceptuality in the first place.[10] And in any case, the proclaimed but illusory plainness was not transparency but precisely a pretence of unmediated access to a presence, an intelligibility, which was always elsewhere – though at the beck and call, we were to construe, of the writer.

In practice feminists, especially since Virginia Woolf, have never ignored the question of their own mode of address, because we know that, as women, we cannot be sure of an audience unless we set out to enlist one. The project has always been to find for feminism a distinctive voice, or preferably voices, designed to ensure attention, without repeating the familiar, authoritarian, patriarchal gestures in the process. (Vituperation, for instance is one obvious patriarchal gesture, intended to humiliate an opponent; obscurantism is another.) And feminist fiction has been even more self-consciously eager to find a narrative mode which does justice to its cause.

How *should* women write? Materialist feminism would perhaps begin by modifying the question. Since the writing that concerns us is not the expression of an interiority, but a political intervention that sets out to be effective, the crucial question seems to be, how should *feminists* write? And the answer is, persuasively, of course. And pleasurably – in order to be read. And intelligibly – in order to be understood. But these (self-evident?) answers pose another problem, and that is how to produce persuasion and pleasure and clarity, without reproducing the illusion of plainness which makes everything so obvious that there is no room for debate. It is the sheer unsurprising obviousness of its propositions that has perpetuated the humanist legitimation of existing modes of domination. Feminism needs surprises, in order to denaturalise that obviousness. It is the magisterial, closed mode of address of so-called good writing that deflects criticism and forestalls debate. Feminism depends on criticism and debate. And above all, feminism is committed to the *continuation* of surprise and criticism and debate, because the project of feminist politics is precisely not to introduce new forms of subordination which replicate the old, merely transferring to women the power that previously belonged to men.

This problem of writing is one that I take very much to heart, having been consistently accused (and not without justification) of producing classic realist texts, raising questions only to resolve them in closure. I find it hard not to – but I pose more unanswered questions now.

The best account of the problem that I have found – and the best proposal of a solution that I know – is Mary Jacobus's essay, 'The difference of view'. That essay is no longer new, but it still seems to me unsurpassed in its identification of the theoretical and practical issues. It argues that feminism cannot afford to reproduce patriarchal forms and conventions. At the same time, it continues, to repudiate them in their entirety is to reject all that is readily intelligible and therefore persuasive: it is, in other words, to risk madness. Jacobus proposes that instead we should inhabit the familiar forms, but inhabit them differently; we should reproduce conventional structures, but reproduce them other-wise, inserting an unexpected alterity which destabilises the soothing, reassuring obviousness and closure of rational argument conducted in the plain style.[11] Feminists, in other words, might do well to reject all efforts to emulate eighteenth-century gentlemen. Or rather, they might demonstrate that it is easy enough to write like an eighteenth-century gentleman, but it is more challenging to introduce sporadic disruptions into the easy flow of what passes for good sense.

This is harder to do, in my opinion, than to theorise. It means, I believe, occasionally transgressing at critical moments the norms of good style, introducing sudden changes of tone in order to highlight a point and, above all, being content to leave a question in place where an answer might be expected. And at this moment in this essay it means not (at all costs) closing off the issue of feminist writing, since I have no comprehensive programme to offer.

VI

Supremely, of course, materialist feminism is self-conscious about its own politics, aware of itself as a political intervention. And it follows that materialist feminist criticism is equally aware of the political questions we need repeatedly to address, even if we are less sure of the answers from one moment to another. To what extent, for instance, is it in itself a political act to analyse the gender relations presented in a literary text? And if it *was* a political act in the 1970s, when feminist readings were a scandal, an explicit defiance of existing institutional practices, is it so still, when the academy is proud to list the numbers of courses in feminist criticism, women's writing or literature and gender? Are there other things that we should do now? Or is it enough to do the same things but, having learnt from our predecessors, try to do them better?

In my view, feminist criticism cannot afford to stand still, to get arrested. Barbara Johnson in the introduction to her second book, *A World of Difference*, formulates a series of questions that now concern her. These might easily be appropriated as a useful check-list for materialist feminist criticism:

> While *The Critical Difference* seemed to say, 'Here is a text; let me read it'; the present volume adds: 'Why am I reading *this* text? What kind of act was the writing of it? What question about it does it itself *not* raise? What am I participating in when I read it?'[12]

The context of Johnson's acknowledged change of focus is perhaps individual, but the questions she adds in the present seem to me to point very sharply to the concerns of materialist feminist criticism. They invoke the politics of reading practices as well as the politics of writing, and they imply an attention to the politics of the institution in which our reading takes place. Materialist feminist criticism might fruitfully reiterate and reformulate those questions at intervals. At any specific moment we might ask ourselves how and why we are performing this particular reading. What difference (to cite the title of an important feminist anthology) does it make?

VII

But there is a danger in all this. (There is so often a danger.) Luckily, materialist feminism recognises the inevitability of contradiction – and does not panic. The danger, as I see it, is this: classification promotes reification. The adoption of a label, however valuable the move appears, always incurs the possibility of fixing meaning and deflecting the process of change. Commitments become dogmas; positions are institutionalised; potential allies are excluded. Feminism's newest category could rapidly become a force for conservatism.

Of course, any radical movement, eager to make alignments, develop analyses and define areas of debate, needs to make distinctions, to identify declared positions which facilitate discussion as well as action. Feminists, like socialists, therefore subdivide into groups with specific commitments based on specific analyses. And from the debates which arise within and between these groups, it becomes possible to delineate a range of ways forward, both theoretical and practical. The traditional categories of feminism – liberal, radical and socialist – or, more recently, French and Anglo-American – have self-evidently had their uses, both analytical and political.

But feminism can learn much from the failures of socialism, as well as from its strengths. And one of the most exemplary of its failures has been the history of internecine struggles between left groups which are held by their opponents to have betrayed the true cause, or travestied the essence of socialism itself. The differences that labels identify are easily cemented as oppositions. From the point of view of feminism, it begins to seem increasingly probable that the traditional categories have eventually come to exclude as many women as they enlist. Certainly socialist feminism has not proved very attractive in the United States. And as Rachel Bowlby has suggested, the notion of French thought as homogeneous, a conviction crucial to the preservation of the antithesis between Anglo-American and French feminisms, is itself an Anglo-American fantasy.[13] That antithesis tells us very little in a world inhabited by Alice Jardine (though *Gynesis* in one sense depends on it, and in another refutes it), by Rosalind Coward, Barbara Johnson, Teresa de Lauretis and Rachel Bowlby herself. Moreover, it runs the perpetual risk of effacing other differences, including non-western differences:

> Possibly, in crossing the ocean between two places whose identities are known and evaluated from the moment of take-off, the transatlantic feminist misses the chance of finding something else – a lost continent, for example – beneath the waters of the Atlantic glimpsed from the plane.[14]

I welcome the advent of materialist feminism, as I welcome theoretical specificity and political alignment. But I fear it too. Names can so easily obscure the need to re-examine and reconstruct our political commitments. Happily, feminists have consistently shown that they know when to discard a label once it has outlived its usefulness.

NOTES

1. Judith Newton and Deborah Rosenfelt, 'Introduction: toward a materialist-feminist criticism', in their *Feminist Criticism and Social Change: Sex, class and race in literature and culture* (New York and London: Methuen, 1985), pp. xv–xxxix; pp. xvi–xviii and *passim*.
2. Newton and Rosenfelt, 'Introduction', p. xix.
3. Shakespeare references are to the one-volume edition of *The Complete Works*, ed. Peter Alexander (London: Collins, 1951).
4. It could be argued that the crisis of epistemology is to be found sporadically at many historical moments since the Renaissance. Lyotard, for example, scandalously finds postmodernism in the sixteenth century: 'It seems to me that the essay (Montaigne) is postmodern' (Jean-François Lyotard, 'What is postmodernism?', in *The Postmodern Condition: A report on knowledge*, trans. Geoff Bennington and Brian Massumi (Manchester: Manchester University Press, 1984), p. 81).

5. Lyotard, *The Postmodern Condition*, p. xxiv.
6. Alice A. Jardine, *Gynesis: Configurations of woman and modernity* (Ithaca, N.Y., and London: Cornell University Press, 1985). See especially pp. 19–24, 38–49, 52–64, 82 and 92–7.
7. For an earlier discussion of this aspect of the issue see Sheila Rowbotham, 'The Trouble with "Patriarchy" ', and Sally Alexander and Barbara Taylor, 'In Defence of "Patriarchy" ', in Mary Evans, ed., *The Woman Question: Readings on the subordination of women* (London: Fontana, 1982), pp. 73–83 (rpt. from R. Samuel, ed., *People's History and Socialist Theory* (London: Routledge & Kegan Paul, 1981), pp. 364–73.
8. I have discussed the debate between new historicism and cultural materialism in more detail in 'Towards cultural history – in theory and practice', *Textual Practice*, 3 (1989), pp. 159–72.
9. Lyotard, 'What is Postmodernism?', esp. pp. 78–82.
10. Catherine Belsey, *The Subject of Tragedy: Identity and difference in Renaissance drama* (London and New York: Methuen, 1985), pp. 83–6.
11. Mary Jacobus, 'The difference of view', in her *Women Writing and Writing About Women* (London: Croom Helm; New York: Harper and Row, 1979), pp. 10–21. Reprinted in Catherine Belsey and Jane Moore, eds., *The Feminist Reader: Essays in gender and the politics of literary criticism* (London: Macmillan; New York: Blackwell, 1989), pp. 49–62.
12. Barbara Johnson, *A World of Difference* (Baltimore and London: Johns Hopkins University Press, 1987), pp. 3–4.
13. Rachel Bowlby, 'Flight reservations', *The Oxford Literary Review*, 10 (1988), pp. 61–72; p. 68.
14. *ibid.*, p. 70.

INDEX

Abd-el-Malek, 150 n.48
Adam, 42
Aeneas, 141
Agnew, Jean-Christophe, 55 n.27, 225, 235 n.12
Agulhon, Maurice, 204, 218, n.5
Alexander, Peter, 149 n.15, 269 n.3
Alexander, Sally, 270 n.7
Alexander the Great, 2
Althusser, Louis, 7–8, 20, 26 n.17, 226–8, 235 nn.14, 15, 236 n.21, 258
Altman, Joel, 196 n.21
Amazon, 207
Amussen, Susan Dwyer, 55 n.23, 191, 198 n.41
Anderson, Perry, 220 n.42
Anger, Jane, 41–2, 52, 54 n.19
Anglo, Sidney, 150 n.43
Archilocus, 202
Ardener, Shirley, 149 n.26
Aristotle, 8, 181
Aubrey, John, 241, 242
Auerbach, Nina, 248, 255 n.18

Babcock, Barbara A. 218 nn.4, 7
Baker, Kathryn A. 235 n.15
Bakhtin, Mikhail, 18, 158, 159, 176 n.20, 216, 220 n.40
Baldick, Christopher 255 n.24
Baltrusaitis, Jurgis, 52 n.1
Barber, C.L., 102, 114 n.52
Barker, Francis, 187, 189, 197 nn.25, 27
Barnet, Sylvan, 195 n.13, 196 nn.15, 20
Barrett, Michèle, 6, 7, 8, 9, 25 n.14, 26 n.16, 217 n.1
Barthes, Roland, 182
Beaumont, Francis and John Fletcher, 156
Belsey, Catherine, 4, 5, 9, 20–1, 22, 24 n.4, 25 n.10, 26 n.27, 52 n.1, 54 n.18, 104, 113 n.51, 148 n.8, 197 n.23, 235 n.13, 236 n.27, 257–70, 270 nn.8, 10, 11
Benson, Larry D., 177 n.35
Bergeron, David, 17, 190, 197 n.36
Berggren, Paula, 53 n.4
Bernthal, Craig, 220 nn.33, 34

Berry, Ralph, 78 n.43, 79 n.51
Bindoff, S.T., 150 n.44, 151 n.57
Bingham, Caroline, 112 n.31
Bloch, R. Howard, 155, 163, 175 n.11, 176 n.14, 177 n.34
Bloom, Harold 61, 75 nn.2, 8, 79 n.46
Blum, Abbe, 108
Boleyn, Anne, 213
Bolton, Sir Edmund, 209
Bono, Barbara, 24 n.4, 52 n.1
Boose, Lynda, 2, 24 n.5, 79 n.52, 117, 118, 123, 127 n.1, 171, 179 n.55, 235 n.13
Boswell, John, 110 n.24, 112 n.31
Boswell, Terry E., 235 n.15
Bowlby, Rachel, 269, 270 nn.13, 14
Bradley, A.C., 243
Bray, Alan, 95, 110 n.24, 112 nn.31, 32
Brecht, Bertolt, 195 n.11
Breton, Nicholas, 42, 55 n.20, 187, 189, 190, 197 n.26
Breward, Ian, 178 n.43
Bridenthal, Renate, 76 n.10
Brink, Jean R., 197 n.38
Brittain, Vera, 113 n.45
Brome, Richard, 211
Brooke-Rose, Christine, 196 n.21
Broude, Ronald, 150 nn.31, 42
Brown, Judith C., 62, 76 n.11, 77 n.12, 113 n.38
Brownmiller, Susan, 132, 148 nn.9, 10, 11
Brucher, Richard T., 151 n.55
Bruster, Doug, 24 n.4
Brydges, Sir Egerton, 197 n.26
Budge, E.A. Wallis, 179 n.54
Bullinger, Heinrich, 55 n.21
Bullough, Geoffrey, 78 n.35, 176 n.15, 179 nn.57, 60
Burgh, B.R., 112 n.31
Burke, Kenneth, 52 n.4, 173, 179 n.62
Burke, Peter, 218 n.11
Burt, Richard, 227, 235 nn.13, 19
Bushnell, Rebecca, 209, 219 nn.21, 22
Butler, Samuel, 18, 206–8, 209, 218 nn.13, 16

Camden, Carroll, 176 n.24

271

Caplan, Pat, 108 n.7
Carmina Burana, 202
Carroll, Berenice A., 77 n.14
Cary, Elizabeth, 194 n.7
Castiglione, Baldassare, 156
Catherine of Aragon, 213
Cavell, Stanley, 123, 128 n.16, 175 n.3, 179 n.55
Certaine Sermons or Homilies appointed by the Queenes Majestie, 30, 52 n.3
Chambers, E.K., 19, 55 n.26, 221, 234 n.1, 248–50, 255 nn.19, 21
Chapman, George, 17, 181, 185, 186, 196 n.19
Charlemagne, 2
Charles I, 209
Charlton, H.B., 252–3
Chatman, Seymour, 127 n.8
Chaucer, Geoffrey, 49, 155, 163, 174, 177 n.35, 179 n.65, 210
Chauncey, George, 110 n.24
Chesler, Phyllis, 75 n.9
Chodorow, Nancy, 109 n.16
Chojnacki, Stanley, 64, 65, 77 nn. 23–6, 28–33
Christine de Pisan, 129, 130, 132, 148 nn.1, 3, 155
Cinthio, G. B. Giraldi, 156, 171, 172
Clark, Anna, 130, 148 n.4
Clark, Katerina, 176 n.20
Clark, Sandra, 55 n.19
Clark, Stuart, 196 n.21
Cleaver, Richard, 43, 55 nn.22, 23
Cohen, Ed., 112 n.31
Cohen, Walter, 2, 10, 24 n.5, 26 n.24, 60, 75 n.5, 78 n.43, 117, 118, 127 nn.4, 6, 178 n.45, 195 n.11, 235 n.13
Coke, Sir Edward, 97
Colie, Rosalie L., 15, 119, 120, 127 n.8
Delaney, Paul, 15, 119, 127 n.8
Collins, Don S., 195 n.10, 198 n.45
Cook, Carol, 109 n.8
Cossa, Francesco, 150 n.47
Coudert, Allison P., 197 n.38
Coward, Rosalind, 7, 9, 26 n.15, 269
Cowie, Elizabeth, 149 n.14
Cowley, Abraham, 208, 219 n.17
Cressy, David, 36, 54 nn.10, 14
Crompton, Louis, 97, 113 nn.38, 40
Cunningham, Karen, 198 n.47
Curtius, Ernst, 202, 217 n.2, 218 n.3

da Vinci, Leonardo, 108 n.6, 109 n.11
Davis, Natalie Zemon, 76 n.11, 218 n.7
De Cecco, John, 110 n.24
Delacroix, 204, 205
Delaney, Paul, 15, 119, 127 n.8
de Lauretis, Teresa, 1, 5, 24 n.1, 25 n.10, 109 n.9, 269

de Lorris, Guillaume, 176 n.13
Delphy, Christine, 6–7, 25 n.14
de Meun, Jean, 155–6, 163, 173, 176 n.13
Derrick, Thomas J., 178 n.41
Dick, Susan, 255 n.27
Diehl, Huston, 148 n.8
Doane, Janice, 255 n.2
Dod, John, 43, 55 n.22
Dollimore, Jonathan, 25 n.5, 107, 114 n.56, 120, 122, 127 n.9, 128 n.15, 195 n.11, 235 n.13
Donne, John, 56 n.27
Doran, Madeleine, 162, 177 n.32
Doyle, Brian, 242, 255 nn.8, 24
Drakakis, John, 54 n.18, 255 n.5
Duberman, Martin, 110 n.24
Dubrow, Heather, 25 n.5

Eagleton, Terry, 59, 69, 75 n.1, 239, 255 n.4
Eaton, Sara, 17, 24 n.4, 181–98
Eco, Umberto, 127 n.8
Edwards, Lee, 108
Eisenstein, Zillah, 25 n.13
Eliot, T.S., 181–2, 186, 194 nn.2, 3
Elizabeth I, 18, 53 n.4, 121, 131, 140, 145, 148 n.6, 150 n.32, 189, 190, 193, 197 n.38, 208, 213, 244, 253, 263
Elliott, Vivien Brodsky, 54 n.13
Elyot, Sir Thomas, 140, 150 n.39, 158, 165, 176 n.21
Engels, Friedrich, 6, 7, 25 n.12
Engle, Lars, 60, 75 nn.3, 4
Engler, Balz, 177 n.37
Epstein, Steven, 110 n.24
Erasmus, Desiderius, 166, 178 n.41
Erickson, Peter, 2, 15, 24 n.5, 108, 117, 118, 125, 126, 127 n.5, 128 n.18
Eriksson, Brigitte, 113 n.38
eroticism, 82–4, 87–90
Evans, Mary, 270 n.7
Eve, 43

Faderman, Lillian, 95, 110 n.24, 112 n.36
Ferguson, Kathy E., 24
Ferguson, Margaret W., vii, 24, 26 n.19, 62, 76 nn.10, 11, 128 n.17, 175, 175 n.10, 197 n.31
Fineman, Joel, 53 n.6, 109 n.8, 110 n.25, 195 n.11
Finkelpearl, Philip, 56 n.27
Firestone, Shulamith, 25 n.13
Fisher, F.J., 54 n.9, 56 n.34
Flahiff, F.T., 127 n.8
Fletcher, Anthony 192, 198 nn.43, 45, 218 n.6
Fletcher, John and Francis Beaumont, 156
Floyd, Thomas, 150 n.38
Foley, Stephen, 19–20, 24 n.4, 119, 237–55

Forde, Emmanuel, 56 n.32
Forgacs, David, 220 n.42
Foucault, Michel, 91, 92, 107, 110 nn.23, 24, 112 n.31, 114 n.54, 136, 149 n.24, 193, 198, n.51, 217
Fox, Alice, 244, 245, 255 nn.11, 13, 14
Foxe, John, 18, 208
Fraser, Antonia, 219 n.23
Fraser, Russell A., 195 n.12, 196 nn.14, 19
French, Marilyn, 123, 125, 127 n.13
French Revolution, 18, 205–6, 209
Freud, Sigmund, 8, 14, 86–7, 92, 93, 96, 108 n.8, 109 nn.10–14
Friedli, Lynne, 113 n.44
Furnivall, F.J., 19, 53 n.9, 248
Fuss, Diana, 110 n.24

Gallagher, Catherine, 25 n.7
Garber, Marjorie, 239, 255 n.4
Gascoigne, George, 150 n.31
Geary, Keith, 78 n.34
Gent, Lucy, 188, 197 nn.28, 30
Geras, Norman, 217 n.1
Gilbert, Arthur, 112 n.31
Gilbert, Sandra, 151 n.63
Gl'Ingannati, 56 n.32
Gluckman, Max, 18, 216, 217, 218 n.8, 220 n.39
Goldberg, Jonathan, 17, 95, 112 nn.31, 33–5, 181–3, 190, 194 nn.1, 3, 197 nn.35, 37, 39, 235 n.13
Goodman, Emily Jane, 75 n.9
Goody, Jack, 63, 77 n.17
Gosson, Stephen, 19, 222–5, 233, 234, 234 nn.2, 4, 6–8, 235 n.9
Gouge, William, 63–4, 73, 156, 158, 159, 165, 167, 176 n.17, 178 n.46
Grady, Hugh, 24 n.4
Gramsci, Antonio, 18, 217, 220 n.42
Greaves, Richard, 192, 198 nn.44, 50
Greenblatt, Stephen, 16, 78 n.42, 81–2, 113 n.51, 120, 127 n.9, 163, 166–7, 177 n.33, 178 nn.40, 44, 194, 198 n.53, 235 nn.13, 18
Greene, Gayle, 25 n.9, 53 n.4, 77 n.14, 78 n.36
Grosart, Alexander B., 219 n.17
Gubar, Susan, 151 n.63
Gurr, Andrew, 223, 234 n.5

Hakluyt, Richard, 243–5
Hale, David, 140, 150 nn.37, 40, 41
Hall, Susanna Shakespeare, 161
Haller, William, 219 n.25
and Malleville, 55 n.23
Halperin, David, 110 n.24
Hamilton, A.C., 150 n.36, 151 n.55
Haraway, Donna, 24 n.2

Harrison, William, 34, 53 n.9
Harsnett, Samuel, 120
Hartman, Geoffrey, 109 n.8, 127 n.9
Hartmann, Heidi, 26 n.16
Harvey–Nash quarrel, 47, 55 n.27
Hawkes, Terence, 19, 120, 127 n.10, 239–43, 247, 253, 255 nn.4, 6, 7
Heinemann, Margot, 195 n.11
Heisch, Allison, 197 n.38
Henderson, Katherine, 54 n.19
Hendricks, Margo, 11
Hennessy, Rosemary, 9–10, 11, 26 n.23
Henry VIII, 95
Hercules, 205–6
Herford, C.H., 56 n.28
Heywood, Thomas
    Curtain Lecture, 176 n.24
    Wise Woman of Hogsdon, The, 19, 228–34, 236 n.26
    Woman Killed with Kindness, A, 17, 184, 186, 195 n.12
Hoare, Quintin, 220 n.42
Hobhouse, Stephen, 255 n.20
Hodges, Devon, 255 n.3
Holbein, Hans, 29
Holderness, Graham, 127 n.12
Holdsworth, Sir William, 148 n.7
Hollander, John, 56 nn.29, 30
Holmes, Sherlock, 22
Holquist, Michael, 176 n.20
homilies see Certaine Sermons
homoeroticism, 92–101, 106–8
    in As You Like It, 101–6
Horowitz, Maryanne C., 197 n.38
Howard, Jean E., 14, 18–19, 24, 24 nn.4, 5, 53 n.4, 55 n.24, 56 n.30, 68, 74, 75 n.6, 77 n.34, 78 n.42, 79 nn.50, 52, 82–4, 96, 104, 108 n.2, 113 n.51, 114 n.52, 117, 118, 127 n.2, 175 n.5, 178 n.45, 183, 186, 195 nn.10, 11, 198 n.45, 221–36, 236 n.23, 255 n.4
Howard-Hill, T.H., 220 n.32
Hunt, Lynn, 205–6, 218 nn.9, 10

ideology, 7–8, 226–8
Ingram, Martin, 56 n.34
Ingram, R.W., 55 n.27
Irigaray, Luce, 114 n.55
Ives, E.W., 77 n.13

Jacobus, Mary, 267, 270 n.11
Jager, Bernd, 150 n.34
James I, 95, 98, 181, 189, 190, 223
Jardine, Alice A., 20, 23, 262, 269, 270 n.6
Jardine, Lisa, vii, 5, 14, 25 n.10, 63, 77 nn.15, 16, 83–4, 108 nn.3–5, 113 n.51, 117, 153, 161, 175, 175 n.4, 177 nn.27, 31, 195 n.10, 242, 255 nn.9, 24

Jerome, Saint, 163, 177 n.35
Johansson, Sheila Ryan, 62, 77 n.14
Johnson, Barbara, 268, 269, 270 n.12
Jones, Ann Rosalind, 217 n.1
Jones, Elred, 150 n.48
Jones, Gareth Stedman, 217 n.1, 220 n.42
Jonson, Ben
    Bartholomew Fair, 151 n.55, 222–3, 234 n.3
    Cynthia's Revels, 13, 48, 52, 56 nn.28, 29
Joplin, Patricia Klindienst, 179 n.64
Jordan, Constance, 176 n.21
Junius, Francis, 188

Kahn, Coppélia 15, 77 n.14, 111 n.25, 124–5, 128 n.17, 133, 149 nn.16, 20, 21, 27, 150 n.46, 235 n.13
Kaplan, Cora, 9, 217 n.1
Kaplan, E. Ann, 194 n.4
Karr, Judith M., 151 n.56
Kastan, David Scott, 235 n.13, 236 n.22
Kelly, Joan, 13, 30–1, 50, 52 n.2, 62, 76 n.10
Kingsley, Charles, 252
Kingston, Maxine Hong, 23
Kinney, Arthur, 108, 195 n.10, 198 n.45
Kiser, Edgar V., 235 n.15
Klinkenberg, Jean-Marie, 127 n.8
Knights, L.C., 55 n.27
Knox, John, 250
Koonz, Claudia, 76 n.10
Krapp, George Philip, 219 n.24
Krieger, Elliot, 36, 38, 53 n.7, 54 n.16
Kruger, Dreyer, 150 n.34
Kuhn, Annette, 6, 7, 25 n.12, 183, 194 n.4, 195 n.8, 198 n.52
Kunzle, David 218 n.4

Lacan, Jacque, 8
Lacanian psychoanalysis, 14, 85–6
Laclau, Ernesto, 217 n.1, 220 n.43
Lancashire, Anne, 196 n.17
Leaska, Mitchell A., 255 n.25
Lenz, Carolyn Ruth Swift, 25 n.9, 53 n.4, 78 n.36
Leventon, Carol, 13–14, 24 n.4, 59–79
Levin, Carole, 176 n.21, 197 n.38
Levin, Richard, 25 n.8, 194 n.7
Levine, Laura, 113 n.42
Lewes, Kenneth, 109 n.22
Lewis, C.S., 178 n.43
Libellus de deorum imaginibus, 210
Licata, Salvatore, 112 n.31
Lieberman, Annette, 75 n.9
Lindner, Vicki, 75 n.9
Little, David, 56 n.34
Locke, John, 266
Locrine, 18, 214–16, 220 n.36
Lodge, Thomas, 150 nn.31, 44

Long, William B, 220 n.35
Lovell, Terry, 9
Lovibond, Sabina, 26 n.26
Luce, Morton, 56 n.32
Lucretia, 130
Luther, Martin, 210
Luxan, Pedro di, 177 n.35
Lyotard, Jean-Françoise, 263, 265, 269 n.4, 270 nn.5, 9

MacCary, W. Thomas, 110 n.25
Macclean, Ian, 149 nn.22, 23
McDonald, Charles O., 196 n.21
McGinn, Donald, 55 n.27
Macherey, Pierre, 75 n.1
McIntosh, Mary, 25 n.14
McKerrow, Ronald B., 220 n.36
McKewin, Carole, 78 n.36
McLaughlin, Eleanor Commo, 175 n.12
McLuskie, Kathleen, vii, 5, 15, 24, 25 n.10, 117, 123, 124, 126, 128 n.15, 195 n.11, 235 n.13
McManus, Barbara, 54 n.19
McMillin, Scott, 220 n.32
McNeillie, Andrew, 255 n.10
Macpherson, C.B., 57 n.34
Malcolmson, Cristina, 12–13, 24, 24 n.4, 29–57, 175, 179 n.64
Manley, Lawrence, 54 nn.15, 27, 56 n.33
Marcus, Jane, 253, 254, 255 n.26
Marcus, Leah, 24 n.4, 79 n.48, 113 n.42
Margoliouth, H.M., 218 n.15
Marianne, 205–6
Marie-Antoinette, 206
Marlowe, Christopher, 198 n.47
    Doctor Faustus, 72
    Jew of Malta, The, 66, 73, 150 n.48
    Tamburlaine, 150 n.31
marriage, Renaissance discourses on, 42–4, 51, 166–7, 172–3
Mars, 210, 211, 216
Marshall, Brenda, 108
Marston, John
    Insatiate Countess, The, 198 n.48
    What You Will, 13, 47, 48, 50, 56 nn.27, 29
Marvell, Andrew, 18, 207, 218 n.15
Marx, Karl, 6, 7, 11, 201
Marxism, 6–8, 10, 30, 123, 217 n.1, 258–9
Marxist criticism, 36–8, 118, 196 n.21
Mary, Queen of Scots, 197 n.38
Mary, the Virgin, 204
Massinger, Philip, 235 n.19
materialism, 6–8, 10, 257–8
materialist feminist criticism, theory of, 1–4, 8–21, 23–4, 30–1, 66–7, 91–2, 106–7, 125–7, 153–9, 174–5, 210–17, 221–8, 233–4, 257–70
Matheolus, 155

Maus, Katharine Eisaman, vii, 97, 113 n.41, 149 n.16, 151 n.55
Menander, 156
Merchant, Carolyn, 150 nn.38, 49
Michels, Agnes Kirsopp, 219 n.30
Middleton, Christopher, 157
Middleton, Thomas, 17, 185, 186, 188, 196 nn.16, 17
Miller, Jonathan, 177 n.36
Miller, R.P., 175 n.12, 176 n.14, 177 n.35
Milsum, Catherine, 24 n.4
Milton, John, 209, 210, 219 nn.24, 25
Minton, Henry, 109 n.22
Miola, Robert, 137, 149 n.27, 150 n.53
Misogonous, 156
Mitchell, Juliet, 9
Mohan, Rajeswari, 9–10, 11, 26 n.23
Mohl, Ruth, 56 n.34
Moi, Toril, 8–9, 26 n.21
Moisan, Thomas, 60, 75 nn.6, 7, 79 n.49
Montrose, Louis Adrian, 114 n.52, 117, 118, 126, 128 n.19, 197 n.31
Moore, Jane, 270 n.11
Mouffe, Chantal, 217 n.1, 220 nn.42, 43, 235 n.17
Mullaney, Steven, 225, 227, 235 nn.11, 13, 236 n.20
Mulvey, Laura, 182–3, 184, 186, 188, 194 n.6, 195 n.9
Murry, J. Middleton, 61
My Stepmother Is an Alien, 22–3

Naogeorgus (Kirchmeyer), 218 n.14
Nash, Thomas, 13, 45, 46, 47, 55 nn.25, 27, 134, 149 n.18
Nature of a Woman, The, 157, 176 n.19
Neely, Carol Thomas, 2, 15, 24 n.5, 25 n.9, 53 n.4, 78 n.36, 117, 118, 120, 123, 124, 127 n.3, 179 n.55
Nestle, Joan, 109 n.18
Neville, Henry, 209
Newman, Karen, 77 nn.27, 34, 79 n.52, 87, 109 n.15, 113 n.51, 154, 170, 175 nn.5, 6, 179 n.52, 198 n.45, 235 n.13
Newstead, Helaine, 24 n.3
Newton, Esther, 109 n.19
Newton, Judith, 3–4, 9, 20, 25 n.6, 52 n.2, 66, 257–8, 269 nn.1, 2
Novy, Marianne L., 123–4, 125, 128 n.14
Nowell-Smith, Geoffrey, 220 n.42
Nuttall, A.D., 60, 75 n.2

O'Connor, Marion F., 24 n.5, 75 n.6, 117, 118, 127 n.2, 175 n.5, 178 n.45, 195 n.11, 239, 255 n.4
Oedipus, 2
Olivier, Sir Laurence, 177 n.36
Omvedt, Gayle, 24, 25 n.12, 26 n.29

Ong, Walter, 196 n.21
Orgel, Stephen, 101, 104, 112 n.31, 113 n.51, 151 n.58
Outhwaite, R.B., 54 n.13
Outram, Dorinda, 206, 218 nn.11, 12
Ovid, 145–7, 151 n.62, 174, 222, 234 n.4

Padgug, Robert, 110 n.24
Park, Clara Claiborne, 53 n.4
Parker, Patricia, 109 n.8, 127 n.9
Parker, Rozsika, 172, 179 n.59
Parsons, Talcott, 217, 220 n.41
Partridge, Eric, 177 n.37
Paster, Gail Kern, 24 n.4
Pateman, Carole, 236 n.27
Pater, Walter, 20, 253, 255 n.25
Patton, Cindy, 88–9, 109 nn.19, 21
Peacham, Henry, 134, 138, 145, 149 n.19
Peacock, T.L., 56 n.32
Pecheux, Michel, 235 n.17
Pecorone, Il, 66, 72, 78 n.35
Peele, George, 150 n.48
Penthesilia, 41
Pequigney, Joseph, 112 n.30
Perkins, William, 43, 51, 55 nn.21, 23, 57 n.34, 166–7, 178 n.43
Peterson, Robert, 112 n.31
Philomela, 145–6, 151 n.62, 174
Plato, 135, 188
Plutarch, 211, 216
Poel, William, 239
Porter, Carolyn, 2, 16, 23, 24 n.5, 26 n.28, 153–4, 175 nn.1, 7
Porter, Joseph, 112 n.29
Porter, Roy, 113 n.44, 148 n.8, 218 n.11
postmodernism, and feminism, 20, 26 n.26, 261–6
Potter, Nick, 127 n.12
Prescott, Ann Lake, 219 n.30
Proud Wives Paternoster, The, 176 n.24
Puttenham, George, 188, 197 n.29

Quilligan, Maureen, 76 nn.10, 11, 128 n.17, 175 n.10, 197 n.31

Rabkin, Norman, 195 n.12, 196 nn.14, 19
Rackin, Phyllis, 104, 108, 114 nn.51, 53
Raleigh, Sir Walter (Elizabethan), 241, 253
Raleigh, Sir Walter Alexander (modern), 19–20, 239–47, 253–4
rape, legislation of, 62, 130–1, 136, 140, 141, 147, 148 n.9
Reiter, Rayna R., 196 n.21
Rhymer, Thomas, 155
Rich, Adrienne, 95, 112 n.36
Rich, Barnabe, 56 n.32
Richards, E.A., 219 n.16
Ridley, M.R., 153, 154, 155, 175 nn.3, 9

Rieder, John, 175
Rieff, Philip, 109 n.13
Robinson, Lillian S., 9, 24, 26 n.22
Rogers, Katharine M., 175 n.12
Rome
  founding of, 18, 141, 210–11, 214
  in *Titus Andronicus*, 134, 137, 138, 139,
    140, 141, 142, 146
  Roman Empire, 2
Roper, Lyndal, 219 nn.26, 27
Rose, Jacqueline, 9, 84, 108 n.6, 217 n.1
Rose, Mary Beth, 5, 25 n.10, 55 n.19, 76
    n.11, 113 n.42, 179 n.61, 196 n.21, 197
    n.40, 198 n.45, 235 n.13
Rosenfelt, Deborah, 3–4, 9, 20, 25 n.6, 66,
    257–8, 269 nn.1, 2
Rousseau, G.S., 113 n.44
Rowbotham, Sheila, 270 n.7
Rubin, Gayle, 77 n.27, 84, 108 n.7, 196 n.21
Ruether, Rosemary Radford, 175 n.12
Ruggiero, Guido, 112 n.31
Ryan, Mary P., 52 n.2

Sanders, Norman, 169, 176 n.23, 177 n.25,
    179 n.58
Sanderson, Robert, 34, 54 n.9
Saslow, James, 101, 110 n.24, 113 n.50
Scarry, Elaine, 186–7, 189, 197 nn.24, 31
Schochet, Gordon, 55 n.24
Schoenbaum, Samuel, 161, 177 nn.29, 31
Schulenberg, Jane Tibbetts, 196 n.21
Schwartz, Murray, 108, 110 n.25
Scot, Reginald, 229, 230, 236 n.25
Sedgwick, Eve Kosofsky, 93–4, 108 n.7, 111
    nn.27, 28
Seidman, Steven, 113 n.47
Serpieri, Alessandro, 15, 119, 127 n.8
Sexton, Joyce Hengerer, 177 n.28
sexuality, in relation to gender, 81–4
Seznec, Jean, 219 nn.28, 29
Shakespeare, William
  All's Well That Ends Well, 149 n.15
  Antony and Cleopatra, 119, 126
  As You Like It, 14–15, 95, 101–6, 113 n.37
  Hamlet, 196 n.18, 201, 260
  Henry V, 249
  King John, 149 n.15
  King Lear, 15, 117–28, 135, 137, 194 n.3,
    215
  Macbeth, 20, 260–1, 264–5
  Merchant of Venice, The, 13–14, 59–79,
    137, 202
  Midsummer Night's Dream, A, 70, 82,
    95–6, 113 n.37, 197 n.31
  Othello, 16–17, 119, 126, 153–79, 184,
    186, 196 nn.18, 22, 202
  Pericles, 96, 113 n.37, 174, 179 n.63
  Rape of Lucrece, The, 15–16, 133, 149 n.15

  Richard III, 177 n.30
  Romeo and Juliet, 135
  Taming of the Shrew, The, 249–50
  Tempest, The, 239, 240, 249
  Titus Andronicus, 15–16, 17, 129–51, 174,
    185, 186, 196 n.20
  Troilus and Cressida, 113 n.46, 146 n.15
  Twelfth Night, 12–13, 29–57, 82, 108
  Venus and Adonis, 52 n.4, 133, 145
  Winter's Tale, The, 17, 37, 96, 113 n.37,
    185, 186, 188, 196 nn.15, 16, 18
Shively, Michael, 110 n.24
Showalter, Elaine, 217 n.1
Sidney, Mary, 194 n.7
Silverman, Debora, 237, 255 n.2
Simpson, Percy, 56 n.28
Sinfield, Alan, 128 n.15, 195 n.11
Sir Thomas More, The Book of, 18, 211–14,
    220 nn.32, 35
skimmington, 207
Skinner, Quentin, 219 n.20
Small, Roscoe, 55 n.27
Smith, Bruce, 112 n.31, 113 n.49
Smith, Joan, 148 n.2, 176 n.22
Smith, Thomas, 34, 53 n.9
Smith-Rosenberg, Carroll, 95, 112 n.36
Snow, Edward, 170–1, 178 n.49, 179 n.53
social mobility, 12–13, 31–9, 44–52, 52 n.4,
    54 nn.10, 11, 12
Sommers, Alan, 149 n.20
Southampton, 2nd Earl of, 63
Speed, John, 215, 220 n.37
Spenser, Edmund, 151 n.56
Spierenburg, Pieter, 192–3, 198 nn.47,
    49
Spivack, Bernard, 175 n.8
Spivak, Gayatri Chakravorty, 23, 179 n.66
Sprague, Gregory, 110 n.24
Sprengnether, Madelon (Gohlke), 22, 117,
    196 n.22
Spurgeon, Caroline, 19, 250–3, 255 nn.22, 23
Stallybrass, Peter, 17–18, 24 n.4, 53 n.5, 108
    n.13 n.48, 150 n.32, 155, 170, 175 n.10,
    179 nn.51, 56, 198 n.46, 201–20, 211,
    219 n.31, 235 n.13
Steane, J.B., 149 n.18
Stein, Arlene, 109 n.17
Stevenson, John, 192, 198 nn.43, 45, 218 n.6
Stoller, Robert, 109 n.20, 111 n.26
Stone, Lawrence, 35, 43, 54 nn.10, 11, 13, 15,
    55 n.23, 63, 69, 77 nn.18, 19, 22, 78
    nn.44, 45
Strachey, James, 109 n.8
Strachey, Lytton, 247
Strier, Richard, 25 n.5, 178 n.40
Strong, Roy, 150 n.32, 189, 197 n.32, 219
    n.18
subversion and containment debate, 5, 18,
    204–5, 227, 235 n.18, 265

Suleiman, Susan Rubin, 149 n.25, 151 n.54, 196 n.21
Supple, Bernard, 56 n.34
Suzuki, Mihoko, 24 n.4, 52 n.1
Swetnam, Joseph, 176 n.24

Taylor, Barbara, 270, n.7
Tennenhouse, Leonard, 15, 17, 53 nn.4, 7, 110 n.25, 120–1, 123, 127 n.11, 189, 190, 197 nn.33, 34, 235 n.13
Terry, Ellen, 248
Theophrastus, 163, 177 n.35
Therborn, Göran, 227, 235 n.16
Thisk, Joan, 77 n.17
Thomas, Keith, 229, 236 n.24
Thompson, Ann, vii, 15, 24 n.4, 117–28, 127 n.7
Thompson, E.P., 77 n.17
Tilley, Charles, 218 n.7
Tilley, Morris, 177 n.25
Tilney, Edmund
    Flower of Friendshippe, The, 43, 44, 54 n.19, 55 nn.22, 23, 156, 166, 167–8, 175 n.2, 177 n.35, 178 nn.39, 42, 47
    Master of the Revels, 213, 220 n.35
Todd, Margo, 178 n.42
Tomaselli, Sylvana, 148 n.8
Toner, Barbara, 148 n.9
Traub, Valerie, 11, 14–15, 24 n.4, 81–114, 196 n.18
Treichler, Paula, 113 n.47
Trent, Council of, 166, 178 n.42
Tricomi, Albert, 143, 149 nn.13, 17, 150 nn.33, 47, 151 nn.51, 52, 55
Trojan origin of Britain, 2, 214–15
Trumbach, Randolph, 97, 110 n.24, 113 n.39
Tudeau-Clayton, M., 177 n.27
Turner, John, 121–2, 127 n.12

Underdown, David, 55 n.26, 191, 198 nn.42, 45, 204, 218 n.6

Vance, Carole, 108 n.7, 109 n.19
van Leer, David, 111 n.28
van Veen, C.F., 203
Veeser, H. Aram, 25 n.5, 195 n.11
Venice, women in, 64–5
Venus, 42, 215, 216
Vicinus, Martha, 110 n.24
Vickers, Nancy J., 76 nn.10, 11, 128 n.17, 175 n.10, 197 n.31
Victoria, Queen, 98
Virgil, 145, 202
Vives, Juan Luis, 177 n.35
Vološinov, V.N., 158, 159, 176 n.20
Vreeland, Diana, 237, 254 n.1

Waith, Eugene M., 148 nn.5, 12, 149 nn.19, 30, 150 n.45, 151 nn. 59, 61

Walker, Alice, 197 n.29
Walkowitz, Judith R., 52 n.2
Waller, Marguerite, 2, 14, 24 n.5, 81–4, 108 n.1
Walton, Shirley, 109 n.19
Warner, Deborah, 148 n.5
Warner, M., 177 n.27
Watson, Jeanie, 176 n.21
Watson, Robert N., 219 n.30
Wayne, Don E., 2, 24, 24 n.5, 55 nn.24, 27, 56 n.28, 117, 118, 127 n.4, 195 n.11
Wayne, Valerie, 1–26, 16–17, 52 n.1, 54 n.19, 108, 153–79, 175 n.2, 176 n.21, 178 nn.39, 42, 47
Webster, John, 52 n.4, 77 n.15, 184, 186, 196 n.14
Weeks, Jeffrey, 108 n.7, 110 n.24
Weiner, Deborah, 24
Wells, Stanley, 148 n.5
Whigham, Frank, 52 n.4, 54 n.17
White, Allon, 211, 219 n.31
Wicke, Jennifer, 26 n.26
Wiesner, Merry E., 76 n.11, 197 n.40
Willcock, Gladys Doidge, 197 n.29
Willett, John, 195 n.11
Williams, Norman Lloyd, 255 n.7
Williams, Penry, 212, 220 n.34
Williams, Raymond, 26 n.18, 53 n.6, 157, 176 n.18
Wilson, F.P., 255 n.19
Wilson, John Dover, 243, 248–9, 255 n.19
Wilson, Thomas, 54 n.9, 178 n.41
Wind, Edgar, 150 n.47, 216, 220 n.38
Without A Clue, 22
Wolpe, AnnMarie, 6, 7, 25 n.12
women, Renaissance debate about, 16, 39–42, 156–68
Wood, Ellen Meiksins, 217 n.1
Woodbridge, Linda, 5, 25 n.10, 54 n.19, 63, 77 nn.20, 21, 156, 161, 176 n.16, 177 n.26
Woolf, Virginia, 19–20, 243–7, 253–4, 255 nn.10–17, 25, 27, 266
Wright, Joseph, 19, 248
Wright, Louis B., 54 n.19
Wright, Thomas, 255 n.25
Wrightson, Keith, 35, 43, 54 nn.12, 13, 55 n.23
Wyatt, Sir Thomas, 81–2
Wynne-Davies, Marion, 15–16, 24 n.4, 52 n.1, 129–51, 176 n.22

Yates, Francis A., 219 n.18

Zaret, David, 57 n.34
Zenobia, 176 n.21
Zitner, S.P., 234 n.4